THE *B*USINESS AND MANAGEMENT OF CONVENTIONS

VIVIENNE McCABE • BARRY POOLE
PAUL WEEKS • NEIL LEIPER

WILEY

John Wiley & Sons Australia, Ltd

First published 2000 by
John Wiley & Sons Australia, Ltd
33 Park Road, Milton, Qld 4065

Offices also in Sydney and Melbourne

Typeset in 10.5/12 pt New Baskerville

National Library of Australia
Calaloguing-in-publication data

The business and management of conventions.

   Includes index.
   ISBN 0 471 34113 4.

   1. Congresses and conventions — Management. 2. Congresses
   and conventions — Planning. I. McCabe, Vivienne.

060.68

Cover photograph: Courtesy of The Melbourne Exhibition
& Convention Centre
Internal design feature: Digital Vision

Printed in Singapore by
Markono Print Media Pte Ltd

10 9 8 7 6 5 4

To my family Bernard and Wyn, Sally and Anne McCabe

CONTENTS

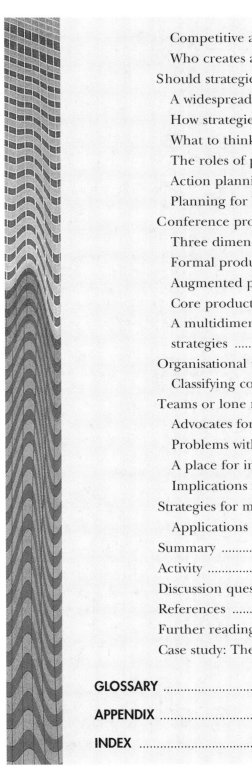

PREFACE

The meetings, incentives, conventions and exhibitions (MICE) industry world-wide has been the focus of much activity during the last 20 years, nowhere more so than in the Asia–Pacific region, where the last decade has seen significant development of both the facilities and infrastructure to support the expansion of this fast-growing area of the tourism industry.

Within Australia, the fledgling MICE industry of the late 1980s has increased substantially and is now estimated to generate $7 billion per year in direct expenditure from both international and domestic markets. The country has embraced the potential opportunities that the MICE industry provides and is acknowledged as a major player in the MICE market. It is recognised world-wide for the quality of both its facilities and infrastructure and for the professionalism of its service. New purpose-built and technologically advanced convention and exhibition centres have been constructed in a number of major capital cities. They have been supported by the development of accommodation, transport and other suppliers to the industry.

The MICE industry is seen as being at the 'blue-chip' end of the tourism industry in an area that continually provides extensive career opportunities. As the industry has grown, new professions have emerged to support this rapidly developing sector. With calls for the continued development of the professionalism of the industry, both the industry association and tertiary institutes have taken up the challenge to provide industry-relevant educational programs and training programs for current and future managers. Courses have been developed at both undergraduate and postgraduate levels. However, to date there has been no academic text specifically designed for use within these programs that provides data and information relevant and applicable to the Australasian region. This text attempts to address this shortfall.

The text introduces the professional environment of the MICE industry, and draws on current business thinking and academic research. It links management principles and practice to the Australian MICE industry. Each chapter focuses on a particular function involved in the business and management of conventions and meetings. The chapters include practical features such as industry insights and snapshots that illustrate a particular point or outline the career path of an individual within the industry. Each chapter also includes a case study, and activities and discussion questions, all designed to encourage students to develop a practical appreciation of the key issues.

The confidence in Australia as a convention destination and the surge of international interest generated by the added exposure of the Sydney 2000 Olympic Games provide a unique opportunity for the continued development of the MICE industry within Australia as the country enters the new millennium.

I wish to acknowledge a number of people who helped or encouraged me in the preparation of this text. First, I would like to thank my fellow authors, Barry Poole, Paul Weeks and Neil Leiper, for their valuable contributions and for their willingness to accept the challenge of writing this book. I am grateful to the following people and organisations for providing information for the case studies, industry insights and snapshots: Trevor Gardiner, Amlink Technologies; Ayers Rock Resort; Brisbane Tourism; Burswood International Resort Casino; Tina Croker; Bill Coulter, Ballina RSL Club Ltd; Dee McGrath, Canberra Convention Bureau; Rob Yeomans, Convention & Incentive Marketing; Sharlene Dadd; Pamela Holsinger, Eventcorp Pty Ltd; Stuart Haynes, Intercontinental Hotel, Sydney; Kingfisher Bay Resort and Village; Lindsay Wallace, Marriott Surfers Paradise Resort; Peter May; Ruth McCarthy; the MIAA; Dale Potts; Kylie Schaeffer; Ann Ewer, Staffords Conference Management; Philip Sunshine, AON Risk Services Australia Ltd; Sydney Convention & Visitors Bureau; Erszi Suranyi, Tourism Queensland and Alfred Merse, Wrest Point Hotel and Casino. I would also like to thank the reviewers from industry and education who provided such valuable and perceptive comments.

I am grateful to my publishing editor, Darren Taylor, for his positive encouragement throughout the project and for keeping me 'on track'. Many thanks should also be given to Maggie Saldais, Sandra Mead and Caroline Hunter, who coordinated and organised the editing process together with the rest of the team from John Wiley.

I would like to acknowledge the academic and administrative team at the School of Tourism and Hospitality Management at Southern Cross University, and in particular Maree Jeffery, for providing such a positive work environment that supported and encouraged this endeavour. A group of people who made a major contribution to this text are the students of the convention, meetings and exhibition management course at Southern Cross who, by their questions and enquiring minds, have challenged me on the journey of trying to conceptualise and understand this fascinating industry.

Finally, I would like to thank Jenny Pittman and Tony Mills for their support, and Wyn and Anne McCabe who provided long distance such constant encouragement to 'keep cracking on'.

Vivienne McCabe
Southern Cross University

ACKNOWLEDGEMENTS

The authors and publisher wish to thank the following people and institutions for permission to reproduce material covered by copyright.

Figures

Page 9 (figure 1.1): reproduced by permission of ICCA; page 9 (figure 1.2): reproduced by permission of ICCA; page 39 (figure 2.1): Don Walter; page 45 (figure 2.2): reproduced with the permission of Richard Gartrell from *Destination Marketing for Convention and Visitor Bureaus*, 2nd Edition, Kendall Hunt Publishing Company, 1994; page 73 (figure 3.2): reproduced by permission of Brisbane Convention and Exhibition Centre; page 74 (figure 3.3): reproduced by permission of Cairns Convention Centre; pages 75–76 (figure 3.4): courtesy of the Singapore International Convention and Exhibition Centre; page 81 (figure 3.5): reproduced by permission of Sydney Convention and Exhibition Centre; page 99 (figure 3.10): D. G. Rutherford, *Introduction to the Conventions, Expositions and Meetings Industry*. Published by Van Nostrand Reinhold. Reproduced by permission of John Wiley & Sons, inc. 1990; page 114 (figure 4.1): Raymond Stone, *Human Resource Management*, 3rd Edition, John Wiley & Sons Australia. Reproduced with permission; page 125 (figure 4.4): reproduced by permission of Sydney Convention and Exhibition Centre and Reddin Consulting Group; page 128 (figure 4.6): Raymond Stone, *Human Resource Management*, 3rd Edition, John Wiley & Sons Australia. Reproduced with permission; page 131 (figure 4.7): from R. E. Quinn, *Beyond Rational Management*, page 48. Reproduced with the permission of Jossey-Bass, Inc.; page 135 (figure 4.8): Schermerhorn, *Management for Productivity*, 3rd Edition. Published by and reproduced with permission of John Wiley & Sons, inc. 1989; page 149 (figure 5.1): reproduced by permission of Sydney Convention & Visitors Bureau; page 157 (figure 5.2): reproduced by permission of the Hilton Sydney; page 161 (figure 5.4): reproduced by permission of the Meetings Industry Association of Australia; page 176 (figure 6.1): reproduced by permission of Sheraton Mirage; page 177 (figure 6.2): reproduced by permission of Crowne Plaza Surfers Paradise; page 178 (figure 6.3): image reproduced by permission of Palm Meadows Resort; page 183 (figure 6.4): reproduced courtesy of Perth Convention Bureau; page 196 (figure 6.6): reproduced by permission of Sydney Convention & Visitors Bureau; page 198 (figure 6.7): advertisement reproduced by permission of Coffs Harbour Convention Bureau and other images supplied and reproduced by permission of Novotel, Bonville International Golf Resort and Pelican Beach Centra Resort; page 219 (figure 7.2): reproduced by permission of Sheraton Mirage; page 254 (figure 8.4): reproduced by permission of the Meetings Industry Association of Australia; page 257 (figure 8.5): Tannenbaum and Schmidt, *How to Choose a Leadership Pattern*. Reprinted by permission of Harvard Business Review. © 1958 by the President and Fellows of Harvard College. All rights reserved; page 272 (figure

9.1): reproduced by permission of Raul V. Hernandez, Carlton Hotel Darwin; page 275 (figure 9.3): reproduced by permission of Raul V. Hernandez, Carlton Hotel Darwin; page 284 (figure 9.8): reproduced by permission of Hotel Sofitel; page 287 (figure 9.9): reproduced by permission of Hotel Sofitel; page 292 (figure 9.10): reproduced by permission of Amlink Technologies; page 293 (figure 9.11): reproduced by permission of Amlink Technologies; page 294 (figure 9.12): reproduced by permission of Amlink Technologies; page 295 (figure 9.13): reproduced by permission of CEO Software Inc.; page 296 (figure 9.14): reproduced by permission of CEO Software Inc.; page 301 (figure 9.15): material provided by Hotel Inter-Continental Sydney. Reproduced with permission; page 349 (figure 11.2): courtesy of Tasmanian Convention Bureau; page 364 (figure 11.5): reproduced by permission of AON Risk Services Australia Ltd; page 371 (figure 11.6): reproduced by permission of AON Risk Services Australia Ltd; page 379 (figure 12.1): reproduced by permission of Amlink Technologies.

Text

Page 7 (table 1.1): reproduced by permission of ICCA; page 8 (table 1.2): reproduced by permission of ICCA; page 10 (table 1.3): International Visitor Survey, various years. Bureau of Tourism Research, Canberra. Reproduced with permission; page 11 (table 1.4): Australian Bureau of Statistics 3401.0. Commonwealth of Australia. © Reproduced by permission; page 12 (table 1.5a): International Visitor Survey, various years. Bureau of Tourism Research, Canberra. Reproduced with permission; page 16 (table 1.6): extract from *Dawsons Venue Directory*. Reproduced with permission; page 46 (second quote): reproduced with the permission of Adelaide Convention and Tourism Authority; page 48 (table 2.1): reprinted with the permission of Brisbane Tourism; page 167 (table 5.1): information supplied by Sydney Convention & Visitors Bureau. Reproduced with permission.

Every effort has been made to trace ownership of copyright material. Information that will enable the publisher to rectify any error or omission in subsequent editions will be welcome. In such cases please contact the Permissions Section at John Wiley & Sons Australia, Ltd, who will arrange for payment of the usual fee.

ACRONYMS

A/V: Audiovisual
AACB: Association of Australian Convention Bureaux
ABS: Australian Bureau of Statistics
AHA: Australian Hotel Association
AIA: Australian Incentive Association
AOC: Amateur organiser of conferences
ATC: Australian Tourist Commission
BCEC: Brisbane Convention and Exhibition Centre
BEO: Banquet event order
BICC: Birmingham International Convention Centre
BTR: Bureau of Tourism Research
CAUTHE: Council for Australian University Tourism and Hospitality Education
CBD: Central business district
CEO: Chief executive officer
CPA (or CPM): Critical path analysis or critical path method
CVB: Convention and visitors bureau
EEAA: Exhibition and Events Association of Australia
F&B: Food and beverage
FOC: Free of charge
IACVB: International Association of Convention and Visitors Bureaux
ICCA: International Congress and Convention Association
IVS: International Visitor Survey
MBO: Management by objectives
MCMB: Melbourne Convention and Marketing Bureau
MECC: Melbourne Exhibition and Convention Centre
MIAA: Meetings Industry Association of Australia
MICE: Meetings, incentives, conventions and exhibitions
OHP: Overhead projector
PCO: Professional conference organiser
PERT: Program evaluation and review technique
PMS: Property management system
RTO: Regional tourism organisation
SBU: Strategic business unit
SCVB: Sydney Convention and Visitors Bureau
SMERF: Social, military, educational, religious and fraternal
SWOT: Strengths, weaknesses, opportunities and threats
TFC: Tourism Forecasting Council
TTA: Tourism Training Australia
VFR: Visiting friends and relatives
WBS: Work breakdown structure

CHAPTER 1

The business
environment of conventions

LEARNING OBJECTIVES

After studying this chapter, you will be able to:

- outline the potential benefits of the meetings, incentives, conventions and exhibitions (MICE) industry to Australia and New Zealand

- briefly explain the development and growth of the MICE industry

- identify Australia and New Zealand's importance within the international convention and meeting industry

- outline the facilities and infrastructure required of the convention and meeting industry

- explain the economic importance of the convention and meeting industry to Australia

- briefly describe some of the political, environmental and technological influences on the convention and meeting industry

- discuss the strengths, weaknesses, opportunities and threats to the convention and meeting industry in Australia

- critically evaluate the future challenges that the convention and meeting industry faces.

INTRODUCTION

Conventions and meetings are one of the fastest-growing and most lucrative areas of the tourism industry. Within Australia they are encompassed in a sector known as the meetings, incentives, conventions and exhibitions (MICE) industry which, as the name suggests, includes a number of different and diverse areas such as conferences, meetings, incentives, exhibitions and trade shows. The MICE industry traditionally has been regarded as part of the tourism industry, with activities that involve both tourists and non-tourists. However, its chief activity, unlike other tourism areas, is business not leisure. In Australia, the sector has attracted increased attention over recent years, in particular since the launch of the National Strategy for the MICE Industry and the successful bid by Sydney to host the 2000 Olympic Games. One of the key features of the MICE industry, which influences both its policy and its strategy, is its potential to attract national and international visitors. Visitors to MICE events often are referred to as participants, delegates or attendees. MICE events provide additional benefits to the country in the form of business opportunities, education and training, and so on, with many of these events being related to business and professional activities. Conventions, meetings and exhibitions also occur for other reasons, such as sports, culture, hobbies and education. MICE activities often occur outside the peak seasons that are associated with leisure travel. They are therefore potentially advantageous to hotels, resorts, restaurants, and so on, in offsetting low and off-peak business periods.

The acronym 'MICE', adopted by the industry, came into being in the mid 1990s. Despite being widely recognised within Australia, the term is not used globally. The term has been subject to much comment, with many calls being made for it to be changed. John Morse has stated: 'It has to go if the industry is to be taken seriously. A mouse is a rodent, making little contribution to anything.' He also noted that by continuing to use the name 'MICE', it is making it difficult for the industry to negotiate with government and business leaders both in Australia and overseas (*Convention & Incentive Marketing* 1997, p. 3). This comment has been taken up by the industry press, who have stated that 'many people have striven for years to gain recognition and respect for this blossoming industry'(*Convention & Incentive Marketing* 1997). However, to date, the acronym is still being upheld within the industry in Australia.

In discussing the industry as a whole in this text, the terms 'MICE' and 'conventions and meetings' are used interchangeably. It is fully recognised that the name MICE relates to meetings, incentives, conventions and exhibitions. However, the focus of this text is on the convention and meeting aspects of the industry. There is little in-depth discussion and analysis of the incentives, exhibitions and special events sectors, other than in general terms as a major and integral component of many conventions and meetings. The exhibition industry warrants separate discussion with regard to its structure, organisation and methods of operation.

This chapter provides an overview of the environment of conventions and meetings as part of the MICE industry. It reviews the convention and meeting industry with regard to its economic, political, technological and environmental impact on the tourism industry and business in general, and sets the framework for the remainder of the text.

THE CONVENTION AND MEETING INDUSTRY: AN OVERVIEW

Conventions, conferences and meetings range in size from small meetings of five to 25 people, to conferences for up to 200 delegates, and conventions attracting in excess of 4000 people incorporating world-class exhibitions. While much kudos is given to the large conventions and exhibitions, a large part of the continuous day-to-day business is in the provision of meetings facilities for a range of corporate, government and association delegates. These meetings are held in venues such as hotels, resorts and conference centres in capital cities, regional towns and rural areas.

The activities that are encompassed within the MICE industry have been identified as a range of management, educational and marketing tools that enable businesses and individuals to receive benefits in the fields of sales, marketing, education, communication, motivation and evaluation. The MICE industry and the products from a MICE event have been recognised as an effective communications medium (Commonwealth Department of Tourism 1995, p. 3).

The provision of conventions and meetings was a sector of the tourism industry that was relatively neglected until the early 1990s. In 1992, the National Tourism Strategy identified the sector as 'having significant growth potential' (Commonwealth Department of Tourism 1992). However, the development and launch of the National Strategy for the MICE Industry in 1995 aimed to identify and address the issues for ensuring the long-term growth of the sector and the economic and social benefits that it would provide to Australia (Commonwealth Department of Tourism 1995). The sector was also mentioned and recommendations made as to its continued development and expansion in an industry report prepared for the federal government's National Tourism Plan (Hutchinson 1997). The MICE sector is seen as a rapidly growing area of the global tourism industry, with many national tourism offices designing and focusing strategies that are geared to developing this market — for example, in Australia, Singapore and Japan.

There are many aspects to the provision of conventions and meetings. One is that they often require the services and facilities of a number of industry stakeholders, such as providers of specialist venues and conference centres, transport, accommodation, catering, social programs, specialist technical support, exhibition facilities, florists, printers, and so on, as well as the services of a specialised professional, such as a professional conference organiser (PCO) or exhibition organiser.

As a result, to a greater or lesser extent many specialists are involved in the provision of such events, all of whom must be coordinated if the events are to be successful (Commonwealth Department of Tourism 1995). This provides a number of challenges for the event coordinators to ensure quality of service for both the organisers and delegates.

A number of important trends have occurred within business in general (Nebel et al. 1994, p. 88) that have impacted on the convention and meeting industry. There is an increasingly competitive environment in all market segments and geographic regions, with consumers demanding more value for the goods and services they purchase. As Nebel et al. identify '[there are] more demanding customers requiring that hotels meet or exceed guest expectations to earn repeat business' (Nebel et al. 1994, p. 88). In addition, there has been an exponential growth in the sophistication, variety and affordability of information technology. These factors, together with increased mobility, the rapid expansion and awareness of tourism and travel, and a recognition that conventions and meetings are an effective means of communication, have been some of the driving forces behind the growth of the industry worldwide over the last 20 to 30 years. Within the Asia–Pacific region, as economies have grown, so has the development of business and professional associations, whose aim is to share knowledge and progress their various national, regional and international businesses (Dwyer & Mistilis 1998, p. 762).

The MICE industry, and its various components, provides a number of potential benefits to an economy:

- It contributes to employment and income both nationally and regionally.
- It increases a country's foreign exchange earnings.
- It helps to generate investment in tourism and recreation infrastructure, thereby increasing the number of available attractions in an area for both local people and visitors.
- It stimulates a country's business activity both nationally and internationally by assisting in strengthening business links between firms. Opportunities are provided to promote both the national interest and international cooperation.
- It provides opportunities to access new technology and the exchange of ideas and to establish valuable business and professional contacts as well as other social and cultural aspects.
- It brings together leading national and international specialists and practitioners in their fields at conventions and meetings. The drawing together of leaders in science, medicine, business and technology can strengthen a country's professional expertise in that discipline.
- It provides a facility for continuing education and training and a forum for developing and maintaining professional contacts.
- A successful convention, meeting or exhibition can be a very effective method of attracting new business or visitors to an area. It can offer a company an effective method for promoting its products or services to a specific target audience. Internationally, it can promote and enhance a country's image as a tourist destination.

- It provides local tourism operators with advanced knowledge of visitor numbers. The relatively long lead times that are associated with the planning and organising of conventions, meetings and exhibitions can assist tourism properties to plan ahead from both a financial and operational perspective (Commonwealth Department of Tourism 1995, p. 7; Dwyer & Forsyth 1996, p. 314).

Australia has gained world recognition for the excellence of its convention, meeting and exhibition facilities. A surge of interest in the country as a conference destination, coupled with the added exposure of the Sydney 2000 Olympic Games, has ensured that the industry has and will continue to boom over the next 10 years (AACB 1994). The MICE industry is seen as an important and lucrative part of tourism revenue generation, estimated to provide around $7 billion annually in direct expenditure from both domestic and international markets (Johnson, Foo & O'Halloran 1999, p. xvii), and is recognised as a high-yield sector of the tourism industry. A key feature of the sector is the substantially higher than average daily expenditure by conference delegates compared with other sectors of the tourism industry. As a result, the MICE market is viewed as highly desirable (AACB 1994) and is seen as a growing market.

The confidence in the continued development and growth of the industry was confirmed by the Department of Industry, Science and Tourism through the publication of the National Strategy for the MICE Industry (1995) and by a former Australian Commonwealth government Minister of Tourism, who stated:

> ■ By the year 2000 more than 250 000 international delegates are expected to travel to Australia to attend conventions, conferences, seminars, trade shows, exhibitions. While these delegates stay only a relatively short time they are a high spending group of travellers and their value to Australian tourism and the economy is becoming increasingly important (Commonwealth Department of Tourism 1995, p. iii). ■

The industry will play a key part in the creation of new employment opportunities, and the National Strategy clearly identified the need for the MICE industry to be competitive, have a customer focus, develop a workforce by training and development and be more professional.

The MICE sector has grown in Australia for a number of reasons:
- There has been considerable development of the country's infrastructure.
- Winning the right to hold the 2000 Olympic Games has enhanced Australia's reputation of capability and efficiency.
- The marketing programs undertaken by the Australian Tourist Commission (ATC), states, territories and the industry have ensured that Australia has become a highly popular tourist destination (Hutchinson 1997, p. 117).

These reasons should be borne in mind in light of the potential benefits and opportunities provided by the sector and the trends in business mentioned earlier.

So what are the characteristics of the MICE industry in terms of events, delegates and the requirements for facilities and infrastructure to support the industry's activities? How large is the domestic MICE industry? What are Australia and New Zealand's positions in the international convention and meeting industry?

■ The international *market*

In the worldwide international meetings market, the United States and the United Kingdom traditionally have been the market leaders in the number of international association meetings held per country. In the period 1995–97 they hosted between 13 and 14 per cent of the total market (ICCA 1997). However, in recent years the United States has lost market share, along with France, Japan and a number of other European countries (e.g. Denmark and Belgium), where there has been a decrease in the number of international meetings hosted. The trend to hold meetings away from the traditional bastion of international meetings in Europe favoured countries such as Australia, an area that has become a very popular conference destination. Part of Australia's appeal is that the country is seen as a sunny, safe and politically stable destination (Tolhurst 1998). Statistics on the international conference and meeting industry indicate that Australia has demonstrated a sustained development in the 1990s, gaining market share consistently in this period. The growth of conventions within the Asia–Pacific region increased by 124 per cent in the period 1980–96 (Hutchinson 1997). Australia progressed from being ranked eleventh by the ICCA on the number of meetings held per country in 1995, to joint sixth with Japan in 1996, and third in the world in 1997 (see table 1.1). The United States and the United Kingdom remained numbers one and two during this period. Preliminary estimates for 1999 and 2000 indicate that the United States and the United Kingdom will remain popular, but that Australia looks certain to take over first place in 2000 (ICCA 1999). In 1997, New Zealand was ranked forty-fifth by the ICCA, hosting just seven international meetings.

The increase in the popularity of Australia as a convention destination has had a resultant increase in its market share of international meetings. In 1992 this was just 2.2 per cent. By 1996 the ICCA identified that Australia accounted for 4.7 per cent of the world's international meetings, with its convention and meeting business accounting for 17 per cent of meetings held in the Asia–Pacific region (ICCA 1997). The increase in market share continued in 1997 to 5.3 per cent, at which time Australia became the number one convention destination in the Asia–Pacific area, holding 22 per cent of the international meetings convened in the region. However, despite being well placed in world ranking and increasing its market share, the MICE sector in Australia is a long way from achieving its full potential for income generation and economic benefit (Hutchinson 1997).

■ Table 1.1
*The top 20
international
association
meeting
countries,
1995–97
(see
appendix for
2000
figures)*

NUMBER OF MEETINGS PER COUNTRY			
Country	1995	1996	1997
1. United States	197	190	148
2. United Kingdom	176	159	147
3. Australia	78	118	118
4. Germany	118	119	107
5. Spain	110	114	103
6. Netherlands	140	124	102
7. France	141	125	98
8. Italy	114	112	93
9. Japan	132	118	82
10. Finland	63	83	68
11. Canada	72	64	64
12. Denmark	79	101	58
13. Sweden	57	66	58
14. Belgium	62	66	57
15. Norway	49	46	57
16. Austria	80	87	55
17. Switzerland	51	62	44
18. Greece	30	38	43
19. Thailand	20	21	42
20. Hong Kong	35	45	42

Note: The ICCA statistics gathered on international meetings follow the criteria that the meetings are organised on a regular basis, rotate between four different countries and attract a minimum of 50 participants.

Source: ICCA (1997)

The United Kingdom and Australia are the only two countries in the world to have two cities in the top 20 convention cities (London, Edinburgh, Sydney and Melbourne — see table 1.2) and Australia is the only country to have four cities in the top 60 (Sydney, Melbourne, Adelaide and Brisbane).

■ Table 1.2
*The world's
top 20
convention
cities, by
number of
meetings
held per city,
1997 (see
appendix for
2000
figures)*

NUMBER OF MEETINGS PER CITY			
City	**1997**	**City**	**1997**
1. Barcelona	48	11. Brussels	27
2. Sydney	44	12. Seoul	27
3. London	41	13. Prague	26
4. Copenhagen	41	14. Melbourne	25
5. Hong Kong	39	15. Edinburgh	25
6. Amsterdam	37	16. Bangkok	25
7. Vienna	37	17. Taipei	24
8. Paris	36	18. Budapest	23
9. Helsinki	34	19. Jerusalem	22
10. Stockholm	30	20. Oslo	21

Source: ICCA (1997)

The number of participants at international meetings has increased by 10 per cent in the period 1992–97, to an average of 707 delegates per meeting in 1997 (ICCA 1997). The size of the meetings ranges mainly from 50 to 1000 participants, with the larger meetings taking place in North America. Meetings in the Australia/Pacific region have demonstrated a tendency to increase in size, whereas those in the United States have tended to decrease. Meeting size in the United Kingdom has remained constant (ICCA 1997).

It is well recognised that international visitors who attend a convention or meeting provide substantial economic benefits to the host country. In order for Australia to build and sustain an increase in the number of international meetings hosted and the visitors attending conventions, it is essential that the country continues to bid to host international conventions. This has been successful to date, with city convention bureaus, such as Sydney, following a determined strategy to bid and attract international conventions. This will be discussed further in chapter 5.

Where international companies choose to site their headquarters can influence their decision as to the destination for their conventions or meetings. Many international corporations have selected Europe and North America (89 per cent) for their base headquarters, with only 6 per cent selecting Asia and 9 per cent the Asia–Pacific area. Twenty-seven per cent of international meetings rotate only within Europe, but twice as many international meetings (55 per cent) are rotated internationally. As such, they provide the opportunity for countries such as Australia and New Zealand to bid for these events. Figures 1.1 and 1.2 outline information as to the headquarters of international companies and the rotation area of international meetings.

■ **Figure 1.1**
Headquarters of international organisations (associations with meetings post-1997) (see appendix for 2000 figures) (Note: total does not equal 100 due to rounding)

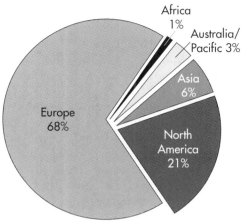

Source: ICCA (1997)

■ **Figure 1.2**
Rotation area of international meetings, 1997 (see appendix for 2000 figures)

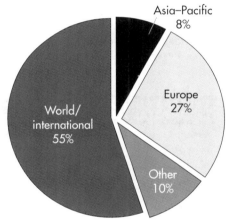

Source: ICCA (1997)

There are indications of a trend towards an increase in the number of international meetings, not only for large organisations, but also for small- and medium-sized businesses (Stanfield 1998). This factor, together with a requirement for more cultural experiences and outdoor and sporting events to be incorporated into meetings along with health and fitness (which continues to be a compulsory ingredient), can only benefit both Australia and New Zealand, whose natural facilities and infrastructure are compatible with these needs. Regional areas within both countries can capitalise on the trends apparent within the international market, as they have with the domestic meetings market (Stanfield 1998).

The majority of association meetings identified by the ICCA take place over a three- to five-day period in convention centres (51 per cent), hotels (22 per cent) and universities (18 per cent). May, June, September and October are the most popular months, with November and December and January to April the least popular periods. The focus of most meetings is medical sciences, general science and industry (ICCA 1999).

■ The Australian *market*

Size and structure

The domestic or national meetings market forms the backbone of the industry within Australia, accounting for approximately 80 per cent of convention and meeting business, as compared to 20 per cent for international meetings. An accurate assessment of the MICE industry in Australia, however, is hampered by a lack of reliable and comprehensive data. The problem is exacerbated by the fact that the estimates that are produced often combine sources that are not necessarily compatible, with the comparisons being drawn from different sources.

In the years 1995–96, the domestic convention and meeting market accounted for 2.7 per cent of all overnight domestic trips, providing an estimated expenditure of $880 million. National association and corporate meetings comprised most of this market. Of a total of 256 472 000 projected visitor nights, 4 917 000, or 19 per cent, were associated with conventions and meetings (Office of National Tourism 1998). Table 1.3 demonstrates the development of the attendance of domestic visitors at conferences and seminars during the period 1987–97, which rose from 2 per cent in 1987 to 3 per cent in 1997 — a slow but consistent growth over the 10-year period.

■ Table 1.3
*Primary
purpose
of trip,
1987–97*

PRIMARY PURPOSE (% OF TOTAL TRIPS)	1987–88	1988–89	1989–90	1990–91	1991–92
Visiting friends and relatives	26	26	27	27	28
Pleasure/holiday	45	44	41	41	41
Conference/seminar	2	1	2	2	2
Other business	13	13	13	14	15
Other/not stated	14	15	17	16	14
Total trips	100	100	100	100	100
Total trips (000)	46 725	46 017	49 962	48 997	48 235

PRIMARY PURPOSE (% OF TOTAL TRIPS)	1992–93	1993–94	1994–95	1995–96	1996–97
Visiting friends and relatives	29	29	30	30	30
Pleasure/holiday	39	39	35	36	35
Conference/seminar	2	2	3	3	3
Other business	14	16	14	14	15
Other/not stated	16	14	18	17	17
Total trips	100	100	100	100	100
Total trips (000)	47 878	48 113	57 898	63 028	62 780

Source: BTR (1999)

Over 98 000 international visitors to Australia in 1997–98 stated that the main purpose of their visit was to attend an international convention or conference (ATC 1998). This figure represents a downturn of nearly 15 per cent on 1996–97, reflected perhaps by the economic downturn in Asia. The main countries of origin of these delegates were Asia, the Americas, New Zealand, and Europe and the former USSR (see table 1.4).

■ **Table 1.4**
Short-term overseas visitor arrivals for the year ending August 1998 (and compared to the year ending August 1997)

Source: ABS (1998)

PURPOSE OF VISIT / COUNTRY OF RESIDENCE	HOLIDAY		VISIT FRIENDS & RELATIVES		BUSINESS		CONVENTION & CONFERENCE		OTHER PURPOSES		TOTAL ALL PURPOSES	
	ARRIVALS	CHANGE	ARRIVALS	CHANGE	ARRIVALS	CHANGE	ARRIVALS	CHANGE	ARRIVALS	CHANGE	ARRIVALS	CHANGE
The Americas	187 690	2.9%	104 265	13.7%	86 899	6.2%	21 509	3.1%	53 385	37.1%	453 748	9.1%
Japan	679 869	-5.2%	17 991	30.1%	29 059	-8.6%	3 625	-22.0%	48 597	24.3%	779 141	-3.4%
Asia (ex Japan)	617 422	-26.8%	171 701	1.4%	112 087	-1.2%	26 912	-25.2%	175 623	0.4%	1 103 745	-17.4%
Central & Southern Africa	21 976	-0.9%	20 471	4.1%	7 359	15.3%	1 797	-15.5%	9 859	65.8%	61 462	9.2%
Middle East & Northern Africa	16 083	10.8%	11 087	-10.8%	3 505	15.8%	1 234	-19.0%	7 613	98.3%	39 522	11.8%
Europe & former USSR	439 163	4.6%	296 839	11.0%	81 359	11.6%	17 937	-24.5%	91 165	52.7%	926 463	9.8%
New Zealand	311 857	0.2%	201 705	2.2%	109 443	6.4%	21 233	-2.9%	56 942	16.9%	701 180	2.8%
South Pacific (ex New Zealand)	51 355	3.5%	24 757	3.6%	10 162	0.8%	4 049	-12.4%	31 175	13.5%	121 498	5.0%
Other	148	–	49	–	96	–	27	–	1 118	–	1 438	–
All countries	2 325 563	-9.2%	848 865	6.6%	439 969	4.2%	98 323	-14.8%	475 477	19.2%	4 188 197	-2.4%

Information on the number of international visitors coming to Australia for the purpose of attending a conference or convention is varied. Table 1.5(a) provides data from the *Domestic Tourism Monitor* (1990–97), which gathers information from international travellers who report conference or convention as the main purpose of their journey. The growth in visitor numbers can be seen clearly; however, the figures are significantly lower than those reported by the ABS and the International Visitor Survey (IVS) for the period 1990–96, shown in Table 1.5(b). Table 1.5(b) provides three groups of figures which, though indicating the growth in international convention delegates to Australia, demonstrate the variances in the potential number of visitors who attend a conference or convention. The ABS overseas arrivals and departure (OAD) data records information on international visitors who indicate convention or conference as the main purpose of their journey. The IVS records data on the number of international visitors who report attendance at a convention or conference as the main or other reason for their journey. The IVS also obtains information from international visitors as to whether they attended a convention, exhibition or trade show, or accompanied someone who did, regardless of the main purpose of their journey (BTR/TFC 1998, p. 24). Despite the variances, it is clearly apparent that the number of convention and conference visitors is increasing, though the specific number may be different depending on the source of the statistics studied. The BTR IVS estimated that in 1996, 6 per cent of all international visitors attended a conference or similar function during their stay in Australia (Office of National Tourism 1998).

■ **Table 1.5(a)** *International visitors by main purpose of journey, 1990–97*

MAIN PURPOSE	1990	1991	1992	1993	1994	1995	1996	1997
Holiday	1 153 900	1 327 500	1 489 000	1 730 900	1 933 400	2 047 100	2 290 000	2 302 500
Visiting relatives	407 100	426 600	440 000	475 200	540 600	631 600	704 100	737 100
Business	231 100	221 500	236 100	267 800	320 800	360 400	391 700	436 100
Convention	41 900	34 700	27 700	44 000	50 800	69 600	98 900	126 800
Other	231 300	206 300	232 900	265 400	259 000	312 500	345 100	371 500

Note: Changes in purpose of journey categories from September 1994 mean that data after that date are not strictly comparable with data for earlier periods.

Source: BTR (1999)

■ **Table 1.5(b)**
Number of conference or convention visitors 1990–96

YEAR	ABS OAD MAIN REASON CONFERENCE	IVS MAIN OR OTHER REASON CONFERENCE	IVS ATTENDED A MICE EVENT
1990	32 500	49 700	115 200
1991	42 800	51 200	111 000
1992	32 300	38 800	100 600
1993	50 200	64 900	131 400
1994	64 900	84 900	130 700
1995	89 700	104 400	155 500
1996	112 900	130 000	211 700

Source: ABS (1998); BTR (1998)

Overseas visitor arrivals are forecasted to grow annually by 5.9 per cent, to reach 7.6 million in 2007 (Office of National Tourism 1998). If it is assumed that the number of convention and conference visitors will grow in the same proportion, then the projected convention visitor arrivals for the year 2007 can be forecasted to be approximately 400 000. Despite the continued growth in the numbers of international convention visitors to Australia, the challenge for Australia is to overcome the impact of the Asian downturn and focus convention marketing on other destinations such as North America and Europe, together with maintaining the benefits of the Olympic exposure after the year 2000.

Timing of conventions and meetings

Consistent and reliable data within Australia and New Zealand as to the most popular months for conventions and meetings are not available. However, it would appear that the most popular period is August to November (McCabe & Bassan 1999), with the quietest months, as would be expected, being January and December. May and June also are popular months with their proximity to the end of the financial year.

Delegate spending patterns

MICE visitors spend more than other visitors per night. The Sydney Convention & Visitors Bureau (SCVB) delegate survey of 1996 indicated that convention visitors spend $4723 per week exclusive of international airfares, while the average visitor expenditure is $3851 per week (Hutchinson 1997, p. 117). The following snapshot presents information on international and domestic convention delegates who visited Sydney in 1997 with the purpose of attending a MICE event.

SNAPSHOT
Profile of convention delegates to Sydney

International delegates

International delegates attending conferences in Sydney stay on average 6.9 nights in the city and 10 days in Australia in total, and spend on average $5722 while in Sydney, or approximately $770 per day. Fifty per cent of the delegates are from Europe (27 per cent) and Asia (23 per cent), followed by North America (13 per cent) and Eastern Europe (11 per cent). Conference delegates from the United Kingdom and Ireland stay in Australia for an average of 12.8 days, while those from Africa and Eastern Europe stay 11.3 days — a factor perhaps of cost and travel time. This is unlike Japanese delegates, who tend to stay for a much shorter period of six days. While in Sydney, conference delegates tend to stay in five- or four-star hotels (79 per cent of all delegates).

(continued)

Just under 50 per cent of all international delegates attending these conferences undertake a pre- or post-conference tour, staying on average a further 3.1 days in the country. Approximately one-third state that the main reason for their tour is to take a holiday, vacation or travel. Queensland is identified as being the most popular destination (56 per cent).

The chief items of expenditure for each delegate, as would be expected, are conference registration fees and accommodation, which amount to just under $2400 of their total expenditure. Domestic airfares, shopping and visiting restaurants equate to a further $2000.

In general, international conference delegates have indicated that they are highly satisfied with their visit to Sydney, rating it 4.2 on a scale of 5, with 5 being excellent.

Domestic delegates

Domestic delegates attending conventions in Sydney demonstrate a predominance towards local participants, with 38 per cent coming from New South Wales. Queensland and Victoria are also popular home states. Approximately three-quarters of all domestic delegates live in capital cities, with one-in-three coming from Sydney, one-in-five from Melbourne and one-in-10 from Brisbane. However, their length of stay in the state capital has declined from 5.4 nights in 1996 to 4.2 nights in 1997. Approximately 50 per cent of domestic participants stay in a hotel while attending conferences, with four-star hotels being the most popular choice (42 per cent). This is in contrast to their international counterparts, where a large group (37 per cent) tend to select five-star hotels.

Domestic delegates spend on average $2089 per delegate for their entire stay in Sydney, or $544 per day. Fifty per cent of this is spent on conference registration fees and accommodation, while other key areas of expenditure include shopping, visiting restaurants, attending social functions at the convention and undertaking tours (25 per cent).

Pre- and post-conference tours are also popular with domestic delegates when coupled with a convention. A quarter of domestic delegates plan to undertake this activity, in particular delegates from Western Australia, Queensland, South Australia and the Northern Territory. The most popular destination is the city itself and its suburbs (61 per cent). Other popular areas in New South Wales include the Blue Mountains and the coast. Visits undertaken to the city, its suburbs and the coast were mainly for visiting friends and family, while tours taken to the Blue Mountains or Hunter Valley were mainly for a holiday or sightseeing.

Source: SCVB (1997, 1998)

■ Facilities *and infrastructure*

The MICE sector utilises a variety of infrastructure and facilities.

Venues

Convention and meeting facilities within Australia and New Zealand are found not only within hotels, motels, resorts and purpose-built convention and exhibition centres, but also in other venues such as historic buildings, national icons, universities and entertainment and sporting centres. These are reviewed in more detail in chapter 2.

Prior to 1987, the area had no purpose-built convention facilities specifically designed to accommodate and stage major conventions. This shortage prompted state governments in Australia to invest in purpose-built convention and exhibition centres. They fully recognised that they would provide little return on investment as a 'stand-alone business', but would attract conventions and their delegates to the city or area, thereby gaining the economic benefit (Commonwealth Department of Tourism 1995). Australia and New Zealand now have world-class, purpose-built convention and exhibition centres in many of their major cities, including Adelaide, Canberra, Melbourne, Sydney, Brisbane, Cairns, Wellington and Christchurch. These centres have been integrated into the tourism infrastructure of each city or area.

There has been a strong and continuing growth in the development of other convention and meeting venues (BTR/TFC 1998). This development has occurred not only in the capital cities, but also in regional centres, where hotels and other venues have either been built or redeveloped in an attempt to gain a share of this lucrative market. For example, the award-winning North Star Caravan Park situated on the northern coast of New South Wales has incorporated a 120-seat convention room as part of the facilities provided by the caravan park. It is rare now for a new hotel to be constructed without some convention or meeting facilities being included in the design. Initially the development took place in major regional cities and towns and areas outside the capital cities, such as Albury/Wodonga, Launceston and Townsville. However, expansion and development of new facilities has now occurred more extensively to incorporate coastal and resort areas, such as Noosa and the Sunshine Coast. For these areas the industry is seen as an opportunity to gain business in the traditional tourist off-peak periods. Many of these venues cater specifically for the local and domestic MICE business.

The complete extent of Australia's convention and meeting capacity is not fully known. However, the convention and visitors bureau in each major city or area produces a *Facilities Guide* that provides information on the full range of MICE facilities available in the area (this is discussed further in chapter 2). Other directories, such as *Dawsons Venue Directory*, provide additional information on venues that provide convention and meeting facilities. Inclusion in *Dawsons Venue Directory* is subject to a fee, so the number of venues featured may not be a true reflection of the total facilities available. Table 1.6 illustrates the convention and meeting capacity available in each state.

■ Table 1.6 *Convention and meeting seating capacity by state*

VENUE	LARGEST ROOM (THEATRE STYLE)	VENUE	LARGEST ROOM (THEATRE STYLE)
AUSTRALIAN CAPITAL TERRITORY			
Canberra Area		Parkroyal Canberra	480
Exhibition Park in Canberra	3200	Canberra Rex Hotel	450
National Convention Centre	2700	Brassey of Canberra	250
Chifley on Northbourne, Canberra	900	Canberra International	200
Old Parliament House	600	Griffin (The)	90
Hyatt Hotel Canberra	500	AMA House	80
NEW SOUTH WALES			
Sydney Airport Area		Museum of Sydney	124
Novotel Brighton Beach	600	UniLodge Sydney (Hotel)	120
Sheraton Sydney Airport Hotel	550	Woolloomooloo Waters	120
Parkroyal Sydney Airport	180	De Vere Hotel	100
		Furama Hotel Darling Harbour	80
Sydney City Area		Chateau Sydney Hotel	70
Sydney Convention & Exhibition Centre	3500		
Sydney Opera House	2690	**Sydney Suburbs**	
Sydney Town Hall	2048	Sydney Superdome	12 500
Westin Sydney (The)	1500	Sydney Showground & Exhibition Complex	4000
Wentworth (The) – A Rydges Hotel	1100	AJC Convention & Exhibition Centre	1500
Sheraton On The Park	940	Panthers Resort	1500
ANA Hotel Sydney	900	Stadium Australia	1500
Wesley Conference Centre	900	Bankstown District Sports Club	1000
Star City	860	Paddington Town Hall	750
Dockside	760	Windsor Function Centre	720
Centrepoint Convention Exhibition Centre	700	Parramatta Riverside Theatres	696
Metro on George	600	Sunnybrook Hotel & Convention Centre	660
Gazebo Sydney Hotel & Conference Centre	500	Epping RSL & Community Club Ltd	600
Sydney Boulevard (The)	500	Gazebo Parramatta Hotel & Conference Centre	600
All Seasons Premier Menzies Hotel Sydney	450	Manly Pacific Parkroyal	600
Millennium Hotel Sydney	450	Ritz-Carlton, Double Bay (The)	550
Nikko Darling Harbour (Hotel)	450	Fox Studios	400
Rex Hotel Sydney	400	Parkroyal Parramatta	400
Sebel of Sydney (The)	400	Rydges Parramatta	400
Carlton Crest Hotel Sydney	350	Swiss Grand Hotel	400
Oxford Koala Hotel and Apartments	350	Curzon Hall	300
Museum of Contemporary Art	300	HIA Conference Centre	300
Sega World Sydney	300	Holiday Inn Coogee Beach	300
Waters Edge	300	Holroyd Centre (The)	280
Parkroyal at Darling Harbour	280	Hawkesbury Lodge & Rum Corps Convention Centre	270
Sydney Marriott Hotel	280	Zenith Convention Centre	251
Mercure Hotel Sydney	260	Chiffley on City View, Pennant Hills	250
Avillion Hotel Sydney	250	Mercure St Leonards – Sydney	250
Portside Centre (The)	250	Coogee Bay Hotel (The)	240
UTS Graduate School of Business	250	Sydney International Aquatic Centre	224
Furama Hotel Central	225	Duxton Hotel North Sydney	220
Renaissance Sydney Hotel	220	Hills Lodge Boutique Hotel (The)	220
Australian National Maritime Museum	210	Kensington Colleges (The)	220
Mercure Hotel Lawson City West	210	Country Comfort Rooty Hill	200
Captain Cook Cruises	200	Panthers Nepean Shores	200
Grace Hotel (The)	200	Stamford North Ryde	200
Novotel Sydney on Darling Harbour	200	Blaxland (The)	188
Sydney Vista Hotel	200	Checkers Country Resort & Conference Centre	180
Theatrette & Conference Facility	188	Courtyard by Marriott Parramatta	140
Ritz-Carlton, Sydney (The)	180	Hawkesbury Conference Centre	140
Holiday Inn Potts Point	160	Newport Mirage	130
Y On the Park – YWCA Sydney	160	Rushcutters Harbourside Sydney	130
Argyle Restaurants & Function Centre	150	Rydges Cronulla Beach	120

VENUE	LARGEST ROOM (THEATRE STYLE)	VENUE	LARGEST ROOM (THEATRE STYLE)
Mona Vale Conference Centre (The)	110	Mountain Heritage Country House Retreat	200
Killara Inn	100	Westbury's Marina Resort	200
Manly Windsor Hotel	100	Coolangatta Estate	180
Middle Harbour Hideaway	100	Country Comfort Monte Pio	180
Sir Stamford Double Bay	100	Country Comfort Port Stephens	180
Wisemans Ferry Country Retreat	90	Horizons Golf Resort & Conference Centre	180
Radisson Kestrel Hotel on Manly Beach	80	Nautilus Coffs Harbour, A Rydges Resort	180
Sydney Huntley Inn Gladesville	80	Milton Park	170
Twin Towers Motor Inn	80	Peppers Anchorage Port Stephens	165
		Rafferty's Resort Lake Macquarie	160
NSW Country		Sails Resort	160
Wollongong Entertainment Centre	5000	Vineyard Resort Conference & Function Centre	160
Country Comfort Mudgee	1200	Apollo Country Resort	150
Albury Convention/Performing Arts Centre	812	Ballina Beach Resort	150
Fairmont Resort	800	Central City Hotel Newcastle	150
Novotel Northbeach	640	Country Comfort Terrigal	150
Novotel Opal Cove Resort	550	Hunter Resort – Hunter Valley	150
Wagga Wagga Leagues Club	500	Leura Gardens Ibis Resort	150
Crowne Plaza Hotels & Resorts Terrigal	420	Sanctuary Resort	150
Jamberoo Valley Lodge	400	Lilianfels Blue Mountains	140
Country Comfort Wagga Wagga	350	Salamander Shores	130
Kirkton Park Country House Hotel	350	Cypress Lakes Resort	120
Noah's on the Beach	300	Hydro Majestic Hotel (The)	120
Seascape Manor	300	Jenolan Caves House	120
All Seasons Premier Pacific Bay Resort	250	Lord Byron Resort	120
Beachcomber (The)	250	Peppers Guest House	120
Bonville International Golf & Country Club	250	Peppers Manor House	120
Charbonnier Hallmark Inn	250	Clan Lakeside Lodge	110
Dooralong Valley Resort	250	Historic Mowbray Park	100
Forresters Resort	250	Leura House	100
Grand Mercure Hotel Bowral Heritage Park	250	Pokolbin Village Resort & Conference Centre	100
Murramarang Resort	250	Colonial Restaurant & Convention Centre	80
Pelican Beach Centra Resort	250	Holiday Inn Esplanade Newcastle	80
Thredbo Alpine Village	250	Little Company Retreat (The)	80
Frog & Toad Function Cetre	210	Lodge Hawks Nest (The)	80
Aanuka Beach Resort	200	Mollymook Shores	80
Bellbird Resort	200	Novotel Lake Crackenback Resort	80
Byron Bay Beach Club	200	Where Waters Meet	70
Country Comfort Albury	200	Peppers The Convent Pepper Tree	45
Macarthur Estate Country Retreat	200		

NORTHERN TERITORY
Darwin

VENUE	LARGEST ROOM (THEATRE STYLE)	VENUE	LARGEST ROOM (THEATRE STYLE)
Carlton Hotel Darwin	500	**NT Country**	
MGM Grand Darwin	500	Ayers Rock Resort	600
Rydges Plaza Darwin	300	Lasseters Hotel Casino	380
		Red Centre Resort	200

QUEENSLAND
Brisbane City

VENUE	LARGEST ROOM (THEATRE STYLE)	VENUE	LARGEST ROOM (THEATRE STYLE)
Brisbane Convention & Exhibition Centre	3988	Brisbane Marriott Hotel	220
Sheraton Brisbane Hotel & Towers	1125	Chifley on George, Brisbane	200
Carlton Crest Hotel Brisbane	1000	Gazebo Hotel Brisbane	150
Parkroyal Brisbane	900	Diana Plaza Hotel	120
Mercure Hotel Brisbane	800	Abbey Plaza Hotel	100
Country Comfort Lennons Hotel Brisbane	500	Conrad International Brisbane	100
Centra Brisbane	450	Dockside Apartment Hotel	100
Novotel Brisbane	350		
Customs House	300	**Brisbane Suburbs**	
Grand Chancellor Hotel Brisbane	300	Brisbane Entertainment Centre	13500
Ridge Hotel	300	Queensland Clunies Ross Centre	680
			(continued)

■ Table 1.6 *Convention and meeting seating capacity by state (cont'd)*

VENUE	LARGEST ROOM (THEATRE STYLE)	VENUE	LARGEST ROOM (THEATRE STYLE)
Bardon Centre (The)	300	**Queensland Country**	
Powerhouse Boutique Hotel	300	Cairns Convention Centre	5000
Robertson Gardens Plaza Hotel	180	Townsville Entertainment & Convention Centre	4500
Mt Ommaney Plaza Hotel	110	Hamilton Island	1000
		Novotel Twin Waters Resort	1000
Brisbane Offshore Islands		Oasis Resort Hotel & Conference Centre	830
Couran Cove Resort	252	Sheraton Townsville Hotel & Casino	810
South Stradbroke Island Resort	120	Cairns International Hotel	600
		Kondari Resort	600
Gold Coast		Rydges Capricorn International Resort	600
Warner Bros Movie World	2000	Novotel Palm Cove Resort	550
Royal Pines Resort	1800	Reef Hotel Casino	500
Club Banora	1500	Radisson Plaza Hotel At The Pier Cairns	400
Sheraton Mirage Gold Coast	1050	Rihga Colonial Club Resort Cairns	380
Twin Towers Services Club	1040	Ivory's Rock Conference Centre	360
Sea World	800	Centra Townsville	350
Surfers Paradise Marriott Resort	800	Noosa Lakes Resort Convention & Exhibition Centre	350
ANA Hotel Gold Coast	700	Club Med Lindeman Island	300
Gold Coast International Hotel	700	Country Plaza International	300
Radisson Resort Palm Meadows	700	Kingfisher Bay Resort & Village	300
Parkroyal Surfers Paradise	530	Radisson Reef Resort	300
Courtyard by Marriott Surfers Paradise	520	Sheraton Mirage Port Douglas	300
Grand Mercure Broadbeach–Gold Coast	450	Sheraton Noosa Resort	270
Mercure Resort Surfers Paradise	400	Courtyard by Marriott Great Barrier Reef	220
All Seasons Mermaid Waters Hotel	300	Holiday Inn Cairns	160
Euro-Asia Legends Hotel Gold Coast	300	Townsville Plaza Hotel	140
Holiday Inn Hope Island, Gold Coast	270	Horizon (The) at Mission Beach	130
Calypso Plaza Coolangatta	160	Sheridan Plaza Hotel	120
O'Reilly's Rainforest Guesthouse	100		
Narrow Leaf Retreat	35		
SOUTH AUSTRALIA			
Adelaide City Area		**South Australia Country**	
Stamford Plaza Adelaide	350	Barossa Convention Centre (The)	1000
Grosvenor Vista Hotel Adelaide	300	Paradise Wirrina Cove	350
Chifley on South Terrace Adelaide (The)	160	All Seasons Premier Barossa Valley	220
		Grand Mercure Hotel Mount Lofty House	150
Adelaide Suburbs			
Stamford Grand Adelaide	800		
Australian Mineral Foundation	400		
TASMANIA			
Hobart Area		**Tasmania Country**	
Wrest Point Casino	1600	Country Club Casino	500
Grand Chancellor Hotel Hobart	800		
Derwent Entertainment Centre	300		
Country Comfort Hadleys Hotel	250		
VICTORIA			
Melbourne Airport Area		Park Hyatt Melbourne	700
Tullamarine Airport Motor Inn	110	Chifley on Flemington Melbourne (The)	450
		Melbourne Exhibition Centre	450
Melbourne City Area		Sheraton Towers Southgate Melbourne	360
Melbourne Park Function Centre	15000	Novotel Melbourne on Collins	350
Melbourne Convention Centre	2500	Rydges Carlton	350
Crown Towers	2400	Duxton Hotel Melbourne	320
Carlton Crest Hotel Melbourne	2100	Le Meridien at Rialto Melbourne	300
Grand Hyatt Melbourne	1300	Windsor – An Oberoi Hotel The	300
Sofitel Melbourne (Hotel)	1200	Eden on the Park	280
RMIT Storey Hall	745	Medina Grand Melbourne	270

VENUE	LARGEST ROOM (THEATRE STYLE)	VENUE	LARGEST ROOM (THEATRE STYLE)
Bayview on the Park	250	Novotel Bayside Melbourne	240
Melbourne Sheraton Hotel	250	Rydges Riverwalk	200
City Conference Centre	200	Settlement Cranbourne (The)	170
Stamford Plaza Melbourne	200	Bruce County	150
All Seasons Premier Swanston Hotel	150	Eltham Gateway Conference Centre	150
Marco Polo Inn	150	Tudor – Box Hill (The)	80
Rydges Melbourne	150	Como (The Hotel)	75
Savoy Park Plaza International Melbourne	150	South Yarra Hill Suites Hotel	25
Downtowner on Lygon	140		
Monash Conference Centre	120	**Victorian Country**	
Radisson on Flagstaff Gardens	80	All Seasons International Hotel	1100
All Seasons Paragon Hotel	70	Mercure Inn Belltower Ballarat	600
Holiday Inn on Flinders Melbourne	65	York on Lilydale Resort	500
Station Pier Condominiums	60	Continental (The)	400
		Cumberland Lorne Conference & Leisure Resort	350
Melbourne Suburbs		All Seasons Ambassador Hotel	300
Showgrounds Exhibition Centre	1800	Pinnacle Valley Resort	250
Moonee Valley Functions & Events	1400	Deakin Management Centre	200
Mansion Hotel at Werribee Park (The)	500	Mt Buller Chalet Hotel	200
Manningham Convention Centre (The)	432	Kooringa Resort & Conference Centre	150
Kimberley Gardens	260	Monash Mt Eliza Business School	130
Elizabethan Lodge	250	Peppers Delgany	88
Novotel Glen Waverley	250	Cammeray Waters	60
WESTERN AUSTRALIA **Perth Area**			
Burswood International Resort Casino	20000	Mercure Hotel Perth	300
Perth Concert Hall	1729	Novotel Vines Resort	260
Rendezvous Observation City Hotel Perth	850	Joondalup Resort Hotel	240
Kings Perth Hotel (The)	800	Underwater World	230
Esplanade Hotel Fremantle	500	Radisson Beach Resort, Dunsborough	220
Duxton Hotel Perth	400	Trade Winds Hotel	200
Lord Forrest (The) – A Furama Hotel	400	Rottnest Lodge Resort	100
Grand Chancellor Perth Hotel	300	Perth Mint	70

Source: Dawsons Venue Directory (1999)

With the main type of business being the domestic meeting market for conferences of under 300–400 delegates (AACB 1994), there is an opportunity for regional areas to bid 'and compete to host conventions and meetings not only from the local area (mainly corporate and government) but also for national and state association business. Policies developed by federal and state government now focus some development of the convention and meeting business in regional Australia. However, regional Australia and other rural areas in general face many challenges in order to maximise their MICE business, not least of which is the perception that they may not have the capability to be serious MICE players. Other difficulties that have been identified include the need to ensure that facilities are up to date and maintained at a high standard, and incorporate advances in industry-specific technology. There is also a requirement for high standards of professionalism in servicing the industry. Furthermore, transport and access issues need to be addressed, such as frequency of flights and distance from major centres. It is also important that resources are available for marketing and identifying creative and more personalised initiatives for this segmented market (Stanfield 1998).

Accommodation.

A wide variety of accommodation at all star ratings is available to support convention and meeting business. International and national hotel groups have all developed a range of facilities in some of the major cities and regions, including Accor Asia Pacific through the Ibis, Novotel and Mercure chains; Hyatt; Hilton; Sheraton, Marriott, All Seasons and SPHC.

However, there is uncertainty as to the amount of accommodation available in certain cities to support MICE activities (BTR 1998). A surplus of accommodation can result in room rates for conventions and meetings becoming very competitive — a trend that is apparent in some cities at certain times (e.g. Brisbane and the Gold Coast) (McCabe & Weeks 1999). On the other hand, a shortage of accommodation during some periods can impact on demand and raise room rates. For example, following the opening of the Brisbane Convention and Exhibition Centre, for certain periods Brisbane suffered from a shortage in the availability of bed stock, as hotel accommodation in the city did not match the requirements generated by the Convention Centre. As a result, convention organisers often were required to 'bus' their delegates to the Gold Coast until bed stock generated by the construction of a number of new three- and five-star hotels came on-line. Other cities such as Perth, Sydney, Melbourne and Darwin also have recognised the difficulty with the supply of accommodation at certain times of the year to meet the demands of convention and meeting business (BTR/TFC 1998, p. 27).

In order to overcome these problems, conventions and meetings may need to be scheduled throughout the year, not only in peak periods. This could be achieved by means of incentives for convention organisers to select dates outside the most popular periods. The successful achievement of a constant level of MICE business in a city throughout the year can demonstrate to potential hotel investors and developers that the industry is financially operational and viable all year round.

Other infrastructure requirements

The current and anticipated growth of the industry has caused the Tourism Forecasting Council (TFC) of Australia to voice concern as to the adequacy of MICE infrastructure both now and in the future. A survey has been undertaken to assess the adequacy of the infrastructure and support services to cater for the future needs of the MICE industry (BTR/TFC 1998). However, it is apparent that the low barriers to industry entry and exit in some areas of infrastructure, such as caterers, entertainment and professional conference organisers (PCOs), means that some industry suppliers can adapt and expand in order to meet demands (BTR/TFC 1998).

THE BUSINESS ENVIRONMENT ·······················

Any review of the profile and characteristics of an industry should also include a discussion of the business environment in which that industry operates. The business environment of the convention and meeting industry includes not only its impact on the nation's economy, but also the political initiatives that have been instigated to support the fledgling industry. Environmental and technological impacts and associated implications on the industry should also be considered.

■ Economic *impacts*

Business and professional people travel throughout the year to attend meetings and conventions. The economic impact of these conventions and meetings is of major significance for the tourism and hospitality industry. For example, most conference participants meet, eat and sleep under one roof — the venue. However, the direct economic impact does not stop with the venue or suppliers such as local restaurants, cultural and sporting activities, sightseeing venues/tours, tourist attractions, local shops and transport facilities, which either provide a service or sell a product to convention delegates. The direct and indirect effects of delegate expenditure is felt throughout the economy of the community, with flow-on expenditure to other firms such as food and beverage suppliers, printers, stationers and so on, from whom the conference organisers may purchase items. The direct and indirect income and expenditure can also produce an induced effect on the economy, whereby the owners and employees of the direct and indirect suppliers spend their income locally on consumer items. This can create increased levels of business and as a result provide additional employment.

As a result, the MICE industry is seen as one of the healthiest and most growth-orientated sectors of the tourism industry. The wide range of stakeholders that may be involved in the provision of a MICE event provides an indication of the potential and extensive economic impact of the sector. This is seen as a major reason for the sector's support by government agencies in many countries.

It is generally recognised that the MICE sector provides about $7 billion annually in direct expenditure to the Australian economy. Approximately $6 billion is attributed to conventions and meetings, and about $1 billion is spent by exhibition attendees (Johnson, Foo & O'Halloran 1999, p. xvii). The MICE sector is seen as a high-yield area of the tourism industry and an important generator of tourism expenditure, foreign exchange earnings, investment and employment. However, there is, as already mentioned, a lack of hard data by which to estimate the magnitude of its effect (Dwyer & Forsyth 1996). The attempts to assess the economic impact of the sector have been rather piecemeal and in some instances the assumptions on which they have been made are questionable (Dwyer & Forsyth 1996). In order for a reliable estimate of the net worth of the industry to be available, an assessment of the direct and indirect effects of the total expenditure, together with the impact of the leakages, and switched and retained income, needs to be undertaken (Dwyer & Forsyth 1996, p. 313). A report focusing on the economic impact of the industry produced by the BTR in mid-1999 has made a significant contribution to improving the situation (Johnson, Foo & O'Halloran 1999, p. xvii).

Government and tourism organisations within Australia stress the value of attracting international conventions and meetings and their potential overseas delegates. There is no doubt that the domestic market — that is, local, regional, state and national conferences and meetings, together with their associated exhibitions — makes up a vast proportion of the business. The convention or meeting industry organiser, however, is not concerned specifically whether a delegate is from overseas or from the region or local area, although this may impact on their organisational arrangements, such as travel and the availability of suitable accommodation. For a conference organiser, the financial success of a convention or meeting is determined by the total number of delegates and the registration fees that they pay, the meals they consume, and the official tours and other formal activities they undertake during the event. The conference organiser is concerned as to whether they can cover the direct expenditure and outgoings for the event, such as the hire of the venue, the provision of food and beverages, conference collateral, marketing, staff costs, and so on.

From the strategic and economic perspective of the MICE industry, the origin of the conference delegate is important, as is both the direct and indirect expenditure made by that conference delegate or on behalf of that delegate (Peters & Jones 1996, p. 2). For example, it has been ascertained that international convention or meeting delegates spend more than domestic delegates in accommodation, pre- and post-event tours, shopping, and so on (SCVB 1998). International delegates therefore boost foreign exchange earnings. However, all groups of convention and meeting delegates are recognised as high yield and high spending, spending on average more than other tourist groups.

This difference in the data and information required and obtained by both conference organisers and other tourism organisations compounds the difficulties in determining the economic impact of the convention and meeting industry. For example, a conference organiser will be able to confirm details of delegates' expenditure such as official travel, registration fees, organised pre- and post-conference tours, and so on, but will not be able to provide (or indeed require) information on the activities undertaken by delegates outside those booked officially and as part of the event, for example shopping, meals and other entertainment. Yet this is required in order to assess the economic impact of the event (Peters & Jones 1996, p. 2) and its direct and indirect effects on employment. A rigorous framework for assessing the economic contribution of the industry has been developed (Dwyer & Forsyth 1995), but the implementation of this framework is constrained by the limitations on the collection of industry statistics. The SCVB delegate study, undertaken annually, has provided some information that can assist in determining the economic contribution, as has the report by the BTR exploring the characteristics and economic contribution of Australia's meetings and exhibition sectors. Economic development units within state government departments also have models to assess the impact of a particular event on the community and the country (personal communication, SCVB 1998).

Employment trends and estimates of the numbers of jobs provided by the industry are just becoming known. The meetings and exhibition sector directly accounts for employing about 85 000 people, or about 1 per cent of the total persons employed (Johnson, Foo & O'Halloran 1999, p. xvii). The industry is viewed as the 'blue-chip' sector of the tourism industry with respect to employment and employment opportunities. Full-time, part-time and casual jobs have been developed or created across many sectors. This is reviewed in more detail in chapter 4.

■ Political *initiatives*

Successive federal and state governments since the late 1980s have recognised the economic benefits and value provided by the MICE industry and have embraced the sector within their tourism strategies. In the early 1990s the Commonwealth government realised that the MICE industry was being recognised nationally and internationally as an area not only with significant growth potential, but also the ability to make an important contribution to both the national and regional economy. 'Australia's Passport to Growth: A National Tourism Strategy' (1992) was one of the earlier initiatives of the federal government and led to the introduction of measures to encourage the development of new niche market segments. As a result, a number of outcomes were developed, aimed at promoting Australia more vigorously as a convention and incentive destination. One of these was the development of the National Strategy for the MICE industry, which aimed to provide a blueprint for growth to ensure that the MICE sector remained competitive beyond the year 2000 (Commonwealth Department of Tourism 1995).

The National Strategy was developed by the federal government in conjunction with the MICE industry, which realised that Australia needed to maintain and develop its international competitive position in this area. Destinations such as Singapore, Hong Kong and Japan had developed world-class convention, meeting and exhibition facilities, with their governments making a commitment to provide large levels of funding for the marketing and development of the sector. Operators of MICE facilities in Southeast Asia were aggressively targeting Australian organisations to hold their conventions and meetings offshore. The National Strategy identified the issues needed to address the long-term growth of the sector and to maximise the economic benefit of this growth to Australia. It aimed to build on the country's strengths in this area, which included the world-class infrastructure available in capital cities, the highly skilled workforce and the safe environment. The National Strategy, through a process of consultation with the various stakeholders of the MICE industry, also explored the impediments to the industry's growth and provided a range of actions on how they might be overcome. Key issues that required action were identified and suggested strategies to overcome them were explored.

The key issues for the industry to address were identified as follows:
• counteract strong international competition, particularly from Asia

- provide sufficient level of infrastructure and accommodation to allow for the growth of the industry
- encourage the availability of long-term finance for investment in facilities such as purpose-built convention and exhibition centres and hotels
- provide efficient and competitive transport services
- facilitate visa arrangements for international MICE visitors
- examine the effects of the taxation system on the MICE industry
- encourage environmentally responsible industry practices
- increase professionalism and service standards
- support industry cohesiveness
- implement marketing strategies to enhance the international awareness of Australia as a MICE destination
- undertake quantitative and qualitative research to encourage investment and allowing planning for growth.
  The issues were assimilated into four major themes:
- a need for further quantitative and qualitative research
- a need to lift standards in all facets of industry operation through training and accreditation
- a need for greater industry coordination and the strengthening of the effectiveness of industry effort
- a need to think regionally, with Australia to establish itself as an important regional centre for MICE events.

These themes have provided the 'backbone' of subsequent initiatives (Commonwealth Department of Tourism 1995).

A change of government in 1996 resulted in the withdrawal of the National Strategy and other tourism strategies (Dwyer & Mistilis 1998, p. 767). However, the National Strategy still continues to provide a benchmark for the industry and a blueprint for its future development. Themes from the National Strategy have continued to be voiced, developed and reinforced on a consistent basis since that time. Some have been, and are being, steadily implemented and the issues addressed. Documents produced by successive federal governments and quasi-government bodies have included the report on *Measuring MICE Infrastructure*, produced by the Bureau of Tourism Research for the Tourism Forecasting Council (BTR/ TFC 1998), *Meetings Make Their Mark* (Johnson, Foo & O'Halloran 1999) and the national tourism plan, *Tourism: A Ticket to the 21st Century: National Action Plan* (Office of National Tourism 1998a). This report included a number of strategies for the MICE industry, which was earmarked as a sector for development within the special interest market segment. Strategies specifically designed to continue the development of the MICE industry included:

- undertake research to provide data on the economic contribution of the MICE sector to the economy
- consider options to support the bidding for and promotion of international meetings
- consider the introduction of a new visa category for MICE visitors
- promote 2001 as 'Meet in Australia' Year
- endorse Meetings Industry Association of Australia (MIAA) accredited operators; support the development of a training package to aid the

professional management of meetings and conferences; and support the establishment of the MIAA Meetings Industry Centre for Excellence (Office of National Tourism 1998).

These strategies highlighted the recommendations for MICE industry development outlined in an industry-commissioned report prepared for the national tourism plan, *Tourism — Getting it Right for the Millennium* (Hutchinson 1997).

State and territory tourism bodies also have actively incorporated and developed federal government initiatives for the MICE sector in their tourism plans, recognising its high yield and economic benefits. For example, in Queensland, since 1992, the state government has funded the development of both the Brisbane Convention and Exhibition Centre and the Cairns Convention Centre. A proposed development for a convention and exhibition centre located on the Gold Coast is planned. Tourism Queensland, as part of the state's tourism strategy, has as one of its objectives to 'support the continued development of the MICE market in Queensland'. There is a specific MICE unit within Tourism Queensland.

Some other initiatives are outlined in the following industry insight.

INDUSTRY INSIGHT
State MICE initiatives

The South Australia Tourism Commission Corporate Plan, 1998–2003, indicates that some of its marketing strategies will be focused and targeted on high-yield business. MICE business is high yield, and therefore one of the Commission's strategic objectives is to 'develop a strong competitive market position' with a subsequent strategy of leverage by developing joint activities to win convention business, increase support of incentive business, and develop better support for the Adelaide Convention and Tourism Authority.

In Western Australia, the Tourism Commission has identified that Perth has a competitive advantage as a business centre compared to other Australian cities. This is due to its proximity to Southeast Asia and the time zone, cultural, social and trade links. Perth is increasingly being used as a regional headquarters for organisations wishing to expand into Southeast Asia. So that Perth can capitalise on both the international and domestic MICE market, a number of sites have been identified for the development of a purpose-built convention and exhibition centre and a $100 million incentive package has been made available by the Western Australian state government to facilitate its development. Early in 1999 expressions of interest were called for from organisations to develop a unique, internationally recognised state-of-the-art centre.

Source: South Australia Tourism Commission (1998); Sydney Morning Herald (23 January 1999); West Australian Tourism Commission (1997)

As already noted, one of the consistently identified shortfalls of the industry, which has been highlighted by a number of government reports as a major impediment to growth, is the lack of consistent and comparable statistical data. Some action has been undertaken to overcome this shortfall. The ABS and IVS figures and the method of collection of the number of international convention visitors coming to Australia has been revised. Furthermore, a number of reports have been or are being prepared by government agencies and industry bodies in an attempt to address the paucity of information.

It is generally accepted that if government is seen to support an industry through such initiatives as the development of infrastructure and facilities, this enhances and encourages private sector investment and potential support for that investment by financial institutions. However, lack of data and statistical information as to the economic growth and development of a sector can discourage financial institutions from investing in an area that they deem to be high risk. This risk is exacerbated if the industry sector also demonstrates a cyclical business pattern with peaks and troughs of business, low barriers to entry and a lack of training, development and professionalism. The result is that cumulatively it will add up to a high-risk business investment. Many of these features are apparent in the MICE sector. Underinvestment within the industry also will occur if there is a feeling of 'go it alone' by private sector investors and a lack of public support in the development of facilities. If public sector investment is not forthcoming then private sector investment may be unprofitable (Dwyer & Mistilis 1998, p. 763).

The demonstration of a sustained and growing market, plus government support through such initiatives as funding for marketing and investment in infrastructure (e.g. the construction of purpose-built convention and exhibition centres), together with the provision of independent consistent and comparable statistical data, will enhance the credibility of the industry, help reduce risk, encourage investment and growth and ensure the sector's economic growth and success.

■ Environmental *impacts*

There is a trend internationally to use environmentally friendly practices within the convention and meeting industry. Convention organisers and tourism organisations have formulated green policies and identified criteria and ratings of 'green' convention cities and destinations. Programs have been put into place to manage the effect on the environment, including waste recycling, reducing the consumption of water, electricity and heat, water recycling and the rationalisation of airconditioning and lighting.

Australia's unique environment, spectacular and diverse range of natural features, wide and unique range of flora and fauna and distinct cultural heritage provide the country with an opportunity to promote and attract MICE visitors who are seeking an event with a special environmental focus (Commonwealth Department of Tourism 1995, p. 35).

Venues such as Kingfisher Bay Resort on Fraser Island, Binna Burra Mountain Lodge in the Gold Coast hinterland, Cairns Convention Centre and Cradle Mountain Lodge in Tasmania have developed their facilities around the environment and have instituted environmentally friendly practices. Kingfisher Bay Resort has focused on a sector of the convention and meeting market as one of its market segments (see the case study at the end of this chapter). The Cairns Convention Centre (see chapter 3) has been designed to be one of the most environmentally friendly convention centres in the world and aims to attract the attention of environmental groups, such as the World Heritage Tropical Rainforest Scientific Conference (Commonwealth Department of Tourism 1995). Tasmania, in the promotion of the state as a convention destination, has promoted its 'green and environmental image'.

Traditionally the convention and meeting industry has been a large consumer of paper and paper products in the form of printed conference materials, satchels, non-reusable convention and exhibition materials, disposable cups and plates, and so on. However, there is a concerted effort being undertaken globally to adopt environmentally-responsible policies and practices. As a result, more 'green' meetings are taking place and eco policies are being put into operation. For example, conference folders and delegates' badges can be made from recycled tyres (see chapter 8) and new plantations of timber can be planted as a form of 'speaker gifts' and as a memento of an area that will remain long after the convention has left the vicinity.

Within Australia, the National Ecotourism Strategy has been designed to encourage the use of ecodesign and environmentally friendly technology. It promotes the design of environmentally sensitive and energy-friendly facilities that use local materials and labour wherever possible. In the building and construction of convention and meeting facilities, the industry, through the strategy, has been invited to take up the programs mentioned earlier, in order to minimise the impact of buildings, services, waste discharge, roads and other facilities, on the environment.

■ Technological *impacts*

The industry has gladly accepted and embraced new technology, and the impact has been felt not only in the area of the equipment used to present conference data and information, but also in the provision of different styles of conferences through the use of video conferencing facilities. At an operational level, the uptake of new technology has been seen within the office management system of conference organisers, at convention and exhibition registration and within venue convention sales and service offices. The days of the conference diary and traditional filing and paper trail systems have been replaced by industry-specific and relevant on-line systems.

Software systems for both conference organisers and venues and exhibition organisers are now available, and Australia is seen to be at the cutting edge in this area of technological development. Fully integrated conference management systems, such as EVENTS for Windows, linked to the Internet enable potential delegates to register for conferences on-line. The use of such systems provides potential cost savings for conference organisers. The advantages include being able to publish conference registration brochures globally with little or no cost per brochure copy and the potential time saved because conference organisers do not have to transcribe and key in information from handwritten registration forms.

In the presentation of conference materials, the traditional tools of the overhead projector and flip chart are fast being replaced by computer-enhanced PowerPoint presentations. Interactive computer technology is taking over from the video laser disc with the use of big screen international productions now very common. Presentations that incorporate video, sound, graphics, 3-D elements and live performances are being designed and used, particularly in the purpose-built convention and exhibition centres (Tolhurst 1998).

The use of technology as a means of communication is also assisting in the production of meetings both nationally and internationally. Advances in video conferencing technology now mean that it can be used not as a novelty but as a legitimate business tool. The flexibility of the technology means that it can be used in many formats. For example, it might be used to provide a time-efficient meeting for approximately 10–12 participants sited in different locations, nationally and internationally, saving in both travel time and costs. Alternatively, it might be used for much larger conferences, perhaps linking together specially designated speakers. Convention and exhibition centres such as Sydney and Adelaide are using live satellite link-ups with international conference venues. For example, at a medical conference in Adelaide, an audiovisual (A/V) link was used to beam into a hospital operating theatre. Delegates were able to watch the progress of a major operation while at the same time interacting with the surgeons in the theatre (Tolhurst 1998).

ISSUES FOR THE CONVENTION AND MEETING INDUSTRY

So what is the current situation with regards to the MICE industry in Australia as it heads towards the twenty-first century? What are its strengths and weaknesses and what opportunities and threats does it face? What are the challenges that the industry must overcome in order to continue to develop and maintain its competitive position within the global MICE market? By obtaining an understanding of these issues, a 'backdrop' for further study and research will be provided.

■ Industry *strengths, weaknesses, opportunities and threats*

The convention and meeting industry in Australia has a number of strengths, with the continent being seen as a politically stable and safe place in which to hold an event. Yet the country is viewed as a fun destination and is therefore sometimes seen as an inappropriate destination for business conventions. There is a good level and quality of infrastructure in place, particularly within the capital cities, although concern has been voiced in respect of the capacity in some cities (BTR/TFC 1998).

The cooperation and coordination of highly professional teams from the Australian Tourist Commission, the purpose-built convention and exhibition centres and the convention and visitors bureaus have been very visible and effective internationally in promoting the country as a convention destination. The pro-active approach to attract and retain conventions and meetings undertaken by the convention centres working in conjunction with the convention and visitor bureaus has made a significant impact. As a result, both international and national organisers and delegates attending events have been impressed and have re-booked for a future occasion. However, in a competitive market there is a continual need to remain creative (SCU 1998).

Currently, there is a huge demand for Australia globally, with tourists wanting to experience the 'real' Australia. This provides a potential opportunity for the country. A possible oversupply of convention and meeting facilities worldwide, however, may affect Australia's competitiveness in respect of travel and accommodation prices. Price competitiveness could therefore become an issue. Domestically, there might be an increase in disposable income as a result of the proposed changes to the taxation system. This could increase domestic tourism within the country and might impact on the MICE industry through the provision of pre- and post-conference tour opportunities (SCU 1998).

In order to take advantage of potential opportunities locally, nationally and internationally, the MICE business of the future will require, on a regular basis, more consistent data and information. The availability of this information will enable the convention and meeting operator to take a more strategic approach to the management of their business, while allowing them to identify and monitor business trends. The multifaceted nature of the industry is such that it can provide a number of opportunities for the development of strategic partnerships and alliances between the various stakeholders (SCU 1998).

Technological innovation and the high use and level of uptake of technology within the MICE sector has the potential to make the industry in Australia more efficient, particularly in the areas of marketing and operations. For example, the proper and effective use of technology could save labour costs.

The current and projected business environments of the MICE industry will require people who are qualified and able to react to and manage change. However, currently, many conference organisers have poor management and limited business skills, with their expertise being mainly in the technical area. Coupled with the low barriers to entry into the industry, this has resulted in a high turnover in the number of professional conference organisations. As a classic small business, many conference organisers are protective of their business, and are reluctant to share information and train and develop their teams. The introduction of an industry accreditation scheme may assist in this area (SCU 1998).

Finally, despite an increase in business growth, there is poor growth in domestic tourism and few specific programs are available to assist regional areas of Australia in attracting conventions and meetings. This factor may hinder development (SCU 1998).

■ Future *challenges and opportunities*

The MICE industry has experienced rapid development and growth globally in many markets. To manage any area of the industry successfully is a complex task that utilises and requires a set of diverse and uncommon skills (Dwyer & Mistilis 1998). Therefore, perhaps some of the greatest challenges and opportunities for the development of the industry in Australia lie in the coordination and cooperation of the industry stakeholders. These take a number of forms:

(a) *Coordination and cooperation in product delivery* As previously identified, a number of stakeholders are involved in the delivery of the convention or meeting product. The coordination of their activities to provide a quality of service that ensures a memorable experience and lasting impression for delegates is a challenge. This is particularly relevant in regional areas where the quality of facilities and infrastructure might be restricted, as might be the levels of competence and professionalism of personnel involved.

(b) *Strategic cooperation and coordination* Within the convention and meeting sector, some businesses compete on a horizontal level — for example, venues in a particular location might bid against each other to host an event. Others might gain from being part of a group or consortia that can bid to gain a national contract for a group of meetings. Also, different businesses, such as venues, local attractions and airline or coach transport companies, might complement each other to provide a total convention experience for the delegate. The varied and complex relationship between the businesses and industry stakeholders provides the industry with excellent opportunities to maximise its cooperation. This can be achieved through initiatives such as strategic alliances, or by informal or contractual arrangements, as has occurred in the exhibition industry, whereby independent companies located in various states have formed cooperative ventures to provide business support and assistance to each other.

(c) *Coordination and cooperation between industry and government bodies* It is essential that the cooperation between the MICE sector and government bodies is maintained to ensure that it continues to develop nationally and internationally. This includes coordinating activities that maximise efforts between the industry associations and government bodies in respect of industry-specific training, marketing and planning. Also key is the training and development of people employed in this highly competitive environment. Education and training initiatives need to be designed to ensure that they meet both the accreditation needs of the industry and the specialised needs of its staff. It has been recognised that the onus and leadership in this area lies with the industry stakeholders and in particular the industry associations such as MIAA. Initiatives in education and training will reflect and assist the continual improvement of service standards (Dwyer & Mistilis 1998).

(d) *Cooperation and coordination in the provision of data and information* The inadequacy of data to assist in the planning and development of the industry locally and nationally has been highlighted. Continued cooperation and coordination between industry operators, associations and government agencies in this area will ensure the supply of appropriate infrastructure and assist the sector to compete nationally and internationally. The industry also needs to clarify and define its terminology so that it is accepted nationally and conforms to internationally accepted meanings.

In order to ensure that the country does not lose opportunities in this area, strategies to overcome these challenges and develop new opportunities need to be addressed and generated. The public and private sectors need to work together to achieve the shared goals (Dwyer & Mistilis 1998).

SUMMARY ··

The MICE industry is seen as a key growth sector of the tourism industry worldwide and is recognised for its high yield and higher than average daily expenditure by conference delegates. Over the last decade there has been substantial development of Australia's position in the worldwide convention and meeting industry. This has been coupled with an expansion in the provision of facilities and infrastructure within the country as a means to attract this lucrative sector of the tourism market. Australia has gained world recognition for the excellence of its MICE facilities and for the quality of its provision of conventions and meetings. The MICE sector and its products are seen as an effective communications medium that requires the services of people such as professional conference organisers and facilities such as venues.

A number of political, economic, environmental and technological initiatives are influencing the direction and development of the MICE sector within Australia. The MICE market is growing, but so is the extent of the competition between destinations internally, regionally and internationally. Despite Australia developing a National Tourism Plan that ensures the long-term growth of the sector and maximises the social and economic benefits to the country, government reports have identified a number of issues that need to be faced. These issues include government support for the industry and the provision of appropriate levels of infrastructure, improved levels of service and training standards, as well as issues relating to the marketing of the sector. They present a number of challenges that, together with the identified opportunities, provide a framework around which the industry can develop.

Activities

1.1 Visit a convention venue in your area and discuss with the convention services manager the environmentally friendly practices that they may be using in the provision of conventions and meetings.

1.2 Contact your local tourist office and identify the methods that are being used to attract MICE business to the area.

Discussion questions

1.1 Discuss the reason why MICE activities could be described as an 'effective communications medium'.

1.2 Identify and review the factors that have led to the recognition of Australia as an important conference and meeting destination.

1.3 Critically discuss the potential benefits that the convention and meeting sector provide to an economy.

1.4 'Lack of data and information has been considered an impediment to the growth of the convention and meeting industry in Australia'. Discuss.

1.5 Identify and explore the factors that have constrained the growth of the international and domestic market for conventions and meetings in Australia.

1.6 Discuss the importance of the National Strategy for the MICE Industry and subsequent government initiatives to the development of the industry.

1.7 Describe how technology can influence the quality of a convention or meeting.

1.8 Critically discuss the future challenges and opportunities to the MICE industry.

REFERENCES ....

AACB. 1994, *Statistical Report on the Scope of the Meetings Industry*, AACB, Sydney.

ABS. 1998, *Overseas Arrivals and Departures*, Cat. no. 3401.0, ABS, Canberra.

ATC. 1998 (*www.atc.gov.au*).

BTR/TFC. 1998, *Measuring MICE Infrastructure*, Tourism Forecasting Council Research Report No. 1, Department of Industry, Science & Tourism, Canberra.

BTR. 1999, *Australian Tourism Data Card*, BTR, Canberra (*www.btr.gov.au/statistics/datacard/dc_ivs_x_purpose.html*).

Commonwealth Department of Tourism. 1992, *Australia's Passport to Growth: A National Tourism Strategy*, AGPS, Canberra.

Commonwealth Department of Tourism. 1995, *A National Strategy for the Meetings, Incentives, Conventions and Exhibitions Industry*, AGPS, Canberra.

Convention & Incentive Marketing, vol. 23, no. 5, May 1997.

Dawsons Venue Directory, 30th Edition, March 1999.

Dwyer, L. & Forsyth, P. 1996, 'MICE Tourism in Australia: A Framework for Impacts', in *Proceedings from the Australian Tourism and Hospitality Research Conference, Coffs Harbour*, BTR, Canberra.

Dwyer, L. & Mistilis, N. 1998, 'Development of MICE Tourism in Australia: Opportunities and Challenges', in *Proceedings of Australian Tourism and Hospitality Research Conference, Gold Coast*, BTR, Canberra.

Harris, R. & Leiper, N. 1995, *Sustainable Tourism: An Australian Perspective*, Butterworth-Heinemann, Sydney.

Hutchinson, J. 1997, *Tourism — Getting it Right for the Millennium*, Report to Minister of Tourism, SCVB, Sydney.

ICCA. 1997 (*www.ica.nl/*).

ICCA. 1999 (*www.icca.nl/*)

Johnson, L., Foo, L. M. & O'Halloran, M. 1999, *Meetings Make Their Mark: Characteristics and Economic Contribution of Australia's Meetings and Exhibitions Sector*, Occasional Paper No. 26, BTR, Canberra.

McCabe, V. & Bassan, H. 1999, 'MIAA Survey of Conferences and Exhibitions', paper presented at MIAA National Conference, Melbourne, June.

McCabe, V. & Weeks, P. 1999, 'Convention Services Management in Sydney Four- to Five-Star Hotels', *Journal of Convention and Exhibition Management*, vol. 1, no. 4, pp. 67–84.

Nebel III, E. C., Rutherford, D. & Schaffer, J.D. 1994, 'Re-engineering the Hotel Organisation', *Cornell Hotel and Restaurant Administration Quarterly*, October.

Office of National Tourism. 1998, *The Meetings Industry Facts*, No. 4, June (*http://www.dist.gov.au/tourism/cfa/cfa%5Ffs4.html*).

Office of National Tourism. 1998a, *Tourism: A Ticket to the 21st Century: National Action Plan*, Office of National Tourism, Department of Industry, Science and Tourism, Canberra (*www.tourism.gov.au*).

Peters, D. & Jones, B. 1996, 'Measuring the MICE Industry', in *Proceedings of the Australian Tourism and Hospitality Research Conference, Coffs Harbour*, BTR, Canberra.

SCU. 1998, MICE Industry Panel for Masters Degree in Convention & Event Management, unpublished paper, School of Tourism & Hospitality Management, Southern Cross University, Lismore.

SCVB. 1997, *Sydney Convention Delegate Study*, SCVB, Sydney.

SCVB. 1998, *1997 Annual Report*, SCVB, Sydney.

South Australian Tourism Commission. 1998, *South Australian Tourism Commission Corporate Plan 1998–2003*.

Stanfield, L. 1998, 'MICE is Booming', paper presented at the 1998 PATA Tourism Executive Development Programme, Ballina, June.

Tolhurst, C. 1998, *Australian Financial Review*, 19 March
(*http://www.afr.com.au/content/980324/survey/survey5.html*;
http://www.afr.com.au/content/980324/survey/survey9.html).

West Australian Tourism Commission. 1997, *West Australian Tourism Development Strategy*.

FURTHER READING ···

Commonwealth Department of Tourism. 1995, *Implementation Progress Report No. 2*, AGPS, Canberra

Dwyer, L. & Mistilis, N. 1997, 'Challenges to MICE Tourism in the Asia–Pacific Region', in M. Oppermann (ed), *Pacific Rim Tourism*, CAB International, UK.

CASE STUDY

Kingfisher Bay
Resort and Village

Kingfisher Bay Resort and Village is located on the World Heritage-listed Fraser Island, an area famous for its ancient rainforest, mighty sand dunes and pristine freshwater lakes and streams, together with an abundance of birds and free-roaming wildlife. The resort, which opened in 1992, was designed with the intention of being a leading-edge ecotourism development and is 'integrated harmoniously with the natural environment'. Since its opening, the resort has been awarded over 20 international, national, state and regional tourism and architectural awards (Harris & Leiper 1995, p. 117). Kingfisher Bay has 152 hotel rooms, 109 self-contained villas and a 180-bed wilderness lodge, providing accommodation for a maximum of nearly 1000 people at any one time. The resort also has a range of conference and meeting facilities, with the main conference suite (which can be subdivided) catering for 300 people theatre-style and 180 people banquet-style. In addition, there are two syndicate rooms plus large shaded verandahs and seating areas which can be used for breakout areas or additional workshop areas.

The marketing of the resort's conference facilities focuses on the natural environment — for example, 'make your next conference a natural winner'. The resort's conference market tends to lean towards the corporate business market, such as medical, pharmaceutical and training conferences. Delegates often fly from Brisbane to the local airport at Hervey Bay and then take the launch transfer to the resort. Locally, Kingfisher Bay conference facilities are used by businesses and organisations in Hervey Bay and the Fraser Coast. It is also a popular location for weddings and wedding receptions that use the island's natural setting. Conferences often incorporate a weekend and tend to cater for between 50 and 100 delegates who may stay for anything up to five days.

A feature of the conference facilities is the vehicle access doors for the main conference suite which make the resort ideal for the launch of new 4WD vehicles. In addition, there is a focus on the natural environment, not only through design and construction, but also in the range of conference activities that are available. For example, conference delegates can undertake team-building activities such as nature walks and all-day hikes, low rope courses and orienteering trails, 4WD ecotours, and cultural and heritage tours. Specific food and beverage options designed for conference delegates also utilise the natural environment, such as a bush tucker dinner or brunch at Lake McKenzie, one of the island's freshwater lakes. In this latter case specific permission has to be sought to use the facility from the National Parks and Wildlife Service.

The resort has been designed to be as environmentally sensitive as possible, and efforts have been focused on minimising the impact on the flora and fauna

both during the construction of the resort and in its everyday management. In the building and construction of Kingfisher Bay a number of environmentally friendly practices were utilised. These include the following:

- All buildings were limited to two levels and are below the tree line, with the exterior colours and finishes designed to blend in with the natural bush colours of the island (Harris & Leiper 1995, p. 117).
- A stipulation of the design and construction phase was the use of local materials and staff wherever possible. As a result, 95 per cent of all goods and services were sourced locally. For example, a range of light fittings made in Brisbane from ripple iron were used.
- The landscaping of the resort mirrors the island's natural vegetation and ensures the protection of the island's gene pool. The existing vegetation that was on-site prior to the construction was protected as much as possible during construction, with hundreds of plants removed and held in an on-site nursery for future planting and thousands raised from seeds and cuttings. In addition, Queensland Forest Service was contracted to raise 60 000 seedlings from seed and cutting stock taken from the island.
- The impact of humans on the dune system around the resort is minimised through the use of either hardwood boardwalks or woodchip walking tracks.
- The central hotel complex, housing restaurants, bars, lounges and reception, was designed without airconditioning, though this has been included in the conference rooms, kitchens and office areas. Natural convection currents and the use of windows and vents have been utilised and save an estimated 480 000 kW of electricity per year. Similarly, the hotel rooms, villas, landscape and streetlighting use low-energy fluorescent lighting which saves a further 375 000 kW of electricity per year. Hotel rooms have airconditioning, which is used at guests' discretion.
- All solid waste is separated into recyclable and non-recyclable materials, compacted and removed to the mainland for disposal. Paper, glass, aluminium, tin and plastics are all recycled. Plastic bags used in the shops on the island are photodegradable.
- The water supply is drawn from the island's huge groundwater reserves and is some of the world's purest water. Water used for watering the gardens and rainwater runoff are filtered back through the sand into the water table.
- Dried sewage sludge, kitchen scraps and paper are recycled through an on-site worm farm and the resultant compost is used on the gardens.

Questions

1 Discuss the ways in which Kingfisher Bay Resort enhances its image as an environmentally friendly convention and meeting venue to the potential conference organiser.

2 Discuss the strengths of the resort as a potential conference venue. What potential weaknesses might the resort have to address?

Source: Kingfisher Bay Resort; Harris & Leiper (1995, p. 117)

2

The business
structure of conventions

LEARNING OBJECTIVES

After studying this chapter, you will be able to:

- outline and explain the structure and organisation of the MICE industry in Australia

- name the industry stakeholders and outline the roles that they play

- define the types of services necessary to conduct MICE business

- describe the types of conventions and meetings that are held

- identify the customers of the MICE industry

- explain some of the terms and definitions used in the MICE industry.

INTRODUCTION

The MICE industry in Australia, as we have seen, is an important and lucrative part of tourism revenue generation. The rising trend in convention and meeting business within the region has been especially apparent since the late 1980s when Australia began to recognise the economic impact from this high-yield sector of the tourism industry. The MICE sector can therefore be viewed as relatively young, especially when it is compared to its counterparts in Europe and the United States. In terms of the product life cycle, the Australasian region is an emerging market, whereas those in Europe and the United States are considerably more mature. However, despite the industry's relative youth, Australia has developed a reputation for both the quality of its world-class facilities and the professionalism of their operation. This has been confirmed, as we have seen in chapter 1, by Australia being ranked third in the world share of meetings (Stanfield 1998). The industry is therefore viewed as a highly desirable area for developing business. Four key features of the industry are:

- the substantially higher than average daily expenditure by convention delegates
- the return of delegates to a venue or destination after attendance at a MICE event
- the fact that MICE activity often occurs in some destinations and venues in shoulder periods of business
- the high yield provided by both domestic and inbound MICE visitors.

The organisation of a convention or meeting incorporates a number of factors. For example, the convention or meeting might occur at a specific place called a facility or venue, and it might involve the provision of food and beverage services, require specialised technical support (such as audiovisual equipment) and include an exhibition of products. It might also require residential and non-residential accommodation, transportation and delegate entertainment and partner programs. To achieve a successful MICE event, therefore, a number of specialists or suppliers who represent these areas will be called on to manage and coordinate their services. Indeed, the successful management and coordination of these suppliers is a key challenge for the industry.

This chapter outlines the structure of the MICE industry in Australia and identifies the key stakeholders and the role that they play as suppliers. It provides an overview of the various types of venues, facilities, products and services offered by the industry. To review the structure of the MICE industry, the following questions will be addressed:

- Who are the industry stakeholders?
- What types of conventions and meetings are held?
- Who holds and plans conventions and meetings?
- Who is involved in the organisation of conventions and meetings?

The process of providing a MICE event is often compared with the design of a wheel (Rutherford 1990, p. 2). At the centre of the wheel is the MICE event, for example a potential conference or exhibition that is to be managed by a conference organiser. All the other specialists who provide services are located on the spokes of the wheel (see figure 2.1). At any given time or point during the planning or provision of the MICE event, one or more of the service specialists (the suppliers) might assume a more pivotal role that is specific to the complete success of the event. An example of this would be a transport supplier who is to provide the coach transfers of international delegates from the airport to the venue. Around the edge of the wheel are the delegates or 'end customers'. At any one time during the event, the delegate will come into contact with a number of the industry suppliers. Their overall experience of the complete event will be influenced by each of these service specialists or suppliers: therefore, the interrelationship between each supplier and the delegates is extremely important to the success of the MICE event. Figure 2.1 details the various stakeholders of the MICE industry. These include suppliers such as hotels and other venues; support services; exhibition service providers; professional conference organisers; incentive travel organisers; and convention and visitors bureaus.

■ **Figure 2.1**
*The process of
providing a
MICE event*

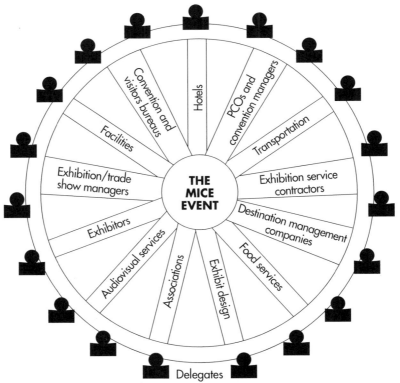

Source: Don Walker, National Association of Exposition Managers (NAEM)

We will now examine the role that these stakeholders provide within the MICE industry.

■ Government *organisations*

Government organisations involved with the MICE industry are the federal government, through the Office of National Tourism and the Australian Tourist Commission (ATC), state government and local government. So how do they operate, and what is their role?

Federal government

Federal government tends to function at a strategic level by helping to shape the environment within which the industry operates. It plays an important role in the promotion of the industry, assisting in the provision of the necessary infrastructure, transport, visa and custom services, and research and statistical data. The Office of National Tourism and the Australian Tourist Commission are the operational sections of the federal government, which focus on the MICE sector as part of their overall brief.

The Office of National Tourism, which is part of the Commonwealth Department of Industry, Science and Tourism, works with the state and territory governments, the Australian Tourist Commission and industry to facilitate the development and growth of tourism in Australia. The department prepares and implements government strategies, policies and programs. In the case of the MICE industry, the Office of National Tourism attempts to reduce any barriers which might hinder its development, as well as providing information that will assist the industry in its decision making (Commonwealth Department of Tourism 1995, p. 22).

In 1995, the department developed and produced the National Strategy for the Meetings, Incentive, Conventions and Exhibitions Industry. The aim of the National Strategy was to:

> ■ facilitate the development of a more viable and internationally competitive MICE industry that takes full advantage of the world-class, high-quality, purpose-built meetings and exhibitions infrastructure developed over the past decade and the opportunities arising from the Sydney Olympic Games in the Year 2000 (Michael Lee in Commonwealth Department of Tourism 1995, p. 1). ■

The National Strategy provided a benchmark for the future direction and development of the industry.

Prior to the development of the National Strategy, the Department had funded a number of projects to assist in the development of the Australian convention and meeting industry. For example, in 1992/93 the 'Convention Means Business' campaign provided a grant to the Association of Australian Convention Bureaux (AACB) to develop a video and supporting information aimed at increasing consumer awareness of Australia as a destination for both national and international conventions.

Australian Tourist Commission

The ATC is the federal government's marketing agency. Its prime task is to market Australia internationally as a tourist destination, with the objective of increasing and maximising the number of overseas visitors who come to Australia. This includes the high-yield business of the MICE industry. To achieve this brief, the ATC, from its national and regional offices, undertakes marketing to consumers and the travel industry in over 30 countries.

The ATC works with state and territory tourism authorities, industry associations and the private sector. It coordinates Australia's tourism industry participation in travel missions and trade shows throughout the world — for example, the European Incentive and Business Travel Meetings Exhibition (EIBTM), a key European trade event for the European meetings, conventions and incentives industry, which is held annually in Geneva and is attended by meetings, conventions and incentives organisers, corporate decision makers and executives.

One of the ATC's areas of responsibility is to promote Australia as a unique and desirable MICE destination (ATC 1996, p. 30). In this instance, it works closely with other MICE bodies to increase the number of international visitors who attend MICE events within Australia. Some of the services and support provided by the ATC for the promotion of the MICE industry both within Australia and internationally include:

- the *Convention Assistance Prospectus*, which is used in overseas offices, and highlights the range of services and promotional material that is available from the ATC
- the Convention Assistance Scheme, which provides funds to assist Australian associations to prepare and put forward bid documents to attract and gain international association conventions to Australia
- promotional materials and assistance for use by corporate organisations and associations when they attend or wish to attract overseas and international conferences to Australia
- direct mail activities such as the 'Fly the Flag' campaign and 'Australia 2001' (see industry insight on page 42) — leads generated from these campaigns are then forwarded to individual convention bureaus for action
- the Dreamtime Incentive Exhibition, an innovative activity organised and hosted biannually by the ATC, with the objective of showcasing Australia as an incentive destination — it attracts overseas incentive buyers, as well as a number of journalists under the ATC's Visiting Journalists program, and includes a familiarisation and post-touring program (the 1996 Dreamtime Exhibition focused on Adelaide, Perth and Darwin, and the 1998 Exhibition on Cairns and Far North Queensland)
- handling overseas MICE enquiries through its regional offices — the overseas offices promote Australia as a convention destination and process initial enquiries
- attendance at overseas trade shows and exhibitions that focus on MICE activities
- the production of the annual international conventions, trade shows and exhibitions calendar, which lists the international conventions, exhibitions and trade shows to be held in Australia (ATC 1996, p. 30).

A specialist convention and events section, situated within the ATC head office, coordinates ATC offices overseas involved in MICE activities.

The following industry insight illustrates how the federal government, through the ATC, works with the MICE industry and its industry associations to promote MICE business.

INDUSTRY INSIGHT
Towards 2001

An illustration of the partnerships and alliances that can operate between the federal government and MICE industry associations can be seen in the 'Australia 2001' campaign. The campaign, 'Meet the Millennium — A New Century, New World, Australia 2001', has been denoted as the single biggest business travel campaign ever undertaken within Australia. The project, which is under the management of the ATC, calls on business organisations within Australia to organise a business travel event (i.e. a MICE program) for their international clients and colleagues in Australia in the year 2001. Australian companies are also being encouraged to hold events at home in 2001 rather than overseas. MICE industry associations have commented that the campaign forms a milestone for the meeting industry in its progress to have the government recognise the industry as an important growth source of the tourism industry (MIAA 1998a).

The focus of the campaign is to encourage Australian businesses to 'invite the world'. ATC offices overseas are using the campaign to bring business travel to Australia. The project is being undertaken in a number of stages, and incorporates the identification and mailing of information packs to key travel and event decision makers from a large number of Australian companies. Subsequent activities include follow-up telephone calls, tailored information packs and potential MICE leads being forwarded to the appropriate convention bureau within the various states. A 'roadshow' is visiting the state and territory capitals and selected regions to emphasise the campaign and gain the commitment of the local business community. In addition, the corporate leaders of a number of industry sectors such as construction, banking and insurance are being contacted with a view to gaining their commitment to host a business travel event in 2001. In the final stages of the campaign associations, common interest groups and government will be targeted to hold an event in Australia in either 2001 or beyond.

The government and the ATC forecast that the campaign will bring an extra $100 million in revenue to the Australian economy.

This campaign leads on from the interest and euphoria shown in Australia for the 2000 Olympics. It will 'piggyback' on the one-hundred years celebration of Federation and will try to capitalise on the post-Olympic boom in tourism and business tourism. It would seem that the government and industry, through this alliance, are determined to continue the business and tourism growth trends started since the initial awarding of the 2000 Olympic Games to Sydney. They are being assisted by the new millennium, the celebration of a century of Federation and the vision of Australia as a new country in a new millennium.

Source: MIAA (1998a)

State government

The MICE industry has been identified as a key area for development by many of the state and territory tourism authorities. Strategies have been prepared to encourage the growth and development of the industry at a state level. In addition, as shown later in this chapter, the state government in some areas has part-funded the convention and visitors bureaus. Within New South Wales, some of the regional tourism organisations (RTOs) have become involved with the industry and developed a MICE strategy for their region.

Local government

Many local government areas have recognised the economic contribution of the MICE sector to their communities and are actively promoting their city or region to the industry (for example, Coffs Harbour). In addition, others are actively involved in the industry through their ownership of venues and facilities that can be used for MICE activities.

■ Industry *associations*

Industry-specific associations are a major part of the development of any new and emerging industry. They are often formed with the mandate to enhance the professionalism of the industry, to act as a means of communication between individuals who have a common business interest, and to create an awareness of the industry and market its services to business and other organisations. Perhaps most importantly they have a role to lobby government on key issues that may affect the operation of that industry group. Within the MICE industry a number of key associations have emerged — the Meetings Industry Association of Australia (MIAA), the Australian Incentive Association (AIA) and the Exhibition and Events Association of Australia (EEAA). Each association represents the members from its particular MICE sector.

Key features of MICE industry associations are that they:

- are national but independent bodies that promote the industry sector to the wider business community
- are non-profit making
- have national and state representation in some cases (e.g. MIAA has regional offices in all states and territories and a national office in Sydney)
- have a membership made up of individuals and companies who are involved in operating within the industry together with other stakeholders
- provide their members in many instances with a range of services that enable them to achieve professional growth and excellence
- represent the interests of their membership to government and other bodies — government in turn often consults with the industry body over current issues and concerns (e.g. MIAA was consulted in the preparation of the National Strategy)
- create opportunities to enable the development of association members

- provide members with a range of publications and general information, newsletters, Web sites, social functions and an annual conference (e.g. EEAA provides support for the industry publication *Australian Exhibitor*)
- provide a range of educational programs and professional development seminars and accreditation courses
- promote the industry and are affiliated with the industry's main bodies.

The following snapshot profiles the Meetings Industry Association of Australia, the industry association for the conventions and meetings industry in Australia.

SNAPSHOT
The Meetings Industry Association of Australia

The Meetings Industry Association of Australia, founded in 1975, is the national, independent body representing the meeting industry. It promotes the meeting industry to the wider business community by marketing the benefits of using meeting professionals. The MIAA seeks to foster professionalism and excellence within all aspects of meeting management in Australia, clearly demonstrated perhaps in its vision statement, 'Australia — The Centre for Excellence in Meetings' (MIAA 1998c). The Association promotes not only the meetings industry as a high-yield sector of business travel and tourism, but also the value and effectiveness of meetings as a communications medium. It creates opportunities for the development of its members and provides a range of services to enable those members to achieve professional growth and excellence. In line with developing the professionalism of the meeting industry in Australia, the Association has established the MIAA Centre for Excellence, which focuses on industry research, and has published and now administers a Code of Ethics. It has also established an industry accreditation program for its members, which is supported by an educational program of residential training courses and professional development seminars.

Source: MIAA (1998b, p. 6)

■ Convention *and visitors bureaus*

In order for a city or area to actively encourage both MICE business and visitors, there needs to be a coordinated approach by all sections of the tourism business community. The establishment of a convention and visitors bureau (CVB) is one way to do this. A CVB acts as a cooperative, representing all the various sectors of the convention and visitor industry (e.g. hotels, restaurants, transport operators, attractions, and so on) and promoting the city or area to a broad range of companies, associations or visitor groups. Gartrell has identified the CVB as 'the single most important marketing organisation for a community, projecting an image for that destination into the various target markets' (1994, p. 16). It can act as a catalyst, bringing together 'the destination team' that enables it to carry out a comprehensive but unified marketing program for the community. This is illustrated in figure 2.2.

■ **Figure 2.2**
The destination team

Source: Gartrell (1994, p. 17)

So what are CVBs? They are not-for-profit organisations.

■ [Their mission is to] solicit and service conventions and other related group business and to engage in visitor promotions, which generate overnight stays for a destination, thereby enhancing and developing the economic fabric of the community (Gartrell 1988, p. 10). ■

A CVB is an example of a destination management organisation. However, in many instances, the key activity and often the exclusive focus of the bureau is marketing and sales. The CVB acts as an intermediary between potential visitors and local business and as such it represents all organisations within a location who have a vested interest in increasing conference and meeting business. The membership of the bureau may include hotels and other venues, tourism and convention suppliers, airlines and ground transport organisations, and caterers and technical facility suppliers, as illustrated in figure 2.2. Typically, a bureau will work with its member organisations, often using their resources, to bid nationally and internationally to obtain a 'city-wide' convention for its area. Once the bid has been secured, it will act as a broker between the potential conference organiser, the host city and its conference infrastructure, from the pre-event planning through to the post-convention tours and activities. A CVB provides a 'one-stop shop' for ideas and information on the region for both visitors and business tourists.

Gartrell (1994, p. 20) has identified a number of main functions and responsibilities in order for the CVB to 'sell the city': develop an image to position the city in the marketplace as an attractive destination for meetings and visitors; coordinate the constituent elements of the industry and public sector; work with meeting and group planners; represent both buyers (the demand side) and sellers (the supply side) so that an autonomous organisation is required to avoid conflicts of interest; provide information and respond to visitor enquiries; and provide leadership for the industry.

The bureau needs to be active and visible within the city or region so that the community can understand the significance of both visitors and the convention and meeting industry to the area. As the Gold Coast Tourism Bureau (GCTB) statement says:

> ■ The primary role of the Gold Coast Tourism Bureau is to provide a cohesive leadership to focus the promotion and marketing of the Gold Coast region as a leading visitor destination, in order to achieve maximum sustainable economic benefits to the members, region and community (Gold Coast Tourism Bureau 1998). ■

This statement can be compared with the following extract taken from the Charter of the Adelaide Convention and Tourism Authority, which identifies its functions and responsibilities as:

> ■ • To market and service Adelaide and South Australia as the quality and value convention destination in Australia.
> • To market Adelaide and South Australia as a key incentive travel destination.
> • To promote the Adelaide and Adelaide Hills region as the prime destination within South Australia which offers value for money, quality experiences, and a product which is characterised by service, friendliness and excellence for the general tourism market and therefore creates economic benefit for the local community (Adelaide Convention and Tourism Authority 1998). ■

In the second statement, there is a clear indication that the CVB is to focus on the MICE industry.

So what services might a CVB provide to a potential conference organiser? In many cases these would include:
- site inspections of the city's hotels and other facilities
- advice and assistance on budgeting and organisation of the event
- suggestions for the structure of the conference program, including social and accompanying partner programs and pre- and post-conference touring packages
- promotional material
- assistance in the preparation of the bid documents, particularly for associations that might wish to host a regional, national or international conference at the destination (we explore in more detail the assistance a CVB provides in the preparation of a bid document in chapter 5)
- liaison between government, civic authorities and the convention organiser.

As an example, the Sydney Convention & Visitors Bureau (SCVB) actively promotes to convention planners that 'One call to Sydney Convention & Visitors Bureau and Sydney is yours' (SCVB 1998b). The SCVB states that it provides a 'free and unbiased service' (SCVB 1998a). Included in its package of services for the convention planner is information on: the pricing and availability of venues and accommodation; familiarisation tours and site inspections; arranging appointments and introductions to MICE industry suppliers; bid document preparation; information for boosting delegate numbers; incentive travel programs; and special events, theme party ideas and pre- and post-conference touring options.

The key promotional document that a CVB produces for potential conference organisers or visitors to the city is the meeting planner, facilities guide or directory. This colourful and extensive publication provides a snapshot of the variety of facilities, hotels, venues and supporting services the city has to offer, plus sightseeing and entertainment that the area can provide. For example, the *Sydney Facilities Guide*, produced by SCVB, includes background information on Sydney, international flight times, climate details and a traveller's checklist incorporating details for arrival in Sydney, money matters and banking information, a plan of Sydney airport and how to explore the city using the various transport options. The guide presents comprehensive information on the various convention venues, listing those with and without accommodation, venues with a difference and exhibition and maritime venues. There is a section on regional conferencing, together with contact details and information on convention and exhibition services. The range of services and facilities provided by the SCVB and a calendar of potential events in Sydney and regional New South Wales are included, together with information on leisure, entertainment, pre- and post-conference tour options and the Sydney 2000 Olympic Games. The guide concludes with information on SCVB members and details of the SCVB Web site, representative offices and contact details (SCVB 1998a).

In addition, as we have seen in the case of Sydney, the CVB undertakes familiarisations to the city for prospective meeting and convention organisers and attends exhibitions and trade shows to promote its area.

Members of the CVB are provided with a broad network of contacts and are actively encouraged to use the promotional patterns/programs provided by the bureau. Membership can range over a number of categories, for example affiliate, bronze, silver, gold and major shareholder. Each category of membership brings a different level of benefit proportional to the level of membership fee. Benefits are focused mainly on marketing and promotional activities — for example, the opportunity to participate in a range of quality publications, member referrals, promotional events and cooperative activities, and use of the CVB logo on promotional material. However, benefits can range over a number of other areas such as networking, updating on information through newsletters, cooperative opportunities, media resources, training and education. This is demonstrated in table 2.1, which outlines some of the membership benefits of Brisbane Tourism.

BENEFITS AT A GLANCE		AFFILIATE	BRONZE	SILVER	GOLD	MSH
Fees		$550	$1100	$2750	$5500	$11 000
Convention sales leads	Confirmed business worth more than $30 000 (distributed by Faxstream)		By appointment	4th day	2nd day	1st day
Conventions mini sales leads	Confirmed business worth less than $30 000		By appointment	By appointment	Direct mail (monthly)	Direct mail (monthly)
General sales enquiries	Non-confirmed business					
Convention & exhibition calendar	Half-yearly list of all meetings confirmed for Brisbane	N/A	4th priority	3rd priority	2nd priority	1st priority
Sales/marketing	Trade & consumer shows fact sheet will be sent and specific leads will be directed to members		4th priority	3rd priority	2nd priority	1st priority
Cooperative opportunities	Advertising media — TV, radio, press publications — trade		4th priority	3rd priority	2nd priority	1st priority
	— consumer		4th priority	3rd priority	2nd priority	1st priority
	Trade and consumer shows		4th priority	3rd priority	2nd priority	1st priority
	— discount		N/A	N/A	5%	15%
	'City of Sun Days' QTTC cooperative advertising	*	*	*	*	*
Advertising opportunities	Meetings and conventions guide: membership directory		4th priority	3rd priority	2nd priority	1st priority
	— discount		N/A	N/A	5%	15%
	Visitors guide, events calendar, wholesale brochure	5th priority	4th priority	3rd priority	2nd priority	1st priority
	— discount	N/A	N/A	N/A	5%	15%
Access to tourism promotional material	Posters	*	*	*	*	*
	Videos (at cost)	*	*	*	free	free
	Visitors guide	*	*	*	*	*
	Events calendar	*	*	*	*	*
Convention promotional material	Conditions apply			free	free	free
Familiarisations	Trade		4th priority	3rd priority	2nd priority	1st priority
	Media		4th priority	3rd priority	2nd priority	1st priority

BENEFITS AT A GLANCE		AFFILIATE	BRONZE	SILVER	GOLD	MSH
Bidding for meetings & incentives	Recognition in all bid presentations (where applicable)			*	*	*
	Recognition in bid documents					
Meeting database	Conditions apply			at cost	at cost	at cost
Direct mailing lists	Access to Brisbane Tourism direct marketing programs (conditions apply)				*	*
Seminars	Members training seminars		*	*	*	*
	Monthly volunteer training seminars		*	*	*	*
Internet Web site access	Linkage to Brisbane Tourism home page (at cost)		*	*	*	*
Information centres	Information centres display of brochures		*	*	*	*
	Bookings of produce					*
Brisbane Tourism reports	Annual report	*	*	*	*	*
	Tourism marketing plan	*				*
	Strategic plan	*				*
Brisbane Tourism newsletter	Receive copy of newsletter	*	*	*	*	*
	Logo representation in newsletter		*		*	*
	Editorial opportunities (conditions apply)					*
Brisbane Tourism logo	Use of logo (with prior approval)	*	*	*	*	*
Members services directory	Listing in members directory	*	*			
	Listing and 25-word description					
	Listing, 25-word description and logo			*		
	Listing, 50-word description and logo				*	
	Listing, 80-word description and logo					*
Membership functions	Invitation to membership networking functions	*	*	*	1 for free	4 for free
	Opportunity to display product information (at cost)		*	*		*
	Opportunity to host functions			*	*	*
Recognition as major stakeholders	Recognition at bureau promotional functions				*	*
	Logo representation in Brisbane Tourism foyer					*
	Receive official bureau corporate gift					*

Source: Brisbane Tourism (1998)

Membership of a CVB therefore provides the opportunity to tap into a wide variety of mainstream marketing and promotional activities. In the case of small operators, this might not otherwise have been a viable proposition.

Many CVBs promote themselves as private, not-for-profit destination marketing organisations. They receive their funding through a mixture of public and private sources, such as membership subscriptions and city council, state and local government subsidies.

Each bureau needs to be independent and impartial in its business affairs in order to ensure a long-term and stable influence within the region's tourism industry. This influence becomes apparent if a conference organiser should make unreasonable demands of a supplier. Alternatively, it can also protect a conference organiser from convention service providers that may not provide a reasonable quality in respect of sales, service or price. It is essential, therefore, that the CVB is autonomous in order to be effective.

Association of Australian Convention Bureaux

The Association of Australian Convention Bureaux (AACB) is the representative organisation for Australian CVBs. Its membership is made up of CVBs from around the country together with other associated organisations such as Qantas and the ATC. The Association provides a number of services for its members, including sales leads for potential international conventions, and has commissioned market reports such as the *Statistical Report on the Scope of the Meetings Industry* (AACB 1994). It lobbies government on key issues such as visa regulations for international convention delegates and administers the ATC Export Marketing Development Grant. The AACB is continually looking at methods for joint cooperation and partnership between the competing bureaus.

■ Venues

The demands that conference organisers place on venues have changed dramatically over the last 10 years. Gone are the days when a traditional ballroom, complete with chandeliers and ancillary noise from the banquet kitchen, was used on a few occasions for an in-house conference. Today, venues that wish to develop a share of the MICE industry need to provide purpose-built facilities that offer multiple usage, are flexible in their design and have suitable lighting and breakout space. In Australasia, hotels and other venues have recognised the value and importance of the industry and have embraced its development by building new facilities and converting existing facilities. They wish to ensure that they reach the required specifications of both conference organisers and delegates.

Venues also are aware of three current trends within the industry:
- the increase in the smaller meetings market (particularly from the corporate sector)
- the need to be cost competitive
- the demand from corporate and association meeting planners for a greater return on their investment.

MICE business can account for up to 50 per cent of the income of many hotels, particularly if the revenue derived from the accommodation and group business is included. Though the number of meetings for over 500 delegates may be limited within a particular city or area, there is opportunity to host smaller meetings. These meetings, frequently required by the corporate sector, and which often support 15–50 delegates, can have a significant impact on a hotel's overall income.

Many hotels traditionally have organised and operated their food and beverage department to maximise the revenue from their 'function capacity' through wedding receptions, gala dinners and balls. The impact and development of MICE business within these venues has furthered the attention on food and beverages and its management and operation. Food and beverage operations have been developed to encompass a wide range of MICE-type events. The aim is to provide the delegates with a food and beverage service experience that is memorable, unique, sophisticated and in many cases uses the latest technology to ensure both a high quality and an excellent standard.

Hotels and venues can be divided into three main categories: residential venues, which provide accommodation plus convention and meeting facilities; non residential venues, which provide only convention and meeting facilities; and special venues. Many of these venues are featured in the facilities guides provided by the CVBs.

Residential venues

There is an endless array of venues that provide both residential accommodation plus a wide range of convention and meeting-style facilities, including city centre, airport, resort and suburban hotels, four- and five-star hotels, small regional hotels, resorts and motels. For example:

- The Hotel Conrad and Jupiters Casino, situated on the Gold Coast, has its own self-contained convention centre with 12 convention rooms. The largest room has a seating capacity for 2300 people.
- The Marriott Surfers Paradise Resort is built on 28 levels, has 330 guestrooms, and features among its wide-ranging facilities a $0.8 million aquatic centre. The self-contained convention area is situated on the first floor and contains a variety of suites, including the Marriott Grand Ballroom with a capacity to seat 600 people for a formal dinner or 850 people theatre-style for a convention. In addition, the facilities provided at the resort include state-of-the-art audiovisual equipment and services.
- The Hotel Nikko, Darling Harbour, Sydney has a separate check-in area for group and convention business.

Resort hotels

In many resort-style hotels, the MICE sector provides the 'bread and butter' business between seasons and is recognised as a high-spend, high-yield business. In addition to providing resorts with extra revenue during the shoulder and low seasons, it can ensure that service standards and staff training levels are maintained. Resort hotels have the added advantage of often being sited in a desirable location with both sporting and recreational facilities to hand. They are therefore popular with both the corporate sector and the association markets as they provide additional opportunities for delegates to add pre- or post-conference activities to the main event. Resorts offer a range of accommodation types, from standard to luxury rooms and suites, as well as large meeting rooms, public areas and plenty of breakout space. In addition to comprehensive banquet facilities, they can provide a range of other food and beverage outlets such as coffee shops, poolside bars and eateries, as well as the more formal restaurants that often specialise in a particular cuisine. Many resorts offer the facility of a health spa and fitness centre which, with today's focus on physical fitness, provides an additional bonus for corporate and association delegates.

In addition, resorts are seen as being cost-competitive against their city counterparts. For example, in order to obtain some particular MICE business, they might offer to reduce the room hire rate for the convention in order to gain the accommodation and food and beverage components of the event. For a large convention there also may be the opportunity to have sole use of the venue for the event. For the larger convention group a resort location in close proximity to an airport is highly desirable.

Central business district hotels

Hotels located in the central business district (CBD) of a city that provide convention and meeting facilities have many amenities to offer a convention or meeting organiser and their delegates. The hotels are usually businesses-orientated, provide facilities such as a business centre and are equipped to handle corporate business. For many businesses, the central location of these venues means that they are easily accessible to business offices, restaurants and entertainment.

Airport hotels

Airport hotels, often sited on the airport perimeter, are seen by many companies as a cost-effective meeting venue for delegates who travel interstate. In view of their location, many airport hotels have added soundproofing or designed the building specifically to reflect noise. Their attributes include the geographical benefits of their location, functionality and a keen price structure compared to their counterparts in the CBD, plus an excellent range of conference and meeting rooms and supporting business services. Some airport venues provide the additional facility to hire the meeting room by the hour.

Suburban hotels

These hotels are popular for meetings where there is little or no need for the variety of amenities provided by a resort. They often gain their business from local companies, be they manufacturing, retail or services.

Boutique hotels

Within Australia, a category of hotels known as boutique hotels, catering for a small number of guests and delegates, has developed. These hotels often provide innovative cuisine, a high level of service and a focus on individuality, and are particularly attractive for small meetings such as executive retreats.

Residential conference centres

Residential conference centres are dedicated to organising and operating conferences and meetings. They provide both excellent accommodation and catering facilities, together with a fully-trained professional conference and meeting team to totally support the event. Many centres have been built to a design specification, focused on enhancing the success of the meeting. They accept no business other than conferences and meetings and as such are an excellent choice for small- to medium-sized corporate and association meetings.

Colleges and universities

Colleges and universities provide inexpensive accommodation and purpose-built convention and meeting facilities usually supported by excellent audiovisual equipment. The facilities, accommodation and catering are often only available in the semester breaks such as the summer vacation period. However, they are particularly attractive to some associations and non-profit organisations that have limited resources.

Cruise ships

Cruise ships are an interesting and different choice for a convention or meeting. They provide a range of accommodation and facilities, often at an 'all inclusive' price. The idea of a sea cruise is usually attractive to delegates, while for the conference organiser the 'encapsulated environment' assists in ensuring the success of the event.

Non-residential venues

Non-residential venues include dedicated or purpose-built convention and exhibition centres, exhibition halls, theatres, arenas and stadiums. Dedicated or purpose-built convention and exhibition centres are designed to accommodate large numbers of people under one roof for a combined convention and exhibition. They usually provide a number of large rooms designed for plenary sessions, halls with appropriate infrastructure to hold exhibitions and trade shows, plus a wide range of meeting rooms, breakout areas, banqueting facilities, a business centre, offices and administration space. The management and operation of these centres is examined in more detail in chapter 3.

Special venues

Special venues might include attractions such as historical buildings, museums, zoos, landmarks and icons, and sporting venues. One example of a landmark and icon is the Sydney Opera House, which enjoys an acclaimed reputation as a national icon and a leading performing arts centre. It offers magnificent function rooms with a total seating capacity of over 5000 delegates, a variety of restaurants featuring modern Australian, international and seafood cuisine, extensive technical facilities and an on-site reservations department for tour, dinner and performance packages (*Dawsons Venue Directory* 1996). The Australian National Maritime Museum, located at Sydney's Darling Harbour, provides a range of conference facilities in a fascinating and stimulating setting. The museum uses its fleet of historic vessels and exhibitions of maritime heritage as a focal point for the various conference and entertainment rooms, such as the USA Gallery and the Whale Hunt Experience (*Dawsons Venue Directory* 1996).

■ Transport *operators*

The transport operators involved in supplying a MICE event can include air, rail, sea, coach, car hire and taxi companies. The logistical aspects of coordinating these operators can be a major consideration for conference organisers.

Airlines play an important role in the transportation process as they handle both international and domestic delegates. Many airlines (e.g. Qantas) have recognised the value and importance of this market area, and have appointed an in-house group travel specialist who focuses on the MICE industry. For the larger conventions and meetings, the travel specialist will negotiate group travel discounts with the conference organiser and will arrange for the airline to become the designated carrier for that convention.

■ Service *support companies*

There is a diverse range of companies that provide support services to ensure a successful convention or meeting. These include audiovisual companies, printers, florists, entertainment companies, interpreters and producers of conference satchels and name badges. They form an integral part of the total impression that is provided to the convention or meeting delegate. For example, the MIAA annual conference in 1996 held in Tasmania drew on the services of a range of support companies, incuding an audiovisual equipment company and a company that specialised in providing transcript services of conference proceedings either on disc or CD ROM.

■ Exhibition *service contractors*

These companies, sited in each capital city, include a range of businesses whose services include exhibition stand design and construction, plant and equipment hire, and the provision of light and power, security, artwork, and so on. They work with the convention, meeting or exhibition organiser to supply the needs of the show, be it a major exhibition or a small trade show required to support a conference. For example, at a recent Stone Fruit Growers conference held in Ballina, the local RSL club (the conference and exhibition venue) utilised the services of a Southeast Queensland exhibition contractor to supply a hockerdome and exhibition booths.

■ Professional *conference organisers*

To be successful, a convention or meeting requires careful planning. A professional conference organiser (PCO) is an individual or organisation who organises and provides convention and meeting planning services to a client for a fee. They manage all the details, activities and interactions of a convention or meeting, from the initial idea through to the actual event and post-event evaluation. The professional conference organiser is the executive arm of the convention or meeting committee. They convert decisions into actions, keep the project on schedule, report to the committee, coordinate the various suppliers and offer consultative expertise. Professional conference organisers are also known as professional conference managers, meeting managers or meeting planners (MIAA 1995). Their role and function is discussed in more detail in chapter 3.

Having comprehensively reviewed the various stakeholders and suppliers to the industry, and the facilities on offer, we now move on to outline types of conventions and meetings and explore who holds and plans meetings.

TYPES OF CONVENTIONS AND MEETINGS

'Meeting' is a generic term that is used to indicate almost any type of get-together. Indeed, Weirich has defined a meeting as a 'coming together of a group of people with similar interests to accomplish some predetermined goal or purposes' (1992, p. 4). Within Australia, the generic term 'meeting' covers all off-site gatherings including conventions, congresses, conferences, seminars, workshops and symposia, all of which bring people together for a common purpose — the sharing of information (Commonwealth Department of Tourism 1995, p. 3). While all of these are basically meetings, each have different nuances that need to be recognised.

Basically, there are four categories of meetings, outlined below. Each meeting has different objectives that need to be met. These are discussed in more detail in chapter 5.

- *corporate meetings*, which businesses use to communicate with staff and distributors
- *association meetings*, which are usually of a practical or technical nature and are related to individual trade associations, professional societies or academic institutions
- *government and intergovernmental meetings*
- *common interest meetings*, for example those held by sports, cultural and social groups (Commonwealth Department of Tourism 1995, p. 3).

In addition to meetings, the MICE industry incorporates:

- *incentive meetings and travel*, which are used as rewards for productivity achieved, or as motivational tools for employees to improve performance or to encourage executives to reach certain goals
- *exhibitions*, which are designed to bring together suppliers of products, equipment and services in an environment where they can demonstrate their products or services
- *trade shows*, which are exhibitions run exclusively for a particular trade or industry and provide forums for the exchange of information between companies and their potential clients — unlike exhibitions, trade shows are only open to members of the particular trade or industry, and attendance is by invitation

- *public shows*, which are run to attract and encourage the public, for example the Home and Leisure Show or Personal Computer Show (Commonwealth Department of Tourism 1995, p. 3).

Managers within the MICE industry must be fully conversant with the various types of meetings. Each has a different image to be projected, and only by being truly familiar with their differences can managers be certain to achieve and understand their customers' requirements.

It is important in the organisation of any meeting to consider the type and style of event required, together with a profile of the prospective delegate, for example general manager or sales trainee. Only then can the formality of the program and the level of luxury desired be established.

WHO HOLDS AND PLANS CONVENTIONS AND MEETINGS?

As noted in chapter 1, the convention and meeting industry forms an effective communication medium. It provides a range of management, educational and marketing tools that enable individuals and businesses to receive benefits in sales, education, communication, motivation and evaluation. The industry has three major groups of customers — corporate, association, and government and non-profit organisations.

■ Corporate *sector*

Business communication is the primary reason for a convention or meeting within the corporate sector. Communication, and in particular intracompany communication, is extremely important, and one of the most fundamental methods of intracompany communication is through meetings. Companies the world over hold meetings, be they small, medium or large — attending conventions or meetings is very much part of professional and business life. Indeed, over 50 per cent of all meetings held in Australia tend to be from the corporate sector (Johnson, Foo & O'Halloran 1999, p. 11). When a company holds a meeting it seeks the maximum return on its investment; while the delegates who attend the meeting seek relevant, practical information that is effectively presented.

The types of meetings found within the corporate sector range from board meetings and training meetings, to the annual sales conference or the launch of a new product. Many of the meetings found within the corporate sector are reasonably small — on average 15 to 50 delegates — and are therefore relatively simple to organise. Some events, however, may be more elaborate, such as the launch of a new product. Over 60 per cent of corporate meetings are single or part-day meetings, and meetings of more than one day represent 35 per cent of all corporate meetings (Johnson, Foo & O'Halloran 1999, p. 11). These events may be held partly over a weekend so that there is minimum disruption to the working week.

The corporate sector can be divided into three distinct areas: manufacturing (e.g. plant, machinery and pharmaceuticals); distribution and retail; and services (e.g. finance, banking, accounting, legal and insurance). Each area has a different requirement of the MICE industry. In the manufacturing sector there may be a requirement for trade shows, while the service sector may concentrate more on seminars and training courses, and distribution companies may focus perhaps on sales meetings. Managers in the convention and meeting industry need to be aware of the requirements of the different market segments so that they can implement a successful and competitive marketing strategy and achieve high levels of customer service.

The organisation of corporate conventions and meetings may lie with a dedicated person within the company, or alternatively it may be allocated to a particular individual within a specific department — for example, a training manager who is responsible for organising the training meetings for each department. Alternatively, for large events, the company may engage the services of a professional conference organiser.

The cost of holding a corporate convention or meeting is normally funded by the company or sponsor of the meeting. Delegates who attend the event often use an expense account. This is in contrast to association meetings where, in many instances, members directly fund their attendance. Corporate meetings seldom raise any direct revenue. Instead, the financial gain from the event may be seen indirectly in such factors as increased motivation of the staff who attend, resulting in higher productivity, improved customer service or higher sales figures.

■ Associations

An association is an organised and structured group of people who have similar interests or businesses. Associations can be professional, technical, religious, fraternal, social, educational or avocation (hobbyist). Most professions or careers (e.g. teachers, doctors, engineers, accountants and librarians) usually have at least one association. Associations are the most visible convention and meeting organisers. There is a vast collection of them throughout the Asia–Pacific region and the world, with many being truly international. Associations can vary in size from small regional groups to large state, national and international organisations.

Associations are an important source of conventions and meetings as virtually every association has regularly scheduled meetings designed to further the interests of their members, exchange information and provide membership activities. The types of meetings held by associations include professional updates and seminars, often on a monthly basis; network meetings; training and development programs; and annual or biannual conferences. Regional and state associations tend to restrict the location of their events to within the state, while some associations move the location and venue of their annual conference each year — for example CAUTHE (Council for Australian University Tourism and Hospitality Education) held its annual conference in Coffs Harbour in 1996, in Sydney in 1997, on the

Gold Coast in 1998 and in Adelaide in 1999. For international associations, each annual or biannual convention may be held in a different country.

Within Australia, the association market accounts for approximately 12 per cent of all conventions and meetings (Johnson, Foo & O'Halloran 1999, p. 11). Associations tend to hold larger meetings than most other groups, particularly those that last more than a day overall, with an average of 110 delegates (Johnson, Foo & O'Halloran 1999, p. 11). International association meetings account for more room nights and a higher income than the average meeting and are seen by venues as a high-yield sector of the industry.

Many associations in Australia have their main office in Canberra, which is recognised as being the 'home of associations in Australia'. This enables them to be near the 'seat of government', so that they can fulfil their lobbying role on behalf of their members. A similar situation exists in the United States, where many associations have their head office in Washington DC.

Membership of an association involves the payment of an annual subscription. Members also must pay to attend any or all meetings. This is a key factor in association meetings. Within the corporate market, companies can dictate to employees who should attend a meeting, but associations have to lure members to their events — in other words, the events need to be marketed. This means that programs have to be structured to be of interest to members; sites selected for events should encourage people to attend; and partner and social programs need to be designed to ensure that attendance at the convention or meeting is an attractive option.

The organisation of members' meetings and conference programs in some of the large associations is undertaken by a separate conference department within the association. For example, the Institute of Directors in London has a director of conferences and a full support team made up of conference and event coordinators to manage, organise and coordinate an extensive convention, meeting and event program. However, in many other associations the board of directors or committee expect the chief executive officer of the association to be responsible for the planning of meetings and activities. If the association can afford to, it may use the services of a professional conference organiser.

Associations gain their funds from membership subscriptions together with any surplus funds made from their activities, such as the annual convention. In many instances, any surpluses gained from the annual convention are a key source of revenue or are used as 'seed funds' for the next conference.

■ **Government** *and non-profit organisations*

Government organisations

Government and intergovernment meetings are another major business sector for the convention and meeting industry, accounting for 19 per cent of the Australian meetings market (Johnson, Foo & O'Halloran 1999, p. 11). City, state and federal government agencies hold meetings of all types, such as for training and planning, or to discuss changes to operational procedures.

These meetings may be held off government premises, and include either government employees or members of the government and the public. The meeting needs of the government sector, however, are somewhat different from those of the corporate sector. The funds for government meetings come from the public purse and as such there is an issue of price-sensitivity, not only in the booking of the facilities but also in the per diem provided to employees for government travel. Government sector meetings also have fewer delegates.

Non-profit organisations

This market comprises unions, religious groups and other common-interest groups such as sports, cultural or social clubs. They tend to be relatively price conscious. Some hotel groups have developed the acronym SMERF for this group of organisations — social, military, educational, religious and fraternal (Astroff & Abbey 1998, p. 19). They have established that SMERF groups have three common characteristics: they are price sensitive; they book meetings during the low season; and their meetings or conferences are often managed by a non-professional conference planner who changes on an annual basis.

WHO IS INVOLVED IN THE ORGANISATION OF CONVENTIONS AND MEETINGS?

In this final section we summarise the main people who might be involved in the management and organisation of a convention or meeting. From the information studied to date we can identify that the main players who might be involved are:

- *company or association* The company or association make the initial decision to organise a convention or meeting. It develops and provides all the information required for the management of the convention and supplies the delegates.
- *venue* A venue provides the services of a convention services manager or banquet manager to organise and arrange the facilities within the venue in accordance with the requirements of the convention organiser. The venue provides the accommodation and all conference and other in-house facilities, and might also provide entertainment and other guest facilities. For larger conventions, the venue might provide assistance with the planning of the convention.
- *professional conference organiser* A professional conference organiser forms a contract with the company or association planning the convention or meeting to organise the total event or occasion on their behalf. The PCO becomes an intermediary between the original planner of the convention (the client organisation), the provider of the venue and facilities, the various suppliers and the actual delegates to ensure that the convention or meeting is a success.

- *convention and visitors bureau* The CVB arranges the overall details of the convention or meeting with the conference planner, whom they put in contact with venues and other suppliers within their city or region. They bid for conventions on behalf of their city or region and sell their own destination on behalf of their membership.

A company or association that wishes to organise a convention or meeting can either: (a) make all its own arrangements, including the organisation of the booking and management and execution of the convention or meeting; (b) decide on a venue and let the convention services manager at the venue take care of the details within the facility, liaising over the details as required; or (c) contract with a professional conference organiser to make all the arrangements on its behalf, not only with the venue but also with the various other suppliers to ensure the smooth-running of the event on the day. A summary of this process is shown in figure 2.3. In chapters 3 and 4 these themes are explored in more detail.

■ **Figure 2.3**
Overview of the process of organising a convention or meeting

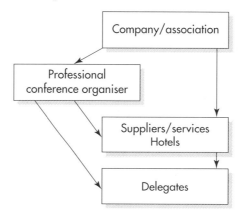

SUMMARY

There are a number of stakeholders involved in the coordination and management of a successful MICE event. They interact with conference delegates at differing points during the convention or meeting. These stakeholders include government organisations, industry associations, a wide variety of venues that provide a range of facilities, convention and visitors bureau, professional conference organisers, transport providers, caterers and other support services and exhibition contractors. Industry stakeholders have different functions and objectives to achieve with respect to the convention and meeting industry. For example, in the case of CVBs, the importance of partnership and cooperation among bureau members, conference organisers and the local community are apparent in order to maximise the potential business opportunities. It is evident that there are a wide variety and range of facilities and services available to potential conference organisers. Each group of stakeholders can gain mutual benefit by working together to ensure the quality and provision of the service provided is to the ultimate satisfaction of the customer, which will ensure potential repeat business.

Conventions and meetings are held by the corporate sector, associations, government and non-profit organisations. Each of these groups operates and has different requirements of the industry. It is essential that conference organisers recognise the varying needs of these organisations and are aware of the differences between the types of meetings. Only then can a 'best fit' be assured in the MICE product or service provided to the customer both in terms of what is required and in the levels of customer satisfaction. These issues are explored further in chapter 3, together with an examination of the implications of managing the suppliers to the MICE industry.

Activity

2.1 From your local tourist information centre, convention and visitors bureau or NRMA directory, establish a list of potential conference venues in your town, city or area. What is the range and extent of facilities available? Who might be attracted to these venues?

Discussion questions

2.1 As a hotel, venue or audiovisual supplier who specialises in the convention and meeting industry, identify and discuss the benefits to your organisation of becoming a member of the local CVB.

2.2 Outline and discuss the methods by which the federal government might assist in the marketing of MICE activities.

2.3 Discuss and evaluate the role of industry associations within the MICE industry in Australia.

2.4 Critically evaluate the role of a CVB within a city or region. Discuss the services it provides for the potential conference organiser.

2.5 Discuss the funding arrangements for a CVB. Why is it important that it remains autonomous?

2.6 Why is it important that a conference organiser understands the differences between the various types of meetings — after all, aren't they all synonymous?

2.7 What is the role of the ATC with respect to the MICE industry? Discuss the mechanisms it uses to promote the MICE industry overseas.

2.8 Discuss the differences in funding arrangements for conventions and meetings between associations and the corporate sector. What are the implications for the conference organiser?

2.9 Describe the types of conventions and meetings held by corporations. How do they differ from those held by associations?

REFERENCES

AACB. 1994, *Statistical Report on the Scope of the Meetings Industry*. AACB, Sydney.

Adelaide Convention and Tourism Authority. 1998. (*http://www.acta.com.au*).

Astroff, M. T. & Abbey, J. R. 1998, *Convention Sales and Services*, 5th ed., Waterbury Press, N.J.

ATC. *Annual Report 1996*, ATC, Sydney.

ATC. 1998, 'Australia 2001' (*www.australia2001.com*).

Brisbane Tourism. 1998, membership brochure.

Canberra Convention Bureau. 1996, personal communication with executive director.

Canberra Convention Bureau. 1999, personal communication with executive director.

Commonwealth Department of Tourism. *A National Strategy for the Meetings, Incentives, Conventions and Exhibitions Industry*, Canberra, 1995.

Convention & Incentive Marketing. 1998, 'Canberra Campaigns for More MICE', vol. 24, no. 5, June.

Dawsons Venue Directory, 25th Edition, 1996.

Gartrell, R. B. 1994, *Destination Marketing for Convention and Visitor Bureaus*, 2nd ed, Kendall Hunt, Iowa.

Gartrell, R. B. 1998, *Destination Marketing for Convention and Visitor Bureaus*, 3rd ed, Kendall Hunt, Iowa.

Gold Coast Tourism Bureau. 1998.

IACVB. 1990, *General Information*, p. 2.

Johnson, L., Foo, L. M. & O'Halloran, M. 1999, *Meetings Make Their Mark: Characteristics and Economic Contribution of Australia's Meetings and Exhibition Sector*, Occasional Paper No. 26, BTR, Canberra.

MIAA. 1998a, *Newsletter*, April.

MIAA. 1998b, *Who's Who in the Meetings Industry*, MIAA, Sydney.

MIAA. 1998c, *Annual Report 1997/8*, MIAA, Sydney.

MIAA. 1998d, *What is a Professional Conference Organiser?*, MIAA, Sydney.

Montgomery, R. J. & Strick, S. 1995, *Meetings, Conventions and Expositions: An Introduction to the Industry*, Van Nostrand Reinhold, New York.

Rutherford, D. G. 1990, *Introduction to the Conventions, Expositions and Meetings Industry*, Van Nostrand Reinhold, New York.

SCVB. 1998a, *Sydney Facilities Guide*, SCVB, Sydney.

SCVB. 1998b, promotional literature, SCVB, Sydney.

Stanfield, L. 1998, 'MICE is Booming', paper presented to 1998 PATA Tourism Executive Development Program, Ballina, June.

Weirich, M. L. 1992, *Meetings and Conventions Management*, Delmar Publishers, New York.

Weissinger, S. S. 1992, *A Guide to Successful Meeting Planning*, John Wiley & Sons, New York.

FURTHER READING

BTR. 1998, *Measuring MICE Industry Infrastructure. A Report for the Tourism Forecasting Council*, Research Report No.1 (*http://tourism.gov.au*).

Clarke, M. 1997, 'Playing Hard', *The Quorum*, September/October.

Getz, D., Anderson, D. & Sheehan, L. 1998, 'Roles, Issues and Strategies for Convention and Visitors' Bureau in Destination Planning and Product Development: A Survey of Canadian Bureaus', *Tourism Management*, vol, 19, no. 4, pp. 331–40.

Varley, J. 1998, 'Cruise Altitude', *The Quorum*, January/February.

Canberra Convention Bureau

In 1995/96, the Canberra Convention Bureau went through a period of considerable change, which resulted in it repositioning itself and its activities from that of a convention and visitors bureau to solely a convention bureau. These changes involved reviewing its activities, incorporating shifts in staff responsibility and organisational structures, and a new corporate image and name change. The bureau has a mission statement to 'market Canberra and the region as a premier MICE destination through the cooperative support of the ACT government and the Bureau's membership'. Under the direction of its executive director, the bureau has revised its marketing strategy.

Membership of the bureau is made up of representatives from Canberra city, hotels, venues, professional conference organisers, audiovisual companies, caterers, large and small retailers and transport companies (on-ground and airlines).

A SWOT (strengths, weaknesses, opportunities and threats) analysis indicated that Canberra had a number of strengths for the bureau, such as being the national capital of Australia, with a number of national icons and attractions, as well as being a diverse destination with four distinct seasons and access to both snowfields and beaches. The city provides a concentration of national associations and gives access to government decision makers. In addition, there is good infrastructure and support services for MICE activities. However, the bureau was aware that there was a negative perception of the city and that the area, despite being the national seat of government, has no international airport and lacks some types of hotel accommodation. In addition, any marketing effort implemented would be hampered by a limited budget.

The bureau has identified a number of opportunities afforded by its access to key decision makers both from within the federal government and from heads of associations, and from the potential of the celebrations of the 2000 Sydney Olympics and the 2001 anniversary of Federation. The revised marketing strategy identifies key markets for the bureau within the ACT, nationally and internationally, and focuses on a number of opportunities in line with the bureau's mission statement.

A new logo has been developed to form the basis for the collateral material produced, the logo being designed to complement that used by Canberra Tourism. A fresh and vibrant meeting planner guide has been developed, which focuses on the 'youthful character' of a city 'thriving on its vibrant political, social and sporting life'. This planner is completely the opposite of its predecessor, which focused on the traditional link of the city with the seat of government. New display material has been produced for use at national and international trade shows, together with an annual calendar of Canberra MICE events. In addition, a number of direct mail campaigns have been undertaken including 'Operation Sell Canberra', which focused on the MICE industry and involved placing a number of major advertisements, to support features on the city, in the two main publications of the Australasian convention and meeting industry — *The Quorum* and *Convention & Incentive Marketing*.

To ensure member satisfaction, the bureau has sought to improve communication and cooperation, with the aim of developing a strong cooperative working relationship with members. Activities have included opportunities for cooperative marketing in areas such as trade show participation, advertising and direct marketing campaigns. A quarterly newsletter includes information on conventions coming to town, together with updates on the various marketing campaigns such as 'Operation Sell Canberra', research data, and information on the bureau's activities such as attendance at trade shows.

The bureau has refocused its sales activity, with a renewed emphasis on the domestic market, and has implemented a convention servicing unit to 'provide an increased level of service to delegates during their stay in Canberra'. The Canberra Information Desk has been introduced and is staffed for all major conferences. The bureau also provides conference organisers with supporting collateral material to be used in the planning stages of an event, such as an information and fact sheet that can be incorporated into registration brochures, a Canberra promotional brochure and assistance with their marketing strategies. The bureau has identified the need for research information and has set up a research base for MICE-specific data in order to monitor delegates' satisfaction with Canberra as a MICE destination, establish delegate expenditure patterns and determine an estimated value of MICE business for the city.

The bureau has continued to develop creative and unique marketing strategies and introduce new products in order to maintain and increase Canberra's MICE business. The 'Operation Sell Canberra' weekend showcase continues to be both popular and successful. In 1998, the bureau introduced a joint promotion — 'A Hop, Skip and a Jump' — with the bureaus in Sydney and Far North Queensland, the objective being to entice potential incentive conference organisers to utilise the three cities for an incentive experience: 'Hop into Australia's gateway city (Sydney), skip into the bush (Canberra) and jump into a tropical adventure (Cairns)'. Also in 1998, the bureau launched a campaign aimed at securing more meetings in the city in 1999. 'Conference in Canberra in 1999' was designed to encourage the Canberra branches of national and international organisations to stage a convention in Canberra in 1999. This initiative was developed further in 1999 with the launch of the Canberra Loan Scheme, which provides interest-free loans from $5000 to $10 000 to associations or similar bodies that wish to hold a national or international convention in Canberra. The loans, which are repayable, provide an important cash injection to associations, charities, and so on, that may not be cash affluent, in order to assist them to kick-start their marketing and promotional campaign for their convention. The first two loan approvals under the scheme generated $3.2 million to the Canberra economy.

Source: Canberra Convention Bureau (1996, 1999). Convention & Incentive Marketing (June 1998, p. 13)

Questions

1 Identify and examine the strengths and weaknesses of the Canberra Convention Bureau prior to the introduction of the revised marketing strategy.

2 What benefits will the marketing strategy and the refocusing of the Convention Bureau provide for the members of the bureau?

3 Discuss and review the marketing and promotional strategies introduced by the bureau since 1995/96. How might they assist in the development of the convention business in Canberra?

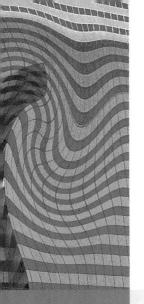

CHAPTER

3 Managing
suppliers to conventions

LEARNING OBJECTIVES

After studying this chapter, you will be able to:

- identify the purpose and scope of purpose-built convention and exhibition centres

- outline the facilities and services provided by purpose-built convention and exhibition centres

- review the management and organisational structure of purpose-built convention and exhibition centres

- outline the structure and organisation of convention departments within hotels and residential venues

- describe the management of conventions and meetings within a hotel

- review the services that professional conference organisers provide to the convention and meeting industry.

INTRODUCTION

Today's business environment is focused on giving more attention to the needs of customers by being more responsive and providing greater value. This is a result of competition, escalating operating costs and changes that have taken place in travel markets worldwide. Conference delegates are being more selective in the conventions and meetings that they attend. There is thus a need to provide a level of service that leaves the delegates wishing to return after the event. Quality of customer service is therefore a key business indicator. As a result, convention and meeting venues have placed greater emphasis both on the service provision and the service encounter to ensure that key staff are fully trained in this area.

This chapter concentrates on exploring the management, organisation and operation of a number of the key stakeholders or suppliers to the convention and meeting industry. These are purpose-built convention and exhibition centres (or, as they are sometimes referred to, dedicated convention centres — DCCs), hotels and professional conference organisers or meeting managers.

PURPOSE-BUILT CONVENTION AND EXHIBITION CENTRES

A purpose-built convention and exhibition centre is a purpose-built, stand-alone facility used principally for meetings, conventions, trade shows and exhibitions. Normally, it will have catering facilities, but need not include accommodation. These centres provide a large flexible space that can host exhibitions, trade shows and conventions, as well as providing smaller rooms for meetings, banquets and other functions such as breakfasts, lunches, dinners, product launches, and so on. Irrespective of size, the centre should be designed for maximum visual appeal and flexibility and to be 'user friendly' to conference organisers, exhibitors and delegates. The centre should be able to host a wide variety of events, be equipped with the latest technology in respect of audiovisual equipment and communications, and offer a number of services.

■ Background

The construction, development and operation of purpose-built convention and exhibition facilities have helped to expand the MICE industry both in Australia and overseas. These centres are structured to meet the needs of conference organisers in the same way as hotels and resorts that specialise in the convention and meeting industry. By understanding the way they operate and how they are organised and managed, the conference organiser can use the services they provide to maximum effectiveness.

Purpose-built convention and exhibition centres have been seen as a means of bringing economic renewal and an enhancement of civic pride to a city or a region. Nationally and internationally, conference, convention and exhibition centres have been developed or expanded in the expectation that they will revitalise the community and the region both physically and economically. The building and construction required to develop such centres has resulted in 'cities jumping on the bandwagon all hoping to reap the rewards' (Fenich 1992, p. 183). Such is the case in Australasia (see figure 3.1), where purpose-built convention and exhibition centres have opened in Adelaide, Melbourne, Canberra, Sydney, Brisbane, Cairns, Auckland, Rotorua, Wellington and Christchurch. New centres are planned for development in Perth and the Gold Coast. Existing centres also have been upgraded and refurbished, for example in Adelaide and Melbourne, as competition increases and as Australia continues to increase its share of the global meetings business. Millions of dollars have been spent both in the construction of new centres and in extensions to existing facilities. The Brisbane Convention and Exhibition Centre cost $200 million to build, while the extension to the Sydney Convention and Exhibition Centre is estimated to have cost $57 million.

The first purpose-built convention and exhibition centre opened in Australia in Adelaide in 1987. Since that time, the country has gone from a position of relative obscurity in both the region and the world meeting industry, to being the number one destination in the Asia–Pacific region (Stanfield 1998).

■ **Figure 3.1**
Location of purpose-built convention and exhibition centres in Australasia

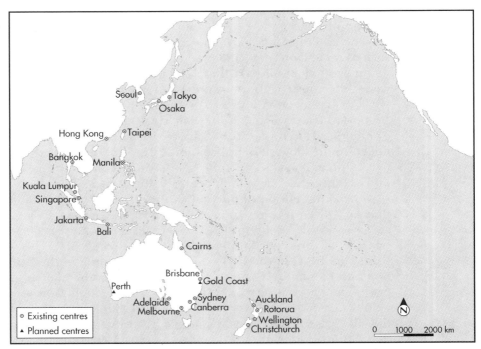

Types *of events*

The types of events held at such centres are wide ranging. For example, they could include medical conventions such as the World Congress of Dermatology, the Congress of Chemotherapy or the Congress of Cardiology, at which the number of delegates might range from 5000 to 10000 and for which there might be an accompanying exhibition. Alternatively, a community service group such as Rotary International might use the facility. The anticipated attendance at an event such as the Rotary International Convention would be in excess of 25000 delegates.

Economic *and social impacts*

There are a number of economic and social factors that support the construction of purpose-built convention and exhibition centres.

The predominant economic impact of purpose-built convention and exhibition centres is the employment opportunities they provide. This is particularly the case for the unskilled or semi-skilled workforce as well as skilled employees. For example, Australian centres typically employ 140 permanent and up to 450 casual staff, 37 per cent of whom are 25 years of age or under (Perth Convention Centre 1999). As such, the development of these centres is 'a plus' for job revitalisation. Other economic benefits include increases in direct and indirect spending for the community, achieved through the multiplier effect — money spent by convention delegates is passed through the local community via the suppliers and their employees. In addition, the construction of the centres can stimulate and support the growth and expansion of other local facilities such as hotels, restaurants, shopping centres and convention-specific suppliers. They can provide additional employment and direct and indirect spending on items such as taxis, laundry facilities and food and beverage outlets. This has been demonstrated in the Darling Harbour area of Sydney and in Brisbane, where the construction of the Brisbane Convention and Exhibition Centre (BCEC) has given rise to the development of a number of hotels built to support the centre, many of which are adjacent to the centre. Another example can be found in Singapore, where a number of hotels have been linked to the Singapore International Convention and Exhibition Centre by means of walkways. The centre is located within Suntec City, an area of offices, businesses, shopping centres and eateries.

A social dimension of purpose-built convention and exhibition centres is that they often provide an enhanced urban image for an area. The centres are used as the focal point for the revitalisation of a particular area and can enable a city to reposition itself and make a comeback. This was the case in Brisbane where, in the 1990s, prior to the building of the Brisbane Convention and Exhibition Centre, convention business had fallen to below 20 per cent. The city was also suffering from competition from other Australian cities (*Convention & Incentive Marketing* 1996). Since the development of the BCEC, the city has re-emerged strongly as a popular convention destination and convention business has risen substantially. In 1995/96 convention-generated spending had risen by 121 per cent to $69.5 million from a figure of $26.6 million in 1994/95 (*The Quorum* 1997, p. 77).

The development of purpose-built convention and exhibition centres is often viewed as a means to counteract urban blight. Consequently, they are, in many instances, sited in areas that require redevelopment and regeneration. For example, in the Sydney Darling Harbour scheme, the Convention and Exhibition Centre, together with hotels, a retail, leisure and entertainment complex and the Maritime Museum, replaced derelict wharves and a run-down dock area. In the United Kingdom, the Birmingham International Convention Centre (BICC) was built on the site of the old Bingley Hall (Britain's first purpose-built exhibition hall, which opened in 1851), and in an area that included wasteland requiring urban regeneration. The BICC now provides a focal point for the area and includes the symphony hall and repertory theatre. It is linked to the central business district (CBD), hotels, shopping and leisure areas by walkways and scenic canals.

The negative impacts frequently are cited as the high cost of development (in many instances, the land adjacent to the CBD is at a premium and this is therefore reflected in land costs), ongoing repayment costs for the construction and indirect costs such as the development of infrastructure to support the development (Fenich 1992, p. 189–90).

Research also has indicated that many purpose-built convention and exhibition centres are viewed as loss leaders (Fenich 1995, p. 313–14). They provide a focal point for luring potential convention delegates to the area, with the delegates' main spending occurring within the community. However, in the Australasian region, these centres are seen as a means to encourage and increase the amount of new convention and exhibition business to a city and its region, despite fears by some operators that they will dilute the existing business.

The development of such a centre therefore affords a number of benefits for a city, including the redevelopment of an area that might have been previously blighted, together with the potential spin-offs of new development. An enhanced urban image is provided, and the local population is able to use the new facilities. In addition, the construction of such centres provides increased employment, and secondary economic activity provides an improved fiscal health for the area. The disadvantages are seen in the potential high cost of construction, both of the centres and their associated infrastructure, and the potential high levels of debt servicing of the initial building costs, which raises the opportunity cost of building such centres. The ongoing high operating costs and potential losses in the operation of the centres also are viewed negatively (Fenich 1992, p. 194).

■ Construction *and location*

The design and construction of purpose-built convention and exhibition centres have developed considerably since the first centres were built. The initial buildings were a mixture of concrete blocks and steel beams, designed more for function than beauty. They were often sited on the edge of the city away from hotels and other facilities (Rutherford 1990, p. 79).

Today, to ensure the marketability of their facilities, purpose-built convention and exhibition centres are generally found in close proximity to hotels and other support infrastructure. They are often located in inner city redevelopment sites adjacent to the CBD. A major influence on the occupancy rates and impact of these convention and exhibition centres is their proximity to support facilities such as hotels, restaurants, retail shops, entertainment and local attractions. They are therefore sited to provide delegates with easy access to accommodation and potentially the city and central business district. Internationally, it is recognised that areas, cities and towns that support a mixture of well-designed multipurpose convention, meeting and exhibition facilities, and promote an image that is exciting, will attract MICE events more easily than those areas where part of the product is missing. Therefore, the more modern purpose-built convention and exhibition centres have been designed and integrated into the tourist infrastructure of the city. They include the latest and most sophisticated technology, which has been incorporated into the building from the start.

The centres should be located close to both public and private transport and their support infrastructure, such as road and rail networks. For example, one mode of access to the Sydney Convention and Exhibition Centre is by monorail, which links the central business district to Darling Harbour and includes a direct stop at the Convention Centre. In Singapore, the MARTA (rapid transport system) station is within two minutes walk of the Singapore International Convention and Exhibition Centre. Air access is equally important, with the desired travel time to and from a city's domestic and international airport being a maximum of approximately one hour. In addition, the international airport should provide frequent, nonstop flights to major destinations. The style of transport by which convention delegates or exhibition attendees arrive at the convention centre will depend on the style of event — for example, a city or local meeting will require more car parking spaces than a large international or interstate convention, where the majority of delegates will arrive by air.

■ External *design and appearance*

Convention and exhibition centres should be modern, purpose built, in character with the city, and meet the specific requirements of the conventions and exhibition industry. They should not be purely sports or music venues (though they may incorporate these facilities).

These centres frequently are located on highly visible sites, with views of the city, river or mountains. As such, the centres often are seen as an icon for a city. This is reflected in their architectural design. Gone are the days, particularly in Australasia, of 'the large featureless concrete box' (Rutherford 1990, p. 79). Recently constructed centres provide much innovation in design, with architects and builders often making use of natural materials from the local area. For example, in Cairns the roof of the convention centre is held aloft by 80-metre long timber beams made of plantation pine, with the aim of conserving the area's natural rainforest resources and encouraging greater local employment. A trend towards a 'sail effect' in roof design seems to be in evidence in the Asia–Pacific region, demonstrated by the centres in Brisbane, Sydney, Cairns, Hong Kong and Vancouver.

In a study of these centres (McCabe 1997), one centre was found to use the historical backdrop of a number of internationally recognised buildings, such as the Houses of Parliament and Westminster Abbey in London, to complement its architectural design and assist in the promotion of the venue as an icon.

In some areas, due to high land costs, a centre may be built upwards rather than follow the traditional horizontal model, which has all facilities on one or two levels (see industry insight). Consequently, in some centres the exhibition and convention floors are situated towards the top of the building rather than on the ground floor (which is more usual).

Purpose-built convention and exhibition centres are beginning to include environmental factors within their design and construction briefs. The Cairns Convention Centre, for example (Australia's first environmentally friendly convention centre), is designed to maximise the conservation of natural resources and minimise the consumption of power and water through 'intelligent design'. The following industry insight illustrates design features used in the construction of purpose-built convention and exhibition centres.

INDUSTRY INSIGHT
Typical convention and exhibition centre designs

1. Brisbane Convention and Exhibition Centre has an unusual design and is hailed as the world's first large-scale 'hyperbolic paraboloid structure', a feature that enables it to provide 24 000 square metres of column-free space. The centre has attracted many design awards, for example one from the British Institute of Structural Engineers, for its sail-inspired roof.

■ **Figure 3.2** *Brisbane Convention and Exhibition Centre*

(continued)

2. The environmentally friendly design features of the Cairns Convention Centre include:
   - a double-layered pleated plate roof, which extends out over the buildings to provide shaded verandahs — the roof is shaped to save energy by screening heat from the interior, encourages natural airflow ventilation, and saves water by channelling rainwater into a tank for future use
   - natural ventilation, which is aided by louvres in the centre walls that adjust automatically to follow the sun
   - an airconditioning system that does not use CFCs and equipment to take humidity from the air.

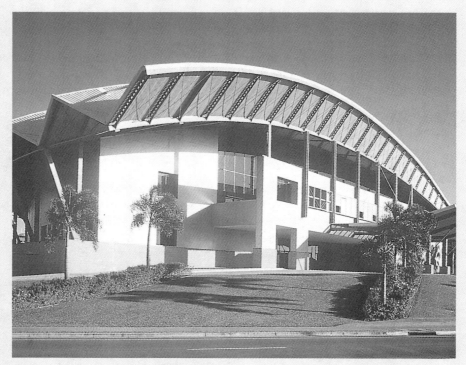

■ **Figure 3.3** *Cairns Convention Centre*

3. The exhibition and convention floors at the Singapore International Convention and Exhibition Centre are sited on the fourth and sixth floors, with the meeting and smaller conference rooms and restaurants on the lower floors of this eight-storey building. Access to the exhibition and conference floors for service providers is by means of an exterior service driveway, which provides direct two-way access for 20- and 40-foot container trucks.

■ **Figure 3.4a** *Singapore International Convention and Exhibition Centre*

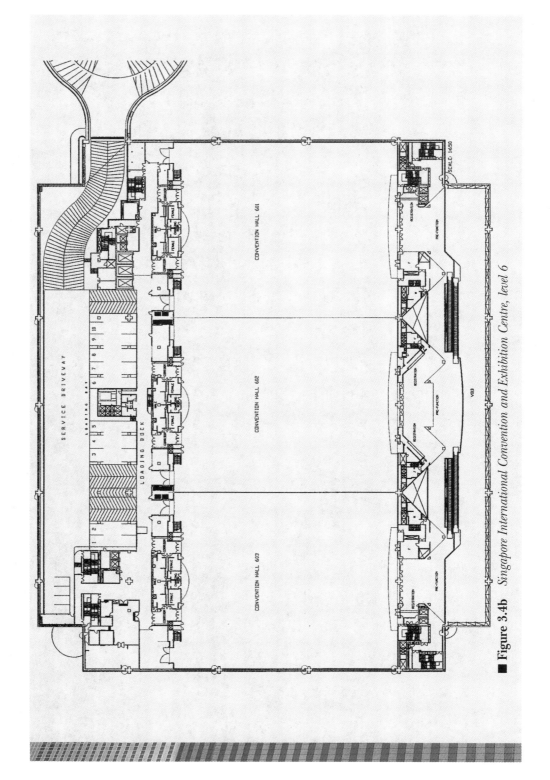

■ **Figure 3.4b** *Singapore International Convention and Exhibition Centre, level 6*

Substantial car parking facilities are required to support purpose-built convention and exhibition centres. These are often built under the centres or on adjacent land, to ease access for delegates. In many centres, the provision of car parking facilities is seen as a means of enhancing revenue.

During the pre-site selection and design process, future expansion and development should be considered. For example, the expansion of the Sydney Convention and Exhibition Centre, on its existing site, has increased its capacity by 12 per cent. The Las Vegas Convention Centre has grown three times in its lifetime and is now at the limit of its site.

■ Interior *facilities*

The facilities provided inside purpose-built convention and exhibition centres include space for conventions and exhibitions, various types and styles of meeting rooms, space for the provision of food and beverages for delegates, and common areas for breakout sessions. There should be sufficient areas throughout the centres to enable the registration of different groups who may be using the facility at the same time.

The internal layout and facilities of the centres therefore should include:
- A large foyer for the registration of delegates and for their refreshment breaks, poster displays and networking.
- Wide hallways to provide access to the auditorium and exhibition halls.
- Exhibition halls and areas with column-free space, adequate floor loading, ceiling height and on-hand services such as water, electricity, drainage, compressed air and under-floor power; food and beverage kiosks; and facilities to cater for large crowds, including toilets and hospitality lounges.
- Ease of access to the exhibition area for pantechnicon trucks.
- Robust infrastructure — the centres must be sufficiently robust to withstand the constant jostling and disruption associated with the regular movement of exhibition and display materials. Delays in the set up and pull down of different events can affect the efficiency of operation of a centre.
- A main auditorium with tiered seating (which should be divisible), simultaneous translation facilities and advanced audiovisual facilities.
- A wide range of breakout rooms all of different capacities to host smaller groups of between 20 and 1000 delegates. They should be interfaced with teleconference and audiovisual facilities.
- Food and beverage facilities to match the capacity of the auditorium. The food preparation areas should include a full-service kitchen, satellite service kitchens and goods receiving and storage areas.
- Lifts, stairs and wheelchair access, and escalators to enable the quick and efficient movement of people throughout the centre and from car parks and main entrance areas to the convention and exhibition space. The lack of escalators can limit the efficiency of a centre.

To be competitive, purpose-built convention and exhibition centres have to be at the forefront of technology both in terms of the audiovisual equipment and the communication equipment they offer. This is a key selling point. The centres should provide facilities such as video conferencing, satellite liaison and data projection. The centres often are used as a telecommunications focus for major national, regional and international events. For example, in 1998 the Brisbane Convention and Exhibition Centre was used as the 'counting house' and telecommunications centre for the Queensland state elections.

Today, purpose-built convention and exhibition centres are contemporary in terms of design, layout, colour schemes and fixtures and fittings. Each centre provides an aesthetically pleasing area geared to attract both the convention and exhibition delegate and the convention organiser. The provision of these enhanced facilities makes it easier for each centre's sales team to sell the facilities of the centre and for the local convention bureau to market the centre. Figure 3.5 summarises the capacities of Australia's purpose-built convention and exhibition centres.

■ Figure 3.5
The capacities of Australia's purpose-built convention and exhibition centres

ROOMS	SIZE	CAPACITIES	
National Convention Centre, Canberra			
Exhibition hall	2400 square metres	Banquet	2000
		Theatre	780
Theatrettes		No. of theatrettes	4
Royal theatre		Banquet	730
(Plenary hall)		(Plenary hall)	
		Tiered	1700
		Flat	800
Ballroom	650 square metres		
Meeting rooms		No. of rooms	5
Adelaide Convention Centre			
Exhibition hall	175 exhibition booths	Booths	175
Convention centre	2 × 3260 square metres	Tiered	3500
		Flat	2800
		Theatre	882
Meeting rooms		No. of rooms	9
Halls		No. of halls	5
Sydney Convention and Exhibition Centre			
Exhibition centre	27 200 square metres	No. of halls	6
Auditorium	2 rooms	Seated	4500
Ballroom	2 rooms	Banquet	2600
Meeting rooms		No. of rooms	30
		Theatre	3997

ROOMS	SIZE	CAPACITIES	
Melbourne Exhibition and Convention Centre			
Exhibition centre	30 000 square metres	Over 3 levels	
Auditorium	3 rooms		450–1423
Plenary hall		Tiered	1300
		Flat	2500
Theatre		Tiered	500
Meeting rooms	10 000 square metres	No. of rooms	33
Halls	5000 square metres	No. of halls	5
Brisbane Convention and Exhibition Centre			
Exhibition centre	20 000 square metres	No. of halls	4
Great hall	4600 square metres	Banquet	2850
		Theatre	4000
Plaza ballroom	2200 square metres	Banquet	1550
		Theatre	1980
Meeting rooms	from 40–950 square metres	No. of rooms	15
		Banquet	12–600
		Theatre	35–1200
Cairns Convention Centre			
Great hall	1720 square metres	Banquet	1500
		Tiered	2400
		Flat	2100
		Cocktails	2000
Meeting rooms	from 65–115 square metres	No. of rooms	7
Halls	430–450 square metres	No. of halls	4
		Banquet	350
		Tiered	294–474
		Floor	126–306
		Cocktails	450

■ **Management** *and operation*

Specific methods for the funding, management and operation of these centres have been developed.

Funding

The majority of purpose-built convention and exhibition centres are publicly owned, either by local or state government, and are operated by a designated board or authority. For example, in the United Kingdom, the Birmingham

International Convention Centre was funded by the city council and an inner city development grant, provided by the European Union, to help create employment and infrastructure. In some instances, convention centres are privately funded and operated, such as the Singapore International Convention and Exhibition Centre or the Sands Expo and Convention Centre in Las Vegas. Within Australia, however, these centres are generally funded by state government, but once operational are normally self-funded.

Rutherford (1990, p. 86) identifies that the convention centre owners are represented by the policy-making body of the facility, which establishes the policy and directions for the centre management to follow. The policy-making body appoints a chief executive officer, managing director or management company to manage the centre and to provide the focal point between the convention centre operation and the policy-making body. In Australia, many of the policy-making bodies have devolved authority to manage the centre to an independent company through a renewable management contract (e.g. Sydney Convention and Exhibition Centre and Brisbane Convention and Exhibition Centre). The management company then appoints a chief executive officer or managing director responsible for the centre, who reports to the centre's policy-making body. This policy-making body is often represented by a board of directors appointed by the owners of the centre.

A purpose-built convention and exhibition centre has to be self-supporting, make a profit and provide positive economic impact to the city. If it is to fulfil the requirements of the policy-making body, it needs to be operated and managed effectively. The specified design and location criteria should ensure that management are able to operate the building smoothly, effectively and efficiently and ensure satisfied customers while maximising returns. Management companies that specialise in the operation of these facilities have developed specific expertise and techniques to ensure their efficiency and effectiveness and a healthy bottom line. They are aware of the challenges to management of operating such a purpose-built stand-alone facility that lacks the traditional support of accommodation and bed stock to support its revenue-earning capacity.

Management and organisational structure

The management and organisation of these centres is sophisticated, with modern management practices being used. A clear statement of both the mission and goals, reflecting the individual focus of each centre, needs to be established by the centre management. Only when these have been determined can the management team plan, organise, develop, design and control the management activities required to enable these goals to be achieved.

The mission statement from the Adelaide Convention and Exhibition Centre reads:

■ The Adelaide Convention and Exhibition Centre shall be recognised as the best convention and exhibition venue in Australia thereby contributing to the growth and value of the South Australian economy and the profits of the State (Adelaide Convention and Exhibition Centre 1998). ■

The centre has been recognised by the industry and has received awards for its management and operation.

In the design of operational management systems, a centre's management team needs to consider:

- the sales and marketing aspects of the business
- the level and availability of client services
- the management, administration and control of the centre, which includes staffing levels, recruitment, selection, induction and training, together with the in-house maintenance levels of the facilities.

Other operational decisions that need to be addressed include the structure of charges for room hire rates and other facilities offered; yield management; the provision of food and beverage services and other ancillary services such as laundry, audiovisual and telecommunications; the availability of parking and the rates to be charged; the charges and cost of heat, light, power, and so on; and the terms of leases for any tenants of the centre, and so on (Rutherford 1990, p. 87).

Typical convention centres tend to follow the structure of functional organisation demonstrated by the generic organisation chart shown in figure 3.6. The chart demonstrates the key breakdown of activities between sales, operations, administration and accounting. Each convention centre has unique characteristics in which the activities of day-to-day management are achieved. Figure 3.7 indicates how the operations department at the Sydney Convention and Exhibition Centre is organised.

■ **Figure 3.6**
Functional organisation chart for purpose-built convention and exhibition centres

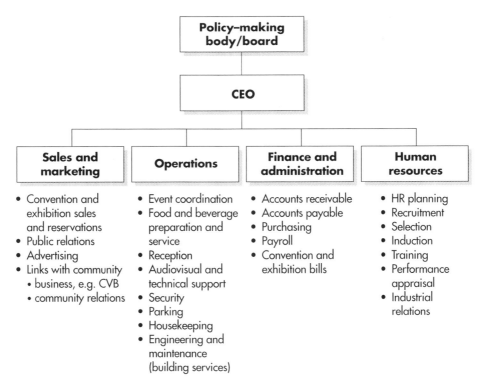

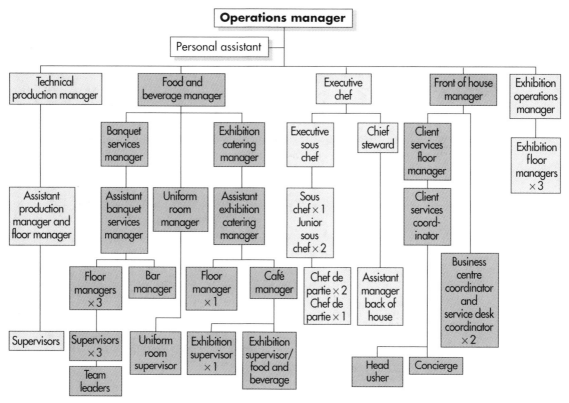

■ **Figure 3.7** *Organisation chart for the operations department, Sydney Convention and Exhibition Centre*

Source: Sydney Convention and Exhibition Centre

The current trend by some centres to be more customer-focused, empower staff and re-engineer some of the operational processes are reflected in the design and formulation of their organisation charts. Key performance indicators are established for each department, and the objectives are set by the department teams to ensure their ownership and commitment to the results.

Staffing

There is general acceptance within purpose-built convention and exhibition centres that staff are a key resource and the key to each centre's success. The structure and fabric of the centres means that many compete on an equal basis. What makes them able to differentiate their product and service is the quality of their staff and how well those staff service the needs and wishes of the customer. More attention is being given to the recruitment, selection and training of high-quality staff, not only in terms of full-time staff but also those employed on a casual or permanent part-time basis.

As a rule, a centre will have a small core of full-time staff plus a bank of casual staff members who can be almost permanent casuals. Contract staff also are employed and there is an emergence of specialist employment agencies that focus on supplying staff purely for the industry. Multiskilling is in practice across many centres, often led by the industry enterprise agreement, with staff moving between departments. In some centres this approach has led to a low staff turnover. However, in order to maintain high levels of customer care, centre management recognises that the casual staff brigade requires training in the standards and procedures of the centre's operations. Many centres within Australia have a commitment to training and developing both full-time and casual staff as a means of ensuring consistency of standards (McCabe 1997). The re-engineering of some of the operational processes, together with the redesigning of jobs, provides staff with the opportunity to see a job through from start to finish, and assists in client and individual job satisfaction.

Sales and marketing

Purpose-built convention and exhibition centres tend to focus on a number of market sectors. As with other conference venues, they tend to woo the lucrative corporate market where possible. However, they are aware that association business, and in particular international association business, is often desirable and beneficial to the city or region as high-spending international delegates often attend these events.

The key focus of a centre's marketing and sales team is to book events into the centre, by developing client contacts, converting enquiries into sales and promoting the venue. The sales and marketing team focuses its efforts to clearly demonstrate the centre's attributes to international and domestic conference and exhibition organisers. Usage of the Internet and Web sites has assisted centres in promoting and presenting their venue to potential clients. Sales and marketing staff assist in putting bids and bid documentation together and as such will often work with the local CVB and other convention, meeting and exhibition suppliers.

Depending on the centre's policy, the sales and marketing team may be broken down into specific market sectors, such as international conventions, corporate business, associations, exhibitions and special events, and account managers may be appointed for these target markets. In Australasia, some centres have an employee who is responsible for targeting international conventions and exhibitions, and indeed some centres have overseas representation, to make sure that this lucrative market is captured. International associations and exhibitions often book a number of years in advance of their actual event. In order to facilitate the letting of their facilities and to secure these events, many centres have established a hierarchy of activities for their portfolio, the aim of which is to attract large events that last for a number of days, for example a week. Smaller events are then used to fill in the gaps. The yield management techniques used by the centres ensure the effective use of the space. Yield management is discussed in chapters 10 and 11. A centre may identify, however, that it has a hierarchy of desirability for different events; this is built into the marketing policy and ensures that the activities of the department's staff are directed to the priority areas.

The client process

An initial enquiry for an event is taken by a member of the sales team, who checks availability, organises a site inspection and negotiates with the client. On receipt of the client confirmation, the event is transferred to the operations department and to the event planning management team, where it is allocated to an individual event manager who is responsible for the event. Their role is to interface, liaise and ensure that the convention centre meets the client's requirements for the event.

The event manager works with the client to develop an operational plan, and assists in determining appropriate food and beverage requirements, room configurations and the amount of space required for the event. They arrange housekeeping, security and other technical services and assist in signposting the organiser to the various subcontractors that will be required (e.g. theming). They also provide and arrange the various client services that the event organiser may require. The event manager is therefore the case manager for the coordination of all activities for a particular event. Following a brief from the sales team, the event manager gathers the event team together, liaises with the client and takes total responsibility for the event within the centre, ensuring that all facets and aspects of the event are brought together. An event manager in a convention centre plays a similar role to that of a convention services manager in a hotel (we discuss this role in chapter 4). Event coordination is considered to be the most critical single relationship between the convention centre, the event manager and the execution of a successful event.

Excellent teamwork within the event management team is essential. As identified in many centres, the event manager is the key person for an individual event. They liaise, coordinate and manage all aspects of the event from the centre's perspective and are empowered to act on behalf of the centre. Despite not having direct control and functional responsibility for many of the centre's staff, for a specific event they have the authority to approach any member of staff to seek assistance to ensure a successful event.

The management of the client process, to ensure the smooth transfer between the sales manager and the event coordinator, is demonstrated in the following industry insight on Melbourne Exhibition and Convention Centre (MECC). In its organisation and management of the client process the MECC management uses many of the practices mentioned above. The client company only has to deal with three people from the initial booking through to the actual execution of the event. Clear boundaries have been established for 'handing over' the client from the sales manager to the dedicated event coordinator and then to the floor manager. This process should minimise any potential communication errors between the client and the centre. The centre has gained ISO quality accreditation for its client service and has demonstrated a commitment to providing quality service (see chapter 10).

INDUSTRY INSIGHT
Melbourne Exhibition and Convention Centre

Melbourne Exhibition and Convention Centre (MECC) believes in the concept of teamwork and limiting the number of people potential clients have to deal with when holding an event at the MECC. From the first telephone call until the booking has been confirmed, the client's only contact at the centre is a sales manager. However, once the booking is confirmed clients are referred to their own dedicated event coordinator, who works with them, takes care of all operational requirements and liaises with other members of the MECC team on their behalf. In the period leading up to their event clients are introduced to a floor manager, who is responsible for running their event on the day and ensuring that all the pre-planning is carried out efficiently and effectively. The venue prides itself on the fact that clients should not have to deal with more than three people at the centre from the initial enquiry through to the conclusion of their event. The MECC's commitment to client service has seen them awarded with ISO 9002 quality accreditation. The MECC became Australia's first convention and exhibition centre to achieve this award.

Source: *The Quorum (1998a, p. 28)*

Food and beverage operations

Convention organisers are very familiar with the need for a high quality of food and beverage service within a centre. In many centres, particularly in the United States, the supply of food and beverages is contracted out to external catering companies. However, within the Australasian region, there is a tendency for the service to be undertaken in-house, with centres priding themselves on the quality of both their food preparation and service. The quality of the cuisine often is a key feature, promoted by management, in the marketing of the centre. For example, the promotional brochure of one centre, which uses an external contractor with an excellent reputation for the quality of its cuisine, states that it has 'a reputation for fine cuisine which is the envy of other venues' (QEII 1996). Another centre has developed thermal heat cooking processes and promotes as a feature the fact that it can serve 1200 meals by silver service in seven minutes (Brisbane Convention and Exhibition Centre 1996).

Within Australia, many in-house convention and exhibition support services are managed on-site, such as housekeeping, laundry, and food preparation and service. This is often undertaken to ensure cost efficiency, minimise expenditure and maximise revenue. This is in contrast to centres in the United States, where there is a tendency to franchise and outsource the majority of these facilities.

Revenue generation

In the absence of traditional bed stock and accommodation to support their revenue-earning abilities, the management teams within these centres have developed numerous and sometimes innovative methods of realising revenue, for example renting out space for shopping centres, restaurants and bistros to encourage public use of the centre.

The traditional methods by which such centres earn revenue are:

- room charges for the hire of the auditorium, meeting and exhibition facilities (this might be on an hourly, half-day or daily rate)
- provision of food and beverages to convention and meeting delegates, such as morning tea, lunch, dinner and cocktails
- provision of restaurants and bars, bistros or coffee shops, which are open daily for use of both visitors to the centre and convention delegates
- provision of audiovisual and other technical equipment and support services
- provision of exhibition support services, such as power, telephone, modem, and so on
- commission on 'bought in' services, such as event theming and florists
- design and provision of signage services and posters
- provision of security services, cleaning, and so on
- charges from car parking
- provision of a business centre and ancillary support services for use by conference and exhibition organisers and delegates
- retail services such as a convention centre shop providing newspapers, business journals, gifts, souvenirs of the city and the centre, perfumes, and so on
- leasing out of other retail space for the provision of banking facilities, a medical centre and convention-specific services such as a convention and visitor information centre.

Some innovative methods of revenue generation include:

- selling space on pillars in the main entrance foyer for banner promotions
- providing workstations, small offices and boardroom facilities for visiting business people, which are charged on hourly, half-day, daily or weekly rates and support the activities of the traditional business centre
- providing escorted educational tours of the centre for public and community groups (some centres provide this service at no charge).

Accounting and administration

Accounting and administration make up a supportive component of the organisation chart and serve the same function as they do in other convention facilities. They provide support to staff who are involved in the frontline activities and deal directly with the external customer — the clients, their delegates and the public.

The following snapshot provides a career profile of Tina Croker, who has successfully developed a career in the management of convention and exhibition centres.

Tina Croker knew from the time that she completed Year 12 that she wanted to be involved in international hotels and to organise events. After completing a business course and with a passion 'to organise and get it happening', she joined The Wentworth Hotel in Sydney, working initially in food and beverage operations, then as banquet secretary, event coordination and finally as assistant banquet manager. A subsequent period overseas provided her with invaluable experience of not only the European scene but also personnel recruitment, where she organised people for jobs and matched jobs to people.

Returning to Australia and wishing to broaden her knowledge of management in the meeting industry, she joined a small Sydney-based PCO, which provided a wide range of experience in both the corporate and association markets and a snapshot of how meeting managers handle convention and meeting business. Then she moved to a production company, which provided an invaluable opportunity to work on the creative side of meeting management and learn the technical aspects of the business.

The Sydney Convention and Exhibition Centre had been opened just six months when Tina joined the team as international conventions coordinator with the brief to organise the highly complex multiday events. This proved to be a challenge in a venue where building work was still under way. Later, she became exhibitions manager at the centre. One of the first events she organised was an 'international headache conference' for 1200 delegates. The builders made plenty of noise during the event, with the result that the centre's CEO had to apologise for the noise caused and provide 'aspirin all round'.

One of the most exciting events that she coordinated was the International Congress of Gastroenterology. In 1990 this was the largest congress that Sydney had hosted, with over 3000 delegates, 15 000 square metres of exhibition space and a complex and extensive convention program. Working closely with the PCO, Tina saw the total event as challenging but fulfilling, including the writing and processing of the required 97 event orders. The congress was rated the most successful event hosted by the city at that time and put Sydney on the map for large international meetings.

While at the centre Tina was invited to join the project team contributing to the design for the Brisbane Convention and Exhibition Centre. 'It was extremely satisfying to see that the architects actually took on board a number of recommendations from the project team.' This included large foyers, pillar-free meeting rooms and outdoor space in order to make the most of Brisbane's climate. Tina joined the pre-opening team at the Brisbane

(continued)

Convention and Exhibition Centre as sales manager, responsible for national and international convention and exhibition sales. When the centre opened in 1995 she became more involved in international business development, representing the centre at international trade shows, as well as being responsible for a sales team that grew from two to 10 people. Developing systems and effective operational procedures, she found it very satisfying to work not only in a world-class venue but also with an enthusiastic team.

In late 1998, Tina was approached to be the general manager of the recently opened Australian Technology Park (ATP) Conference Centre in Sydney. The ATP has been internationally acclaimed as a model for technology parks, marrying the charm and ambience of nineteenth-century buildings with the latest in high-tech facilities for conferences, meetings, exhibitions and special events. The ATP includes 7000 metres of exhibition space, a theatre seating 520, and multiple breakout spaces to accommodate the same number. Tina sees the position as one that will provide her with the opportunity to 'work with a dedicated team to build up the business within a dynamic environment'.

Source: Tina Croker, Australian Technology Park Conference Centre

Having reviewed the concept of purpose-built convention and exhibition centres, their management, organisation and method of operation, we now focus on the management and organisation of MICE activities within hotels and other residential venues.

HOTELS AND RESIDENTIAL VENUES

Hotels, resorts and other residential venues are another group of major stakeholders and suppliers to the MICE industry. With the conference organiser and the client organisation they form a key component in the partnership to provide a satisfactory MICE event.

■ Background

The convention and meeting industry has had a considerable impact on the business mix of those hotels and venues that have developed dedicated facilities and services for the provision of conventions or meetings. Over the last 20 years, to facilitate these developing market segments, new departments and sections within departments have evolved, resulting in considerable changes to the traditional hotel organisation chart. Departments have been developed where the key focus is the specific interaction between the venue and the conference organiser and whose task it is to ensure the coordination of the activities of the hotel or venue regarding conventions and meetings.

So what facilities and services are provided by hotels and other such venues? At a cursory glance it would appear that conventions and meetings require only accommodation and meeting rooms. A further inspection reveals that it is not only accommodation that is required, but also food and beverage services, room hire and a host of other activities and revenue-earning items such as audiovisual equipment, theme equipment, business services, florists and printing. The conference venue of today is much more intricately involved in the planning and provision of conventions or meetings. Revenue generation from conventions, meetings and other functions has increased substantially for many of those hotels and venues that have focused and developed the infrastructure to support these markets. In a survey of CBD four- and five-star hotels in Sydney and Brisbane (McCabe & Weeks 1999), revenue generation from conventions, meeings and functions (excluding the accommodation component) ranged from 10 to 20 per cent to 31 to 40 per cent of total hotel revenue. However, if the accommodation component is included, it could be up to 25 per cent higher. With such a percentage of the venue's revenue focused on conventions, meetings and functions, the effects of dealing with such groups ripples through every department of the hotel and influences not only the revenue but also the management, organisation and operation of the venue. As a result, hotels and resorts have focused on ways to design and organise their staff and manage their properties towards the lucrative convention and meeting market, so that they are well prepared to compete for a significant proportion of convention and meeting business.

■ Key *players*

There are a number of key players involved in the provision of conventions and meetings within a venue. The hotel general manager as one would expect has the ultimate responsibility for the success of any convention or meeting running within the venue. Other departments involved include banquet operations, convention services, food and beverage, sales and marketing and the rooms division. In the larger convention hotels, the convention and meetings business is divided up and dealt with by specific professionals, while in smaller venues many of the tasks are collected under one job role such as the banquet and conference manager. However, at one time or another, to varying degrees and intensity, almost every department within a hotel or resort will become involved with the convention or meeting. But it is with the sales manager, the convention services manager and the banquet operations manager that the activity is focused most keenly in relation to the capabilities of the hotel and its provision of the requirements for the conference organiser.

The sales manager either initiates, contacts and sells the venue's convention or meeting facilities to the customer who is planning the event, or responds to the telephone call from the potential client. The role of the sales manager is to generate new and repeat business prospects on a regular basis. In some venues this task may be undertaken by one or more people, whose sole function is to focus their sales activity and techniques on the convention, meeting and function market. The employment of a dedicated person, who has a key focus on the convention and meeting market, is seen as a positive step. It is important that this person is knowledgeable about this type of business and the facilities that the venue can provide. They must be careful not to oversell aspects of the service that the venue will not be able to deliver.

The convention services manager effectively has the responsibility for carrying out the hotel's obligation once a convention or meeting has been booked and the contract signed. According to Montgomery and Rutherford (1994, p. 490), convention service managers coordinate and service the convention. Indeed, often they are referred to as the 'person who makes things happen' and it is said that 'service coordination can make or break a meeting'. Hoyle et al. (1989, pp. 156–7) note that convention services managers are responsible for representing the hotel to convention and corporate meeting officials and their guests. Their role begins once the booking has been made. They work closely with all departments and coordinate the activities of these departments to ensure the maximum service to conventions and other groups once they are in the venue. A study undertaken in the United States has indicated that typically a convention services manager has the authority and responsibility to determine the strategy and tactical details of a meeting or convention while it is in the hotel (Montgomery & Rutherford 1994, p. 490).

The banquet operations manager is responsible for ensuring the production and operation of the convention or meeting on the actual day of the event. They are responsible for ensuring that the requirements established by the convention services manager and the client are carried out by the venue to the satisfaction of the client and its delegates.

■ Organisational *structures*

Many hotels and resorts follow the traditional organisational structures and line hierarchy. In order to respond to the convention and meeting business, they tend to organise themselves along one of three standard structures. These are described below and illustrated in figure 3.8.

1. The convention services department reports to the food and beverage director. Either banquet operations reports directly to the food and beverage director through convention services or the convention services manager and the banquet operations manager report directly to the food and beverage director.
2. The convention services department reports to the sales and marketing department and liaises with the food and beverage director. In this situation, the banquet operations manager reports directly to the food and beverage director.
3. The convention services department reports directly to the hotel general manager and has the same level of authority as the food and beverage director and the sales and marketing director. In this situation, the banquet operations manager may report directly to the convention services department or alternatively to the food and beverage director.

1.

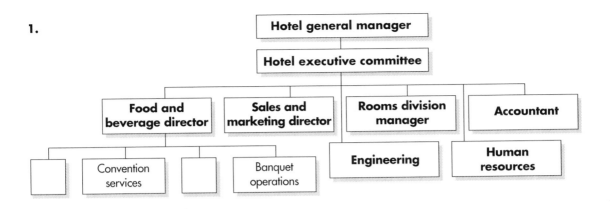

2.

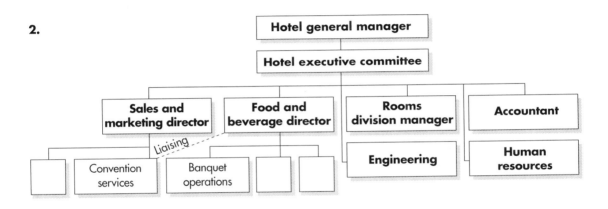

3.

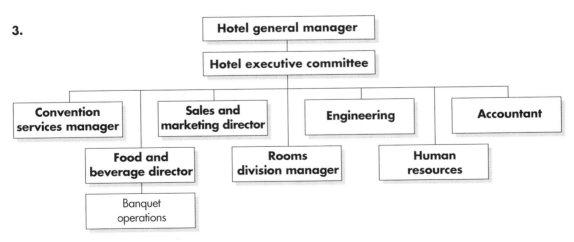

■ **Figure 3.8** *Three types of organisational structure for hotels with convention and meeting facilities*

The positioning of the convention services department within the hotel's organisational structure is often a point of contention. There appear to be three schools of thought (Montgomery & Strick 1995; Astroff & Abbey 1995):

- the person responsible for the convention services department should report directly to the general manager
- the convention services department should be a segment of the sales department
- the convention services department should be a segment of the food and beverage department.

The first case is believed by some to give too much freedom to the convention services manager. Irrespective of who the convention service manager reports to, it is important that they have 'line authority', in respect of servicing the convention needs, over food and beverages, accommodation, housekeeping, and so on. Only then can they ensure that the client's requirements can be satisfied.

In Australia, the majority of hotels still cling to the traditional positioning of convention services within the food and beverage department. However, in some instances, the convention services manager may report to both the food and beverage director and the sales and marketing director (McCabe & Weeks 1999). This could provide conflict in respect of unity of command and in the lines of authority. In other instances, the convention services manager reports directly to the hotel general manager. Although many convention services departments still hold to traditional lines of reporting, significant changes are being made by some hotels to better reflect the growing status of convention services departments and their financial input into the hotel's revenue base (McCabe & Weeks 1999).

Research undertaken by Montgomery and Rutherford (1994) and Nebel, Rutherford and Schaffer (1994) has indicated that the role and function of convention services and the convention services manager within hotels could change in view of the trends in business and academic thinking. If the organisational structure of convention services within hotels is re-engineered away from the traditional functional structure into becoming more 'process orientated', the convention services department could become more customer orientated. It could overcome some of the traditional weaknesses of the functional organisation, such as lack of communication, difficulty of cross-functional coordination and unclear responsibilities for overall performance.

The job of convention services manager is known by various titles, such as conference coordinator, banqueting and conference manager, and conference and catering manager. Regardless of title, the position can bring much prestige and responsibility. As mentioned earlier, the convention services manager is the one person who can make or break a convention or meeting. They are considered to be the single communication link between the hotel and the conference organiser and, on behalf of the hotel, handle the needs of the conference organiser for their event. Therefore, when considering the design of the organisational structure for the hotel or venue, it is important to ensure that the convention services manager has the authority to get the job done quickly and efficiently.

The convention services managers deal with:

(a) new business from sales and marketing — once the client contract has been signed the convention services manager handles the business up until the day of the function, when it is handed over to the banquet operations manager

(b) repeat business — this may be handled in two ways: either through the sales and marketing department or, as occurs more frequently, the client makes direct contact with the convention services manager.

■ The client *process*

Within hotels, conventions, meetings and functions tend to be broken down into two distinct segments: conferences, meetings and functions requiring a small number of accommodation rooms, such as 15 to 30; and those with a large accommodation requirement, such as over 30 rooms (McCabe & Weeks 1999). In the latter case, the group booking section of the reservations department deals with the residential aspects of the event, and all other activities associated with the event are managed by the convention services manager. For a repeat meeting or function with a small accommodation component, the entire booking and management of the event may be undertaken by the convention services department or by the sales department until the contract is signed, when it is handed over to the convention services department.

If the size of the convention and meeting business in the hotel warrants the position of convention services manager, then traditionally it has been beneficial to separate the sales and service components, with the sales department handing over the event once the booking is confirmed. However, it is very important that the convention services manager is involved in the initial sales discussions with the client, particularly if the event is large. This eases the situation and reduces the need for the client to be handed to three or four people. The convention services manager also needs to manage the liaison and coordination between in-house departments such as food and beverage, security and audiovisual for the client, thereby enabling a system of 'one-stop shopping' for the client.

So what is the process when a potential client contacts the hotel in order to book a conference, meeting or function? In many instances, the first point of contact is the switchboard operator, who then transfers the call to either the sales and marketing department or directly to the convention services department. There are three approaches to the client process:

(a) The sales manager sells, arranges and works with the client conference organiser from the initial contact until the completion of the event. The advantage of this is that if the sales person is involved in both the sales and service of the meeting, they will not be concerned with only obtaining the business and therefore selling something that cannot be provided.

(b) Once the booking has been made and confirmed, the sales person steps aside and hands the client and the business to the convention services manager, who finalises the details and coordinates the meeting through to its end. In this situation, the convention services manager follows through the meeting until the actual day of operation, when they hand over the function to the banquet operations team. The convention services manager may then check the progress of the event during the day and make contact with the client at the end of the event, to ensure that they are satisfied and discuss any future requirements.

(c) The sales person follows through the event from initial enquiry until the actual day of the function, when they hand over the client and the event to the banqueting operations team. They may then check on progress with the client during the day and at the end of the event to establish that the client is satisfied and to negotiate any new business needs.

In many hotels and venues, the focus of the convention and meeting business tends to be on smaller meetings and conferences, often resulting in group accommodation bookings of between 15 and 30 rooms per day. In these instances, the business organisation of the event may be quite simple — for example, room hire, morning and afternoon tea, business lunch, use of some audiovisual equipment, and so on — and there is a trend to 'one-stop shopping', whereby the convention services manager is responsible for both the sales and servicing. This simplifies the process for the client conference organiser and often increases customer loyalty by building up the relationship between the convention services manager and the client conference organiser. It can allow more creative and innovative ideas and result in increased revenue for the venue, as well as a more effective event for the organiser.

If the booking is a large convention with a number of accommodation rooms, then the sales and group booking area of the hotel is often involved in the negotiation and release of the rooms. They work either in conjunction with the convention services manager or directly with the client.

Transition points

When should a potential conference be handed to the convention services department? This varies greatly and there are no hard and fast rules. What is important to the customer is that the transition between the sales person and the introduction to the convention services manager is handled as smoothly as possible. The potential opportunities for customer transition are detailed below and are summarised in figure 3.9.

- *During the site inspection and the initial client negotiation* Though the sales person may be the point of client contact up until the contract is signed, they may involve the convention services manager in meeting the potential client during the site inspection or during the initial negotiations. This is important for the client conference organiser and provides reassurance of the capabilities of both the hotel and the person who will be handling the organisation of their conference or meeting.

- *Before the contract is signed* This is particularly the case with large conventions or meetings. The organiser may wish to meet the convention services manager to ensure that the promises made by the sales person can be met by the venue. This provides an excellent opportunity for the client conference organiser to explain to the convention services manager about their particular event and its requirements, and also enables the convention services manager to reassure the organiser about the in-house management of their event.
- *After the contract is signed* The sales person arranges a meeting between the convention services manager and the client conference organiser, and the convention services department begins to work on the operational aspects of the event. This enables some of the major details to be resolved early, which is particularly important in the case of large events.

■ **Figure 3.9**
Customer transition points

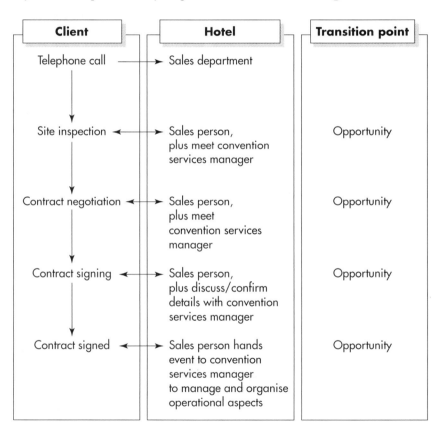

In all instances, the sales person needs to be sensitive to the needs of the client conference organiser and provide reassurance, particularly if the client is new or is inexperienced in conference organisation. This is often the case when dealing with association business, where the organisation of the event may be in the hands of a number of volunteers. The time frame of the event also influences when the convention service team commences work on the event. For example, detailed work on a large convention may commence one to two years prior to the event. Currently, with the trend to shorter lead times in the booking of conventions and meetings, work might begin almost immediately. It depends on the size and complexity of the booking. If the sales department takes the initial booking then it is useful for them to keep in contact with the organiser and the event. The handover of the event between departments and personnel needs to take into consideration client trust. Only if the various transition points are managed satisfactorily and the client is totally satisfied will the venue gain the repeat business.

PROFESSIONAL CONFERENCE ORGANISERS

A professional conference organiser (PCO) is an independent person or organisation specialising in planning and organising conventions and meetings. As stated in chapter 2, PCOs organise conventions and meetings for a living. PCOs are also known as meeting managers, planners or coordinators, conference managers, event managers and special projects managers. Many organisations offer some of the aspects of convention and meeting management as part of their service (e.g. public relations companies and some venues), while others have their own in-house meeting or event departments managed by a corporate or association meeting planner. Globally, however, there are a growing number of individuals and companies whose core business is to specialise in all aspects of convention and meeting management. The entrepreneurial PCOs not only manage conventions and meetings for their clients but also have set up their own company with all its inherent management, business and organisational challenges. An association or corporation that does not have the facility of an in-house conference organiser may choose to contract their event to a PCO.

The position and profession of PCOs have emerged and developed over the last 15 to 20 years. In line with the growth and development of the industry, their role has become more sophisticated and they have developed their levels of expertise and professionalism. The services provided by PCOs have become more complex and extensive. They have to be true managers and participate in planning, organisation, leadership, coordination and communication and, more importantly, control the details attendant to the management and marketing of a convention or meeting. Their job involves managing all the details, activities and interactions of a convention or meeting, from the time of its conception through to the actual event, and concluding with the evaluation. If a convention or meeting is held without the PCO paying full attention to these management activities, then the event may be unsuccessful both in relation to the quality of provision and delegate and client satisfaction, as well as in terms of its financial return.

To be successful, PCOs should not only develop and maintain a reputation for excellence in the service that they provide but also demonstrate creativity, dependability, honesty, integrity and show complete ethical behaviour. As PCOs work for a number of clients at any one time, they must demonstrate utter discretion and confidentiality in all client matters.

The major aspects of an event that PCOs will be involved in are:
- conceiving the idea for the event
- undertaking regular scheduled meetings with the client
- selecting the site
- negotiating with the venue and other suppliers
- planning the program
- managing and monitoring the finances and budget for the convention or meeting
- promoting the event and delegate attendance
- managing and executing the convention or meeting on-site
- finalising the bills, evaluating the event and holding the post-event meeting with the client
- preparing final report and event evaluation.

In addition, in some cases they also may raise sponsorship funds.

The role of PCOs is to form the 'executive arm' of the convention committee or client organisation (MIAA 1997, p. 3). They are responsible for converting client decisions into actions, ensuring that the convention project is kept both on schedule and on budget, reporting to the convention committee or organisation executive, coordinating the suppliers to the convention and offering consultative experience. The convention committee or the client organisation, to be most effective, should therefore act as the policy maker for the event, set objectives and goals, act on the recommendations of the PCO and monitor the progress of the event. It is important that the role of the PCO be clearly established with the convention committee or client organisation to ensure that communication is effective and the roles and responsibilities clearly defined.

The client brief prepared for the PCO by the client organisation will depend on the level and extent of services required. However, it should include information on the following:
- background of the host organisation/s
- name of the event
- objectives of the event
- proposed dates
- preferred location
- theme
- accommodation requirements (venue and category required)
- anticipated attendance numbers and place of origin of delegates
- status of event (international, national, regional state, other)
- type of event (congress, symposium, conference, meeting, corporate, association, government, exhibition, other)
- frequency of event (inaugural, annual, biennial, one-off event, other)
- program format (number of days, plenary sessions, concurrent sessions, poster sessions, roundtable discussion groups, workshops, associated tours, pre- and post-tours, pre- and post-workshops)

- speakers (total number of speakers, number of invited speakers, where they come from, speaker entitlements, other speakers, call for papers, interpretation required)
- social program (number of social events, type of events)
- accompanying persons program (expected number of accompanying persons)
- funding (government, corporate, industry, sponsorship, exhibition, registration fees, details of underwriters)
- finance (budget and procedures)
- marketing and promotional needs
- any other special requirements unique to the event
- history of the event (if held before) — previous locations, breakdown of attendees, registration fees, sponsorship raised, number of exhibitors
- list of services required from the PCO.

It is recognised that some of the above information may not be known or to hand at the time of seeking a PCO, or relevant to a specific event (MIAA 1997, p. 7).

Chapter 4 looks at some of the skills required of PCOs.

The sequence and focus of the tasks undertaken by PCOs are demonstrated in figure 3.10. The main activities are sited on the perimeter of the circle. The personnel featured in the centre of the circle represent the various suppliers to the convention and meeting industry that PCOs may have to liaise, interact and work with in their role as intermediary between the client organisation and the provider of the event. The frequency of these interactions can be intensive, occasional or irregular and will depend on each event.

The communication and coordination of the services or products that other suppliers provide is therefore a key focus for PCOs. To ensure a successful event PCOs, through their network, need to be well aware of the quality and reliability of each of their suppliers. PCOs have ultimate responsibility for the professionalism and quality of the event. However, other suppliers servicing the event can impact dramatically on its success or failure and as such can influence the reputation of PCOs. This is discussed further in chapter 9.

How do PCOs charge for their services? As previously identified, PCOs charge for the management services they provide to an organisation. These charges take a number of forms:

- a flat management fee, which might include the conference registration service
- a management fee plus a per capita registration and secretarial fee
- an all-inclusive fee
- a percentage of the total conference budget
- a profit-sharing arrangement between the PCO and the organisation holding the convention — this enables the PCO greater opportunity to increase their overall revenue for the convention and for the client organisation it can result in a reduced 'up-front fee' or a more lenient payment schedule (MIAA 1997).

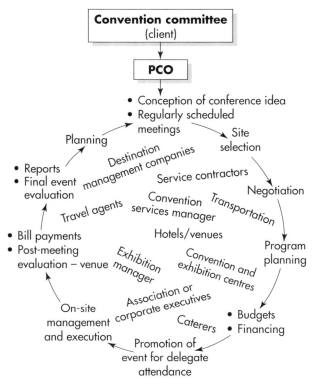

Source: Adapted from Rutherford (1990, p. 108)

A separate fee normally will be charged for the organisation of an exhibition that may be held in conjunction with a convention, or for identification and negotiation with potential sponsors for the event.

SUMMARY

Purpose-built convention and exhibition centres, hotels and other residential venues are key stakeholders and suppliers to the MICE industry. They work in partnership with conference organisers and their client organisation to ensure that the MICE event is provided to the ultimate satisfaction of the delegates.

Australia has actively pursued the building of purpose-built convention and exhibition centres over the last decade, realising their economic potential and associated impact on the development of the fledgling MICE industry. The design and construction of these centres enhances the provision of appropriate and flexible convention, meeting and exhibition space that is equipped with the latest technology and is designed to accommodate large events. The centres have particular features in respect of site location, design and the facilities provided, and some are incorporating the latest developments in environmental design. There are specific managerial and operational challenges for management teams to enable them to operate these centres efficiently and effectively.

Within hotels and residential venues, the convention services manager, the sales and marketing department and banquet operations undertake the management of conventions and meetings. As elsewhere in the industry, client management and satisfaction is key. This has led to the use and development of a variety of organisational structures, all focused on ensuring the provision of a convention or meeting that will satisfy both the client organisation and its delegates. In particular, the communication of information between the venue's various departments is key to the ultimate success of the event. Client management in relation to their transfer between the venue's departments is critical. Mismanagement of this client transfer, together with a lack of communication between the various personnel in the venue, could result in ultimate client dissatisfaction and loss of repeat business.

The profession of PCO has developed over the last 15 to 20 years. As the MICE industry has grown, PCOs have become more sophisticated and have developed their levels of expertise and professionalism. PCOs are involved in a comprehensive and extensive range of activities in their management and organisation of an event. They are the 'executive arm' of the conference committee and client organisation (MIAA 1997, p. 3).

Activities

3.1 From a brochure, Internet site or physical site inspection, undertake an analysis of the facilities and services provided by two purpose-built convention and exhibition centres. Compare and contrast the data gained from each centre against the information provided in the text.

3.2 A pharmaceutical company based in Melbourne wishes to organise a three-day annual conference for approximately 200 of its employees. The residential conference, which is to be held in eastern Australia in late spring, will be attended by representatives from the company's offices in the Asia–Pacific region. On behalf of the company, prepare an initial brief for a PCO to manage and organise the conference. Identify and discuss the aspects of the brief that will require further clarification.

3.3 Using the information provided in the question above, establish two groups and role play the actual negotiation and discussion that might occur in the initial briefing of the PCO by the client organisation. Group A is the organising group from the pharmaceutical company and Group B is the PCO given the outline brief for the conference. At the completion of the role play, discuss the issues raised.

Discussion questions

3.1 Identify and discuss the factors that should be taken into consideration when selecting a site and location for the construction of a purpose-built convention and exhibition facility. Prepare a check list of the issues to be considered.

3.2 Discuss the positive and negative economic impacts that the construction of a purpose-built convention and exhibition centre might have on a city or region.

3.3 Critically evaluate the factors that should be considered when designing the organisational structure of a purpose-built convention and exhibition centre.

3.4 Discuss the role and function of PCOs. How does their role differ from the role of convention services manager in a venue?

3.5 Discuss the advantages and disadvantages of the convention services manager reporting to:
(a) the director of sales and marketing
(b) the director of food and beverage
(c) the hotel general manager.

What are some of the points to consider, in terms of organisational efficiency and customer satisfaction, if the banquet operations manager were to report to the director of food and beverage and the convention services manager to the director of sales?

3.6 What does the term 'transition points' mean?

3.7 From the perspective of a venue, identify and explore the issues relating to client management in the booking and organising of a convention or meeting.

REFERENCES

AACB. 1997, 'Conventions Australia', *The Quorum*, January/February, p. 77.

Adelaide Convention and Exhibition Centre. 1998 (*http://www.sacentral.sa.gov.au/agencies/acceh/acceh.htm*).

Astroff, M. A. & Abbey, J. R. 1995, *Convention Sales and Services*, 4th ed, Waterbury Press, N.J.

Australian Exhibitor. 1995, 'Exhibition Design, Marketing and Management', May/June.

BCEC. 1996, facilities brochure (*http://www.brisconex.com.au*).

Convention & Incentive Marketing. 1996, 'Dedicated Centres on the Front Line', February, pp. 14–15.

Convention & Incentive Marketing. 1998, 'BCEC Keeps on Keeping On', September.

Fenich, G. G. 1992, 'Convention Centre Development: Pros, Cons and Unanswered Questions', *International Journal of Hospitality Management,* vol. 11, no. 3, pp. 183–96.

Fenich, G. G. 1995, 'Convention Centre Operations: Some Questions Answered', *International Journal of Hospitality Management,* vol. 14, no. 3, pp. 311–24.

Hoyle, L. H., Dorf, D. C. & Jones T. J. A. 1987, *Managing Convention and Group Business,* The Educational Institute of the American Hotel & Motel Association, East Lansing.

McCabe, V. S. 1997, Purpose Built Convention and Exhibition Centres — Management and Operation, unpublished research paper.

McCabe, V. S. & Weeks, P. 1999, 'Convention Services Management in Sydney Four- to Five-Star Hotels', *Journal of Convention and Exhibition Management,* vol. 1, no. 4, pp. 67–84.

MIAA. 1997, *Professional Management of Meetings, Conventions and Events,* MIAA, Sydney.

Montgomery, R. J. .& Rutherford, D. G. 1994, 'A Profile of Convention Services Professionals', *Cornell Hotel and Restaurant Quarterly,* December, pp. 47–57.

Montgomery, R. J. & Strick, S. 1995, *Meetings, Conventions and Expositions: An Introduction to the Industry,* Van Nostrand Reinhold, New York.

Nebel, E. C., Rutherford, D. G. & Schaffer, J. D. 1994, 'Re-Engineering The Hotel Organisation', *Cornell Hotel and Restaurant Administration Quarterly,* October, pp. 89–95.

Perth Convention Centre. 1999 (*http://perthcc.com.au*).

Queen Elizabeth II (QEII) Conference Centre. 1996, conference and facilities brochure, London.

The Quorum. 1997, 'Once More with Feeling', May/June.

The Quorum. 1998a, 'Joining Two Great Venues Under One Roof', March/April.

The Quorum. 1998b, 'Simply Irresistible', March/April.

The Quorum. 1998c, 'Convention Centre Survey', May/June.

The Quorum. 1998d, 'Single Minded', October.

Rutherford, D. G. 1990, *Introduction To The Conventions, Expositions and Meetings Industry,* Van Nostrand Reinhold, New York.

SCEC. 1998, facilities brochure.

SCVB. 1998, *Sydney Facilities Guide,* SCVB, Sydney.

Singapore International Convention and Exhibition Centre. 1996, facilities brochure.

Stanfield, L. 1998, 'MICE is Booming', paper presented at the 1998 PATA Tourism Executive Development Programme, Ballina, June.

FURTHER READING ....

Asian Business Review. 1995, 'Australia's Newest Convention Centre', April, p. 96.

Brisbane Convention and Exhibition Centre

Brisbane Convention and Exhibition Centre (BCEC) opened its doors in May 1995 and within the first three days had hosted 17 events and dealt with a total of 70 000 people, including the PC95 exhibition with 24 085 delegates. Since that time, business at the centre has gone from strength to strength as its reputation as an excellent venue has developed worldwide.

The centre is recognised as one of the largest and most advanced facilities of its kind in the Southern Hemisphere. In the period since it opened until late 1998, the BCEC had hosted over 2000 events. It has bookings until 2006, when it will be the host venue for the seven-day Rotary International Convention. This convention is expected to attract 25 000 delegates from 28 000 Rotary Clubs worldwide and inject $60 million into the Queensland economy. Brisbane and the Gold Coast will provide an estimated 175 000 accommodation nights. With approximately two-thirds of the delegates coming to Brisbane from overseas, this convention is seen as an opportunity to 'show the world how great we are'.

So what makes the BCEC successful? One factor is the range, scope and flexibility of its facilities that include a great hall that seats 4000, or 9000 if the adjoining exhibition hall is utilised; four exhibition halls that each provide 5000 square metres of column-free space; a grand ballroom of 2200 square metres that can host a banquet for 1550 guests; and 17 breakout rooms that range in size from 27 square metres to 1000 square metres. In addition, each exhibition hall has its own organiser's office and fully-furnished area for private entertaining, plus direct lift access from the off-street loading bays and individual storage areas. Furthermore, within the centre there is a fully-equipped business centre, information desk, restaurant, bar and coffee shop. Car parking is available for 1600 cars.

The centre is supported by a fully-integrated in-house audiovisual production facility and incorporates the latest technological support and infrastructure. It has been identified as the most modern facility in Australia and is at the technological cutting edge in the provision of communication facilities. Flexibility and technological excellence have also been considered in the provision of food and beverage services, with food from the finest French cuisine to the traditional Australian barbeque being available. Full convention support services are available to potential conference organisers through an in-house event coordination team.

An initiative of the Queensland government, the centre is set amid gardens and waterways in the city's South Bank parklands, the cultural precinct of the city. There is good access to the CBD and an effective transportation and road system is in place (e.g. rail, ferry, bus, taxi, and so on). The city's international and domestic airports are within 20 minutes drive of the centre.

The BCEC has developed a reputation not only for flexibility and technical infrastructure but also for the quality of its staff and the service that they provide. They have been acknowledged by conference organisers as completely adaptable and enthusiastic, rising to meet the challenges set.

Brisbane views the BCEC as one of its major drawcards, along with the fact that the city is seen as a safe, relaxed, friendly and pleasant place. The physical and technical facilities at the BCEC are believed by the city to be unmatched in Australia and are seen as playing an important role in the city's increasing success at attracting convention business. The centre works in cooperation with Brisbane Tourism, the city's visitors and convention bureau.

In the period since it opened, the BCEC has established itself as a market leader in the convention and exhibition business worldwide and has developed a reputation as a leading venue for the medical, scientific and information technology sectors. In 1998 it hosted the World Wide Web (WWW) conference and in 2001 will host the International Congress on Toxicology. This has benefited Brisbane, Queensland and Australia and has been instrumental in the success of Brisbane in the convention field, with the quadrupling of the city's convention wins in the period 1995–98. Prior to the opening of the BCEC, the city had $26.8 million worth of confirmed convention and exhibition business. In mid-1998 this figure was $104 million. The BCEC's economic impact on the city is estimated to be more than $100 million per year.

By 1997 the BCEC was operationally financially 'in the black' for the second year running and had exceeded targets since opening. The centre has established representation in the United Kingdom, Europe and North America, along with an office in Melbourne. Its innovative marketing and commitment to building and maintaining customer loyalty was demonstrated by its third birthday celebration in 1998, attended by 800 clients, business people and media personalities. This event enabled those participating to celebrate the success of the BCEC with the centre's senior management team and network, and for the BCEC to showcase not only its full capabilities but also those of Brisbane.

The continued substantial growth of business at the BCEC has led to its management submitting plans to the South Bank Corporation (owners of the centre) to expand the facility and provide additional space for a multipurpose exhibition and conference complex with a capacity for a further 7000 people. If approved, this expansion will begin before the end of the year 2000.

The centre's slogan of 'All it takes to make it happen' could well be considered appropriate.

Source: BCEC (1996); Convention & Incentive Marketing (1998); The Quorum (1997, 1998b, 1998c, 1998d); Australian Exhibitor (1995)

Questions

1 Critically review the economic and social impact of the BCEC on Brisbane.

2 Identify and discuss the factors that have led to the success of the BCEC.

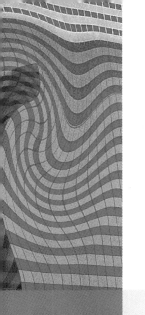

CHAPTER 4

Managing human
resources for conventions

LEARNING OBJECTIVES

After studying this chapter, you will be able to:

■ describe how effective human resource management can provide
competitive advantages and contribute to the development and
sustainability of the MICE organisation

■ evaluate the importance and relevance of human resource
management practices for the MICE industry

■ outline the role of human resource planning for the MICE
organisation

■ review the process of recruitment, selection and induction for the
MICE organisation

■ understand the relevance of training and development for the
MICE industry

■ implement a process for leading, organising and motivating the
convention and meeting team.

INTRODUCTION

The globalisation of business markets, increased competition, and customers who demand more value for the goods and services they purchase are factors that are well accepted as we enter the new millennium (Go et al. 1996, p. 2). In the worldwide turmoil of business and financial markets, tourism and hospitality organisations are being forced to focus their attention on the needs of the customer. New ways are being found to 'delight the customer', in order to become more responsive to their needs, provide added value, achieve customer satisfaction and gain competitive advantage. The quality of an organisation's service relies on its employees and, in particular, those in the 'front-line'. They play a major part in influencing the customer's perception of service quality and their overall satisfaction. This trend to ensure the provision and delivery of improved customer service is of particular relevance to the MICE industry.

The MICE industry is recognised as being at the 'blue-chip' end of the tourism market. It is seen as an attractive employment area for those entering the workforce for the first time and for those who may be seeking a career change. Potential entrants to the industry view it as dynamic and one that provides many career opportunities and the prospect for rapid career advancement. However, the MICE sector is not immune to the shortages in labour supply and high staff turnover found within the tourism and hospitality industry. If there are not enough employees of the right quality available at the right time, then a fall in standards and levels of customer dissatisfaction may occur. The management of people is therefore a key challenge and resource issue for the industry as it enters the twenty-first century. This has been indicated by the National Strategy for the MICE industry, which highlighted the need for training and development of staff, the continual striving for increased professionalism and the need to continue to build on quality of service (Commonwealth Department of Tourism 1995, p. 37). Fundamental to the provision of a high quality of service and to the building of competitive advantage is the need to ensure that the human resource aspects of the organisation are well managed and that employees' talents are both recognised and fully utilised (Go et al. 1996). If the MICE industry is to meet this challenge, it will need to ensure that sound leadership and management skills are in place.

To be competitive and harness employee skills, a manager needs to be focused on people and have a 'people perspective'. It is important that human resource issues are considered, for example, when deciding on the strategy and objectives of a business. The principle here is that if the employees are looked after, then they will subsequently look after the customer. A satisfied employee will equal a satisfied customer, who in turn will equal repeat business. People management skills are therefore very important for the conference organiser.

This chapter examines and discusses the management of a business' key resource — its people. It begins by identifying current issues facing the industry and discusses some of the employment opportunities available within the MICE industry. A systematic approach to the management of human resources is outlined, followed by an evaluation of the management roles, skills and competencies that are required in order to lead and motivate the team. Managers within the MICE industry need to have skills that meet the human resource challenges of the future, while ensuring the occurrence of individual and team development, in order to provide a quality service and achieve ultimate customer satisfaction.

KEY HUMAN RESOURCE ISSUES

There are a number of key issues that the industry faces in respect of management and the provision and development of staff.

1. If the industry is to continue to build competitive advantage, then there is a need to ensure that a human resource plan, together with an effective recruitment and selection process, is in place within MICE organisations. Many areas within the industry find it difficult to recruit sufficient people to satisfy their requirements. The industry also needs to retain its staff. The hospitality industry traditionally has had a reputation of high staff turnover, particularly in the operational departments of food and beverages and housekeeping. Shortages of staff in these areas can affect the operation of conventions and meetings within hotels and venues.

2. Apart from basic skills training, it is apparent that there is a lack of supervisory and management training and development within the industry. Management and supervisory skills are generally weak and as a result can compound the basic human resource difficulties of high labour turnover and an inability to recruit the right calibre staff.

3. The professional management of human resources is often not in place. There is a lack of people care, which can result in employee dissatisfaction and subsequent organisational problems. The tourism and hospitality industry and MICE organisations are working in a highly competitive global marketplace. Jobs such as front-line and management positions, which have a key impact on customer service and satisfaction, are being redesigned to reflect this development. Historically, front-line personnel have been undervalued within the industry and were seen as replaceable, entry-level employees (Go et al. 1996, p. 2). Yet these are the very people who deal directly with customers, and have the highest influence on customers' perception of service quality and therefore customer satisfaction. It is an important fact that everyone working within the convention and meeting industry is someone else's customer. They may be dealing directly with the final customer or they may be part of the service chain, providing backup support to front-line staff.

4. Traditionally, the management of human resources in the industry has been weak. It needs to be recognised that all managers have a responsibility for their teams (i.e. human resources) and that human resource management is everyone's business — managers, supervisors, peers and each individual within the organisation.

The structure of the MICE industry (see chapter 2) ranges from small organisations that employ a handful of staff, to large venues with a substantial number of employees. Human resource issues and management needs are therefore extensive. In the small, owner-operated businesses, such as professional conference organisers (PCOs), each member of the team is expected to undertake a wide range of tasks and therefore can gain experience in a number of roles. However, there is limited opportunity for career progression. Only a few people within the team, for example, the owner/manager, are involved in senior management decisions and full client liaison. This contrasts with large venues, such as purpose-built convention and exhibition centres or convention hotels, where a full organisational structure, established roles and responsibilities, and career progression and development are in place. Despite the differences in size and complexity, the human resource issues in both types of organisation are key to the ultimate success of the business.

The MICE industry provides many job opportunities, a number of which have developed in the last 25 or so years. The linchpin of a convention is the conference organiser or manager. There are many different titles for this job, but basically this is the person who organises the convention or meeting and is either from the sponsoring or client organisation, or based within the venue that supplies the facilities. It has been only in the last 25 years that the job of conference organiser has become formalised and recognised. Prior to this time, the planning and organisation of a meeting within the corporate world might have been undertaken by the managing director's secretary for events such as board meetings, or the sales manager's secretary for events such as the annual sales conference. For an association, a committee member (possibly from the region holding the event) would be given the job. In nearly all these cases, the people who undertook the task did not have the relevant or necessary skills and hence the standard of meeting could be haphazard. Likewise, conference organisation and management within a venue was often undertaken by the duty manager or the food and beverage manager, again with the same lack of skill and experience of this specific area of business. Now a new profession, that of conference organiser, has emerged and with it a whole plethora of new job roles and opportunities.

The job opportunities that are available within the convention and meeting industry can be broken down into a number of groups.

■ Conference *organisers*

Conference organisers or meeting managers undertake a range of different roles and responsibilities, often dependent on the type of organisation within which they are employed.

Associations

In chapter 2, an association conference organiser was identified as often being a full-time employee of the association. In the absence of such a person, the role is undertaken by the executive director or another employee. An association conference organiser is responsible for organising membership meetings and annual conventions, distributing meeting notices, organising meeting reservations and registration, and venue liaison, including issues such as accommodation and meeting rooms, food and beverage and speaker requirements, and welcoming members, guests and speakers.

Corporations

A corporate conference organiser is an employee of a particular corporation, and is employed specifically with the responsibility to plan and execute the details of conventions or events for the individual organisation, its management, employees and owners. A corporate conference organiser coordinates and manages MICE events for a single company with a set range of products or services.

Professional conference organisers

A PCO or independent conference organiser specialises in all aspects of conference management as the central core of their business (MIAA 1998a). The role of the PCO was discussed in detail in chapter 3. In a study of PCOs in Southern Queensland, Hill (1996) established that PCO job titles range from event coordinator and event manager, to account manager and conference supervisor.

Venue convention services manager

Career opportunities within the convention sector of a venue are found in the areas of convention services, convention sales and banquet operations. Job titles and career progression might range from convention secretary and convention or conference coordinator, to the supervisory and management role of convention services manager. Alternatively, within the area of banquet operations, opportunities exist for kitchen staff who may specialise in the large-scale production techniques of the banquet kitchen, banquet waiting and bar staff, audiovisual technicians, and banquet captains or supervisors who can progress to the role of banquet operations manager.

■ Convention *sales*

Positions within the area of convention sales can be found in both venues and PCO organisations. A convention sales manager or a convention sales executive might have specific responsibility for a geographic region or for a particular client base.

■ Other *opportunities*

Other career opportunities exist within conventions and visitors bureaus (CVBs) and state and national tourism offices, where a wide range of positions are found, ranging from conference organisers to conference sales or account executives. Some corporate organisations have specialised in the development and marketing of specific conventions, conferences or meetings to various sectors of business and the community, for example motivational meetings and economic modelling seminars. Career opportunities for conference organisers exist in this sector.

■ Roles *and responsibilities*

So how does the job and role of a conference organiser or manager in a venue differ from that of a conference organiser in a corporate organisation, association or PCO?

A convention services manager within a venue deals with a wide variety of MICE events, all with different specifications (e.g. product launches, sales conferences, training meetings and exhibitions). They also liaise with a large number of organisations, all with different requirements. As we saw in chapter 3, the convention services manager coordinates the different departments within the venue to ensure that the meeting is delivered as required in respect of food and beverages, audiovisual requirements and accommodation. This is achieved by teamwork, as the convention services department in many instances has no direct responsibility for any of these areas. The convention services manager works within the budgetary guidelines of the venue and, as already discussed, is responsible for ensuring that the client organisation and its delegates are satisfied with the event.

Within a commercial company, the events planned by a conference organiser or meeting manager may be similar each year (e.g. the annual sales conference, training courses, etc.). There is therefore a need for creativity in order to maintain delegate interest. A corporate conference organiser will be familiar with the products and services offered by the company, its culture and organisation, working environment and various personalities involved. Though the client for each activity may be different (e.g. sales manager, training manager), a fundamental point is that they all work for the same company in the achievement of its goals and philosophy. The corporate conference organiser should build up rapport with the various suppliers that they may use from the MICE industry.

The services provided by a PCO are used by both corporations and associations, which may prefer to employ an independent conference organiser for reasons of cost or efficiency. The main difference between a PCO and a convention services manager is that a PCO has to deal with both sides of the equation — the client company and the venue and other suppliers. A PCO has certain responsibilities to coordinate, communicate, control and evaluate for a conference. There are a number of challenges to PCO management:

- controlling deadlines, with so many people involved
- coordinating the many people involved
- pioneering — each event is different in terms of its design and management; few conventions or meetings are replicated in their entirety
- adequately controlling the huge amounts of information, dates, budgets, and so on.

A PCO needs to be sales and marketing orientated, for they have to sell the services of their business to a potential company. In addition, to maintain client interest, they need to demonstrate a portfolio of creative and innovative ideas and keep abreast of current trends.

Other ways that the roles and responsibilities of a convention services manager differ from a PCO or a conference organiser in an association or corporation include:

(a) *Diversity* The range of tasks that a convention services manager in a venue deals with is more diverse than that of a corporate conference organiser. A corporate conference organiser may only be concerned with similar types of meetings each year. However, this means that they have to consistently create and maintain interest.

(b) *Responsibility* A venue convention services manager must liaise with the different departments within the venue, such as food and beverages, rooms and front office, to make sure that the necessary arrangements are carried out. However, they have no direct control over or responsibility for these departments. A corporate conference organiser has some degree of autonomy over how the meeting will run, but still has to liaise with other corporate personnel.

(c) *Constraints* A venue convention services manager will be under certain operational constraints — for example, the size and physical capabilities of the convention and meeting facilities and the venue's staff resources and experience, as well as the budgetary constraints imposed by senior management in order to achieve minimum acceptable profit levels (this encompasses items such as room rates and food and beverage charges). A corporate conference organiser will have an overall financial budget for each conference or meeting — for example, $50 000. Therefore, both the venue convention services manager and the corporate conference organiser need to negotiate in respect of the charges for a conference — one wants to make money and the other wants to save money.

(d) *Relationships* A venue convention services manager forges relationships and builds rapport with their clients (corporate conference organisers and PCOs). They must ensure that they are satisfied with the services provided by the venue. Many of the relationships that a corporate conference organiser will develop will be with clients from internal departments within the organisation. It is beneficial to both parties that they work for the same organisation, have the same culture and philosophy and are familiar with the product or service that is offered by the company.

Having explored the range and scope of jobs available for conference organisers, we now review human resource practices.

*E*FFECTIVE HUMAN RESOURCE MANAGEMENT PRACTICES

To ensure an effective and efficient human resource management operation, an organisation must introduce a consistent and systematic process which will assist it to identify and analyse its needs and make decisions on an informed basis. The influence and impact of human resources should link into, and be part of, the business planning and goals and objectives of the organisation. Only if an organisation's business direction is known can a realistic and effective human resource plan be put into place.

As previously discussed, the MICE industry is made up of a wide variety of organisations. There is a predominance of small, owner-operated businesses, for example PCOs, many of which maintain a core team of approximately three to five people. Their human resource requirements and development are substantially different to those larger organisations, for example venues and purpose-built convention and exhibition centres, where a team of 100 full-time staff, plus a large number of casual and part-time employees, is not unusual. However, despite the differences of scale, it is equally important and relevant that all organisations follow a systematic but consistent process for their human resource operations. Simple policies and procedures should be developed. Equally relevant to MICE companies as in other industries is the generic human resource process which encompasses the following activities:

- human resource planning
- job analysis
- recruitment and selection
- staff orientation
- training and development
- performance appraisal
- discipline and termination processes
- remuneration and compensation
- industrial relations issues.

■ Human resource *planning*

Why is human resource planning important in the MICE industry? As with other industries, the key purpose of human resource planning for MICE organisations is to ensure the effective management of human resources in the long and short term. It is undertaken in order to make sure that the required quantity and quality of employees is available when and where necessary. It is the method by which an organisation translates its overall objectives into the practicalities of clarifying the number of people required to meet these objectives.

Human resource planning is important at a national, strategic and operational level within the MICE industry. For the governing bodies of the MICE industry, there is a need to set up and establish programs, initiatives and systems that encourage entry to the industry. At an operational level, the people employed by the many businesses associated with the MICE industry are seen as being critical to the success of each business. It is essential, therefore, to ensure that there are sufficient, suitably qualified people, not only in managerial positions but also within key front-line positions where staff are in constant contact with the end customer.

Cyclical and seasonal patterns of business are also a feature of the MICE industry. The human resource plan should ensure that sufficient people are available to cover these peaks and troughs. For example, some convention and meeting organisations employ a core of key people on a full-time basis. To augment this team and attempt to overcome the difficulties presented by the cyclical nature of the business, there is a trend to employ permanent part-time staff and have a regular bank of permanent casual staff who are employed on a per session basis.

Human resource planning is therefore the process by which an organisation ensures that it has the right number of suitably qualified people in the right jobs at the right time. In order to satisfy this process, a MICE organisation reviews its present supply of staff and compares it against the projected demand for staff. It then decides whether to add, reduce or reallocate the employees within its organisation. The process for preparing a human resource plan is generic and systematic and should be conducted in four stages:

- stage one — forecast labour demand
- stage two — analyse labour supply
- stage three — balance supply and demand considerations
- stage four — formulate staffing strategies to meet organisational needs.

This is an ongoing cyclical process. In the more complex and large organisations it can involve a number of quantitative and qualitative forecasting techniques (Stone 1998, p. 52). Figure 4.1 demonstrates a human resource planning model.

A key component of human resource planning is labour demand forecasting. This involves estimating in advance the number and type of employees that will be required by a MICE organisation and is linked to the overall objectives of the business. In calculating these estimates, consideration should be given to projected business (product or service demands) — for example, the number of conference bids gained and the use or introduction of new technology such as specific software packages for conference management — and staff turnover rate — a projection of how many employees might leave each area through resignation, retrenchment, retirement and termination. This rate can vary within a convention venue — for example, the labour turnover rate in convention services may be minimal, while in banqueting operations it may be quite high. Also to be considered are the financial resources available and any planned developments or expansion — for example, a PCO who wishes to enter the incentive market may need to recruit a specialised staff member to develop this area. Establishing the number and types of jobs that may be required to be filled enables the MICE organisation to match current staff and skills against the potential opportunities and openings.

An audit of both the internal supply of people and the availability of staff within the external environment should be undertaken. To forecast the

■ Figure 4.1
Human resource planning model

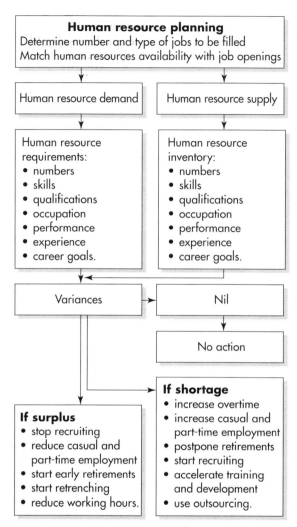

Human resource planning
Determine number and type of jobs to be filled
Match human resources availability with job openings

Human resource demand

Human resource supply

Human resource requirements:
• numbers
• skills
• qualifications
• occupation
• performance
• experience
• career goals.

Human resource inventory:
• numbers
• skills
• qualifications
• occupation
• performance
• experience
• career goals.

Variances

Nil

No action

If surplus
• stop recruiting
• reduce casual and part-time employment
• start early retirements
• start retrenching
• reduce working hours.

If shortage
• increase overtime
• increase casual and part-time employment
• postpone retirements
• start recruiting
• accelerate training and development
• use outsourcing.

Source: *Adapted from Stone (1998, p. 53)*

labour supply, a skills inventory of all current employees should be prepared. This will encompass such information as job title, age, education and qualifications, experience, job history, duties and responsibilities, projects completed, specific skills (e.g. languages, competency in use of specific conference and exhibition software), training courses completed and specific job preferences (e.g. an employee may wish to move from one area of job responsibility to another). The skills inventory can be simple in its preparation and can be recorded manually. It is a useful document for MICE managers: it enables them to identify which employees may be specifically qualified to do a different job; it provides information on the skills that are present or perhaps lacking; and it can assist in the easy transition and movement of staff between areas and in succession planning by identifying personnel who may be appropriate for promotion. Results from the supply analysis can assist in the long-term recruitment, selection and development of employees.

To make sure that there is a sufficient supply of staff, the external labour supply environment also needs to be considered. This covers issues such as the physical environment (the climate, location and general attractiveness of the area in which a MICE organisation is located); the social, demographic, cultural and political environment (e.g. national, international and regional economics); the education level of the workforce; population mobility; and demands for specific skills (Nankervis et al. 1996, p. 69). For example, as already noted, the construction and development of many purpose-built convention and exhibition centres, together with their support infrastructure, has resulted in the development of many additional services, suppliers and employment opportunities to an area.

A number of universal trends have occurred that are particularly relevant to the external labour supply for the MICE industry.

1. The number of women in the workforce is increasing. The MICE industry is attractive to women, and utilises many of their specific business and management skills, such as empathy, teamwork, attention to detail, logical and creative thinking, and participative management style.
2. Education levels are increasing. Stone (1998, p. 59) has identified that over 70 per cent of young Australians completed their Higher School Certificate in 1995, compared to less than 50 per cent in 1985.
3. There has been an increase in the number and importance of service sector jobs, particularly within the Australian tourism and hospitality industry, as a result of points 1 and 2 above.
4. There has been a growth in the number of tertiary institutions providing programs in tourism and hospitality, some of which include a course on MICE operations and management. The development of such programs assists the industry by ensuring that there are enough suitably qualified people with the necessary skills and experience to work in the industry.
5. Worldwide there is a trend towards casual or part-time work. This is a result of a number of factors, including more competitive pressure, the need for more flexible staffing, changes in technology and unfavourable industrial relations legislation (Stone 1998, p. 60). The MICE industry is particularly suited to the employment of casual and part-time staff due to the cyclical nature of its business.

In order to balance the supply of and demand for staff, MICE managers need to review aspects such as recruitment strategies, which includes looking at using a mix of full-time, part-time or casual workers, the design or redesign of particular jobs, remuneration packages and career development paths. Retrenchments within this sector of the industry are not a frequent occurrence as many people leave through natural fallout.

Human resource planning forms the basis of and influences many human resource activities, such as recruitment and selection, training and development, career management and staff appraisal, retirement and retrenchment. Failure to prepare a human resource plan can result in unfilled job vacancies, expensive replacement training or, in fact, little training at all. This can result in standards not being met, demotivated employees and customer dissatisfaction. The range of human resource activities that are influenced by human resource planning is demonstrated in figure 4.2.

■ **Figure 4.2**

Human resource activities that are influenced by human resource planning

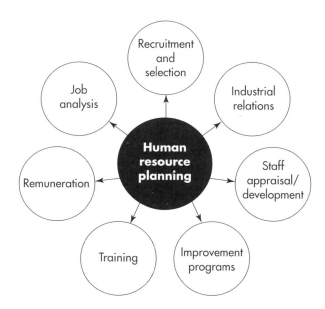

Human resource planning can assist MICE managers in the recruitment of staff by determining the future needs of the organisation. Together with job analysis, it will indicate how many and what types of people need to be recruited. The provision of an effective recruitment program also can assist in the selection process, by providing a pool of suitably qualified people from which to select. Human resource planning can aid in training and development programs and assist in the retention and development of staff. For example, many MICE businesses, such as venues or PCOs, use multi-skilling as a way to both develop their staff and ensure maximum flexibility. It is important that staff be given the opportunity to develop their job skills through training and development and career management as this can reduce labour turnover.

■ Job *analysis*

Job analysis is the process of obtaining information on and determining the essential duties, tasks and responsibilities of a job. It involves a systematic investigation of the job. Job analysis assists in the preparation of job descriptions, job or person specifications, human resource planning and the redesign of jobs. It helps in accurate recruitment and selection and sets standards for undertaking performance appraisals. For example, in the preparation of such a job analysis, the scope and range of tasks undertaken by a PCO might be identified to include the following:

- establish the design and objectives of the event
- select the site and facilities (i.e. the venue)
- negotiate with the venue and other suppliers
- budgeting
- handle delegate registrations
- select and organise transport
- plan the program and supporting information plus partner programs
- organise pre- and post-conference tours
- set up and establish the registration desk and procedures
- arrange support services (e.g. convention bureaus and other outside services).

Many basic tasks within a PCO business, such as data input for delegate registration and satchel compilation, though repetitive, are essential, and require great attention to detail on the part of the job holder.

The type of information that is collected when analysing a job should answer the following questions:

- What is performed?
- Where is it performed?
- How is it performed?
- Why is it performed?
- When is it performed? (Stone 1998, p. 123)

Job analysis helps to clarify the requirements of a job and the various interrelationships between the departments. It can help to reduce overlap and duplication between jobs, thereby encouraging efficiency.

■ Job *descriptions*

The analysis of the tasks and duties of a job is often a preliminary step in the preparation of a job description. This is a written statement that explains:

- why a job exists
- what the job holder does
- how they do the job
- the conditions under which the job is performed.

A job description can vary in appearance and content. It should include information on the job title, and clearly outline the status of the job. This is of psychological importance to the employee. It should identify the role of the job within the overall organisation, and the person to whom the employee reports. The most important section of the job description covers the actual duties and responsibilities, relationships, roles and goals of the job, for example working conditions and accountability.

The job description for a convention services manager might include the following:

- plans and executes conferences
- develops standard operating procedures
- establishes standards of operational performance
- sets objectives, goals and policies relating to MICE business

- carries out training of staff and instigates meetings of convention services teams
- prepares forecasts and budgets
- maintains up-to-date equipment lists
- establishes business contacts and disseminates information.
  These could be broken down into four categories:
1. administrative responsibilities
2. working relationships with sales and marketing departments and food and beverage operations
3. interdepartmental relations within the venue organisation and structure
4. client service responsibilities (Montgomery & Rutherford 1994, p. 49).

A convention coordinator, often found in smaller venues, might also deal with room set-ups, client liaison, bookings, marketing and event evaluation. If appropriate, these would be included in the job description.

Common problems found in the preparation of job descriptions are that often they are poorly written and therefore provide little guidance to the job holder. In addition, a job description is not static; it should be revised on a regular basis and reviewed if the job holder leaves the job. In the current work climate, it is common practice for job descriptions to be updated by employees. Figure 4.3 outlines the job description for a conference manager in a corporate organisation.

A profile of the role, skills and experience of convention services managers is provided in the industry insight on page 120.

■ Job or person *specifications*

Job or person specifications reflect the skills, experience, personal qualities and competencies needed of the successful job holder, that is the skills required to do the job. These can be broken down into the following areas: experience; qualifications; skills; abilities and knowledge; personal qualities; and special requirements. The job specification identifies the type of potential employee that should be recruited and how they might be assessed. When preparing a job specification, it is useful to identify the essential skills and the desirable skills. So, for example, in respect of education and training, essential skills might be an advanced diploma from TAFE plus successful completion of the MIAA basic meeting management course, and desirable skills might be successful completion of the MIAA advanced meetings management course.

No matter what type of organisation a conference organiser works for, certain professional and personal qualities are required in order to undertake the diverse requirements of the job. These qualities include good negotiation skills, being culturally adept, diplomatic and creative. Having excellent communication skills, being people oriented, tactful and polite are also necessary. These qualities, which are described in more detail on page 121, would be incorporated into the specifications for this job.

■ **Figure 4.3**
*Job
description
for a
conference
manager*

CONFERENCE MANAGER

REPORTING TO   MANAGER, MEETINGS DEPARTMENT, OCC
MANAGING DIRECTOR, OCC

OVERALL JOB PURPOSE
Manage all logistical and administrative aspects of meetings organised by OCC on behalf of clients

RESPONSIBILITIES
* Manage all elements in relation to organising a meeting
  Book venues and accommodation, if applicable
  Confirm all arrangements in writing to venue
  Be aware of venue contracts and obligations relating to deposits and cancellation
  Coordinate mail-out of invitations/registration brochures
  Receive RSVPs and develop delegate lists
  Coordinate audiovisual equipment
  Coordinate exhibition display contractors, if applicable
  Arrange food and beverages
  Prepare printed name badges
  Coordinate telephone confirmation, if applicable
  Organise flights and ground transfers
  Coordinate complimentary parking at the meeting venues
  Manage meeting on-site
  Book temporary staff as necessary

* Maintain accurate and easy-to-read files for each meeting
  Prepare regular written progress reports to client on each live job
  Attend work-in-progress meetings as applicable
  Liaise closely with relevant OCC account manager
  Attend meetings with clients

* Research and prepare proposals to be presented to clients
  Provide recommendations and generate new ideas where possible
  Develop cost estimates using OCC's in-house model
  Prepare invoices to clients at the end of an event
  Reconcile budgets and report to OCC's financial accountant
  Develop new business and generate sales leads

* Keep up-to-date with new products, venues and trends in the meetings industry
  Be aware of pharmaceutical industry and OCC clients

Source: Reproduced with the permission of OCC Australia Pty Ltd

Convention services managers in four- and five-star hotels in eastern Australia are predominantly female (66 per cent), aged between 26 and 35. They have been employed within the convention industry for a period of one to five years and in their current position for between one and two years. The majority have completed a Higher School Certificate together with a further qualification from TAFE (e.g. associate diploma) or university. If they have taken a degree course, it could be in a subject such as history, art or hospitality. Many have undertaken professional development programs run 'in-house', covering issues such as train the trainer, leadership skills and customer service. Some are studying for a further degree through an industry university partnership program.

Specific job responsibilities for convention services managers are identified as:

- maximising space utilisation
- preparing and maintaining budgets for the department
- ensuring clients are 'looked after' and 'making things happen' in respect of conventions held in the hotel
- ensuring convention and event information is disseminated throughout the hotel
- recruiting convention services department staff
- training and mentoring the convention services team
- undertaking direct liaison with clients regarding large or complex conferences
- ensuring the standards of convention and meeting service and operations are met by the hotel.

There is an indication that some managers are responsible for providing a 'one-stop shop' for conference and banquet clients.

Key competencies for convention services managers include an 'in-depth' knowledge of multiple market segments, a good grasp of the convention and meeting business services available in the local area, and a broad-based and sound knowledge of the management and organisation of all hotel departments and their staff capabilities.

Two of the hallmarks of the job of convention services manager are seen as the long hours and the need to adapt to varying personalities, all of whom have differing competencies.

There is evidence that a large proportion of the interactions between conference organisers and venue staff are conducted mainly through the convention services manager and their department. Conference organisers often see them as being the key to the success of their event, because of their knowledge of the venue and its capabilities and limitations. However, conference organisers do need to build confidence and trust in convention services managers. In Australia, many conference organisers will change their choice of venue for an event in order to follow the career moves of a good convention services manager. A career challenge is therefore created for venue management in how to provide responsibility, challenge and job enrichment for the convention services manager, yet still keep them in a position that offers no real prospects for promotion. In one venue the answer has been to give the convention services manager additional responsibility for the development of convention standards of operation and management across the group's convention properties. In addition, this particular convention venue has been designated as the 'flagship and benchmark property' for the group in regards to convention standards and quality.

Source: McCabe & Weeks (1999)

Professional and personal qualities required to become a conference organiser are:

- **Good negotiation skills** — These skills are critically important, because the conference organiser interacts with a wide variety of people including senior management, suppliers, staff and guest speakers.
- **Culturally adept** — The conference organiser will meet people from many different nationalities and cultures. It is essential that they are familiar with international protocol and are sensitive to the needs of conference attendees and speakers from different cultures.
- **Diplomacy** — In order to overcome the intricacies that are required in client negotiations, as well as finding out and meeting the client's objectives for an event, the conference organiser must be diplomatic at all times.
- **Creative** — In the light of rising delegate expectations and increased competition, it is essential for the conference organiser to design events that are different in style and format. They have to find new ways of working that have both practical validity and provide something different. Yet this all has to be within budget. The conference organiser has to be creative in their program design, selection of speakers, entertainment and logistics. They must ensure that these are all pertinent to the goals of the event, while at the same time ensuring that the event is a memorable occasion.
- **Excellent communication skills** — The conference organiser has to be able to communicate with people at all levels, from those involved in technical operational details (such as electricians and audiovisual technicians) to the client, senior management and the CEO.
- **People orientated** — The conference organiser must have empathy with the client, delegates and suppliers (i.e. be able to put themselves in their customer's shoes).
- **Tactful and polite** — The conference organiser meets and deals with many people, so a touch of humour and the ability to empathise is essential.

- **Excellent organisational skills** — Conference organisers need to possess analytical skills and demonstrate attention to detail. They need to be able to undertake and break down tasks step by step, yet still keep sight of the big picture. Good project planning skills are essential, as is familiarity with industry specific technology and software.
- **Other skills** — Other skills required are the ability to follow through projects and to use initiative.

A conference organiser has to thrive on challenge and have high levels of energy, nerves of steel and a 'passion for excellence'. They must appear calm in the midst of apparent confusion and chaos and have immediate solutions to problems. During the organisation of a convention they are very visible and should have the capability to work long days (12 hours if necessary), yet be able to maintain an outward calm (Weissinger 1992, p. 9).

The mix of essential and desirable characteristics for the job of conference organiser will depend on the particular job and the requirements of the organisation. For example, a small PCO organisation seeking an experienced conference organiser to join its business might identify a different range of essential and desirable characteristics than a large firm of PCOs seeking to recruit a specialist function and event organiser. This is demonstrated in table 4.1, which compares the essential and desirable characteristics for an experienced conference organiser and a specialist function and event organiser.

■ **Table 4.1**
Essential and desirable characteristics for two types of conference organiser

AN EXPERIENCED CONFERENCE ORGANISER	SPECIALIST FUNCTION AND EVENT ORGANISER
Essential characteristics might include: • 'X' years experience in the field of convention and meeting organisation with specific experience in the management and coordination of conventions and meetings of various sizes • Completion of industry specific training programs • Excellent organisational and administrative skills, including the ability to follow through with tasks and get things done • People orientated, empathetic and sensitive to the needs of delegates and speakers • Proven ability to interact with wide range of people at all levels within the business environment • Excellent written and verbal communication skills • Highly motivated, with ability to foster a cohesive team • Ability to use initiative.	**Essential characteristics might include:** • Experience within the events or hospitality industry, with 'X' years experience in food and beverage supervisory management, including operational and logistical coordination of functions and events • Tertiary level qualification such as diploma in hospitality management • Proven experience of ability to design and implement a variety of innovative and creative functions and events • Customer focus, plus proven ability to provide high-quality functions and events • Excellent communication skills, plus the ability to negotiate with clients and suppliers • Proven administrative experience and attention to detail, with the ability to get things done.

AN EXPERIENCED CONFERENCE ORGANISER	SPECIALIST FUNCTION AND EVENT ORGANISER
Desirable characteristics might include: • Conversant with industry specific software packages • TAFE advanced diploma or university degree in tourism, hospitality or business • Familiarity with current trends in convention and meeting technology • Ability to use project planning techniques.	**Desirable characteristics might include:** • Familiarity with international protocol • TAFE advanced diploma or university degree in hospitality or tourism • Project planning skills • Ability to use industry specific software packages.

The following snapshot outlines the career progression of a graduate with a business degree in tourism and explores the sales role within a purpose-built convention and exhibition centre.

SNAPSHOT
Kylie Schaefer, Sydney Convention & Exhibition Centre

The opportunity to be involved in sales and marketing, plus the excitement of working in a purpose-built convention and exhibition centre with an excellent reputation worldwide, was the successful combination that attracted Kylie Schaefer to join the Sydney Convention & Exhibition Centre just over three years ago.

Kylie had just returned to Australia from a period working in London. A key component of her degree program, a Bachelor of Business in Tourism from Southern Cross University, had been the facility to gain industry experience overseas. Kylie spent the final six months of her degree program (the internship component) working in front of house within a central London hotel. This was followed by further work experience within the hotel and a period travelling before she finally returned to Sydney to begin her chosen career path in sales and marketing.

So what else has maintained her attraction to sales and marketing and the MICE industry for the past three years? ' It's the buzz, the excitement — no day's ever the same, no event ever the same — lots of variety. This is a small industry where you get to know a lot of people, the hours are demanding, but you don't mind if you enjoy the job.'

As assistant sales manager/national, her job is focused predominantly on the corporate market. The sales and marketing department at the Sydney Convention & Exhibition Centre is divided into international and national sales. Five people are employed within national sales — a sales development manager, an assistant sales manager, a sales executive and two sales coordinators whom Kylie oversees on a daily basis. All the team reports directly to the sales development manager.

So what does Kylie's job involve? 'Sourcing leads, researching companies, for example on the Net, initiating or responding to sales enquiries, researching
(continued)

prospects and making appointments to see them.' Kylie is involved in taking an initial enquiry through to the contract stage, after which it is handed over to an event coordinator at the centre who will oversee the actual event. This involves site inspections, putting together client proposals and the day-to-day client liaison. She has been in her current position for approximately 18 months and in this time the job has changed to become a more pro-active and 'out on the road' sourcing business. Together with the assistance of a sales executive she focuses on the Sydney market. 'I like the job — it's rewarding and challenging to make the client happy — matching their requirements to those of the centre. The client wants to hold a successful event; you make sure that they do.'

Despite being focused on the corporate sector, she continues to maintain relations with a key client base of conference and event coordinators who contact her personally when booking an event at the centre.

Prior to her current role, Kylie worked for 14 months as a sales co-ordinator within the centre, dealing with incoming client sales calls, reservations enquiries and site inspections across all market segments. This proved to be invaluable experience for her current position.

So what do the next five years hold for Kylie careerwise? 'Staying within sales and marketing within the MICE industry.'

Source: Kylie Schaefer, Sydney Convention & Exhibition Centre

■ Recruitment *and selection*

The hiring and retention of employees has become a key focus for business in Australia today and the MICE industry cannot afford poor employee selection. Nankervis et al. (1996, p. 208) have identified that in the current environment greater attention should be given to the selection process than ever before in order to maintain competitive advantage. Yet this is difficult given the recent rapid growth and development of the MICE industry in Australia and the shortage of suitable qualified people. However, it has been found that individuals who have been screened using carefully developed job specifications learn their job readily, are more productive and are able to adjust to new tasks with little difficulty. As a result, the organisation benefits and turnover is minimised.

Recruitment has been defined as a 'process of attempting to locate and encourage potential applicants to apply for existing or anticipated job openings' (Nankervis et al. 1996, p. 184). Recruitment strategies therefore attempt to create a pool of appropriately qualified experienced people so that selection strategies and decisions can be initiated.

Selection is the process of gathering legally defensible information about job applicants in order to determine who shall be hired for long-term or short-term positions (Kramer, McGraw & Schuler 1997, p. 322). Selecting from a pool of applicants from within or outside the organisation to fill an existing job opening is a major human resource function for a manager.

Before the recruitment process begins, a number of questions should be asked: Is it necessary to fill the position? Is there any money in the budget? Is there someone in the company who can do the job? Within Australia, a large number of positions are filled without the need for external advertising. Vacancies are filled internally by promotion or by transfer between departments. In this way, a MICE organisation can capitalise on the costs previously invested in the recruitment, selection, induction and training of current employees. The promotion of employees from within the business provides an excellent incentive for employees, is a form of motivation and improves morale within the organisation. It maximises the opportunities to allow employees to multiskill and assists in the provision of career paths.

The sources of recruitment for potential employees differ and depend on the type of job and the level of expertise that is required. For example, the recruitment of a senior manager within a MICE organisation might well be handled by a firm of executive search consultants, while the job of banquet supervisor might be advertised in the employment section of a national newspaper. Such an advertisement will incorporate information identified in the job specification and description. The most popular areas to place job advertisements for positions within the MICE industry are:

- *newspapers* — national and local newspapers are a highly relevant source for attracting potential applicants for positions (see figure 4.4, which shows examples of advertisements from Australian national newspapers)

CONFERENCE & INCENTIVE MANAGER

- **International Hotel Group**
- **Change of Scenery!**

A rare opportunity to join this world renowned hotel group to manage and grow key market segments for two unique resorts at a highly desirable destination.

You will be responsible for achieving budget through your strong relationships with key suppliers and your ability to sucessfully negotiate and win business.

Critical to your success will be your demonstrable leadership and organisational skills and a track record of exceeding customer expectations. An excellent remuneration package is negotiable for the right candidate.

Time for a change? To register your interest call Beth Barclay on (02) 9233 7755 or fax your resume to (02) 9233 8876 or email to reddin@syd.com.au

REDDIN

In preparation for the opening of our expanded Centre and the lead up to the 2000 Olympics, two roles have become available.

Concierge

Responsibilities to include greeting guests, responding to inquiries concerning events, providing information on The Centre and Darling Harbour, operating the cloak room and providing back up support to our Business Centre. You will have 1–2 years experience in a concierge/portering role.

Catering Supervisor — Exhibitions

This hands-on role involves overseeing Exhibitor Catering. Duties include pre-event planning, briefing staff, assisting with stock control, department rostering and staff training. You must have at least 12 months experience as a supervisor in a high volume catering operation.

To apply you must be well presented, possess excellent communication skills and computer skills. If you have a superior customer service attitude and can work days, evenings and weekends, please send your resume to:

Gloria Elias-Fallone,
Assistant Human Resources
Manager
Sydney Convention &
Exhibition Centre
Locked Bag 14
Pyrmont NSW 2009
or Fax (02) 9282 5099
by Friday 7 May 99.

SYDNEY CONVENTION & EXHIBITION CENTRE DARLING HARBOUR

■ **Figure 4.4** *Examples of MICE job advertisements*

- *Internet sites* — job vacancies are now being advertised on the Internet, with industry associations such as MIAA featuring a bulletin board of positions vacant and wanted (MIAA 1998b)
- *trade and professional journals* — some vacancies can be advertised through trade or professional journals, but unless the journal is published frequently, this may not be a viable alternative.

Sources that assist in the recruitment process include private employment agencies, executive search firms and educational institutes such as TAFE colleges and universities. Indeed, a number of MICE organisations have actively developed relationships with particular educational institutions in order to recruit and select their new employees from students completing relevant programs. Employee referrals, such as recommendations from existing employees, or speculative résumés and applications, are other recruitment sources. The latter should be acknowledged and, if appropriate, kept on file until a suitable vacancy becomes available, at which time the potential applicant might be called for a selection interview.

The overall aim of the recruitment process is to make people aware that the vacancy exists and to persuade them to apply for the position. The selection process should follow three stages:

1. The potential applicant should complete an application form or submit a curriculum vitae or résumé.
2. All applicants should undertake an interview. This might include some job skills testing.
3. A reference check should be undertaken on the person selected for the position.

Figure 4.5 details the activities involved in the recruitment process and their relationships.

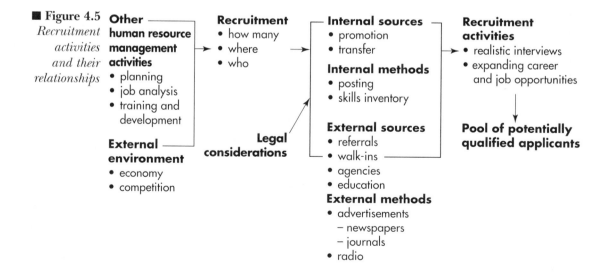

■ Figure 4.5 *Recruitment activities and their relationships*

■ Induction *and orientation*

The induction and orientation of new employees into an organisation is very important. Research has indicated that the highest labour turnover rates are found among newcomers to an organisation, and that this turnover occurs mainly in the first month of joining an organisation (Kennedy & Berger 1994, p. 59). The aim of an induction or orientation program is to socialise and familiarise new employees with their position and organisation so that they can begin to operate effectively and efficiently as quickly as possible. This is particularly the case in the MICE industry, where many new employees may be joining organisations with only a small number of staff. The induction or orientation of a new employee begins at the time that the initial offer of employment is made, and continues up until the first performance appraisal interview.

Basic orientation programs normally include aspects such as the history, philosophy, vision and culture of the organisation; a brief outline of its policies and procedures; fire safety and security training; and familiarisation with the organisation and its key personnel. Orientation programs typically last from one day to one week, depending on the organisation. Traditionally, many orientation programs do not consider the emotional factors that are paramount for new employees during the early stages of working in their new position. Yet if the programs are to be successful and achieve their objectives and hopefully reduce the number of employees leaving in the first month, then they should recognise these emotional stresses. The goal of orientation programs should be to diminish individual feelings of social and emotional vulnerability, decrease stress and allow new employees to learn the interpersonal and operational skills necessary for success in their new position. A buddy or mentoring system is a further way to ensure that new employees are assimilated into an organisation. With the predominance and trend to use part-time and permanent casual employees within MICE organisations, orientation programs should be planned to include these members of the team.

■ Training *and development*

The training and development of staff is a key development area for the MICE industry. To maintain and improve the competitive position of the industry, increase professionalism and improve standards of quality, there is a need for both operator (skills-based training) and manager development programs. Many owner operators such as PCOs require not only specific technical skills for the MICE industry but also general business management and strategic skills. As the industry embraces the new millennium, there is a need for senior management education and training.

It has long been recognised that training can enhance individual, departmental and organisational performance. In the current and future work environment, a company should see training and development as an investment in their employees' careers. In order for effective training and development programs to be produced, there needs to be a systematic, integrated approach in both the identification of the training needs and the introduction of the training process. Employee performance appraisals often provide a useful source of information on these training needs and can highlight specific areas of weakness or deficiency. This process is outlined in figure 4.6.

■ **Figure 4.6**
Performance appraisal and training needs

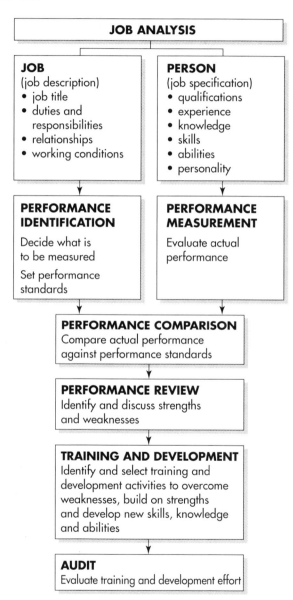

Source: Stone (1998, p. 321)

So how is industry-specific education, training and development carried out within the MICE sector?

Industry training

Currently, education, training and development are carried out at a number of levels and are provided by a variety of institutions and industry bodies.

'In-house' training programs are provided by numerous organisations, such as the Marriott Corporation. These programs offer mainly operational, skills-based training, such as telephone skills, food and beverage service or junior management or supervisory training, in areas such as customer service, train the trainer and the role of the supervisor.

The Meetings Industry Association of Australia (MIAA) has developed and operates a number of specialised training programs for the MICE industry. These are available to its members and are linked to an accreditation program developed by the Association. The Association offers a range of educational programs, including short residential courses in meeting management. The accreditation program has been designed to recognise both valid educational and training courses undertaken by members and current relevant industry experience. It is seen as a way to increase professionalism and upgrade members' education and training standards.

Technical and supervisory management training

Tourism Training Australia (TTA), the tripartite industry training committee comprising government, industry and union representatives, has worked with the MICE industry to identify current and future training needs to ensure that the industry has the required levels of skilled staff and managers. Competency standards and associated relevant curricula have been prepared for use by TAFE colleges specialising in tourism and hospitality courses.

Students undertaking university programs, particularly those in tourism and hospitality, have been provided with the opportunity to study the MICE industry through various curricula including a range of courses such as food and beverage operations and management, marketing and tourism and hospitality studies. Some universities in Australia and New Zealand have recognised the importance and diversity of career opportunities from this segment of the tourism and hospitality industry and have provided a range of specialist units that focus on the MICE sector (e.g. Southern Cross University in Northern New South Wales). In addition, students from many programs are encouraged to gain work experience within the industry. Partnerships between industry and educational institutions have been developed, with the objective of ensuring that the studies have both educational and industry relevance. Some companies have favoured these developments and are actively providing convention scholarships (such as Amlink Technologies), linked to formal work experience, as a means of encouraging potential entrants to the industry. Specific postgraduate qualifications have also been developed by some Australian universities in order to ensure education and development for future managers, for example the master's degree in convention and event management provided by Southern Cross University.

MICE operators, and particularly the owners of independent PCOs, face a number of dilemmas with respect to training and developing their employees and the costs versus the benefits. If they train and develop a team member but are unable to provide opportunities for promotion, that person may leave and the investment in training and development will be lost to the organisation. Yet in strategic terms, if standards are to improve, it is essential that training and development occur throughout the industry. Increased levels of training and development within an organisation have the potential to reduce labour turnover and in the longer term will provide a wider pool of suitably qualified applicants and employees.

MICE organisations therefore need to develop a systematic training and development plan for their operation. This should be linked to a performance appraisal system, with training needs being evaluated and developed on an annual basis. Training and development should not be reserved for full-time employees. Perhaps more important for the businesses is a more formalised bank of permanent casual staff, for example members of the banqueting team, who benefit from 'in-house' training and are aware of the standards required at that venue.

The removal of the federal government's training guarantee scheme has meant that there is currently no government support or encouragement for these training developments, yet the industry needs to sponsor and encourage employees to seek and embrace a program of continual learning in this rapidly developing industry.

LEADING AND MOTIVATING THE TEAM

Managers in the MICE industry, as in other areas, have found that in this changing world, managerial strategies that were once effective in one situation may not be effective in another and may be effective today but not tomorrow. Their business has to be both flexible and adaptable while also being stable and controlled. The business must be able to grow, acquire resources and be aware of the influence and impact of the external environment. However, at the same time, managers need to ensure that internal formal communication methods and information management are efficient and effective. On the one hand, an emphasis is needed on the importance and value of human resources — the people; while on the other hand, a focus is required on the need to plan and set goals. These values are not mutually exclusive, and it is possible for an organisation to perform effectively in all areas (Quinn et al. 1996, p. 14).

Many conference organisers, as we have seen, must lead and coordinate a group of people for whom they are not directly responsible. Yet the successful management of this team to meet its standards, deadlines, and so on is critical to ensure ultimate customer satisfaction. So how can the MICE manager ensure that the team is motivated and focused on the task at hand? What skills, knowledge and attitudes are required from within the managerial tool bag so that they can lead the team and ensure its ultimate effective and efficient use?

■ Managerial *leadership*

In order to provide effective leadership, managers often have to undertake roles and meet expectations that are both conflicting and competing. Quinn et al. (1996) have identified eight managerial leadership roles, together with their key competencies. These are outlined in figure 4.7. Their model is particularly relevant for MICE managers, who should be fully conversant with these roles and their key competencies in order to become master managers.

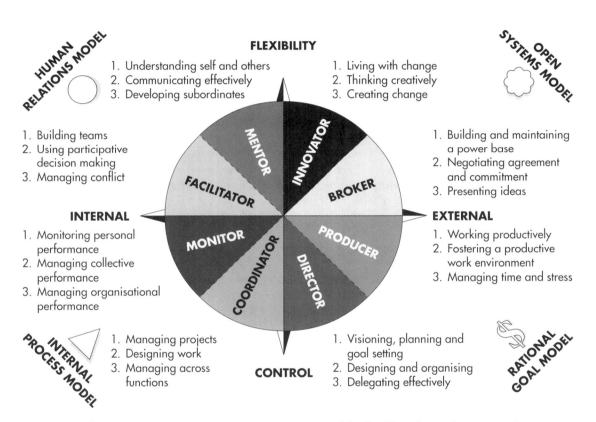

■ **Figure 4.7** *Becoming a master manager — managerial leadership roles and competencies*

Source: *Quinn et al. 1996, p. 16*

In the role as 'director', the conference organiser focuses on clarifying expectations through activities such as planning and goal setting. They establish objectives, such as determining the objectives for a particular conference; define roles and tasks, for example when working with a team of conference coordinators; outline any problem areas and select a solution; generate rules and policies; and give instructions, for example on conference room booking policies. The key competencies required in this instance would include the ability to plan and set goals, design policies, organise the team and delegate effectively.

As a 'producer', the conference organiser has to be task orientated and work focused. They need to maintain high levels of interest, motivation and energy, together with personal drive and productivity. In this role they also should be able to motivate other members of the team and help increase their productivity so that they can accomplish the pre-established goals. The key competencies required would include the ability to work productively, manage their time and stress and foster a productive work environment.

In the 'monitor' role, the conference organiser must be aware of what is going on in their job and work area and at the same time ensure that the team members follow instructions and are able to achieve the tasks identified in their job. A monitor is good at analysis, can handle data and forms, and is able to control and undertake analysis (Quinn et al. 1996). This role is particularly relevant, for example, in making certain that the administrative aspects of the conference, such as conference pre-registration and the preparation of event orders, are carried out effectively. The key competencies required would include the ability to monitor both their own and others' performance and to manage and monitor both the performance of the team and the organisation.

Dependability and reliability in the work environment, together with the ability to schedule, organise and coordinate the team, are the leadership skills required of the conference organiser in their role as 'coordinator'. Additionally, they should be able to handle any crisis, and look after the technological, logistical and housekeeping aspects of the conference. The key competencies would include the ability to manage projects (this is examined further in chapter 8), design jobs and the work environment, and manage across the various functions and environments.

In the 'facilitator' role, the conference organiser encourages collective effort, builds cohesion and teamwork and manages interpersonal conflict, facilitating group problem solving and team building. As a 'mentor', the conference organiser has to be helpful, considerate, open, fair and approachable. The key competencies would include the ability to listen, give compliments and credit where due, and to help to build the skills of the team members, provide training opportunities and plan for each team member's success. They need to understand both themselves and others within the team, communicate effectively and be able to develop subordinates.

The 'innovator' role focuses on adaptation and change. The conference organiser in this instance focuses attention on the changing environment, identifies important trends and conceptualises new ideas or events. Key competencies required would include the ability to tolerate risk and uncertainty, and be creative and innovative, as well as having a vision — skills very apparent, as noted earlier, for a professional conference organiser. In the 'broker' role, the conference organiser has to be politically astute, persuasive and influential. They represent the business, and so the key competencies would include the ability to negotiate with clients and others, market their services and facilities and act as a liaison and spokesperson.

The managerial leadership roles identified by Quinn et. al. are as applicable for a junior manager/supervisor as for a senior MICE manager. It is only the extent and use of the role that changes at the different levels within the organisational hierarchy. For example, in the broker role, the president of the industry association will act as a liaison or spokesperson for the industry as a whole, whereas a conference organiser will liaise and negotiate with a client concerning their conference.

If the MICE manager is to lead and motivate the team, they need to be competent in all these areas and be familiar as to when they might use the appropriate managerial leadership role. For example, in many instances the conference organiser will act as a coordinator and facilitator and use these skills and competencies. This would be particularly the case when working with a conference committee or across the various departments within a venue. During the initial planning stages of a conference the 'innovator role' may be paramount. As a conference nears its start date, the skills of the 'producer' and 'director' may become more evident, to ensure that the many specific tasks are completed at the right time and to the correct standard.

In their role as a manager and supervisor, the conference organiser should focus on three areas:

- *Task* — It is important to focus on the task and identify 'What are we here for?' Both the conference organiser and the team need to know why they are doing a job, and they need to have a focus to aim for and establish objectives to achieve this aim. The objectives should be established with the aid of the team, with the conference organiser checking on the method and progress.
- *Team* — In assisting the team, the conference organiser needs to emphasise the common interests of the group, look after the group (e.g. make sure that they have sufficient resources), keep a watching brief on team members, consult with the group, and set and maintain high standards. They should also give credit and praise as appropriate and listen to suggestions.
- *Individual* — The conference organiser should try to assist each member of the team to realise their objectives and achievements and, where possible, try to help to remove any motivational dissatisfiers. The conference organiser should consult with each person, give praise for initiative and listen to suggestions. It is important that the conference organiser leads by example.

■ Motivation

In looking after the individual and team interests, the conference organiser becomes aware of the motivational aspects involved in the leadership of a team. This is one of the most challenging aspects of management. It can manifest itself through employee morale, work output, absenteeism rates, the amount of effort expended by the employee, labour turnover, loyalty and achievement. All managers should be aware of what makes the high fliers fly, and why some employees wish to achieve and accept increased responsibility while others remain passive or even in some instances hostile. The motivation to work is different for each employee. However, if the MICE business is to succeed, then its employees must be competent, the company must be efficiently organised and it must provide employees with the necessary materials and resources to do the job. In addition, employees should have a desire to do their best not only for their own satisfaction but also to ensure the success of the company.

So what is motivation? It can be defined as: 'The willingness to exert high levels of effort toward organisational goals, conditioned by the effort and ability to satisfy some individual need' (Robbins 1986, p. 121). A simple motivational process is

$$need \rightarrow action \rightarrow goal$$

The definition of motivation suggests that although individuals may work towards common group or organisational goals, the willingness to do so reflects an individual's needs. By understanding the individual needs that drive an employee's behaviour, the manager and organisation can help to motivate their work towards the achievement of organisational goals. The needs of each employee vary from one person to another, and in order to accommodate these many and diverse needs, a variety of motivational strategies should be implemented throughout the organisation.

So what really motivates employees? Money? Status? Power? Self-fulfilment? There are a number of motivational theories and strategies. They can be separated into content and process theories and include:

- Maslow's hierarchy of needs — content theory
- Alderfer's ERG theory — content theory
- Hertzberg's two-factor theory — content theory
- McClelland's manifest needs theory — content theory
- Vroom's expectancy theory — process theory
- Adams' equity theory — process theory

The content theories explain 'why' someone is motivated to undertake an activity, while the process theories describe 'how' the individual becomes motivated in the first place and sustains that motivation over a period of time.

So how do these theories apply to the MICE manager? There are many references and discussions about the theories of motivation. There is not the space here to cover them all, so only Vroom's expectancy theory is discussed and how it might relate to convention and meeting management. Vroom's expectancy theory is based on the relationship between job effort, performance and outcomes of performance.

Expectancy theory identifies that employees are motivated to undertake behaviours for which they are rewarded. For example, an individual will be motivated if they believe that a reasonable amount of effort will lead to a satisfactory performance that will then provide the desired rewards. Expectancy theory purports that whether a person is motivated depends on two 'expectancies' and one 'valence'. An 'expectancy' is a probability that something will occur. A 'valence' is an assigned value of a reward.

The first 'expectancy' is the probability that an employee will make a connection between the level of effort and performance that derives from effort. For motivation to occur, an employee has to believe that if they put forward a reasonable amount of effort, then there is a high probability that they will meet the expected performance standards.

The second 'expectancy' is the probability that an employee will be able to link performance to the rewards received for that performance. For example, high levels of motivation will occur only if the employee believes there is a high probability of being rewarded for satisfactory performance.

The 'valence' refers to the value that is attached to a reward. For example, for a reward to have a high value as a motivator it must have a high value for the employee. The employee will only be motivated to work if the reward is something that they will find desirable. This theory is outlined in figure 4.8.

■ **Figure 4.8**
Elements in the expectancy theory of motivation

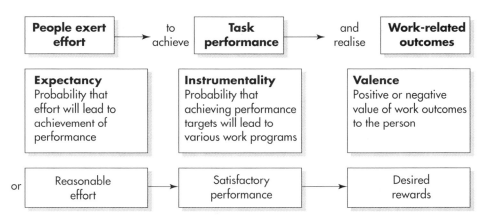

Source: Adapted from Schermerhorn (1989, p. 365)

How do MICE managers apply the expectancy theory of motivation to their teams? There are three ways:

1. *Link effort to performance* Managers need to make sure that each member of the team has the necessary skills to perform their job satisfactorily. People should either be recruited with the required skills or they should undergo training in the required areas. Managers also need to make sure that employees are aware of what constitutes 'satisfactory performance'.

2. *Link performance to outcomes* Employees need to be aware of the possible outcomes that can result from their performance. This could be done by performance appraisal, goal and objective setting and management by objectives (MBO).

3. *Understand the valence or work-related outcomes that the employee desires* Managers need to be aware of the 'outcomes' that are important to their team. This information can be obtained through consultation. Managers should be consistent in their allocation of rewards so that an employee can be confident that they will be rewarded adequately.

The 'desired rewards' (valence) can be either extrinsic rewards (usually monetary) or intrinsic rewards, which focus more on job factors. Examples of extrinsic rewards include direct wages or salary, bonus plans, profit sharing, superannuation, medical care, a company vehicle, and pay and time-off for attending work-related training programs and seminars. Other extrinsic rewards might be in the form of status symbols such as the receipt of formal awards and recognition, or the size and location of an office and the quality of its furnishings. Examples of intrinsic rewards might be found in social rewards such as after-hours social gatherings, informal recognition, friendly greetings, compliments and praise, or through self-rewards gained from the job, such as interesting and varied work, a sense of achievement, self-recognition and self-praise, flexible working hours and autonomy on the job (Schuler et al. 1992, p. 258).

In the MICE industry it would appear that there are many opportunities to gain intrinsic rewards. For example, many of the jobs within the sector are challenging, interesting and provide much variety. For the conference organiser, there is the satisfaction of seeing through the total job from start to finish, and receiving praise from both the client and delegates for a well run event. In addition, there are opportunities to meet a wide range of people, undertake both domestic and international travel, and be involved in a range of social activities that might be part of a conference. There is also the chance for part-time and flexible working hours in some areas. All of these factors could be identified as providing valence and assisting, along with extrinsic rewards, in the motivation of employees.

SUMMARY

The MICE industry has identified that effective managerial leadership of employees enables organisations to both satisfy and 'delight' the customer, while at the same time building competitive advantage. The expansion of the industry within the Asia–Pacific region has been recognised by potential employees who see it as an area of career opportunity.

However, as in other areas of the tourism and hospitality industry, a current human resource challenge is that of a shortage of suitably qualified people. Strategies for addressing this situation include the use of a systematic process for human resource management. This incorporates the preparation of a human resource plan, job analysis, the implementation of a recruitment and selection strategy, and the recognition of the value of industry-specific education, training and development programs for both junior and senior managers.

Managers within the MICE industry are required to implement a variety of managerial strategies, together with leadership and motivational techniques, in order to be effective. The provision of a convention or meeting requires the conference organiser, as a manager, to lead, motivate and coordinate a team of people for whom they are not directly responsible. In order to achieve this successfully, they need to undertake a number of managerial roles and utilise a variety of key managerial competencies. The importance of the task at hand, the conference team and the needs of the individual employees involved in the event should always be borne in mind. Human resource issues and management are a key component in the successful provision of a quality convention or meeting and ultimate customer satisfaction.

Activities

4.1 From the following advertisement for a conference manager for the Association of Retirement Homes for the Elderly, prepare a job description and job/person specification.

Conference Manager

The Association of Retirement Homes for the Elderly is seeking a conference manager to lead its convention and meeting activities.

The Association of Retirement Homes for the Elderly represents non-profit organisations dedicated to providing high-quality healthcare, housing and services for the elderly. Its membership consists of approximately 3000 not-for-profit nursing homes and continuing care retirement communities.

The conference manager is responsible for planning and implementing the Association's committee-related meetings, as well as a variety of internal social functions and projects. The conference manager organises the annual convention, as well as the annual general meeting. The person appointed will work in conjunction with the Association's marketing director to produce the annual conference brochures, and with the Association's executive director to produce a schedule of local and regional meetings.

The successful candidate should have a minimum of three years experience in the convention industry, preferably with an association, and have a recognised degree or TAFE qualification. The position requires a demonstrated ability to develop and attain established goals. Excellent oral and written communication skills, organisational skills and interpersonal skills are required, together with attention to detail and accuracy. The position requires the ability to meet deadlines and manage multiple projects, work with responsibility, make rapid decisions in anticipation of problems and/or opportunities, and follow through all tasks. Experience in Microsoft Word and Excel is required. Knowledge of the EVENTS software package is essential.

Please send your résumé, together with a letter of application, to . . .

4.2 Interview someone operating in a 'front-line' position in the MICE industry, for example a convention services manager in a venue, and determine:
(a) the motivational strategies used by this person's employer
(b) the individual's level of motivation.

Discussion questions

4.1 Critically evaluate why effective human resource management is important to MICE organisations.

4.2 Compare the role of a conference organiser in a corporation and an association with that of a convention services manager. What are the areas of similarity? How do their roles differ?

4.3 Discuss the advantages of human resource planning for MICE organisations.

4.4 How does human resource planning in MICE organisations contribute to the effective recruitment of staff?

4.5 Discuss how training and development within MICE organisations might affect:
(a) customer satisfaction
(b) employee motivation and satisfaction.

4.6 Identify the key areas that should be included in an orientation/induction program for a conference coordinator who is taking up a position:
(a) with a PCO
(b) in a purpose-built convention and exhibition centre.

4.7 As a convention services manager in a venue, what steps would you take to determine how best to motivate your team? Explain the importance of these steps.

4.8 Identify and compare the skills and competencies required of the MICE manager in their roles as 'director', 'coordinator', 'mentor' and 'producer'.

REFERENCES

Commonwealth Department of Tourism. 1995, *A National Strategy for the MICE Industry*, Canberra.

Go, F. M., Monachello, M. L. & Baum, T. 1996, *Human Resource Management in the Hospitality Industry*, John Wiley & Sons, New York.

Hill, F. 1996, 'A Career in the Meetings Industry — Career Paths of Meeting Planners', unpublished research report for graduating seminar, Southern Cross University, Lismore, NSW.

Kramer, R., McGraw, P. & Schuler, R. 1997, *Human Resource Management in Australia*, 3rd ed, Addison Wesley Longman, Melbourne.

McCabe, V. S. & Weeks, P. 1999, 'Convention Services Management in Sydney Four- to Five-Star Hotels', *Journal of Convention and Exhibition Management*, vol. 1, no. 4, pp. 67–84.

MIAA. 1998a, *Professional Management of Meetings, Conferences and Events*, MIAA, Sydney.

MIAA. 1998b (*http://www.miaanet.com.au*).

Montgomery, R. J. & Rutherford, D. G. 1994, 'A Profile of Convention Service Professionals', *Cornell Hotel and Restaurant Administration Quarterly*, December, pp. 47–57.

Nankervis, A. R., Compton, R. L. & McCarthy, T. E. 1996, *Strategic Human Resource Management*, 2nd ed, Nelson ITP, Melbourne.

Quinn, R. E. 1998, *Beyond Rational Management*, Jossey-Bass Inc, San Francisco.

Quinn, R. E., Faerman, S. R., Thompson, M. P. & McGrath, M. R. 1996, *Becoming a Master Manager: A Competency Framework*, 2nd ed, John Wiley & Sons, New York.

Robbins, S. 1986, *Organizational Behavior: Concepts, Controversies and Applications*, 3rd ed, Prentice-Hall, Englewood Cliffs, N.J.

Schermerhorn, J. R. 1989, *Management for Productivity*, 3rd ed, John Wiley & Sons, New York.

Schuler, R. S., Dowling, P. J., Smart, J. P. & Huber, V. 1992, *Human Resource Management in Australia*, 2nd ed, Harper Educational, Pymble.

Stone, R. J. 1998, *Human Resource Management*, 3rd ed, John Wiley & Sons, Brisbane.

Weissinger, S. S. 1992, *A Guide to Successful Meeting Planning*, John Wiley & Sons, New York.

FURTHER READING ··

Adair, J. 1987, *Not Bosses But Leaders*, The Talbot Adair Press, Guildford, UK.

Nebel, E. C., Rutherford, D. G. & Schaffer, J. D. 1994, 'Re-engineering the Hotel organisation', *Cornell Hotel and Restaurant Administration Quarterly*, October, pp. 88–95.

Rutherford, D. G. & Umbreit, W. T. 1993, 'Improving Interactions Between Meeting Planners and Hotel Employees', *Cornell Hotel and Restaurant Administration Quarterly*, February, pp. 71–7.

Stone, R. J. 1995, *Human Resource Management*, 2nd ed, John Wiley & Sons, Brisbane.

Vinnicombe, S. & Colwill, N. L. 1995, *The Essence of Women in Management*, Prentice-Hall, London.

Eventcorp Pty Ltd

Eventcorp Pty Ltd is a multi-award-winning conference, incentive and event management company that has been operating for 10 years. The company commenced its operations in Brisbane and opened an office in Sydney in 1997. It employs 15 full-time staff. In an industry known for its high staff turnover, and yet that is dependent on the quality of the team to provide a successful event, how does Eventcorp address the recruitment and selection of its team?

The company uses a variety of recruitment methods, such as advertisements in national newspapers and the trade press, and recruiting through university internship programs and via the marketplace through word of mouth. The company has successfully recruited a number of its employees from university internship programs. The current national operations supervisor has been with the company for four years and joined Eventcorp through their university internship program. The coordinator of registrations joined the company after having gained industry experience through a university internship program with a PCO.

Eventcorp believes that there are three areas that impact on an individual and their suitability for a job:
- how they present themselves
- their skills and experience
- the person and their temperament.

The first two areas can be taught, but the key area is that of temperament and this is different with every individual. The company has a sophisticated and comprehensive system in place with respect to its human resource management and the recruitment and selection of the team.

So what is involved in the recruitment and selection of a member of the team? What processes are followed? For the appointment of a new member of staff to the operations team, the managing director and national operations supervisor will meet to identify and prepare a 'job survey'. This 21-question document identifies the type of person the company is seeking in terms of their temperament and personal qualities — whether they are accepting, able to coordinate and have analytical skills, drive and motivation and social skills — and a personality profile is prepared.

Next, a job analysis is undertaken. The key job responsibilities are outlined and performance measures are identified, together with any issues that the employee may face — such as working environment, reporting relationships and supervisory responsibilities. Both the attractive and negative parts of the position are listed, as are the opportunities for career advancement.

From this information an advertisement is prepared. At the same time, the data are input into a computer program, and details are produced on the type of person being sought, and their strengths and weaknesses, together with a list of potential questions for the preliminary interview. The interview follows a two-stage process.

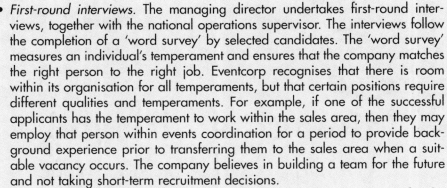

- *First-round interviews.* The managing director undertakes first-round interviews, together with the national operations supervisor. The interviews follow the completion of a 'word survey' by selected candidates. The 'word survey' measures an individual's temperament and ensures that the company matches the right person to the right job. Eventcorp recognises that there is room within its organisation for all temperaments, but that certain positions require different qualities and temperaments. For example, if one of the successful applicants has the temperament to work within the sales area, then they may employ that person within events coordination for a period to provide background experience prior to transferring them to the sales area when a suitable vacancy occurs. The company believes in building a team for the future and not taking short-term recruitment decisions.

  The results of the 'word surveys' are provided to the interviewers for the first-round interviews. These interviews follow the form of a pre-prepared form that is aimed at providing information on each candidate as a person and on skills they have. Results from each candidate's interview form are reviewed, and a short list is established for second-round interviews. The applicants are notified as appropriate. A reference check is undertaken before the second-round interviews. This is seen as essential.

- *Second-round interviews.* The second-round interviews, again with the managing director and national operations supervisor, last for approximately one hour and may include additional members of staff such as the financial controller, the manager of information technology (IT) or the sales manager. Questions posed will reflect the skills and requirements of the job, for example analytical skills, creativity and operational capabilities. Finally, once a candidate has been selected, the salary and terms and conditions are negotiated and they are provided with a work contract. This six-page legal document incorporates information such as the salary, plus benefits for the position, the location of the job, the probation period and a confidentiality agreement.

All new staff recruited to the company undertake a two-day induction program that covers areas such as IT, reception, event management and coordination and administration, together with housekeeping and security issues. The company has a performance appraisal system in place, and new recruits have an appraisal after their first three months and again at the end of their first year. This is followed by an annual appraisal.

The result of the implementation of this recruitment and selection process and human resource system is a reduction in staff turnover, a harmonious office and a happy team.

Source: *P. Holsinger, Eventcorp Pty Ltd*

Questions

1 Critically evaluate the recruitment and selection process used by Eventcorp.

2 Prepare four interview questions that might be asked at the second round of interviews for an event coordinator.

Managing site and
venue selection for conventions

LEARNING OBJECTIVES

After studying this chapter you will be able to:

- establish the aims and objectives for a MICE event

- determine the variables that the conference organiser should consider in their selection of a destination

- identify the factors to consider in putting together a bid proposal for a MICE event

- establish appropriate site and venue selection criteria for a convention or meeting

- evaluate a venue with respect to its site and design parameters

- undertake a meaningful site inspection

- evaluate the efficiency of a venue's convention and meeting operations and measure its quality of service.

INTRODUCTION

The selection of a destination, location and venue is one of the key decisions made in the planning of a convention or meeting. The decision involves matching the goals and objectives of the event and the needs of the delegates to the attributes that are provided by the destination and venue. The organisation that wishes to hold the convention or meeting has to be confident that both the destination and its venues are able to orchestrate the event successfully. In order to ensure that the right decision is made in the selection of a destination and venue, conference organisers continually search for information that provides details of the characteristics and key attributes of destinations and their venues, facilities and staff.

This chapter focuses on the practicalities of destination (site) and venue selection. It explores the factors that influence this decision from a number of perspectives, and identifies the mix of facilities that assist the client organisation or conference organiser in the selection of a destination and venue for their convention or meeting.

ESTABLISHING THE AIMS AND OBJECTIVES OF CONVENTIONS AND MEETINGS

Conferences and meetings have been identified as a means of achieving the following aims (Montgomery & Strick 1995, p. 67):

- to enhance communication by providing a pool of shared knowledge
- to provide a forum for the generation of new ideas
- to generate a spirit of cooperation that contributes to the formulation of a collective entity
- to obtain increased commitment to decisions by involving more people in the decision-making process
- to provide an opportunity to promote the collective aims of the organisation.

Conferences and meetings are often held to create change in the attitudes, skills or efforts of the potential delegates. It is therefore important when formulating the aims and objectives for a particular conference that the required change is given due consideration. The changes that can occur can be categorised under the following headings:

1. *Change in information* This might include educating delegates with respect to new products, markets, policies and company direction. The content of the program might include specific information that delegates will need in the future.
2. *Change in understanding* The purpose of the conference might be to explain or defend new policies or procedures that are to be introduced into the organisation. As a result, the delegates might be expected to

rethink their procedures or think in new ways in order to meet future challenges that the company might face.

3. *Change in skills* This is an important subject for many conferences, for example time management, improving product knowledge and human resource management issues. Many conferences look to focus on skill changes in order to create a more effective work environment.

4. *Change in effort* The objective of the conference might be to encourage and motivate delegates to work more efficiently or effectively, work harder and be more enthusiastic. Often this is called a motivational conference.

5. *Change in behaviour* As a result of attendance at the conference, participants might be required to do things differently, for example how they handle problems or the pressures that they face.

In addition, some conventions and meetings may be held for the purpose of an incentive or reward. This is discussed further in chapter 6.

Before an organisation begins to plan a convention or meeting, it should decide what it wishes to achieve from the event and establish its aims and objectives. The goals and objectives that are set should be both specific and measurable. It is essential that these objectives are defined, for without specific objectives the meeting will have no direction or cohesiveness and, most importantly, might not produce the results that are required. The conference organiser should be briefed by the organisation as to whether it requires the meeting to provide delegates with a serious educational experience, to boost their morale, to entertain or to solve a specific problem within the company. Often, it may be a combination of several factors (Montgomery & Strick 1995, p. 69).

For the conference organiser, getting potential clients to sit down and determine the purpose of their convention or meeting and what they wish to achieve from the event is often one of the most difficult stages to achieve. However, it is important that this process is undertaken, for without a clear understanding of the purpose and goals of the meeting it is difficult for the conference organiser to progress and produce a memorable event that will satisfy both client and delegates. The setting of the aims and objectives of the meeting should be undertaken prior to the identification of the factors that may influence site and venue selection.

In determining the objectives of the conference, thought should be given to the needs of the potential delegates. It is important to find out information about the prospective audience, for example what they got out of the last meeting and why they thought it was valuable. Information on past meetings should be sought, for example what they wanted more or less of, how much time they had to network and talk to other delegates and whether this was sufficient. One of the key factors of conventions and meetings worldwide is the opportunity they provide to network. As a result, potential delegates often wish to establish who else be might attending the event, and the delegate list has become an important component of the conference satchel.

◍ITE SELECTION

In the selection of a destination or venue, the conference organiser and client organisation are seeking reassurance from the team involved that it is professional and competent, can make sure that everything happens at the right time, and is able to 'make it happen' by bringing the convention or meeting together. Thus they need to know that the destination and venue are able to meet their needs and provide an event that will fulfil and hopefully exceed all expectations. They seek a partnership with the destination and venue, to make sure that the event is successful and that the delegates are truly satisfied.

■ **Preparation** *of convention and meeting briefs*

There are a number of factors that a conference organiser should take into consideration in the selection of a potential destination or site. However, before this decision is made, a prospectus or event brief should be prepared. This document enables the conference organiser to determine the physical requirements of the convention or meeting event, and includes such information as:

- the size of group
- a profile of potential delegates
- the characteristics or history of the organisation/group
- the desired image or prestige
- the preferred dates or time of the event and alternative dates
- an estimation of the number of rooms and type of accommodation required
- a breakdown of the number, size, type and potential usage of convention or meeting rooms required
- notes on the times when rooms are required
- the preferred mode of transport to access the venue or location
- the type of food and beverage services required
- exhibition space requirements
- the physical requirements of the program
- any special activities or functions
- an estimation of the acceptable rates/budget.

This document is put together by the conference organiser and forms a basis for the development of the conference. It is an essential component of the planning process (see chapter 8) and is updated continually. These variables can be a key factor in the selection of the final destination, site and venue.

A synopsis of the full prospectus or event brief is sent to the convention and visitors bureau (CVB) or directly to a number of potential venues, who are asked to put forward a proposal or 'bid' to host the event. The CVB will either put together a 'bid' from its area to host the convention or meeting or, if this is not appropriate, distribute the brief to its member organisations (e.g. venues), who may then respond to the proposal. The latter option would be followed, for example, for a small corporate conference of 100 delegates to be held over two days. The 'bid' process for CVBs is discussed later in this chapter. The high delegate spending patterns mentioned earlier in the text mean that MICE business is highly desirable. As a result, one telephone call or fax to the CVB or a venue will result in a plethora of information for the conference organiser, company or association. Because of the attractiveness of MICE events, many CVBs and venues actively invite and woo associations and companies to use their destination for their events. However, the conference organiser still needs to determine that the site is suitable for the occasion.

The selection of the site location and venue may not be the sole responsibility of the conference organiser. Frequently, the conference organiser acts as a resource, providing the information on the proposed location, and the association or corporate organisation makes the final decision. Generally, the destination, area, city or region is selected in the first instance, and then the venue is determined.

■ Destination *selection*

There are a number of key factors that may influence the selection of a destination:

- the range and availability of accommodation
- the type, range and availability of convention, meeting and exhibition space
- the convenience of the destination
- the cost of the destination
- the image of the city or destination
- the drawing power of the city or destination
- the availability of recreational and entertainment activities
- the access to transport and infrastructure.

For Australia, the cost of air transport and the time taken to travel to the destination have been key hurdles to be overcome in attracting international conventions to the continent. The excellent facilities and infrastructure provided, the presence of natural attractions and a reputation for providing a safe and secure environment, along with the drawing power of cities such as Sydney, have all assisted in encouraging MICE business to Australia. In a bid to secure international convention delegates, excellent convention packages have been developed, and can include both extensive pre- and post-convention tours. In their promotional literature, cities such as Cairns actively promote the fact that 'the cost of international air travel and the time taken to travel to the destination are reducing, which makes Australia a very affordable destination'.

What other variables impact on the selection of a site or venue?

Size of the group

The expected number of participants to a convention or meeting is very important. For example, a large international convention with an exhibition and an anticipated attendance of 15 000 delegates may be limited in its geographical location. In this instance Melbourne, which promotes itself as having the largest exhibition facilities in the Southern Hemisphere (provided by the Melbourne Exhibition and Convention Centre) and has an international airport, may well be selected instead of Canberra. Small- to medium-sized meetings (under 250 delegates) are not restricted in their location as there are plenty of potential locations that can host such events; it is simply a matter of finding one that is appropriate for the organisation.

Characteristics of the organisation

The organisational characteristics of the company need to be considered in the selection of an appropriate site or destination. For example, if a company always holds its conferences or meetings in the same city or location, perhaps where its headquarters or regional centres are located, then it will not be necessary to undertake the site selection process. Alternatively, the corporation could stipulate a site, for example, within 30 minutes drive of the company headquarters. Some companies or associations select a number of sites and then rotate their meetings around these locations, thus reducing some of the financial burden, such as airfares, for members.

The type of organisation also is important. For example, a scientific association might choose a particular university venue because of its international prominence in one field of scientific research. Alternatively, if specialised equipment is required during the convention or meeting, then this also can influence site selection. Some associations or companies may not choose a destination because it is opposed to the very nature of the company or association, its business and philosophy.

Furthermore, the type of delegate may influence site selection. For example, a car manufacturer that is holding an incentive conference might choose a glamorous location (such as the Gold Coast) and a five-star resort at the time of the Indy Grand Prix, in preference to a CBD venue in a regional city.

Timing

The timing of the conference or meeting should be considered. A resort hotel in the peak holiday season may not be appropriate for the potential convention or meeting. Whether the conference is to be held during the week or at the weekend is another factor to be considered, with some venues offering special rates at off-peak times. Many resorts and venues in luxury locations provide off-season rates for potential convention and meeting business.

Season and climate

The season and prevailing climate at the proposed time of the convention or meeting also should be borne in mind, particularly if pre- and post-conference tours, recreational activities and sightseeing are to be included as an addition to the convention package. When dealing with international conventions and meetings, it is important to remember time zones, and seasonal and calendar differences between the Northern and Southern Hemisphere and their impact on work patterns.

Holiday periods

Holiday periods are normally a quiet time for conventions and meetings, particularly for the corporate sector. However, certain associations focus their events particularly towards the shoulder holiday periods in order to increase attendance. More economical accommodation options and venues, such as university halls of residence and conference facilities, usually are available at this time.

Other events

Other events that are occurring at the same time in the area or at the venue also can affect site or venue selection. Many destinations actively promote events that are occurring in their area at different times of the year as a means to either attract or retain conference delegates and tourists to an area — for example, events such as the Indy Grand Prix, the Melbourne Grand Prix, regional or city festivals, or exhibitions such as the Motor Show. These events can encourage some MICE activities and provide an excellent opportunity for pre- and post-conference tours and activities. However, the staging of these events can mean that many venues in the area are fully booked, or that they prove a distraction to serious meetings.

As a means to encourage convention and meeting bookings, many cities produce annual convention and event calendars (produced by the local CVB). The calendars list and highlight the main events, conventions, meetings and exhibitions that are being held in the city, together with the date and length of each event, the approximate number of delegates and the venue selected. These calendars are normally produced annually and project the confirmed MICE events over the next 10 years. They are circulated to member organisations and other relevant organisations and assist them in planning their conferences. The calendars also can assist conference organisers in the planning and timing of potential conventions and meetings. For example, should they wish to hold a medical conference, it might be appropriate to time the event to coincide with a medical exhibition that is to be held in the city. Figure 5.1 illustrates some of the items in the calendar of events produced by the Sydney Convention & Visitors Bureau (SCVB). The SCVB calendar is produced annually and provides basic information on each event. In addition to the information mentioned above, it includes contact details for the conference organiser, together with the type of event (e.g. seminar, exhibition). This information is useful for venues and other industry suppliers that may wish to market their facilities or services to a particular conference organiser.

| 27 MAY 1999 | **WORLD MASTERS OF BUSINESS** | Delegates |
| | *Venue: Sydney Entertainment Centre* | 10 000 |

Ms Bettina Brown
Project Manager
WORLD MASTERS OF BUSINESS
Level 1, 69–75 Reservoir Street
Public Exhibition   SURRY HILLS NSW 2010   **New Listing**

Ph: (02) 9211 7467   Fax: (02) 9212 3649   Email: bettinab@infosalons.com.au

---

28–30 MAY 1999	**BIG BOY'S TOYS**	Delegates
	Venue:	25 000
	Sydney Showground and Exhibition Complex at Homebush Bay	

Mr Gary Kendall
Managing Director
KENDALL-RICHARDSON BIG BOY'S TOYS PTY LTD
PO Box HP 274
Public Exhibition   HERMIT PARK QLD 4812

Ph: (07) 4725 1188   Fax: (07) 4725 2343   Email: big_boys_toys@ultra.net.au

---

| 28 MAY 1999 | **KARA MANAGEMENT LUNCHEON AND SEMINAR** | Delegates |
| | *Venue: Sydney International Aquatic Centre* | 300 |

Ms Jane Coles
Operations Supervisor
SYDNEY INTERNATIONAL AQUATIC CENTRE
Locked Bag 2127
Seminar   HOMEBUSH BAY NSW 2127   **New Listing**

Ph: (02) 9752 3666   Fax: (02) 9752 3699

---

28 MAY 1999	**YOUNG WOMEN — NEW FUTURES, EDUCATIONAL**	Delegates
	PLANNING FOR BETTER POST SCHOOL OPTIONS	80
	Venue: Crows Nest TAFE	

Ms Robyn Woolley
Joint National Executive Member
CROWS NEST TAFE
149 West Street
Seminar   CROWS NEST NSW 2065   **New Listing**

Ph: (02) 9448 4429   Fax: (02) 9448 4408

| 29 MAY 1999 | **CERAMIC STUDY GROUP MONTHLY MEETING** | Delegates |
| | *Venue: Macquarie University* | 100 |

Mrs Paquita Farmer
Secretary/Public Officer
CERAMIC STUDY GROUP
PO Box 1528
State Meeting   MACQUARIE CENTRE NSW 2113   **New Listing**

Ph: (02) 9869 2195   Fax: (02) 9869 4722

■ **Figure 5.1** *Extract from the SCVB calendar of events*   *Source: SCVB (1999)*

Cost

The budgeted cost per delegate also influences the destination and venue decision. The corporate sector often has a higher budget per head, particularly for departments such as sales and marketing, than perhaps government and association meetings. There is a trend for companies to request a total price when budgeting for the event. Additional costs such as transport to the venue should not be forgotten.

Pre- and post-conference tours, recreational activities and entertainment

The availability of entertainment activities can affect both the destination and venue selection. The provision of extensive and innovative partner programs, that do not just comprise shopping trips, recreational activities for company conference delegates such as golf and other entertainment activities are all part of the overall conference package that should be addressed by the conference organiser when selecting a destination. For an international event, a number of activities can enhance the overall convention experience and ensure that MICE events are attracted to the destination. Such activities could include holding a Maori welcome ceremony during the opening activities of a convention, providing the opportunity to sail in a square-rigger on Sydney Harbour, or providing an evening of entertainment that focuses on the region and comprises an Aboriginal dance company such as Bangarra.

Transport

The availability of adequate transport and the accessibility of the destination are other factors to consider in site and venue selection. In Australia, conventions and meetings may attract participants from the local area, as well as interstate, intrastate and international delegates. Transport needs must therefore be addressed, air services in particular. For example, consider a site with some transport difficulties such as an island located off the coast of Queensland. Though the island may be an excellent destination for a corporate retreat, the only transport may be a 10-seater aeroplane that flies to the destination three times a week. Delegates may be held virtually captive by the air schedule and the conference organiser and venue may need to provide other means of transport. Alternatively, at a large convention, delegates may have to be accommodated in several hotels within the area, so transport will need to be organised to and from the main convention venue. The selection of a site with public transport, such as monorail and trams, or the provision of a 'shuttle bus' between locations may need to be considered.

THE BID PROCESS

In the overall process of providing a convention or meeting, it is important that a good relationship is built up between the potential buyer, who is the conference organiser or client organisation, and the destination, its CVB and venues. This relationship begins prior to the actual bid, when the initial contact is made. It continues to develop throughout the bid or proposal process and, if the destination or venue is successful, throughout the whole pre-convention planning and operational stages of the actual event.

Within the industry, CVBs are key stakeholders in the bid process. Part of the brief for many CVBs (see chapter 2) is to provide assistance in the preparation of bid documents or to bid to attract certain large events to their area. Many of these conventions and meetings are held by associations and, as such, international and national association conventions are an important target market for CVBs.

■ CVBs *and associations*

CVBs are, as already noted, keen to attract MICE business to their destination — in particular, national and international association conventions. For a destination to be selected to host an association's annual conference, it must be included in the list of potential sites that the association considers. To be successful, the CVB and venues should have an understanding of the association's decision-making process for its selection of a potential site and venue.

All associations have a different structure and decision-making procedure. It is important that CVBs are aware of the variables that might affect an association in its site selection process for its annual conference. Clarke and McCleary (1995, p. 62) have identified the importance of the 'buying centre' (i.e. the number of people involved in the decision-making process) in an association's selection of an appropriate destination for its annual conference. A typical 'buying centre' for an association comprises five to eight people, made up of, for example, the board of directors, executive committee, site selection committee, association president, conference organiser or association executive. A CVB should therefore research its target 'bid' association and identify who is involved in the 'buying centre'.

The decision to select a particular destination and venue is based on the information that is supplied to the association by the destination. An association may review a number of destinations each year; the typical number is six to eight, although as many as 18 may be reviewed in some instances (Clark & McCleary 1995). Therefore, CVBs need to establish how many sites are being considered and ensure that their destination is included in the initial group of potential destinations. If a small number of sites is being considered, then a destination can focus its efforts on becoming the city or area that is selected.

Factors that affect an association's decision to select a potential destination include:

1. *The 'buy class'* — Associations often use the process of a 'modified rebuy' (Clarke & McCleary 1995) in selecting an area for their event. That is, they may look for a destination or venue that 'offers something new'. The basic product that they require is the same, but some different elements are sought. Alternatively, some associations automatically

rebook a location after a certain number of years, for example they return to Canberra every five years.

2. *Risk* — The amount of perceived risk that a destination or venue has is important, and can be subdivided into financial, consequential, social and physical risk.

   (a) Financial risk — some associations, particularly those that derive a substantial amount of income from their annual convention, favour a destination that has drawing power for their membership. Thus, they avoid holding an event in a location that may not appeal to members.

   (b) Consequential risk — many associations prefer a destination or venue that has been previously viewed by the conference organiser or by association members. They want to make sure that the convention will work at a particular destination and so reduce the risk of failure.

   (c) Social risk — associations will try to avoid potential sites that do not have a good reputation or have an image that is contrary to that of the association.

   (d) Physical risk — associations will try to avoid destinations that demonstrate an image of physical risk for potential delegates, such as riots, crimes against tourists, terrorist attacks and water pollution.

3. *Power relationships* — CVBs need to identify the power relationships within an association. For example, the president of an association may just be a figurehead, with 'expert' power being held by a powerful PCO. Thus, CVBs need to ask the right questions of the 'buying centre' members to identify where the decision-making power is held (Clark & McCleary 1995).

■ Familiarisation tours *and site inspections*

In order to address the risk factors identified above, CVBs organise for potential conference organisers or members of client organisations to visit destinations and undertake familiarisation tours ('famil tours'). 'Famil tours' bring together to one city at the same time several executives from different organisations with the support of a sponsoring airline, local hotels and attractions, the purpose being to provide a general overview of the destination's capabilities for handling conventions and trade shows (Gartrell 1994, p. 200). A site inspection, on the other hand, is undertaken for executives of the same organisation, such as an association. The inspection is tailored to the organisation's specific needs and meeting requirements (Gartrell 1994, p. 200).

When demonstrating the advantages of an area, CVBs need to demonstrate ways to reduce the previously mentioned potential risks that client organisations may perceive. For example, to overcome the concerns of financial risk, CVBs can demonstrate how the destination can increase attendance to the convention or meeting and therefore increase its revenue. The drawing power of a destination can be conveyed to association members through advertisements in its newsletter, or by mail-outs to potential participants to the event. Social risks, for example, can be overcome by building an image of the destination as a desirable location and by targeting associations that are compatible with that image. To overcome physical risk, the destination needs to demonstrate that precautions have been taken to ensure the safety of delegates and residents of the area.

The purpose of the 'famil tours' is to show how things work within the destination and that professional staff are in place to handle an event. In the case of association conventions it also may be useful to engage the support of the local chapter of the association in this process. A typical 'famil tour' would include:

- a general orientation of the destination or city including the location of the convention and meeting facilities, attractions, CBD or retail areas, restaurants, and so on
- an explanation of the transport mechanisms that are available to and from the area and between the various convention and meeting facilities and hotels
- inspection tours of the relevant hotels, venues, and so on and convention and meeting facilities
- an overview of any events, attractions or activities that are unique to the destination
- details of any particular selling points of the destination, such as amenities or services, which make the destination unique or special.

When compiling 'famil tours' or site inspections, CVBs should bear in mind the factors that affect association and corporate decision-making and tailor the program to ensure that those concerns are addressed.

The following snapshot provides some insights into the preparation, production and submission of a proposal to host a convention or meeting.

SNAPSHOT
Preparing successful convention or meeting proposals

The preparation of a proposal to host a convention or meeting provides an opportunity to continue building the relationship between the potential customer — the conference organiser and the client organisation — and the venue or destination. It is important that this document, which is a communication tool, should be both customer focused and tailored to the specific needs of the client. As a presentation tool, it is a key component in the quest to host a convention or meeting.

Information on the specific services and facilities that are to be provided for the convention or meeting, such as food and beverage services, accommodation, specific functions, prices, and so on, should be clearly defined in the document. It is important that the client is aware of what is being provided.

(continued)

The content of the proposal should also:

- be customer focused and targeted to the specific client and event — the material should be personalised (many proposals are sent with a few amendments to the standard letter and often are filled in incorrectly)
- be tailored and individual, demonstrating that the company has 'thought about' the event and its potential requirements
- demonstrate professionalism and integrity and be ethical
- demonstrate flair, creativity, innovation and interest in the event and the 'bidding' document
- be flexible and open to negotiation
- name the specific person or team who will be responsible for the event, which enables a more personalised approach and assists 'one-stop shopping'.

If the proposal is from a PCO to a potential client organisation, it might also contain the following information:

- to demonstrate credibility, details such as the history of the company or background experience of the PCO and team, the type and scope of events that have been organised and managed by the company, and any specific experience, such as experience in scientific or medical conferences, as appropriate
- contact references or testimonials from previous clients

In the presentation of the document, the following aspects should be considered:

- The layout, style and format should be professional and may include the use of graphics. Relevant supporting information, such as appropriate brochures, may be provided.
- The pitch of the proposal — the tone, clarity and use of language — must be matched to the client.
- The proposal should clearly address the points and information should be easily accessible.
- The proposal should follow the four Cs — it should be clear, concise, complete and correct — and it should be *error free*.
- The use of company stationery, logos, collateral and other material should demonstrate consistency.

It is important to review the proposal before it is sent, to ensure that there are factors that make it different to the proposals from the potential competition. If the proposal is to be faxed or e-mailed, the layout should be reviewed to ensure that it is of a high standard and that clear copies are transmitted. The proposal should be accompanied by a 'covering letter' that leads the potential reader to the key areas to review within the document. Mention should be made that a follow-up call will take place to discuss the proposal, together with any queries — that is, that contact by the potential conference organiser, venue or destination does not stop at this point.

Source: McCabe & Lawrence (1999)

Site and venue selection usually occur at the same time. The conference organiser will want to evaluate both the site and the range of suitable venues and facilities. In order to decide which venue is most appropriate, the conference organiser systematically evaluates each potential property against their pre-established criteria until an appropriate venue is apparent. General factors that are taken into consideration link back to the event brief and in some areas are similar to the influences on site selection, that is group size, timing of the event, costs, organisational culture and preferences, transport and accessibility. However, there are a number of other factors that should be borne in mind when selecting a venue. These can be divided into two main areas — the physical attributes and the features of service quality.

Studies undertaken of corporate and association planners indicate that the site attributes that are considered to be the most important criteria in their selection of a venue are:

- the number, size and quality of the meeting rooms
- flexible food and beverage and room rates
- the number, size and quality of the accommodation stock
- the quality of food and beverage services.

Also considered to be important are good audiovisual capabilities, the facility to separate corporate delegates from other hotel guests and the ability of the venue to create a memorable event. It would appear that conference organisers are prepared to make trade-offs regarding the various attributes that they require of a venue. For example, if a venue is not able to offer the optimal combination of the required attributes, then a decision is made based on the presence of some of the requirements compensating for the absence of others (Vogt, Roehl & Fresenmaler 1994, p. 120). But what do conference organisers require of a venue?

■ Physical *attributes*

There are a number of physical attributes that can affect the selection of a venue.

Location

As in other areas of tourism and hospitality, location, location, location is the key. Consideration should also be given to the type of delegate and the style of event. For example, a city centre venue, with its proximity to the CBD, restaurants, bars, transport systems and other hotels, might suit a business convention or meeting. A suburban venue usually has excellent parking facilities and may be located near a shopping centre, but if it is away from the airport and other main transport links, it may be a more appropriate venue for locally-based companies.

Convention and meeting rooms

It is important to consider not only the space available, but also the configuration of the conference rooms, meeting rooms and exhibition space. Many venues have a multipurpose conference room that can be subdivided into smaller rooms, together with a range of smaller meeting rooms and breakout areas. The multipurpose room can be used as a main plenary area, or for other functions such as dinner dances or exhibitions.

Aspects of the convention facilities that should be inspected include:

- the number, size and distribution of the conference and meeting rooms, together with their availability at the time of the event
- the proximity of the conference and meeting rooms to other areas, such as the food and beverage outlets, cloakrooms, toilets and telephone
- the soundproofing capabilities, particularly for the larger conference rooms that may be subdivided by movable walls
- the availability of sound systems and the acoustics within the rooms
- the provision of suitable lighting
- the provision and location of electric power sockets
- the floor loadings and entry access points, together with their dimensions
- the visual clearance in the conference and meeting rooms, and any potential obstructions or distractions that may affect the successful execution of the event (particular points to check are pillars that may obstruct the view, ceiling heights, L- and T-shaped rooms that limit overhead projection lines and low-slung chandeliers)
- the availability of natural light and/or blackout facilities
- the location of and access to the conference and meeting rooms, together with the siting of lifts and escalators and disabled access, and the logistical problems of moving people through the building or area in a short space of time
- the proximity and access of the conference and meeting rooms and exhibition area to the loading bays for the delivery of equipment.

Much of this information should be readily available in the conference and meeting brochure or guide that is produced by the venue. As well as providing diagrams and details of each of the venue's conference rooms, such as their size, details and capacities (dependent on style of set-up), the brochure should provide a wide range of other information, including menus for all occasions, wine and beverage lists, audiovisual and other technical equipment, theme programs, accommodation, details of terms and conditions of business. Some of this information is demonstrated in figure 5.2, which illustrates the capacity and details of convention facilities at the Hilton Sydney. Note the detail of information provided, which includes ceiling heights, floor loading, dimensions of access doors and lifts, and the location of microphone sockets and power points. The floor plan from the Hilton Sydney provides a very useful tool for the conference organiser for timing and planning the conference program. It includes the information mentioned above and also details the proximity of the various rooms and potential exhibition space, and the siting of washrooms and lifts.

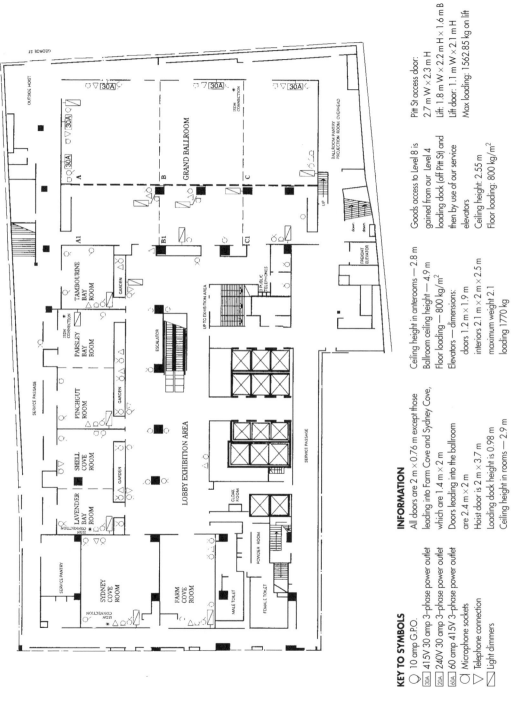

KEY TO SYMBOLS

○ 10 amp G.P.O.
[30A] 415V 30 amp 3-phase power outlet
[20A] 240V 30 amp 3-phase power outlet
[60A] 60 amp 415V 3-phase power outlet
○ Microphone sockets
▽ Telephone connection
▱ Light dimmers

INFORMATION

All doors are 2 m × 0.76 m except those leading into Farm Cove and Sydney Cove, which are 1.4 m × 2 m
Doors leading into the ballroom are 2.4 m × 2 m
Hoist door is 2 m × 3.7 m
Loading dock height is 0.98 m
Ceiling height in rooms — 2.9 m

Ceiling height in anterooms — 2.8 m
Ballroom ceiling height — 4.9 m
Floor loading — 800 kg/m²
Elevators — dimensions:
  doors 1.2 m × 1.9 m
  interiors 2.1 m × 2 m × 2.5 m
  maximum weight 2.1
  loading 1770 kg

Goods access to Level 8 is gained from our Level 4 loading dock (off Pitt St) and then by use of our service elevators
Ceiling height: 2.55 m
Floor loading: 800 kg/m²

Pitt St access door:
2.7 m W × 2.3 m H
Lift: 1.8 m W × 2.2 m H × 1.6 m B
Lift door: 1.1 m W × 2.1 m H
Max loading: 1562.85 kg on lift

Source: Hilton Sydney (1998)

■ **Figure 5.2** *Floor plan for the convention areas of the Hilton Sydney*

The importance of inspecting the venue's convention rooms is borne out by the following example. One new prestige hotel in the centre of the city booked its conference and exhibition facilities to a truck manufacturer for a new product launch. On the day prior to the event, the truck that was to be the focal point of the product launch was delivered to the venue. It was at this point that the conference organiser and the venue realised that none of the access doors to the designated convention/exhibition rooms was wide enough to enable the truck to be unloaded and positioned in the space!

Accommodation

A careful evaluation of the venue's guest accommodation and other public areas should be undertaken, to ensure that they meet the potential delegates' needs. An assessment should be made with respect to level of luxury, location, cleanliness, accessibility and the configuration of rooms.

Other variables

Other points to check include:

- Renovation and building plans — a check should be made with the venue to establish whether any renovation or building work is to take place in the venue at the time of the event, and if there is, then steps need to be taken to avoid any disturbance or detraction from the event.

- Other groups using the facility at the same time — it is important to establish whether there are any clashes in style of event with other groups or perhaps a competitive organisation using the venue at the same time.

It is very important that the conference organiser explain the purpose of the meeting to the venue, so that the staff have a full understanding and can take it into consideration. For example, if the event is to be a reflective meeting and the room chosen is adjacent to one where a noisy and boisterous lunch party is to occur, there will be a clash of objectives and potentially an unhappy conference organiser, client and delegates.

Figure 5.3 provides an example of sections from a checklist that might be used by a conference organiser when selecting a venue. This checklist is extensive and covers all aspects of the physical facilities and attributes of the venue and its logistics. Also included would be an assessment of the standard of the accommodation and meeting facilities. A section of the checklist might focus on the level and quality of service provided by the venue (see page 162). This would include all areas that might affect the overall conference, such as concierge, front office, and food and beverage preparation and service. Having completed a checklist for each venue visited the conference organiser can then assess which is the most satisfactory for the event.

The industry insight (see page 160) provides a synopsis and an example of the criteria that the MIAA has developed to assist architects and venues in the design of convention, meeting and exhibition facilities.

GENERAL

VENUE NAME:. . . . .

VENUE ADDRESS: . . . . TEL. NO./FAX NO.:. . . . .

STAR RATING: 3-STAR . . . . .4-STAR. . . . . 5-STAR . . . . . . .OTHER

CONTACT DETAILS: NAME . . . .

                      POSITION . . . .

                      TEL. NO.: . . . . .FAX NO.:. . . . . .E-MAIL: . . . .

LOCATION OF VENUE: . . . .

DISTANCE FROM AIRPORT:. . . . .

DISTANCE FROM CBD:. . . . .

FACILITIES PROVIDED

ACCOMMODATION   No. and breakdown of guest rooms:. . . . .

                          Access to rooms: . . . .

                          Situation/views: . . . .

                          Facilities provided:

FOOD & BEVERAGE No. of restaurants:. . . . .

                          Style of restaurants: . . . .

                          Capacity of restaurants: . . . .

                          Bars   No.:. . . . . Location:. . . . .

                          Room service

RECREATIONAL/LEISURE/OTHER FACILITIES:. . . . .

. . . .

PUBLIC AREAS:. . . . .

CONVENTION AND MEETING FACILITIES

MEETING ROOMS Number . . . . Size . . . . Capacity . . . .

                    . . . .

                    . . . .

EXHIBITION SPACE Number . . . . Size . . . . Capacity . . . .

                    . . . .

                    . . . .

Availability and capacity of breakout space . . . .

Disabled access . . . .

Availability of storage space . . . .

MEETING ROOMS   Ceiling heights . . . .

                        Floor loadings . . . .

                        Location of electrical sockets . . . .

                        Unobstructed views. . . . .

                        Availability of   Natural Light ❑ Blackout facilities ❑

                        Stage ❑

                        Ventilation/airconditioning ❑

                        Range of a/v /technology available ❑

                        Rooms soundproofed ❑ Good acoustics ❑

■ **Figure 5.3** *Sample sections from a venue selection checklist*

INDUSTRY INSIGHT
Guide to the design and operation of meeting and exhibition venues

Architects and owners of venues who are considering designing or introducing MICE operations should be aware of the physical requirements and design of convention and exhibition facilities both at the design stage and in its management. To ensure the continued development of new and existing sites and their facilities, the industry, through the MIAA, and after consultation with a number of architects, has developed criteria that focus on the design and operation of meeting and exhibition venues. The key design criteria provide developers, designers and owners of convention and exhibition facilities with a checklist of the main elements, with the aim being to create and provide the most suitable environment within which clients and venue staff can operate efficiently and effectively. The checklist also provides PCOs and other industry professionals with the opportunity to express clearly to the venue their customers' needs and requirements for a convention.

Every design element that might impact on the physical operation of conventions and exhibitions is outlined, together with the corresponding design issues. The critical management decisions that affect the serviceability of facilities and thus their attractiveness for a conference organiser are also identified. For example, the external ease of access to the venue should take into consideration individuals arriving by car or public transport, groups arriving by coach and any trucks and service vehicles that might use the venue. Delivery access, storage and parking all need to be considered. The key design criteria in relation to access might therefore include:

- easily identifiable entrances and exits, and clear external signage, which might need to be illuminated at night
- a level ground floor with loading docks of sufficient size for all services, including client vehicles
- doors of sufficient width and height or demountable/retractable walls to permit truck access.

The decisions that management might need to consider in relation to access include:

- clean, well-lit and secure areas with plenty of trolleys for client use
- in larger venues, the loading dock staffed at all times and a security management and monitoring system in place.

In addition to access, other issues that are covered include plumbing, power, light and ventilation; catering; venue floor and wall finishes; and meeting rooms and public spaces and their facilities, services, fittings and furniture. An illustration of the depth and breadth of information for A/V equipment is demonstrated in figure 5.4.

ELEMENT C6	SERVICES — AUDIOVISUAL EQUIPMENT
COMMENTARY: Speakers, audiences and organisers have seen the improved communication that is possible when there is flexibility in the shape and layout of rooms, when lighting can be controlled freely, and when speakers use a variety of media (video, computer, response systems, stage effects, live action, pyro, etc.). All this creates the need for decisions by the venue management in deciding what to provide and on what basis. This element should be considered in conjunction with elements dealing with communications, power, light, production and meeting room services.	
KEY DESIGN CRITERIA — PROVIDE:	1. Flexible, comprehensive and adjustable provision for audiovisual equipment rather than fixed. 2. Movable panels and storage that can be erected easily to neatly enclose audiovisual operator and equipment at the back of meeting rooms (bio boxes are of questionable value). 3. Ceiling grids (concealed for preference) that can fly video/data projectors, lights and other equipment. 4. In-house music able to be easily adjusted by meeting organisers.
KEY MANAGEMENT DECISIONS — CONSIDER:	1. Flexible approach to provision of equipment and services — ability to have either in-house or external operators and equipment providers. 2. Providing minimum amount of equipment at no extra charge, including stage risers, a lectern, at least one microphone and a sound system adequate for the spoken word, some basic focusable lighting, 35 mm slide projector, overhead projector, screens for front and rear projection in various sizes, and an electronic whiteboard. 3. Media splitter box in main meeting room. 4. Providing experienced in-house technical people to set up, operate and pull down equipment if it is supplied by the venue. 5. Providing a prospectus of available equipment in plain English. 6. Maintaining and replacing equipment on a regular basis. 7. Equipping staff with technical and interpersonal skills to deal with clients, or developing a commercial relationship with an audiovisual supplier that provides all services on a preferred supplier basis. 8. Distinctive identification, e.g. clothing or badges, for venue audiovisual services staff. 9. Information indicating safe load capacity (weight) for ceiling grids for suspension of equipment. 10. Swipe-card registration and voting systems. 11. Set-up flexibility permitting a screen to be mounted in the centre of the stage area, and lecterns to either side.

■ **Figure 5.4** *Key design criteria for A/V equipment*

Source: MIAA (1996)

■ Quality *of service*

The quality, consistency and reliability of both the service and the product are a key factor to consider in the selection of a venue. Great service both prior to and during the event can make the convention or meeting an unparalleled success. Poor service can result in dissatisfied customers and a reputation that will be hard to overcome. Venues that have spent some time developing the trust of a conference organiser can lose that confidence as a result of poor service, broken promises and inappropriate behaviour. If these incidents happen frequently, a venue can gain a reputation as being difficult to work with, and this can impact on its level of business (Rutherford & Umbreit 1993, p. 72).

One of the basics to providing quality service is communication. In the provision of a convention or meeting there is a period of elapsed time between the initial meeting and the actual event. During this time, the conference organiser might meet with the venue staff a considerable number of times, covering the initial enquiry, site inspection, negotiation of the contract and confirmation of the booking, to working with the venue staff in the planning and organisation of the event and through to its execution and evaluation. Though some meetings might take place within a matter of days or weeks, many events have a lead time of a number of months or years. During this time, the personnel at both the venue and conference organisation could change, as could the market and industry conditions. The ability to sustain and maintain both the communication and quality of service over such large periods of time is paramount.

The attitudes of the venue staff also can be a key deciding factor in the selection of a particular venue, and first impressions are very important. For example, was the response to the initial enquiry prompt and courteous? Who responded to the call or contact and what was the tone of the response? Was it a standard response, or did they take an interest in the potential business opportunity provided by the enquiry and the event? The level of service and the efficiency of staff should be noted during the site inspection too. Were the staff courteous and friendly? Did they focus on 'delighting the customer'? The site inspection provides venue staff with a further opportunity to actively listen to the requirements of the client, ask relevant and appropriate questions, and find out about the potential event. At the same time, they can demonstrate that they understand the convention and meeting product, for example the requirements of a product launch compared with a training meeting.

At all times, a conference organiser should expect prompt, clear and courteous service in dealing with venue staff, be they the sales and marketing department during the negotiation phase, the convention services manager or the banquet operations manager and team during the event. Indeed, many conference organisers have learned to judge a venue's capacity for successfully hosting a convention or meeting by the outcome of their pre-convention experience. There are a wide variety of potential interactions between the venue staff and the conference organiser during the many stages leading up to, during and after a convention or meeting. These include communication style meetings, the organisation and execution of the event, the development of relationships with the venue and other suppliers to the event and the opportunities to take the initiative or be involved in managing a crisis. All provide opportunities for the venue to achieve potential success or disaster in its relationship with the conference organiser (Rutherford 1993, p. 72).

With regard to the level of service quality provided by conference hotels, the following functional components of the total conference product and service have been suggested as major contributors to the overall quality perceived by the conference organiser and delegate:

- the dependability of hotel management and staff
- managers experienced in dealing with conferences
- polite, friendly staff who respond immediately to requests
- staff who do their utmost to assist the conference organiser and delegates (Oberoi & Hales 1990, p. 713).

The technical components of a conference (the physical attributes, such as comfortable seating, conference rooms serviced throughout the day, the provision of purpose-built conference rooms and the availability of equipment) were not seen to significantly influence the perceived overall quality provided to the delegate. A convention and meeting venue should recognise the importance of anticipating customer requirements rather than reacting to consumer dissatisfaction. There is also evidence of a disparity between what conference organisers and venue managers perceive as important in the provision of the conference product (Riley & Perogiannis 1990, p. 18). The venue needs to address this issue to ensure that it understands clearly the requirements of conference organisers, not only during the initial site inspection but also for the whole process of providing the convention or meeting. This issue of quality of service is discussed in more detail in chapter 10.

■ Information *sources that influence site and venue selection*

Conference organisers obtain details of potential sites and venues from sources such as venue guides, (e.g. *Dawson's Venue Directory,* or the facility planners and guides produced by CVBs), individual hotel and venue convention and meeting brochures and from the Internet. In some instances, they are contacted directly by a venue's sales and marketing staff, undertake site and venue inspections and network with their peers. But is there any one source that is more effective than another?

Sources that are seen as being most useful for conference organisers can be divided into three areas (Vogt, Roehl & Fesenmaler 1994):

1. *The initial decision to consider a venue* Corporate and association planners indicate that factors that could affect their initial decision to consider a venue are a recommendation from another conference organiser or from someone within their own organisation, or a visit by a member of a

hotel sales team. In addition, testimonials from previous end users, venue's Web sites and CVB guides are also popular.

2. *Sourcing a potential facility* The top information choices for selecting facility sites are prior experience, talking to other conference organisers and looking at the existing conference and meeting information held within the office filing cabinets. Convention and meeting facility information available on the Internet is also a potential source.

3. *Receipt of information of potential venues* Between specific events, the most useful sources for receiving information about potential convention and meeting venues are convention and meeting guides accompanied by a personal letter, a personal invitation to visit a facility and undertake a site inspection, and obtaining information by direct mail.

This information is important for sites and venues to consider in the preparation of their marketing and sales strategies and will be explored more comprehensively in chapter 6 and chapter 7.

SUMMARY

Prior to deciding on the destination and venue for a convention or meeting, it is necessary for the conference organiser and client organisation to determine what the organisation wishes to achieve from the event and establish the aims and objectives for the event. An outline of the basic physical requirements and the aims and objectives of the event form the basic event brief that provides the conference organiser with a blueprint against which a destination or venue can be evaluated.

There are a number of factors and variables that may influence the selection of a destination by a conference organiser and client organisation. The professional compilation and presentation of a bid document by the potential destination or venue, addressing the needs of the client organisation, is key in gaining the opportunity to host a particular convention or meeting. Also important are the 'famil tour' or site inspection process, which affords the conference organiser and client organisation the opportunity to view, discuss and evaluate the destination and its facilities. As with the selection of a destination, there are a number of factors that may affect the choice of venue. These include not only the physical attributes of the venue such as its location and the facilities available, but also the more intangible aspects such as quality of service.

Activities

5.1 The CVB in your capital city has submitted a bid to host the annual conference for:
   (a) the Association of Librarians
   (b) a large cosmetics company (such as the Body Shop or Red Earth).
   The annual conference for each organisation attracts approximately 500 delegates. Prepare a 'famil tour' that will encourage each organisation to place their conference with your city or area. Briefly outline the contents of the bid document that you would submit to each organisation.

5.2 Visit a venue in your area and, using the sample venue checklist in figure 5.3, undertake a site inspection. Identify the strengths and weaknesses of the venue.

5.3 As a conference organiser, you have been asked to organise and manage the National Ecotourism Conference for approximately 400 delegates. The event is to be held over three to four days. Prepare a list of appropriate destination and venue selection criteria for the conference.

Discussion questions

5.1 How might the aims and objectives of a convention or meeting influence the selection of a site or venue?

5.2 Identify the aims and objectives for a management development program for a group of travel agency managers. Outline the factors that should be considered in the development of a brief for this management development program.

5.3 What is a 'famil tour'? Identify the steps that should be taken by a venue to ensure that a 'famil tour' is successful.

5.4 What is the difference between a site inspection and a 'famil tour'?

5.5 Discuss the factors that might affect the selection of a destination and a venue for an international congress.

5.6 What is a bid? Why is it important? Discuss the steps involved in developing a bid proposal.

REFERENCES ···

Clark, J. D. & McCleary, K. W. 1995, 'Influencing Associations' Site Selection Process', *Cornell Hotel and Restaurant Administration Quarterly*, April, pp. 61–8.

Gartrell, R. B. 1994, *Destination Marketing for Convention and Visitor Bureaus*, 2nd ed, Kendall Hunt Publishers, Iowa.

Hilton Sydney. 1998, venue conference and function brochure.

McCabe, V. S. & Lawrence, M. 1999, 'Writing Successful Proposals', presentation to MIAA Queensland Education Seminar, Brisbane, April.

MIAA. 1996, *The MIAA Guide to the Design and Operation of Meeting and Exhibition Venues*, MIAA, Sydney.

Montgomery, R. J. & Strick, S. K. 1995, *Meetings, Conventions and Expositions: An Introduction to the Industry*, Van Nostrand Reinhold, New York.

Oberoi, U. & Hales, C. 1990, 'Assessing the Quality of the Conference Hotel Service Product: Towards an Empirically Based Model', *The Service Industries Journal*, vol. 10, no. 4, pp. 700–21.

Riley, M. & Perogiannis, N. 1990, 'The Influence of Hotel Attributes on the Selection of a Conference Venue', *International Journal of Contemporary Hospitality Management*, vol. 2, no. 1.

Rutherford, D. G. & Umbreit, W. T. 1993, 'Improving Interactions Between Meeting Planners and Hotel Employees', *Cornell Hotel and Restaurant Administration Quarterly*, February, pp. 68–80.

SCVB. 1997, *Calendar of Meeting and Events, March 1996*, SCVB, Sydney.

SCVB. 1997/98, *Annual Report*, SCVB, Sydney.

Vogt, C. A., Roehl, W. A. & Fesenmaler, D. 1994, 'Understanding Planners Use of Meeting Facility Information', *Hospitality Research Journal*, vol. 17, no. 3, pp. 119–30.

FURTHER READING ··

Hoyle, L. H., Dorf, D. C. & Jones, T. J. A. 1987, *Planning and Managing the Meeting: The Planner's Perspective*, Educational Institute of the American Hotel and Motel Association, East Lansing.

McGeogh, R. & Korporaal, G. 1994, *The Bid: How Australia Won The 2000 Games*, Heinemann, Australia.

Weirich, M. L. 1992, *Meetings and Convention Management*, Delmar Publishers, New York.

Weissinger, S. S. 1992, *A Guide to Successful Meeting Planning*, John Wiley & Sons, New York.

CASE STUDY

Bidding for MICE events in Sydney: SCVB

Recognised in 1997 as the number one convention city in the world (SCVB 1997/98), Sydney has developed an excellent reputation for successfully hosting MICE events. The city is known for its unique destination appeal and natural heritage, but has also developed a prominence for the quality of its infrastructure and services to support these events. In the financial year 1997/98, Sydney Convention & Visitors Bureau (SCVB) won 24 conventions to the city, which over the next few years will attract 28 450 delegates and an estimated 14 000 accompanying partners, providing a total of 144 050 bed nights and generating $111 564 470 in direct spending to the city. Of the 24 conventions gained, 21 are international conferences, such as the 8th World Congress in Intelligent Transport Systems to be held in 2001 with an expected 10 000 delegates, the World Congress in Medical Physics and Biomedical Engineering to be held in 2003 with 1500 delegates and the 19th World Energy Congress to be held in 2004 with 5000 delegates. The average size of meeting secured during the period was 1185 delegates. These events further enhance an expansive portfolio of confirmed bookings (see table 5.1).

■ **Table 5.1** *SCVB bid wins by calendar year to be held*

YEAR	BIDS	ATTENDANCE	DELEGATE DAYS	EXPENDITURE
1997	23	42 050	239 450	$193 956 000
1998	23	18 900	101 550	$70 802 550
1999	32	45 950	316 450	$174 155 600
2000	26	37 070	178 600	$120 553 720
2001	15	27 350	133 900	$102 295 600
2002	5	26 100	130 500	$101 492 750
2003	7	26 000	142 000	$106 229 500
2004	4	7 640	38 060	$29 134 300
2005	1	5 500	22 000	$16 258 000
2006	0	0	0	$0
2007	1	6 000	36 000	$26 604 000
Total	137	242 560	1 338 510	$941 482 020

Source: SCVB (1997/98)

In 2002, Sydney will host the World Congress of Cardiology, which with 15 000 delegates and 5000–10 000 potential accompanying partners, will be the largest medical meeting ever held in Australia, generating $48 million to the city and state.

In bidding for the opportunity to host conventions and events, Sydney cannot compete with the level of government funding and subsidies provided by many of its overseas competitors. However, the city wins bids on its own merits; it has destination appeal plus the expertise and qualifications to host major congresses and conventions. For international conventions, Sydney is seen as providing value for money and a recognised quality of service, plus excellent food and beverage options, audiovisual and technological support, comprehensive exhibition facilities, access to suitable pre- and post-conference tours, and a track record of success, all of which compliment the professional teams on hand to coordinate conventions.

The SCVB concentrates much effort on identifying new business opportunities both for its members and for Sydney (and utilises the support of its overseas offices in Europe and North America). It actively monitors international meeting patterns and identifies opportunities for Sydney to host these major events. The SCVB promotes itself as a not-for-profit organisation, which provides a free and unbiased service to put conference organisers in touch with the best Sydney has to offer.

The SCVB works in conjunction with national and international associations to develop an individually tailored bidding strategy for each convention. This includes:

• identifying the bid criteria
• preparing a customised bid document
• sourcing written endorsements from key political and tourism industry contacts
• locating the appropriate venues and support facilities to include in the bid
• preparing the preliminary budget
• planning and hosting site inspections for key national and international decision makers.

The SCVB recognises that a 'desirable destination' is not the only facet of winning a bid and that there is a need to demonstrate both the comprehensive infrastructure of facilities and service quality. The potential conference host needs to be confident of the outcomes of placing its convention in Sydney. There is an excellent working partnership between the SCVB and state and federal government, with all bids being evaluated in respect of their economic impact to the city, state and nation. Where appropriate, assistance for funding for the staging of the event is sought. This is an important stage, for the cost of preparing and winning a potential MICE event can range from $10 000 to $60 000, and for some large conventions can be as much as $250 000. Each bid is assessed on its own merits and funds are allocated appropriately.

Over the last few years, Sydney has won the opportunity to host many major international conventions. Once the bid has been won, many associations place a moratorium on the number of years before a bid will again be valid. The SCVB is now focusing on winning the opportunity to host more of the smaller conventions, such as those for 500 delegates, due to the international trend towards smaller meetings.

The SCVB is extremely professional in putting together each bid document, which is identified as a 'business proposal' and is presented in an attractive manner. The importance of background research is recognised, together with the need to obtain government and tourism industry support, the coordination and involvement of any local branch of the association group and other key stakeholders involved in the process. The SCVB is constantly on the lookout for information to update its bid documentation and has an in-house 'bid' library that includes such information as cosmopolitan Sydney, the multicultural nature of the city, foreign language skills, and so on. In the current business climate of speedy responses, this facility can assist in reducing the time taken to compile and design the tailored bid proposals. The SCVB coordinates, produces and distributes copies of the bid document to the potential client; this can range from one copy to 80 copies, delivered all over the world. Once the bid has been submitted, the SCVB will also assist the local executive committee of the association to present the proposal to its international head office and will support the bid document with speeches, slides and video assistance. Alternatively, the SCVB will present the bid on behalf of the association to the major decision makers. This may be a small executive committee or a large congress that will vote on the proposal.

The SCVB recognises the need to build relationships, work closely with the client at both a local and international level and build trust. The SCVB supports the client once the bid has been secured by providing information and assistance in areas such as the preparation of a comprehensive marketing and promotional strategy for the convention and the instigation of delegate boosting techniques. It also assists in the appointment of a local PCO who will manage the event.

The securing and successful execution of a convention is of key importance to an association (as noted in chapter 2). A convention is a means to showcase the local industry or association and its achievements to its international body and colleagues; generate profits to enable further development or expansion; and highlight the profile of the association and its membership, which can result in increased membership and the development of strong relationships and pride within the association or industry. The SCVB, by working in partnership with an association in its preparation of a bid, aims to develop and enhance these benefits for the local chapter of the international association, while at the same time encouraging lucrative international convention delegates to Sydney.

Source: SCVB

Questions

1   Critically evaluate the factors that have contributed to the success of the SCVB 'bid' process.

2   Discuss the long-term and short-term challenges to the SCVB's bid process.

6 Managing the
marketing of conventions

LEARNING OBJECTIVES

After studying this chapter, you will be able to:

- understand the contemporary Australian marketing environment in which MICE industry professionals must operate

- identify customer needs inherent to both corporate and association conference organisers when choosing a MICE destination or venue

- determine how market segmentation, product positioning and product differentiation apply to the marketing efforts of various service providers within the Australian MICE industry

- understand the overall marketing relationship and orientation of primary and secondary service providers to identified level I and level II decision makers

- appreciate how the issues of business objectives, capacity and demand, price and marketing mix apply to select primary and secondary service providers in the Australian MICE industry

- evaluate how relationship marketing can be conducted between select service providers and MICE decision makers.

INTRODUCTION

Marketing in the tourism and hospitality industries has increased in importance over the last two decades as more MICE professionals and their industry partners appreciate the fact that satisfying customer needs is the foundation of a successful tourism or MICE-related business. This chapter deals with contemporary services marketing issues as they relate to the MICE industry in Australia. It is assumed that students and industry professionals alike who refer to this marketing overview have some cursory understanding of fundamental marketing principles as they apply to service industries. This chapter does not revisit the basics of marketing at any length, but rather builds on the basics of contemporary services marketing theory and concepts and how they relate specifically to the Australian MICE industry. An overview and analysis is provided of the major players (both end users and service/facility providers) as they fit within the overall marketing distribution network and structure. Thus, special attention is given to how primary and secondary service providers direct their marketing activities towards the main decision makers who ultimately choose the convention or meeting venue or destination. In addition, the subject of relationship marketing is discussed in order to present a coherent overview.

Since the 1990s, the MICE industry in Australia has grown to become a significant part of the overall business mix of the primary and secondary service providers involved. Thus, effective marketing by these MICE service providers has become paramount to ensure their continued competitiveness and profitability.

THE CURRENT MARKETING ENVIRONMENT

As the tourism and hospitality industry has changed and evolved over the last two decades, so too has society in general and its influences on professional marketers. Primary MICE industry service providers (stakeholders) in Australia, such as five-star hotels, resorts, CVBs (convention and visitors bureaus), and purpose-built convention and exhibition centres have faced increased competition since the late 1980s. Hotels and resorts, in particular, which historically directed their marketing efforts towards a core business of individual business and leisure travellers, have found themselves in an overall more competitive market (Vogt et al. 1994, p. 120). Sydney has suffered particularly from an oversupply of facilities created by a weakening in demand and the emergence of new developments in MICE infrastructure (*The Quorum* 1997). This increased competition has led hotels and resorts to target the MICE industry to an increasing extent as a share of their business mix. Blue Line Cruises, a Sydney Harbour cruise and charter operation, has further reinforced such a marketing orientation by doing the same (Dennis 1998). Because of this competition these primary service providers must market their facilities and services more effectively, which means more effective communication strategies.

In addition to an increasingly competitive marketplace, the dynamics of the convention and meeting industry are changing in relation to shortened 'lead times'. Such changes in booking time frames have obvious marketing and service delivery implications. *The Quorum* (1997) has reported a developing trend in the Australian MICE industry, whereby MICE events, large and small, are being booked in shorter lead times (i.e. within two weeks). This may be due somewhat to technological advances such as greater use of e-mail and the Internet. The marketing implications for a primary or secondary service provider are that such data needs to be updated constantly and timely service follow-up needs to be implemented for all leads, and there is added pressure on related decision makers in organising such MICE events. If a company or individual advertises that specific service standards can be achieved, it is imperative that they be delivered. The use of advanced technology offers both benefits and many pitfalls for marketers. On the one hand, such accessible technology is facilitating the dissemination of product information more effectively and easily. However, there seems to be a growing consumer disillusionment with databases that are not maintained regularly, and with other forms of direct marketing, particularly telemarketing. The huge growth in the amount of related information being sent to potential buyers may be reaching a saturation point with regard to its effectiveness. Also, the cost of direct mail and the maintenance of related databases dictate that marketers must select their target audiences carefully.

Perhaps the above situation is also affected by a higher consumer awareness of the related products on offer by the MICE industry. Customers are becoming more conscious of their product and service options in purchasing a venue and site. As the MICE industry in Australia has grown, so too have consumers' expectations. Customers are more educated than in the past, particularly in relation to hotels and what they offer (*The Quorum* 1997). Finally, as many contemporary marketing texts and media continually discuss, the demographics of consumers are changing. The population is ageing and, as a result, consumers will have different needs. These different needs will no doubt also affect the MICE industry in Australia.

■ Societal *issues*

Society's norms are changing. Within the last two decades, the general population's attitude towards a myriad issues and activities has changed or emerged. This potentially has profound marketing implications. The concept or pressure to 'Buy Australian' has expanded from one essentially centred in the retail sector (with selected products primarily made in Australia being labelled 'Buy Australian') to encompass the service and MICE industry. As outlined in chapter 2, the 'Towards 2001' campaign actively encourages companies and associations to organise their business meetings and activities within Australia. Marketing can be described as a process of persuading customers to use a particular product or service. Various means can be employed to do this. For example, persuading local organisations to 'Buy Australian' could be classified as an 'emotional' appeal (Davies et al. 1981, p. 300). Other persuasion appeals, such as 'peer pressure' and logical argument, may be used by MICE industry marketers to win over and retain customers.

Psychographic or lifestyle-related attributes (Richardson 1996, p. 71) have also changed in society in recent years. It is important that the MICE industry understands and adjusts to such changing market needs. One particular area of growing psychographic market change is in the area of health consciousness. Large and small primary service providers, such as the Runaway Bay Resort on South Stradbroke Island (south of the Gold Coast), are focusing on meeting these new consumer needs by providing health and fitness opportunities for their guests (*The Quorum* 1997). It is generally accepted that members of modern society are facing increased job stress. Support facilities in hotels and resorts, such as health clubs and fitness centres, can offer the benefit of relaxation.

Other societal issues to have emerged in Australia since the late 1990s are concerns with the responsible serving of alcohol and responsible gaming. These are now impacting on how primary service providers market themselves to the MICE industry. For example, one particular gaming venue in Australia now promotes itself as an 'entertainment' venue as opposed to a 'casino', thus reflecting an understanding of society's generally negative perception of gambling.

The 'greening' of products and services will further impact on marketing approaches in the new millennium. Will consumers actively seek out and pay more for those service providers who take on a more conservationist and environmentally friendly approach? Research in Australia is inconclusive at this stage, but a trend supporting this theory may be appearing. Those primary service providers understanding these emerging consumer needs may be well-served to orient their future marketing efforts to take such psychographic changes into consideration.

■ **Economic** *environment*

There may be definite marketing opportunities for primary and secondary service providers to the Australian MICE industry over the next few years. A perceived tighter economic business environment in Australia has seen a trend whereby conventions and meetings (large and small) are of a shorter duration, although only by a day or so. Some are also being conducted over the weekend to lessen the impact on weekday work periods (*The Quorum* 1997). Such trends were also highlighted in the 1997 consumer delegate research conducted by the Sydney Convention & Visitors Bureau (SCVB), which showed that the duration of delegate stays in Sydney had reduced from 5.4 nights in 1996 to 4.2 nights in 1997. Given the shorter duration of conventions and meetings, primary service providers might need to 're-package' their products accordingly, as consumer needs change.

Since the financial disruption in the Asian region from July 1997 to the end of 1998, the inbound MICE market from these areas has almost certainly declined. Those organisations that market Australia, such as the ATC (Australian Tourist Commission) and the SCVB, might adjust their target marketing more towards Europe and the United States. This course of action is likely not only because of the downturn in general travel from the Asian region, but also because of the increased affordability of Australia with the depreciation of the Australian dollar in relation to the British pound and the American dollar. If such destination service providers do realign their target marketing, they will also need to re-evaluate the marketing message being communicated to adjust to the target market needs. As an illustration, in the SCVB's 1997 research, North America showed the highest incidence (60 per cent) of international delegates who arrive in Australia accompanied by a spouse or friend. Thus, from a service provider's perspective, it would be beneficial to develop related activity packages for those individuals who accompany delegates from the North American region. Conversely, for the United Kingdom and Ireland only 42 per cent of delegates were accompanied, so the marketing focus (destination benefits) there would be communicated somewhat differently.

■ Legal/regulatory *issues*

Marketers must continually be aware of the legal and regulatory implications of their activities. As previously stated, the issues of responsible service of alcohol and responsible gaming are matters of increased concern, not only for society in general, but also for those government and consumer departments and organisations that monitor such activities. Organisations and industry marketers must understand their 'duty of care'. As Simons (1996, p. 270) has stated, those organisations that operate liquor licences (MICE service providers) and market their alcohol-related services in an inappropriate manner, such as offering happy hours and lower prices for women, may be seen as socially irresponsible, while also jeopardising their licence.

Government regulations and operations also impact on the effectiveness of certain MICE industry service providers and thus their marketing efforts. For example, the 10 per cent bed tax for Sydney's CBD hotels certainly might affect the city's financial attractiveness to both international and domestic convention and meeting delegates. The Sydney ferry service competes directly with private cruise and charter operations, and has a lower operating cost base than the private sector participants.

Hospitality and travel industry marketers, then, would be well-served by understanding the societal changes now occurring within Australia. Operating and promoting products and services in a socially and ethically acceptable manner not only will ensure adherence to the relevant legislation, but also will perhaps be tapping into a new consumer thermometer for choosing a convention or meeting venue or location.

■ Market *segmentation*

All customers are not alike. Market segmentation involves grouping potential customers within a market in such a way that their responses to the service provider's marketing efforts will be about the same (Richardson 1996). Such groupings should share consistent needs and expectations with respect to the service provider. The MICE industry is segmented into meetings (small and large), incentive groups, convention groups and product launches. Historically in Australia, primary service providers (hotels, resorts, and so on) have been slow to recognise that these market segments have different needs when selecting a MICE venue or destination. Many hotels and resorts in the past have considered groups (10 or more customers or rooms booked) as being homogeneous in their needs. This has been evident in the marketing collateral material produced, with one piece of conference information, or one F&B (food and beverages) price list, provided for all segments, with no formal thought or delineation between each one. In addition, many hotels and resorts have conducted site inspections in the same manner.

To market effectively, service providers must acknowledge that distinct differences exist between these market segments. Incentive customers or end users are being 'rewarded' for their productivity within their organisation. Thus, the event they will be attending is less of an educational value and more designed to thank them for a job well done (i.e. sales targets met or exceeded). Therefore, if marketing efforts are directed towards attracting this particular MICE segment, it is important to understand the customer's motivation and reason for involvement. Incentive houses or planners generally purchase up-market or five-star products, involve peer recognition of each individual's efforts and incorporate elaborate 'theme' parties or similar events to create a memorable stay. There seems little reward for a hard-working employee in booking them into a three-star hotel. With incentives there is less emphasis on actual meeting time and organised educational sessions. A three-star facility, for example, may therefore choose to target the convention or meeting market, because its product features and benefits do not meet the needs of the incentive customer.

Convention group organisers and their participants are a different market segment and have different needs again. They have more need of large and small meeting spaces, hold exhibition and trade displays and undertake fewer social activities. Those attending association conferences are a different market segment yet again. They generally pay their own way at the convention and may therefore be more price-sensitive than those attending company events where they are hosted. Thus, service providers need to not only understand the convention delegate and conference organiser's specific needs, but also direct their marketing efforts towards satisfying these needs if they are to enhance their effectiveness in obtaining the business.

■ Product/services *positioning*

It follows that once a primary or secondary service provider has chosen to target one or more of the particular segments that make up the MICE industry, they must then position their product accordingly. Product positioning involves the development of an appropriate marketing orientation, or service and marketing mix, to occupy a specific place in the minds of the customers within the market segments targeted (Morrison 1996, p. 204). Positioning involves communicating the product or service benefits that meet the needs of the particular segment targeted. This can be done effectively with print advertisements, as shown in figure 6.1.

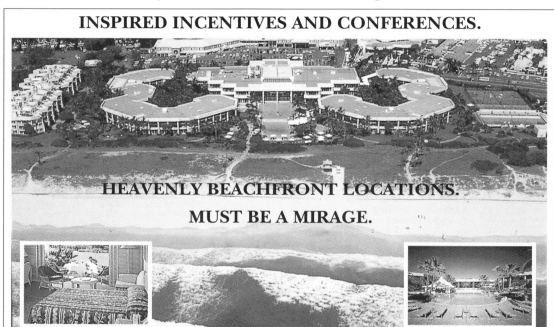

INSPIRED INCENTIVES AND CONFERENCES.

HEAVENLY BEACHFRONT LOCATIONS.

MUST BE A MIRAGE.

PORT DOUGLAS
$**195***per person twin share
GOLD COAST
$**160***per person twin share

If your dream incentive is flavoured by exciting events arranged with extraordinary flair and imagination ... if you picture it in an oasis of five star style and breathtaking tropical wilderness by a pristine beach . . . then it must be Sheraton Mirage Port Douglas.

If you imagine holding a conference highlighted by ingenious and spectacular themed events . . . if you see it staged in first class splendour right on a golden surf beach, surrounded by

Sheraton MIRAGE
GOLD COAST AND PORT DOUGLAS

all the wonders of Australia's premier holiday playground . . . then it must be Sheraton Mirage Gold Coast.

If the facilities are second to none, the food sensational, the service exceptional, the creativity inspired, the venue simply heaven on earth and the value outstanding . . . indeed, if it all seems too good to be true, it must be a Mirage.

For further information or to book your meeting, conference or incentive, call one of our conference specialists in either Port Douglas on (07) 4099 5888 or the Gold Coast on (07) 5591 1488.

SEAWORLD DRIVE, MAIN BEACH, QUEENSLAND 4217. TELEPHONE: (07) 5591 1488. FACSIMILE: (07) 5591 2299.
DAVIDSON STREET, PORT DOUGLAS, QUEENSLAND 4871. TELEPHONE: (07) 4099 5888. FACSIMILE: (07) 4099 4424.
*Conference packages include Garden Room accommodation, full breakfast daily in Lagoons or Terraces, set lunch during conference with morning and afternoon teas, use of meeting room and selected A.V. equipment, valet parking. Gold Coast rate valid until 20/12/98 and from 1/4/99 to 30/5/99. Port Douglas rate valid until 30/9/99. Rates subject to availability. Conditions apply.

■ **Figure 6.1** *Incentive and convention advertisement for the Sheraton Mirage Gold Coast and Port Douglas*

The Sheraton Mirage is attempting to position its product at the Gold Coast and Port Douglas as an up-market venue for both incentives and conventions. Note that the price references included in the advertisement may also reinforce this positioning. Because incentive award winners want and need prestige, creative theme events and very memorable travel experiences, the Sheraton Mirage has effectively positioned this advertisement for its resorts to meet these discerning needs (called positioning by benefit). The advertisement was also strategically placed in the publication *Convention & Incentive Marketing*. The readership of this Australian trade publication is primarily oriented to both professional incentive organisers and corporate conference organisers. Thus, the advertisement effectively targets the market segment by the nature of the publication's readership.

Another example of effective product positioning is highlighted in the advertisement shown in figure 6.2. The rebranded Crowne Plaza Surfers Paradise, also on the Gold Coast, has chosen to position itself on a 'price' or value-for-money basis and demonstrate its convenient location through the provision of a winter incentive for conference organisers. The special all-inclusive package includes conference room hire, standard audiovisual equipment, coffee on arrival, morning and afternoon tea, a working lunch and car parking for a limited period. Such a package would well suit the needs of a more price-oriented client within the convention and meeting segment. This type of positioning also allows the rebranded property to gain valuable market share and continue to build a broad client base.

Positioning the product/service can be effectively undertaken through the use of print advertisements placed in appropriate trade journals. The convention and incentive advertisements shown in figures 6.1 and 6.2 clearly illustrate positioning strategies through the use of price, services and benefits.

Meet in the Middle $42*

All inclusive Day Package. Conference room hire with standard a/v equipment. Coffee on arrival, working lunch, morning and afternoon tea. Free car parking.

Soaring above the Gold Coast in two striking towers, Crowne Plaza Surfers Paradise (formerly Parkroyal) is right in the middle of all the action – a mere 15 minute stroll to the centre of Surfers Paradise, Jupiters Casino and major shopping, and just 250 metres to golden surf beaches. From small meetings to the grandest of banquets, the eight flexible conference rooms can be tailored to suit any event. Call now for the **Special Conference Organisers' Winter Incentive**.

For reservations call **(07) 5592 9900**

CROWNE PLAZA

SURFERS PARADISE

THE PLACE TO MEET

Crowne Plaza Surfers Paradise, 2807 Gold Coast Highway, Surfers Paradise 4217. Telephone (07) 5592 9900
Email: meetings@crowneplazasurfersparadise.com.au Website: www.surfersparadise.crowneplaza.com
Conditions apply. Subject to availability. Valid to 31/7/03 for new bookings only.

■ **Figure 6.2**   *Convention advertisement for Crowne Plaza Surfers Paradise*

■ Product *differentiation*

Product positioning is tied closely with product differentiation. Service providers to the MICE industry strive not only to meet the needs of select target market segments, but also to appear 'different' from their competitors in positioning strategies. Product differentiation can also be referred to as positioning by product class dissociation (Morrison 1996, p. 210). The service provider attempts to appear different from its competitors. The advertisement in figure 6.3 exhibits such an attempt by the Palm Meadows Resort. First, the resort endeavours to promote and position itself as a viable convention and meeting venue with professional staff, world-class F&B outlets, a good location and many other attributes claimed by primary MICE industry service providers. Then it attempts to differentiate itself from its competitors (which may boast the same services and facilities) by offering a leading 18-hole golf course.

We'll go the *extra 6319 metres* to make your convention a *success*.

Palm Meadows Resort has everything you could ever wish for in your next conference or function . . . state of the art facilities, luxury accommodation at the Radisson Resort Palm Meadows, attentive professional staff, world class restaurants and bars and a central Gold Coast location, just minutes from the beach and Jupiters Casino.

However, it's the little extras that make us the perfect choice . . . including one of Australia's leading resort golf courses (a 6319m Par 72), providing 18 holes of some of the most exhilarating golf of your life or simply a sweeping backdrop of manicured fairways and shimmering lakes.

To plan your next convention or meeting for up to 120 delegates at Palm Meadows Resort, or even a corporate golf day, contact our Conventions Coordinator today on (07) 5594 2800.

Gooding Drive, Palm Meadows

PALM MEADOWS

■ **Figure 6.3**   *Convention advertisement for Palm Meadows Resort, Gold Coast*

As discussed earlier, acknowledging demographic and psychographic changes occurring in the marketplace will allow service/facility providers to position and differentiate their product accordingly. For example, hotels can promote the benefits of health-related facilities and activities, and resorts can market the advantage of their location, proximity to water and entertainment activities, or the availability of an 18-hole professional golf course. As more and more service providers place an increasing marketing emphasis on the MICE industry, it is becoming more crucial that they show how they are different from the expanding competition base. Thus, differentiating a product on the basis of service or facility benefits offered will be vital to gain significant market share in the future.

■ Product *features and benefits*

The foundation of effective marketing for a primary service provider to the MICE industry is knowing its product or service, knowing it well and approaching it from the correct perspective. A correct perspective involves a clear understanding of the product or service features and the resulting customer benefits. This in turn involves customer segmentation on the basis of benefits, which many marketing experts feel is the best and most effective manner in which to segment the market (Morrison 1996, p. 173). This form of market segmentation is considered effective because customers do not necessarily buy the facility or the service; they buy the benefits they receive from the service or facility. Table 6.1 illustrates how an Australian MICE industry service provider — a purpose-built convention and exhibition centre — may outline such a marketing profile for its facility.

■ Table 6.1
Product/ service feature and benefit profile for a purpose-built convention and exhibition centre

PRODUCT FEATURE	CUSTOMER BENEFIT
Four separate kitchens	Fast, quality and consistent service for large groups
Located next to two hotels	Affordable accommodation with convenient access for convention delegates
Located on scenic waterway	Memorable and relaxing social activities
Professional and experienced staff	No hassles with client coordination 24 hours per day

One of the first activities a service provider marketer must complete is to put together a comprehensive feature and benefit profile for their organisation. This should be done once the marketer has decided which MICE industry segments to target. Then, in the light of relevant customer research (which will uncover customer needs for the market segment to be targeted) the marketer can effectively position and promote their facility and service in a manner that satisfies those needs. The focus should always be on marketing the benefit and not the facility itself. Compiling a feature and benefit profile is an important founding step in developing the direct sales activity, which is overviewed in chapter 7.

■ The marketing *mix*

So the service provider marketer has selected the appropriate MICE market segments they wish to target and direct their marketing energies to, determined through some sort of market research the customer needs inherent to the segments chosen, completed a feature and benefit profile of the product and decided on which benefits to position and differentiate the product. Now all that is necessary is to communicate those benefits successfully to the target customers or decision makers.

In Australia today the professional marketer can communicate benefits through a range of communication channels:

• collateral material
• advertising
• publicity and public relations
• direct marketing
• direct sales
• sales promotion.

Collateral material (e.g. brochures, information handouts, and so on) should be developed for the specific market segment targeted. The production of a single brochure to satisfy all possible customer needs is not effective. As outlined previously, such collateral material should highlight and promote the benefits of the product that are important to the specific customer segment. However, given this specific benefit positioning, it is also important for the marketer to realise the importance of the general 'branding' identity of the product or facility. A brand is a name, symbol or image (as in a logo or other visual communication icon) that identifies the product or services of the selling organisation (Kotler et al. 1996, p. 283). Such branding, or the use of a visually consistent logo, colour combination and/or layout of the images, is important in eliciting product recognition. As Kotler explains, the symbol of the golden arches used by the McDonald's organisation has established an important and solid visual identification for the company's marketing efforts.

Advertising, as has been shown earlier in the chapter, should also target the specific market segment. The Sheraton Mirage advertisement in figure 6.1 is specifically targeted to the incentive or corporate conference organiser or decision maker, with a particular communication message addressing perceived customer benefits. The company also understands the correct communication medium to use, choosing *Convention & Incentive Marketing* magazine through which to reach these important decision makers. Note that the advertisement also includes an obvious area of general product 'branding': the product brand at the bottom indicates that it is a Sheraton Mirage product and logo. Such visual devices used in all Sheraton Mirage product advertising reinforce in perhaps a more subliminal manner the overall quality image of the product.

The following snapshot provides an outline of the publication *Convention & Incentive Marketing* and its role as a news magazine serving the MICE industry in Australia and New Zealand.

CIM (*Convention & Incentive Marketing*) magazine is a national Australian monthly news magazine serving convention, meeting, exhibition and incentive planners throughout Australia and New Zealand, and has an audited distribution of over 15 000 per month. Readers vary from chief executives and general managers, to professional conference organisers, executive directors and secretaries. The average number of readers per copy is 3.9, and the average reader attends 4.2 conferences per year. CIM states, from their research, that 97 per cent of respondents make the buying decision regarding venues, transportation, destinations and incentive programs.

The publication is marketing-oriented and has expanded over the years to include topics related to the growing incentive travel market. The format of the glossy publication comprises up-to-date industry news, as outlined in a 'News briefs' section. In addition, a calendar of events is supplied, along with an update on the 'people' in the industry and their career movements. CIM includes topical stories relating to all aspects of the MICE industry, both organisational and marketing-oriented. These stories may relate to the Australian MICE industry or to countries within the region such as Singapore, Indonesia and New Zealand. Rob Yeomans, publisher of CIM, offers editorial comments each month relating to what is happening in the development of the industry. Such an editorial perspective is encapsulated in the following industry perspective on New Zealand.

Rob has been impressed with the strides being achieved in the New Zealand market over the last couple of years with an increase in industry professionalism. 'Auckland is currently going through the "do we expand the Aotea Centre or construct a new purpose-built convention and exhibition centre" debate.' He feels that different MICE market segments require different product facilities and benefits. 'No amount of politicking will make it right for an entertainment centre (which is what the Aotea Centre is) to operate 100 per cent efficiently as a convention and exhibition centre.' He asserts that entertainment centres are operationally diametrically opposed to the running of convention and exhibition centres. He goes further to cite research by KPMG in Auckland that supports the fact that a purpose-built convention and exhibition centre is what is needed. He feels the market is there for New Zealand to 'bite the bullet' and go the whole way and build a state-of-the-art convention and exhibition centre for Auckland. 'This done, within five years everyone will probably wonder what the argument was all about — and they will probably be looking to expand it.'

Source: *Rob Yeomans, Convention & Incentive Marketing*

Publicity and public relations are very important components of a marketer's communication mix strategy. Some might say that they are even more important than advertising. Publicity and public relations might involve the production of press releases, product publicity (the production of feature stories on the product in various media — e.g. magazines and television shows), corporate communications (internal and external) and lobbying (Kotler et al. 1996, p. 558).

In today's 'fast paced' commercial environment it is getting more difficult to communicate effectively through general advertising. The amount of information bombarding the consumer is ever-increasing and the public is becoming more aware and sophisticated. The MICE consumer, therefore, may be less willing to believe general advertisements glorifying the benefits of a certain facility or service claim. Properly planned and executed public relations campaigns can be extremely effective in building product and service credibility in the eyes of the customer. This might simply be due to the fact that people tend to believe what appears in a newspaper or magazine as a news story, but not what appears in an advertisement. The issue then is credibility. Where possible, many MICE industry service providers supplement any advertisement that they make with a corresponding 'editorial story', which is generally provided as part of the overall package purchased by the advertiser. The advertiser may set the tone and product branding with the advertisement, but follow it up with more detailed product information, thus gaining credibility with the editorial copy.

Negative destination images or publicity in the general consumer media — because of the credibility factor discussed above — must be addressed by the relevant service providers. For example, poor images of the American MICE destinations of Miami and Los Angeles are well established. These perceptions are based primarily on reports of violence in these areas and other negative publicity that has appeared in the American national and international press (Oppermann 1998, p. 44). In a 1994 survey of meeting planners on the issue of perceived safety of destinations, Los Angeles ranked third and Miami second as the most dangerous destinations behind New York (Bega Research cited in Oppermann 1998). Such negative publicity rarely can be overcome simply by advertising. Responses and 'good news stories' must be channelled through the same media that the negative stories appeared in, in order to begin an effective campaign to overcome the bad publicity.

Good news stories can be an effective marketing tool in the positive positioning of a MICE venue or destination. Such stories contained in media releases or planned feature stories should concentrate on what is different about a facility, providing the media or journalist with an 'angle'. The media will always look more favourably on a positive news item that is different or that might have a human interest component.

An effective form of external publicity for destination marketing is the newsletter. The Perth Convention Bureau produces a quarterly four-colour glossy industry newsletter called *The Perth Bugle*. A newsletter can be an effective direct marketing exercise, as demonstrated in figure 6.4 by the front cover of the spring 1998 edition of *The Perth Bugle*. The primary reason

SPRING EDITION   OCTOBER 1998

PERTH NEWS & VIEWS FOR THE MEETING & INCENTIVE TRAVEL PLANNER

BUREAU TO OFFER $10,000 SCHOLARSHIP TO ASSOCIATION EXECUTIVE

A $10,000 scholarship is being offered to an association executive as part of a move by the Bureau to foster the development of not-for-profit organisations in Western Australia.

The scholarship will enable the successful applicant to attend their association's international convention. In the event that the association is not affiliated to its international body, the scholarship will also cover a joining fee.

The scholarship was announced by Professor Fiona Stanley, founding director of the TVW Telethon Institute for Child Health Research.

Professor Stanley has accepted a role as an 'Association Ambassador' to encourage WA-based associations to bid for their national and international conventions as part of a major campaign to attract meeting business to Australia in 2001.

"The scholarship will be welcomed by many cash-starved organisations which simply do not have the funds to meet the cost of sending a representative to their international conferences," said Professor Stanley.

"There are hard-working volunteers and paid executives who deserve recognition for their efforts. This scholarship is timely and will be keenly sought after."

The scholarship will cover accommodation and costs of travelling to an association's international convention.

Perth Convention Bureau Executive Director Anne-Maree Ferguson said the scholarship would complement its existing scheme to assist local associations in bidding for their national and international conventions.

Under the scheme - known as the Convention Assistance Package (CAP) - associations can qualify for up to $4000 in cash plus further in-kind support.

Professor Fiona Stanley

"Since the CAP's introduction in 1991, more than $500,000 has been given to associations to help them stage their conventions in Perth.

"This business has been worth an estimated $160 million to the State's economy in delegate generated support," Ms Ferguson said.

SOUTH AFRICANS CAN'T GET ENOUGH OF WA

A four-day site inspection for 10 South African buyers in association with the Sydney-based Australian Incentive Travel Company confirmed that the republic offers great potential as a source of incentive travel business for Western Australia.

The enthusiasm of the buyers for the quality of WA product was evidenced by two buyers who indicated they would be bringing their groups to Perth.

The buyers toured Fremantle Prison and the Swan River, met former Australian Test captain Kim Hughes, took part in a car rally from the Swan Valley to Fremantle, and enjoyed dinner at the themed English pub, the Elephant and Wheelbarrow.

Jody Johnson, the Bureau's Regional Manager UK/Europe, said that site inspections were the best way to sell Western Australia to international buyers.

CLICK HERE FOR A DC&EC UPDATE

Anyone who wants to voice an opinion on Perth's proposed Dedicated Convention and Exhibition Centre (DC&EC) now has an opportunity to do so on a unique web site (www.perthcc.com) sponsored by the Bureau.

The site - headlined New Century, New Meeting Place - provides factual information, industry comment, news and development progress reports.

It even allows visitors to vote on their preferred site for the DC&EC - and with another click of the mouse to view a running 'scoreboard' of how the votes are stacking up.

There is a section for comment by the industry, and another for input of opinion by all visitors to the site.

"This is an opportunity for people in the industry to have an input into the DCEC planning by offering their views and suggestions," said David Coffey, director of the site's creators, the Dac Group of Perth.

■ **Figure 6.4**   *1998 spring edition of* The Perth Bugle

Source: *Perth Convention Bureau*

that the newsletter is so effective as a marketing tool is that it is an effective communication vehicle. 'Newsletter' implies 'news'. A positive feature story where the bureau offers association executives a 'scholarship' will enhance the bureau's corporate image. This in turn will hopefully place the bureau in a favourable light with respect to decision makers in the MICE industry.

Direct marketing has become a widely used marketing tool since the 1990s. Direct marketing refers to a form of marketing where services or products are marketed from the producer to the consumer (decision maker) without an intermediate channel of distribution (Kotler et al. 1996, p. 535). Direct marketing commonly takes the form of direct mail (as seen with the newsletter discussed above) or telemarketing. Direct sales and relationship marketing might also be a form of direct marketing.

Primary service providers to the MICE industry might direct mail venue or destination information, such as brochures, to targeted decision makers. In the United States, of the US$2 million spent annually on average by each state on their promotion as a MICE destination, the bulk of this money is allocated to advertising (Zhou 1997, p. 144). Within this advertising expenditure, one primary objective is the generation of requests for information packages, that is brochures, that have been prepared by the state. This type of information request by consumers might be considered an 'active search' (Vogt et al. 1994). The production of such collateral marketing material and its targeted dissemination to key MICE industry decision makers can effectively promote the destination or venue in question. Recipients of such material with no prior knowledge of the attraction have reported that they were more likely to visit once they had seen the brochure (Etzel & Wahlers cited in Vogt et al. 1994).

On the other hand, sending a targeted MICE decision maker an unsolicited information kit or brochure highlighting the benefits of a product or service may also be of value. Vogt et al. (1994) term such a transaction a 'passive' search on behalf of the MICE decision maker or conference organiser. Their research indicates that 38.7 per cent of such passive direct mail pieces are viewed as being useful in the decision-making process.

Direct sales involves a sales representative from the service provider conducting a personal and face-to-face sales call to the decision maker or conference organiser in order to promote the benefits of using the service provider. The result of such activity is to obtain a sale or commitment from the decision maker to use the service provider's venue or destination. This topic is discussed in greater detail in chapter 7.

The final part of the marketing mix strategy involves the use of sales promotion. Sales promotion is another marketing activity where customers are given a short-term inducement to make more of an immediate purchase (Morrison 1996, p. 355). Such inducements might include discount coupons, samples and contest offers. A resort, for example, might send a special limited accommodation offer at a significant discount (or for free) to targeted decision makers inducing them to stay at the resort to experience the benefits themselves.

All the above strategies are further incorporated within chapter 7 when the process of developing a market action plan is discussed in detail.

■ **Overview** *of the Australian distribution system*

The stakeholders in the Australian MICE industry are many and varied. These participants range from decision makers and consumers, such as conference organisers, professional conference organisers and the companies and associations themselves, to primary and secondary service providers, such as hotels and resorts, purpose-built convention and exhibition centres, airlines, tourist bureaus and support caterers. Such complexity is also evident in the North American MICE industry, where 98 per cent of its businesses are classified as small business (Gartrell 1991, p. 157). This complex diversity confuses many, yet, as Gartrell asserts, each entity maintains a critical interrelationship and interdependence with the others in order to deliver the desired products and services. The Australian MICE industry is no different. Because of this complexity, marketing efforts need to be highly focused and directed.

The model outlined in figure 6.5 has been designed to bring some clarity to this complex marketing distribution network. The model outlines the marketing orientation that select service providers might take in relation to segmenting and positioning their product for key MICE industry decision makers. The model does not include all possible decision makers and service providers, but provides a practical overview of the most prominent decision makers and service providers involved in the Australian marketing distribution network.

■ **Figure 6.5**
Marketing orientation model of key service providers in the Australian MICE industry

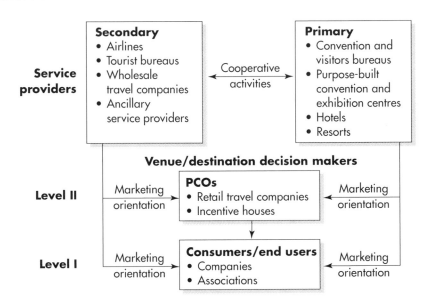

The model provides an overview of the relationship between key decision makers (level I and level II) to whom service providers (primary and secondary) direct their marketing efforts. Two groups of decision makers have been identified: level I incorporates the end users or actual consumers of the service provided (i.e. company or association), whereas level II comprises those involved in the choice of venue or decision but who work on the direction of the company or association. The level II decision makers are made up primarily of professional conference organisers, retail travel companies and incentive houses. As shown in the figure, primary and secondary service providers can direct their marketing efforts either to intermediate organisations or individuals such as PCOs, or directly to the company or association itself, or a combination of both. However, for the purpose of the discussion to follow, it is asserted that within the Australian MICE industry today the majority of marketing efforts are directed by primary service providers towards level II decision makers. Such a marketing orientation might result because of the ability of those primary service providers to more easily target the travel-related organisations that hold, to a lesser or greater extent, some sway in the decision process.

This marketing orientation is supported by a criteria for segmentation choice outlined by Kotler et al. (1996, p. 254), whereby a suitable market segment can be targeted if it adapts well to the following characteristics: measurability, accessibility and substantiality. The number of professional conference organisers can be determined and measured easily within Australia and in key generating markets. These decision makers are accessible and marketing efforts can be easily directed to them through advertising, direct mail and direct sales calls. And finally, level II decision makers control a substantial amount of MICE business and have influence over the actual clients or consumers who may be more difficult to reach with a focused marketing communication.

■ Level I *decision makers*

Associations

Associations are one customer segment that is an end user of MICE products or services. Associations may be small and local, national, or international like the Lions Clubs. Varying in mandate and purpose, they form a large potential market for industry service providers. As outlined in chapter 2, the tourism industry itself has many trade associations, for example AFTA (the Australian Federation of Travel Agents). AFTA meets annually with an association conference of about 400–600 participants. For every large industry, there is most certainly a national or international association that might need to meet as a group. Therefore, service providers, both primary and secondary, can direct select marketing communications to the decision makers within these associations.

Two problems arise for service providers attempting to market their venue or destination directly to associations as a market segment. First, the large heterogenous mass of association members themselves can number in the many thousands. Trying to reach each member with a marketing communication may be not only expensive but also cumbersome and time consuming. Also, a single individual or association member rarely controls a major purchase decision for an organisation (Clarke et al. 1996). Second, they may attempt to direct their marketing communications more specifically to the decision maker/s within the association itself who have influence over the venue or destination chosen. This marketing orientation is directed to the 'buying centre', as discussed in chapter 5. However, attempting to determine and persuade the key players involved can be time consuming and burdensome. Research by Clarke et al. has indicated that no one individual in an association is responsible for site selection and no dominant pattern has emerged in the make-up of these buying centres.

Given the above issues, there are certain marketing considerations to be made when marketing products or services to an association or its members. Price and timing are two variables that might dictate a marketing focus. Association members generally pay their own way and expenses when they attend an association conference, thus value for money could be an important product benefit (Lewis & Shoemaker 1997). Also, such conferences generally take place during the spring and autumn, the traditional soft periods in tourism demand, thus allowing some price flexibility (Oppermann 1996). This price sensitivity has also been alluded to in research conducted by Bonn et al. (1994), who have found that association conference organisers surveyed were more concerned with 'water-related' activities (perhaps as opposed to land-based activities) than corporate conference organisers. An explanation they put forward is that such water-related activities are less expensive generally than land-based activities such as golf. Perceived 'environmental-related' factors such as climate, beaches and swimming also were seen to be important in their research and thus perhaps should be considered with respect to any marketing initiatives directed to this market segment.

Companies

Companies or for-profit organisations are also level I decision makers. As outlined in chapter 2, a corporate conference organiser might elect to utilise the services of a level II decision maker (PCO or incentive house), or they might liaise directly with a primary service provider to arrange the conference or incentive meeting. However, it is felt that as the complexity of conference and incentive planning increases, individual corporate conference organisers, or those within the company responsible for organising meetings or conventions, will increasingly utilise the services of a level II decision maker.

From a service provider's marketing perspective, it still might be less difficult to target those within companies who are the 'internal' meeting planners than similar decision makers within associations. Also, certain companies within Australia have chosen to incorporate the position of conference organiser within their own company if the volume of work is great enough. They deal directly with primary and secondary service providers in arranging group movements. Such an arrangement might have benefits for the company because total control is maintained internally and the process may be very cost effective. The latter case might apply if the group movements are large enough and if the internal conference organiser is successful in arranging price structures at a 'net' rate less any intermediary's commission. Also, it might be easy to access and communicate marketing initiatives to this targeted decision maker. Thus, for service providers it might be more appropriate and cost effective to market their services or products directly to a corporate conference organiser than to an association.

With both association and internal corporate conference organisers, certain product or service attributes have been outlined as important factors for choosing a site. It would be beneficial for those service providers marketing their products and services to attempt to acknowledge such 'customer needs' and direct marketing strategies that promote the satisfaction of those needs. In descriptive studies Bloom et al. (cited in Vogt et al. 1994) found that site attributes such as number, size and quality of meeting rooms, negotiable food and beverage rates, accommodation quality, and quality of food service rated as important in the decision-making process. One other important factor emerged from the same research. Prior experience, perhaps via a physical site inspection or previous stay, emerged as the most frequently used information source when selecting a facility. Therefore, it would be of benefit to marketers to complement their marketing activities with well-planned familiarisation or educational visits to their venues or sites.

■ Level II *decision makers*

Professional conference organisers

A PCO, as outlined in chapter 2, is an intermediary who acts on behalf of a company or association in the organisation of meetings, conferences, or events/incentives. They are professional organisations or individuals who may have substantial control over destination and venue choice and who can be readily targeted by primary and secondary service providers.

A large proportion of marketing efforts by service providers in Australia are directed to these organisations or individuals. The reasons are many. First, PCOs are dedicated in their attention to one aspect of the travel market — that of organising group meetings and travel. Second, they are accessible and easily identifiable within the marketplace. And third, it is generally cost effective for service providers to focus their limited marketing resources to a select target group who control a great amount of the business. As with any customers, all PCOs are not alike and do not handle the same kind of MICE business. Thus, within this target market it would be beneficial for service providers to determine the PCOs' individual business and client mix in order to further understand their specific MICE needs. Then they can orient their marketing efforts accordingly to meet those needs. PCOs are good territory for 'relationship' marketers. This topic is discussed to a greater extent later in the chapter.

Retail travel operations

A travel agency is an intermediary organisation that links travel principals (service providers) and consumers through the provision of a range of services associated with the sale of travel products (Harris & Howard 1994, p. 16). There are well over 3000 retail travel agencies in Australia. The retail travel agency network is made up of a variety of groupings or types of operations. Many agencies are independent, have a small number of employees and are owner-operated. Then there are the larger chains (e.g. Traveland or Harvey World Travel), where a franchise relationship might exist between the owner and the parent company.

Small independent agencies handle a variety of business, commercial and holiday, domestic and international. Chains do the same, but often large chain operators have a dedicated section servicing group and conference travel. Generally speaking, the MICE-related business that retail travel agencies handle is meetings and special interest group travel, with less emphasis on large conferences and incentive travel. Incentive travel involves a greater amount of expertise and resources to service properly and therefore this business usually goes to more dedicated PCO operations and incentive houses. Also, the group business for independent and chain retailers often is related to their primary commercial base (holiday/business travel) and is handled as a courtesy, in that the agency already has a good working relationship with the client.

Therefore, service providers could successfully target this retail segment as a source of MICE-related business, remembering the specific mix of business the retail travel agency controls. It is easier to target the decision makers within chain or franchise operations because these organisations might have the resources to employ a dedicated MICE business consultant, whereas smaller independent operators are more difficult to target because of their size and marketing accessibility.

Incentive houses

Incentive houses in Australia are companies whose business objective is to increase productivity from their clients' employees through a variety of motivational and other reward measures. The travel product is one of many possible 'incentives' that such houses offer their clients as an employee motivator. The incentive house or company also might use other motivational elements such as cash, appliances and recognition. However, travel continues to be a high motivator for participants in any incentive program. Incentive travel now accounts for about 10 per cent of the large premium and incentive industry in the United States (Astroff & Abbey 1995).

An incentive house might design the entire incentive program for a client that wishes to increase its sales and/or profits. An incentive program can run over just a few weeks or can involve a year-long program with intermediate rewards such as watches and appliances, building up to the major reward of a domestic or international holiday. The travel-related needs of an incentive house and its clients is very different to that of a normal business meeting or convention.

Because an incentive program may run over several months — for example, a sales contest for employees of a car dealership — the service provider chosen (e.g. a five-star resort) must be able to provide the incentive house with a variety of marketing tools or collateral material to enhance the incentive program. These tools might consist of special postcards mailed to employees as a continuing 'teaser' of the main holiday to be won if they reach their sales target. Other marketing items are chosen to tangibilise the service provider's product. Special brochures highlighting the luxury of the resort, small bags of beach sand from the resort's lagoon and coconut shells with a special message all help to aid the incentive house in visualising the reward to be won. Service provider marketers must understand the important underlying needs and motivations of the incentive traveller and client in order to target this MICE industry segment effectively. Incentive house travel planners must choose their destination and venue very carefully in order to ensure that the site or resort will draw the greatest amount of people involved within the incentive program as possible.

As noted earlier, an association was set up in Sydney in the early 1980s to enhance the professionalism of the Australian incentive industry, and thus was born the AIA (Australian Incentive Association). By far the main players and stakeholders involved in the emerging organisation were those related to the travel industry. Each year the AIA holds an annual convention where service providers can network with those level II decision makers specialising in the incentive industry.

Incentive houses are an important market segment for service providers to target because they deal in high-yield business. However, only those service providers that offer products in the premium end or five-star category should seriously target this market. Those service providers that do choose to target this lucrative part of the MICE industry can do so effectively because incentive houses are measurable, easily accessible (they can be located through lists and contacts via the AIA) and are substantial in the amount of revenue it is possible to generate. Other marketing concerns that relate specifically to this target market segment are pricing and the size of the group movements involved. Incentive planners in the United States have been found to determine their travel-related budgets on a per-person basis (Kotler et al. 1996). Such a trend is also evident in the Australian incentive travel industry. Also, incentive reward winners might travel in a group of up to 1000, or on an individual basis with only a partner or friend.

■ Primary *service providers*

The discussion now turns from the venue or destination decision makers in the Australian MICE industry to those primary service providers that market their products or services to the relevant decision makers outlined above. The primary service providers (see figure 6.5) are hotels, resorts, CVBs and purpose-built convention and exhibition centres. The analysis to follow views each service provider's 'marketing orientation' from the perspective of the service provider's primary business objective, capacity and demand issues, pricing issues, marketing mix activities and service issues. Related issues of market segmentation, product positioning and differentiation also are included where applicable.

Hotels

For the sake of this discussion, hotels are defined as those accommodation facilities that are rated as four- to five-star and are located in the CBD of major Australian capital cities or gateways/airports. As such, these hotels might target any or all of the MICE industry segments outlined above. Such target segmentation will depend on the hotel's features and the benefits it can offer the various segments, as well as its overall business objectives and marketing mix strategy.

Four- and five-star hotels located in Australian capital cities generally depend on a high level of individual domestic corporate business. This is complemented by business from individual holiday travellers. Each hotel's primary business objective is to attain the highest annual average room rate at the highest possible occupancy level, thus ensuring the highest possible profitability. Because of the expansion in the five-star hotel sector in Australia in the 1980s, and the resultant competition, hotels have chosen to go after the MICE industry market with greater enthusiasm in order to 'top up' their normal business mix with that of meetings, conventions and incentives.

Given this expanded business mix orientation, hoteliers must direct their marketing efforts in light of certain capacity and demand issues. Hotels have a fixed capacity with regard to their number of accommodation and meeting rooms, but they operate in an environment of shifting demand and seasonality. The MICE industry can be targeted to overcome some of these capacity and demand limitations. Shoulder season fluctuations in demand can be stabilised by booking meetings or conferences/incentives in a low period of normal corporate traveller activity. In addition, city hotels, because of their general reliance on the corporate market can experience falls in accommodation bookings from Friday through to Sunday evenings, but they have an opportunity to fill this gap with a MICE market segment.

Pricing can be an important marketing tool in moving demand to softer accommodation periods. Special weekend or off-season convention or meeting packages can be put together to attract such a market. Pricing also is an important tool in the overall positioning of the hotel as it relates to the perceived quality of the product or service offered. Hotel marketers must be careful not to confuse their clients when discounting by varying the prices too dramatically, as price is seen as an indicator of quality (Lewis & Shoemaker 1997). Australian hoteliers have learned to a certain extent that rate wars do not work and can lead to a downward spiral in pricing (*The Quorum* 1997). Hoteliers are therefore offering value-added packages where the meeting space is offered FOC (free of charge), or one room is provided on a FOC basis for every 10 full-price revenue rooms booked. The marketing advantages for hotels in such price and product packaging are that this allow the hotels to perhaps 'bury' their special discounted room rates along with select food and beverage and other service/facility costs into one price, so that not only the customer but also the hotels' competitors might be less inclined to make direct comparisons.

Service delivery issues also must be addressed when targeting any or all related MICE industry segments. Five-star CBD hotels generally are designed and operated to cater for the individual corporate or holiday traveller. If hotels pursue the MICE market, they must ensure not only that they can satisfy the segment's specific needs in relation to price and product attributes, but also that the service delivered is consistent, is of high quality and is compatible with the existing market segments catered for. This means the hotels might need the space and staff to check in 100 to 200 guests at any one time, ensure that their luggage is appropriately positioned, tagged and directed to their rooms in a timely manner, and ensure that the F&B requirements of the group do not take over the hotel's normal restaurants and displace existing guests. There is little sense in going for a new market if it ultimately is going to displace and upset an important market segment base that is already established.

Five-star CBD hotels are usually well positioned in the market to target any segment of the MICE industry and to satisfy each segment's particular customer needs. Conference organisers and decision makers have indicated that the following product attributes are important in the selection of a MICE venue or destination (Cox, as cited in Baum 1990). Location is the number one consideration in choosing a venue. Is the facility or hotel close to transportation? Is it near shops and entertainment areas? Second, function rooms must have good visual and audio capabilities. Food often emerges as an essential consideration, not only in quality but also in speed and ease of service. And transportation access is very desirable. Thus, it is important for hotel marketers to orientate their marketing efforts in a manner that satisfies these identified needs and where their hotel can perhaps 'stand out' and differentiate itself from its competitors going after the same market.

Resorts

Four- and five-star resorts in Australia offer many similar attributes and facilities to four- and five-star CBD hotels, with certain exceptions. Resorts are generally located in recreational areas (e.g. snowfields and beaches), offer a range of F&B choices and meeting facilities, and offer more recreational facilities than CBD hotels. The latter case is due to a basic difference in the market mix of resorts as opposed to city hotels. Whereas city hotels primarily cater to satisfy the needs of corporate travellers, resorts primarily draw on holiday travellers to fill their rooms. Thus, resort marketers' focus and marketing efforts are different because their customer is different.

A resort's business objective, however, is the same — to maximise occupancy and room and F&B revenue over the year. But because a resort's customers and needs are different, the market has different dynamics. Such differences are evident in the capacity and demand aspects in marketing a resort. Low or soft seasons for a resort lie to a greater extent outside traditional school holiday periods in Australia. Whereas in January a five-star city hotel might have lower occupancy rates (a low business travel month), a resort might achieve its greatest occupancy level for the year (a peak holiday travel period). Therefore, for a resort to target the MICE industry effectively, it would wish to move demand to its lower period of occupancy (winter or off-season travel periods).

Resorts usually cater more for the association and incentive market and less for the convention and small meeting market due to their location and distance from commercial centres and company headquarters (Oppermann 1996, p. 176). Resorts might be a preferred destination for incentives and thus might be more easily marketed to this particular segment than hotels.

Pricing can also be an important marketing concern for resorts, which results in convention 'packages' for similar reasons to those listed earlier for hotels. One way in which resorts can maintain some price integrity — or stability in the eyes of the market — is to offer a percentage discount off established room and F&B prices rather than discounting the actual price of the product or service offered. Thus, it is easier for resort marketers to then adjust the discount levels offered as opposed to trying to raise actual rates. This maintains the resorts' 'rack' rate integrity within the market, but also allows some price flexibility in turn, affecting the perceived quality of the product to a lesser extent.

Another area of concern historically for resort marketers oriented to the MICE industry is the problem with F&B pricing. Many incentives and conventions are still booked in excess of 12 months in advance, making it difficult for F&B managers to cost their products accurately for consumption at such a long-term date in the future. But the decision makers must make decisions now and make venue and destination commitments in light of today's budget. The better resorts can confirm and satisfy this customer need, the better they will do in attracting such business.

There is a further pricing problem when resorts go after the MICE industry. Generally, MICE movements involve groups of people occupying the same style of room for the same period, resembling a normal holiday traveller in every way except for the additional support services provided, such as meetings spaces, specially arranged recreational activities, and so on. Resort marketers must be aware that decision makers or PCOs could simply buy, say, 100 package tours to their resort from a wholesale tour operator, at a normal discounted rate, instead of negotiating a similar or worse rate directly with the resort's sales and marketing department. Such rate pressure is experienced by many Australian resorts and professional marketers must understand how to overcome these customer perceptions. Usually, the more professional conference organisers or incentive houses understand the unique needs of their group and therefore understand that the resorts will need to have additional support staff in order to ensure the efficient handling of the group. Such personalised service and support comes with a cost, which the normal package holiday traveller would not be expecting. Therefore, from the beginning, it is beneficial for resort marketers to attempt to package the customer's MICE function in a personalised manner (i.e. a packaged price), so that such cost comparisons are more difficult to make. The resorts might elect to charge full rate for the room accommodation, but offer any meeting space FOC. In Australia, such a marketing carrot seems to occur to a greater extent with resorts rather than city hotels. This might be because the resorts are maximising their revenue through food and beverages and accommodation room sales (*The Quroum* 1997). Conversely, accommodation room rate integrity can be maintained by giving away a free breakfast — however, this option generally puts the director of F&B a bit offside since it is their budget that is affected.

An additional problem can develop when resorts wish to sell and advertise special convention packages. Such advertising and marketing efforts can be directed to the consumer or to the level I decision maker (i.e. company or association member) and can be done through various consumer media. It is highly recommended that if any such 'consumer' advertising is planned, the 'trade' industry is advised and educated first, via 'trade' publications. This ensures that the distribution network understands and is aware of the package, if and when a consumer walks into their office and makes enquiries. It can be discouraging (and self-defeating) for marketers to place their professional intermediaries in the unenviable position of looking stupid and unaware in the eyes of the consumer.

Overall, resorts seem better able to cater for related group service demands than five-star CBD hotels. This is evident because, historically, resorts generally have received more of their holiday customer arrivals in the form of group arrivals by coach, and so have more room to check in groups and attend to their specific needs. However, resort marketers must still be aware of the problems associated with the displacement of regular holiday guests in restaurants and other service areas. These concerns can be overcome with the development of appropriate product features, such as special check-in areas and another swimming pool, to meet the specific needs of the MICE segment targeted.

As with CBD hotels, resort marketers must be aware of the specific customer needs associated with each segment of the MICE industry in order to target their venue's marketing efforts successfully. The attractions of a resort destination for a conference organiser might include:
• a desirable location
• a lack of city distractions
• recreational and sporting activities are easily accessible
• partners can be well catered for in activities
• large MICE groups may have run of the house
• resorts are often well-equipped for handling special theme nights (*The Quorum* 1997).

Just as the independent corporate or business traveller market spawned the concept of 'all-suite' hotels in the 1980s, a resort conference facility hybrid has now been developed in the United States. Conference resorts are designed and operated specifically to handle small or medium-size meetings (Cabanas 1992). Whereas in the past resort marketers concentrated on the holiday market for the majority of their business mix, and topped that up with some meeting business, the introduction of specialty conference resorts may do just the opposite. This trend might also emerge in Australia.

Convention and visitors bureaus

Another primary service provider to the MICE industry is the city or regional convention and visitors bureau. Historically, convention bureaus are non-profit marketing organisations that assist other primary service providers (hotels, resorts, attractions, and so on) to attract MICE business to their destinations or facilities (Kotler et al. 1996). These organisations are often funded through local tourist-related taxes, such as bed taxes, and are administered on behalf of local and state government. An effective city convention and visitors bureau can be crucial to the overall success a city or region has in attracting MICE events. Every capital city in Australia has a convention and visitors bureau. The Sydney Convention & Visitors Bureau is probably one of the most active, due to Sydney being the primary gateway to Australia and New South Wales. The Melbourne Convention & Marketing Bureau (MCMB), with an annual MICE marketing budget of more than $8 million, is the largest destination marketing organisation in Australia (*The Quorum* 1997).

The business objective of most CVBs is to work in partnership with other local service providers to enhance and promote the overall attractions and venues of the bureaus' members to the MICE industry. The key word in this description is 'partnership'. A CVB is a cooperative marketing organisation working on behalf of both large and small service providers. The CVB might be of great marketing assistance to those smaller service providers (with substantially fewer resources) that on their own would have difficulty in coordinating and targeting the MICE industry effectively. These bureaus also strive to support and assist MICE planners with the myriad decisions involved in the convention management process (Gartrell 1991). Two related phases in this process are 'need identification', or the search and sale phase, and 'need fulfilment', or the service support phase.

CVBs are not too concerned with the capacity and demand problems of individual service providers because they are primarily marketing an overall destination. Price is not fundamental to their marketing efforts, unless perhaps the destination in general is perceived as too expensive. However, CVBs can become a voice for their members when government action impacts the price competitiveness of the city — for example, the impact of the New South Wales government's introduction of a 10 per cent bed tax on Sydney's CBD hotels.

Customer research can also be an important activity of CVBs. Since 1995, the SCVB has conducted customer research to identify and quantify the impact of conventions on Sydney. Such research, as cited here, also provides much-needed clues as to customer expectations and needs in relation to MICE services and facilities provided (SCVB 1997).

Other than research, the main role of CVBs is to augment and offer proactive initiatives to member service providers in marketing their destination. This activity expands across all aspects of the marketing mix. One important part of a CVB's marketing mix strategy is the production of relevant and branded destination and service collateral, which might be used by the CVB on its own, or with other marketing material in conjunction with a service provider. For example, the SCVB can act effectively as the first point of

sydney australia

One call to Sydney Convention & Visitors Bureau and Sydney is yours . . .

Sydney Convention & Visitors Bureau (SCVB) should be every planner's first contact point when organising meetings, incentive travel programs, conventions, exhibitions and corporate events in the beautiful harbourside city of Sydney.

Sydney is an exciting and alluring destination which has professionals in all aspects of business tourism who will ensure your event is successful and memorable.

SCVB can put you in touch with Sydney's venues, accommodation, retail outlets, transport, attractions, restaurants, arts and entertainment, convention and exhibition services, meeting managers, exhibition and special event organisers, inbound tour operators, and finance and tourism development corporations.

The success of your event is a goal we share.

Source: SCVB

contact for general MICE industry enquiries regarding Sydney. Figure 6.6 shows the front cover of a promotional brochure produced by the SCVB regarding this point. This effective marketing piece is promoting the SCVB as a 'one-stop-shop' for information for MICE planners. The brochure offers assistance to MICE planners with respect to:

- the price and availability of venues
- the arrangement of site inspections
- the preparation of bid documentation
- special event and theme party ideas
- pre- and post-conference touring options.

In addition, the SCVB acts as a centralised source of information on service providers, supplying copies of the *Sydney Facilities Guide*, the *Member Services Directory*, the SCVB newsletter, *Bureau Bulletin*, the calendar of meetings and events, and the 'Imagine Sydney' incentive industry brochure. Obviously, the SCVB understands that different MICE market segments have different needs, hence the production of a specific promotional brochure for the incentive industry. The SCVB is taking marketing advantage of the Internet too, maintaining is own Web site to provide MICE planners with access to relevant information (see *http://www.scvb.com.au*). The SCVB also provides supplementary marketing material, such as:

- four-colour tour or brochure shells, which can be used as an economical convention or association program outline and announcement brochure — the tour shells include select destination images (and branding logos) and give MICE planners a simple tool on which to overprint their specific message
- postcards, clip-on koalas and posters used for incentive mailings
- presentation folders and destination videos — such as *Images of Sydney*, *Convention Sydney* and *Imagine Sydney* — which also effectively target the needs of each particular MICE market segment.

This supplementary material can be utilised by individual service providers to augment their individual marketing efforts, so it is imperative that primary and secondary service providers work closely with the CVB in their city. The CVB can source for the service provider's benefit those MICE planners who have shown an interest in the city, support the service provider's own marketing efforts with select collateral material and offer joint marketing activities in which the service provider can participate.

In addition to the production of collateral material, CVBs can initiate effective destination print advertising in both trade and consumer publications. Figure 6.7 shows such an advertisement coordinated by the Coffs Harbour Convention Bureau. This cooperative print advertisement effectively promotes Coffs Harbour as a potential and viable destination for conferences and incentives. It markets the destination first, then shows MICE planners the availability of professional and appropriate accommodation related to their meeting needs. A full-page advertisement is possible because of the cooperative efforts of the bureau's members in funding select one-off marketing initiatives. Individually, the service providers would not have the impact or perhaps the resources to mount their own print advertisement marketing campaign.

Coffs Harbour

"Coffs Harbour has so much to offer . . . quality venues and resorts for conferencing, a fantastic range of experiences for incentive groups, accessibility and most importantly – incredible value for money!"

NEW SOUTH WALES

Coffs Harbour Convention Bureau
PO Box 2168, Coffs Harbour, NSW 2450
Telephone: (02) 6648 4767 – Facsimile: (02) 6652 1773
email: conventionbureau@coffscoast.net.au

NOVOTEL OPAL COVE RESORT

Situated on the quiet shores of Korora Bay just minutes from Coffs Harbour. Nestled amongst mountains, natural parkland, lagoons and white sandy beaches, the four star Resort comprises 136 rooms and 38 self contained villas.

The award winning Conference Centre offers seven fully equipped function rooms catering from small board meetings of 5 up to larger conventions seating 550 theatre style.

Direct off-the-street access to the convention centre reduces all the difficulties for trade shows, exhibitions, car and product launches.

Pacific Highway, Coffs Harbour
Phone: (02) 6651 0510
Fax: (02) 6651 0572

BONVILLE INTERNATIONAL GOLF RESORT & COUNTRY CLUB

Bonville International's breathtaking 18 hole Championship Golf Course is NSW's Premier Resort Course.

All accommodation suites line the first fairway, within minutes of the Clubhouse, Restaurant Bar and gaming room.

Function rooms, outdoor venues, floodlit tennis courts and a billabong pool make Bonville International the perfect property for your next conference.

For enquiries or a conference pack Phone (02) 6653 4002

www.bonvillegolf.com.au

. . . Much more than a great Golf Course

PELICAN BEACH CENTRA RESORT

We believe we can provide the environment and service to ensure your incentive visit, conference, seminar, function, product launch or meeting will be the success you would rightly expect.

Consider our winning (*North Coast Tourism Awards*) track record:
1995	Resort of the Year
1996	Superior accommodation
1997	Superior accommodation (Distinction)
1997	Meetings Industry
1997	Industry Training (also 1998)
1998	Deluxe Accommodation

We will organise both on and off site activities. We would welcome the opportunity of discussing your requirements with you.
Call our conference manager
Contact: Neale Barnier
PO Box 6302
Coffs Harbour, NSW 2450
Telephone: 1800 028 882
Fax: (02) 6653 7081

■ **Figure 6.7** *An example of a cooperative destination advertisement*
Source: *Coffs Harbour Convention Bureau*

Direct sales opportunities are also facilitated by CVBs between buyers and sellers (service providers). For example, the Sydney Convention & Visitors Bureau conducts 'Sydney on Sale' and 'Destination One', which comprise one-day trade shows where, under one roof, the various stakeholders can come together to discuss and view new developments and services offered by Sydney's service providers.

In addition to the myriad support services outlined above, CVBs can assist local conference organisers in preparing destination bids for their parent association or company. This can be in the form of hands-on staff and professional assistance in preparing a professional destination presentation utilising the above-mentioned marketing tools, or in the form of financial backing, as with the ATC's Convention Assistance Scheme (*The Quorum* 1997).

The local CVB, then, can be an effective marketing partner for MICE service providers. CVBs are supportive and helpful, but must in the end show no overt favouritism in their dealings and support for individual members in the local industry.

Purpose-built convention and exhibition centres

As with CVBs, purpose-built convention and exhibition centres work largely in a cooperative role with other service providers to the MICE industry. As outlined in chapter 3, these centres generally offer the most available space for large conventions and exhibitions, in addition to select food and beverage services or facilities. The Sydney Convention and Exhibition Centre underwent a $57 million expansion program in the late 1990s. The Skyline Terrace was opened as an outdoor/indoor venue and now comprises a dining and conference venue for up to 250 delegates or up to 400 for a cocktail reception (*The Quorum* 1997).

Purpose-built convention and exhibition centres normally do not have accommodation facilities but, if marketed properly, are able to join with other service providers and local CVBs to offer MICE planners a complete meeting product. Thus, the centres often operate at a loss because of the huge development costs involved and because space cannot be sold at actual prices (Oppermann 1998). The benefit to the city, then, is the overall contribution that the convention centre brings to other service providers in the area.

Pre-established marketing concerns relating to CBD hotels also may apply to purpose-built convention and exhibition centres. As outlined above, such a centre can be marketed effectively if its location is such that it allows easy access to accommodation and entertainment facilities. The market positioning of purpose-built convention and exhibition centres can also benefit if they are branded more as 'corporate entertaining venues' than as simply 'cold' buildings (*The Quorum* 1997).

It is vital, then, for purpose-built convention and exhibition centres to work alongside CVBs and other service providers in close proximity in order to market the venue effectively to everyone's benefit. The centres can produce product-related collateral material that can be used by other service providers in promoting the destination, assist in site inspections, participate in cooperative advertising campaigns and work in cooperative public relations activities.

■ Secondary *service providers*

Whereas primary service providers are perhaps more directly reliant on the revenue generated by the emerging MICE industry, secondary service providers such as airlines, tourist bureaus, wholesale travel companies and ancillary service providers also play an important part in the marketing and product distribution network (refer back to figure 6.5). Secondary service providers in Australia rarely market their products or services directly to level I decision makers, but often work on behalf of level II decision makers in a cooperative effort with primary service providers.

Airlines

As perhaps the main transportation vehicle for the MICE industry in Australia, the business objective of the airlines is to maximise revenue or yield from each flight, as well as to maximise the load factor (the number of people on a flight as a percentage of overall capacity). The two main domestic/international airlines operating in Australia today are Ansett Australia/Ansett International and Qantas. Both commercial air carriers rely on a broad-based mix of business to operate profitably, and this business mix is divided mainly between individual business customers and holiday/VFR (visiting friends and relatives) customers. However, each airline does and will cater for the transportation needs of the MICE industry. As secondary service providers, Australian domestic airlines do not market and promote their services as aggressively as primary service providers to the MICE industry. Therefore, they have different marketing concerns and strategies to primary service providers with regard to servicing and selling to the MICE industry.

In relation to capacity and demand issues, historically airlines have viewed all MICE segment business as the same — that is, simply a group movement (a minimum of 10 passengers travelling together). From a marketing perspective, Australian domestic airlines really do not need to know the ultimate aims of the groups they are transporting or why they are there — only that they must be transported in an efficient and timely manner within the operators' budget constraints. Although, having noted this, it might be appropriate for the airlines involved to work towards developing suitable incentive marketing collateral to augment that of the incentive houses or PCOs; but only if the airlines can offer the customers tangible service options relating to their specific needs.

It is important for primary service providers and level II decision makers to understand how the airlines' capacity and demand constraints can impact on their own marketing efforts. There is little sense, for example, in a regional Northern Territory resort successfully bidding for an 800-person incentive movement if the transportation option (the domestic airline) cannot effectively move the people to the destination in a timely and economical manner.

The largest seat capacities for Australian domestic airlines are available between capital cities and major resort centres. Yet, even on such high-capacity routes demand problems can occur. Airlines might be hesitant to commit an entire aircraft to one single passenger group for two reasons. First, the load factor on the return journey might be adversely affected by the onward group, and second, airline seats are a perishable product and might be difficult to resell if the group reduces in size or cancels. As a result, airlines enforce very specific carriage restrictions and cancellation fees on group movements. Capacity also can be affected by the destination's seasonality. School holiday periods in Australia not only restrict the availability of ground services and accommodation, but also seat availability on aircraft.

Such capacity/demand concerns can lead to corresponding pricing issues for airlines. Airlines' capacity control the types of airfares offered on any one flight by limiting the number of discount seats available, primarily in the economy or coach section of the aircraft, which makes up the majority of seats offered on any one flight. This capacity and price control is coordinated through a 'yield management' program. Yield management effectively manages revenue and inventory by pricing differences on the elasticity of demand (Kotler et al. 1996). An effective yield management program might establish fences to prohibit customers from one segment receiving prices intended for another. From an airline perspective this means, for example, that business travellers might pay a premium price because they book their seats at the last moment and require flexibility in changing their flight plans. On the other hand, MICE travellers might pay much lower fares because they have more time to plan and can commit to predetermined travel dates set well in advance and accept strict amendment penalties. However, such lower 'group' or MICE-related airfares are often limited, so that the airline does not discount too many seats on any one flight. Such a situation can be avoided by chartering the entire aircraft for sole use by the MICE customers, but this option is limited, for the reasons noted above. Thus, the marketing implications for MICE movements relating to price can be either supported or restrained by the airlines' yield management system and the size/type of aircraft available on any given route.

It is therefore appropriate for both level II decision makers and primary service providers to be aware of the service and marketing limitations relating to the air transportation of MICE customers.

Both Qantas and Ansett Australia operate special 'group' reservation services to assist in the planning of such movements. Both airlines also understand the special service handling aspects of MICE customers, offering special 'group check-in' areas at all domestic airports along with priority tagging and handling of luggage.

A cooperative marketing exercise with an airline might be an appropriate strategy to pursue even given the above issues. For example, a MICE service provider interested in the in-bound international MICE market might conduct joint marketing activities with Qantas. Qantas flew 42 per cent of the delegates to Australia in 1997 (SCVB 1997) — up substantially from 33 per cent in 1996. Qantas also flew 59 per cent of these delegates to their pre/post-conference destination. The closest international airline was Singapore Airlines, which carried 9 per cent of delegates in 1997. It should be noted that Ansett International had not entered the Asian international market at the time of the survey.

Tourist bureaus

As with city convention and visitors bureaus, Australian regional areas operate tourist information bureaus and centres as part of the overall regional tourism areas or organisations. Such centres usually are funded by local and state government, but also may incorporate revenue-generating operations such as accommodation booking services.

The South Australian region, for example, is broken down into five separate tourist regions, each with a dedicated manager (Richardson 1996). The managers provide marketing support and liaise with both local tourism operators and government. Each region is provided with funding that must be matched dollar for dollar by the local tourist association in support of the region's marketing efforts. This allows smaller regional service providers an opportunity to broaden their individual MICE marketing efforts in coordination with their local tourist association.

Wholesale travel operations

Wholesale travel operations are also known as tour operators. The term is applied to organisations that package other people's (i.e. service providers) products such as accommodation, transportation, food services, attractions, and so on (Richardson 1996). Tour operators range from small owner-operated coach companies that organise local weekend special group tours to large airline-owned tour operators dealing with both domestic and inbound/outbound international group movements.

Tour operators are the intermediaries in the Australian travel network, liaising between the principals of the industry (i.e. hotels, resorts, airlines) and the retail travel agency distribution network. Their product generally comprises destination brochures offering a packaged range of holidays incorporating transportation to and from the city of origin, ground transfers and accommodation. These brochures are displayed and promoted through select retail travel outlets throughout Australia, which in turn are accessible to the consumer.

Tour operators, then, are able to buy rooms, airline seats and local tours in bulk and therefore at a price advantage not usually available to the consumer or retail travel agency. The tour operators usually will only market their packages through the retail travel network, which in turn may use such products as an easy, affordable, off-the-shelf package for small- or medium-sized MICE groups. This can prove to be an effective way for small retail travel agencies or individual PCOs, which normally would not enjoy any special discount access to service providers, to service the MICE market. However, as noted earlier, primary service providers such as resorts and hotels might be hesitant towards such arrangements, due to the dilution of their revenue via the tour operator intermediaries.

The majority of Australian tour operators do not direct their marketing focus especially to the MICE industry, although they may handle related business in cooperation with level II decision makers. Tour operators today are for the most part owned and operated by the airlines. Over the last two decades the airlines, both domestic and international, have enhanced their vertical sales distribution network by purchasing or developing their own wholesale travel operations. They have done so primarily in order to control the choice of transportation company in the product mix of packaged holidays. Thus, Ansett Holidays is a subsidiary of Ansett Australia, Jetabout Holidays operates with Qantas as the parent company, and Malaysian Airlines operates with MAS Golden Holidays.

The primary focus of these tour operators is to cover operating costs and ensure a continued flow of passengers for the owner airline. They do this by focusing their marketing efforts towards the retail travel agency network, which acts as their agent to the population in general.

Small level II decision makers might therefore work in cooperation with a wholesale tour operator in marketing and designing a MICE event. The tour operator might have access to specific destination information, support services, entertainment and transportation options, and supporting collateral material that will assist the PCO or travel agent. The tour operator also might provide substantial benefits to the small PCO and travel agent with the service delivery of the MICE event. The tour operator can handle the booking of all airline seats, ground transfers and initial room blocks, allowing the PCO or retail agent to work on other less core issues regarding the MICE event.

Ancillary service providers

Ancillary service providers offer a vital component to the successful running of a MICE event. They provide tours and transportation, tour escorts and guides, sporting activities, theme parties, flowers, speakers, entertainment, audiovisual equipment and all the other parts that go together to make up the whole event (Weirich 1992). These ancillary service providers have enormous potential to make the MICE event either very successful or a disaster. So, it is imperative that the primary service provider marketing the event or venue ensures that such suppliers are not only efficient but also capable of delivering on the marketing and service standard promises made.

Working together with a focused marketing orientation, these suppliers can support and complement the primary service provider's marketing efforts. This can be achieved by the supplier assisting the marketer in tangibilising its product for the decision maker. If the supplier is a food and beverage operation, for example, it might provide samples of select unique food items presented in 'theme' costumes by the theme company, in a joint marketing initiative with the service provider. Relationship marketing, which is discussed in the next section, means having not only an effective relationship with the decision makers to whom you are directing your marketing efforts, but also a sound marketing relationship with your support service providers.

Because of the inherent complexity of the Australian MICE industry and the stakeholders involved, it is important for primary service providers to target their marketing efforts effectively towards those decision makers deemed to return the highest benefits. Marketing today has changed its focus from maximising the profit on each individual transaction to maximising mutually beneficial relationships with consumers and other parties (Kotler et al. 1996). Therefore, the focus is on building good relationships, which will in turn generate profitable transactions. Such an orientation is based on the premise that a small proportion of customers can account for a large share of the service provider's sales.

Kotler (1996) has outlined and distinguished five different levels of relationships that can be applied to the MICE industry:

- *basic* — the service provider sells the service or product but does not conduct any post-sales follow-up with the customer
- *reactive* — the service provider provides the service or product and encourages the customer to call if they have any questions
- *accountable* — the service provider follows up after the sale to solicit service delivery and product quality feedback
- *pro-active* — the service provider follows up with the customer on a regular basis to obtain consistent product or service feedback
- *partnership* — the service provider works continuously with the customer and with other customers to discover ways to deliver better value.

How, then, do select primary and secondary MICE industry service providers develop the most beneficial relationships (pro-active and partnership) with key level I and II decision makers? In the case of primary service providers such as hotel and resorts, various relationship marketing strategies must be developed. However, individual hotels and resorts will rarely accommodate the same conference or incentive group each year, although they might host small meetings on a continual basis. With respect to large group movements such as incentives, an individual venue would rarely host the same group twice in a row, but more likely several years apart. Therefore, it is difficult for an individual venue's marketing staff to develop such pro-active long-term relationships with its end users or customers.

Thus, from a hotel or resort perspective, the strategic marketing 'relationship' must be arranged by the corporate or hotel regional office. Many of the hotel and resort management companies or chains operating in Australia operate a capital city regional marketing office or offices. These regional offices might incorporate the chain's dedicated reservation office for Australia, national operations support staff, and domestic and international corporate sales and marketing staff. It is the role of these regional office marketing and sales staff — who are not tied to any one specific chain venue and who are well placed to develop relationships with select level I and II MICE decision makers — to foster such beneficial relationships. These 'corporate'-based marketing staff can then develop long-term personal relationships with individual PCOs, retail group consultants and incentive houses in their geographic region, and can thus promote all the chain's hotels or resorts. For example, a PCO might develop a close working relationship with Sheraton corporate marketing staff, and arrange to send an incentive group to the Sheraton Port Douglas one year, and then to the Sheraton in Sydney the following year.

CVBs can have the same problems as individual venues in developing these strategic marketing relationships. Thus, CVBs might work in cooperation with other destination marketing organisations, such as the ATC, in generating leads and sales opportunities. In this situation, it is assumed that the ATC office has already developed such a relationship with MICE decision makers in its respective geographic area.

Airlines are in a similar position to that of hotel chain regional offices in developing relationships with select level I and II decision makers. The main Australian domestic airlines, Ansett Australia and Qantas, generally have state sales offices that have such a responsibility. The state-based airline marketing staff build relationships with the level I and II decision makers in their respective geographic territory or city. The goal of such relationships is to ensure that, whenever possible, the PCO or incentive house uses the service provider's airline when moving any MICE groups.

The foundation of relationship marketing, then, is the premise that a company should not try to pursue and attract every customer, but build strong strategic relationships with those seen as the most profitable in the long term. Many companies discover that between 20 and 40 per cent of their customers are unprofitable (Kotler et al. 1996). Also, the largest customers might not be the most profitable. Large customers might require more client servicing and be more demanding in price considerations, and small customers might be too small to cover related servicing costs, so the medium-sized customers might be the service provider's most profitable, and those with whom it should look at building long-term relationships.

The marketing orientation incorporated by a MICE service provider therefore should include those decision makers with whom a strategic relationship can be developed. In so doing, the service provider will better understand the basis of the marketing concept — that is, understanding customer needs. The fulfilment of these relationships is accomplished by marketing professionals who then spend years becoming familiar with and developing a rapport among such decision makers (Gartrell 1991). Building relationships then becomes the foundation for mutual problem solving.

The role and responsibilities of the director of marketing for the Marriott Surfers Paradise Resort are illustrated in the following industry insight. The MICE sector is a key area of the resort's business activities, and relationship marketing is very important.

Lindsay Wallace is the director of marketing for the Marriott Surfers Paradise Resort, Gold Coast. Opened in May 1992, the 330-room deluxe resort property caters to leisure guests and conference and incentive attendees. The resort has won three Tourism Queensland awards, the AHA (Australian Hotel Association) Best Marketed Hotel Award (in 1996), and continues to be recognised with the Marriott Corporate Award for customer service and satisfaction.

In her position as director of marketing for the resort, Lindsay has overall responsibility for the international sales team, catering sales, reservations, convention services and public relations efforts, which involves managing 22 staff. In addition, she and her team prepare the resort's business plan each year, as well as quarterly updates and monthly marketing reports. Lindsay has held her current position at the resort since 1994. Prior to this, she was the director of sales for the resort and has worked in similar areas for Sheraton, Holiday Inn and the Gold Coast Visitors and Convention Bureau. She holds a Bachelor of Business degree in Hospitality Management from the University of Queensland.

In relation to targeting the MICE industry, Lindsay states that she and her marketing team drive sales through relationship marketing, 'we concentrate our financial resources on our sales and convention service management staff as this customer "buys" through trust, image and friendship rather than just price, location and availability'. The majority of MICE-related marketing funds are spent on the production of the resort's dedicated conference and incentive planner, which is sent with proposals to customers. The planner details the attributes of the destination and the resort, and provides specific details pertaining to the resort's services, facilities, venue capacities, menus, activities and audiovisual capabilities, and any other information required by the conference organiser.

The Marriott Surfers Paradise Resorts target MICE niche markets have been identified through market analysis and research. For example, one MICE niche market that the resort targets is the medical and pharmaceutical meeting market. This is due to their year-round meeting patterns, mix of corporate and association events that provide demand across seven days a week, and the fact that this market segment travels with families who enjoy the resort facilities while the professional participants attend the educational sessions.

Overall, minimal marketing funds are allocated to advertising to the MICE industry in general. Funding that is set aside is spent on venue directories such as the regional meeting planner, and periodic feature inclusions in specific meeting and incentive publications and niche publications that target the event planner within the specific industry identified.

Source: *Lindsay Wallace, Marriott Surfers Paradise Resort*

Marketing in the MICE industry has increased in importance over the last two decades as the industry has developed. MICE service providers face increased competition at a time when customer expectations and product knowledge are increasing. The dynamics of the industry are changing as it is impacted by the numerous societal, economic and legal/regulatory changes taking place in today's marketplace, concerning issues such as 'health consciousness', the responsible serving of alcohol, responsible gaming and the 'greening' of the industry.

All MICE customers are not alike, and to market effectively, service providers need to be aware of the distinct differences that exist between the market segments and to understand the specific needs of each of these market segments. Once MICE service providers have chosen which market segments they wish to target, they must position their product accordingly. To be successful, they also need to differentiate their product from the competition.

The stakeholders in the MICE industry are many and varied, so marketing efforts need to be highly focused and directed. Two levels of decision makers can be identified (level I and level II), to whom primary and secondary service providers direct their marketing efforts. Primary service providers generally direct their marketing efforts towards level II decision makers, who are easily accessible and control a substantial amount of MICE business. Secondary service providers often work on behalf of level II decision makers in a cooperative effort with primary service providers. Each service provider's marketing orientation can be viewed from the perspective of its primary business objective, capacity and demand issues, pricing issues, marketing mix activities and service related issues.

Marketing today has changed its focus from maximising the profit on each individual transaction to maximising mutually beneficial relationships with consumers and other parties. Such relationship marketing activities are an effective way in which to maintain the most profitable customer base through corporate oriented marketing strategies.

Activity

6.1 Choose a service provider in your area or one with which you are familiar and explain how societal changes evident in today's external environment will impact on its promotional and marketing strategies.

Discussion questions

6.1 How do association and corporate conference organisers differ in their needs with respect to the choice of a MICE venue or destination?

6.2 What is the relationship between level I decision makers and level II decision makers?

6.3 What is the marketing relationship between primary and secondary service providers to the MICE industry?

6.4 Explain the capacity and demand issues and pricing issues that confront a resort in its efforts to market its product and service effectively to the MICE industry.

6.5 What marketing assistance do CVBs provide to level II decision makers in their efforts to market a destination or venue successfully ?

6.6 What role do wholesale travel organisations (tour operators) play in marketing a MICE event?

6.7 What are the primary concerns of an airline in dealing with the transportation of MICE groups?

6.8 How can ancillary service providers assist the marketing efforts of primary service providers in tangibilising their product or service for MICE decision makers?

6.9 What is relationship marketing and how can it be used effectively by a primary service provider to enhance its strategic marketing goals?

REFERENCES

Astroff, M. & Abbey, J. 1995, *Convention Sales and Services*, 4th ed, September/October, pp. 61–2, Waterbury Press, N.J.

Baum, C. 1990, 'Attract Corporate Meetings to Fill Your Hotel Rooms', *Hotels*, August, pp. 25–6.

Bonn, M., Brand, R. & Ohlin, J. 1994, 'Site Selection for Professional Meetings: A Comparison of Heavy-Half vs Light-Half Association and Corporation Meeting Planners', *Journal of Travel & Tourism Marketing*, vol. 3, no. 2.

Cabanas, B. 1992, 'A Marketing Strategy for Resort Conference Centres', *Cornell Hotel and Restaurant Administration Quarterly*, June, pp. 45–9.

Clarke, D., Price, C. & Murrmann, S. 1996, 'Buying Centres: Who Chooses Convention Sites?', *Cornell Hotel and Restaurant Administration Quarterly*, vol. 37, August.

Davies, M. R., Keis, K. E., Nutting, J. B. & Tronc, K. E. 1981, *The Business of Communicating*, McGraw-Hill, Sydney, pp. 298–305.

Gartrell, R. 1991, 'Strategic Partnerships for Convention Planning: The Role of Convention and Visitors Bureaus in Convention Management', *International Journal of Hospitality Management*, vol. 10, no. 2, pp. 157–65.

Harris, R. & Howard, J. 1994, *The Australian Travel Agency*, Irwin/McGraw-Hill, Sydney.

Kotler, P., Bowen, J. & Makens, J. 1996, *Marketing for Hospitality and Tourism*, Prentice-Hall, Englewood Cliffs, N.J.

Lewis, R. & Shoemaker, S. 1997, 'Price-Sensitivity Measurement', *Cornell Hotel and Restaurant Administration Quarterly*, April.

Morrison, A. 1996, *Hospitality and Travel Marketing*, 2nd ed, Delmar Publishers, Melbourne.

Oppermann, M. 1996, 'Convention Destination Images: Analysis of Association Meeting Planners' Perceptions', *Tourism Management*, vol. 17, no. 3, pp. 175–82.

Oppermann, M. 1998, 'Perceptions of Convention Destinations: Large-Half versus Small-Half Association Meeting Planners', *Journal of Convention & Exhibition Management*, vol. 1, no. 1.

The Quorum. 1997a, 'Industry Puts Harder Accent on Service Delivery', March/April.

The Quorum. 1997b, 'Striking Deals', September/October, pp. 61–62.

Richardson, J. 1996, *Marketing Australian Travel and Tourism: Principles and Practice*, Hospitality Press, Melbourne.

Simons, M. 1996, 'Liquor Licensing Liability of Licensees for the Service of Liquor to Intoxicated Patrons Involving Claims with Third Parties', *International Journal of Hospitality Management*, vol. 15, no. 3, pp. 269–82.

SCVB, 1997, *Sydney Convention Delegate Study*, Sydney.

Vogt, C., Roehl, W. & Fesenmaler, D. 1994, 'Understanding Planners' Use of Meeting Facility Information', *Hospitality Research Journal*, vol. 17, no. 3, pp. 119–30.

Weirich, M. L. 1992, 'Suppliers to the Meeting Industry', *Meetings and Conventions Management*, pp. 114–33.

Zhou, Z. 1997, 'Destination Marketing: Measuring the Effectiveness of Brochures', *Journal of Travel & Tourism Marketing*, vol. 6, no. 3/4.

Burswood
International Resort Casino

Perth's Burswood International Resort Casino covers over 100 hectares of parkland and incorporates the Burswood Park Golf course, a 414-room five-star hotel, a 24-hour casino and a freestanding convention centre. The convention centre features a large Las Vegas-style theatre showroom and the largest enclosed exhibition and special events venue in Perth — the 20 000-seat Burswood Dome. The five-star hotel offers delegates a variety of facility benefits. Guests can enjoy nightly entertainment, the choice of nine restaurants, a flutter in the casino or a round of golf on the challenging 18-hole golf course. The hotel offers 17 river suites in addition to its complement of normal rooms, and a wide range of leisure facilities including a swimming pool, heated pool, recreation gym, tennis courts, spa, massage centre, children's amusement room and child-care facilities. Resort shops include a hairdresser, ladies' fashion boutique, gift shop, jewellery shop, florist and beauty salon.

The resort's sales manager, Jane Wishaw, states that Burswood's success is due to its competitive edge in providing quality service, integrated conference and exhibition facilities, themed events and appropriately designed training, sports, sailing and golfing programs. 'We have built a reputation for delivering customer service that exceeds the expectations of our clients', she states. 'An example of this capacity is our ability to design Asian banquets or specialised cuisine to very specific requirements. The resort is now hosting more than 80 national and international conventions, incentives and exhibitions each year, and we expect this to grow up to the 2000 Sydney Olympics.'

She asserts that the key to their success has been to ensure delegates at a Burswood conference enjoy a 'quality and memorable experience'. Jane goes further to state, 'By developing partnerships with our clients we commit Burswood to achieving the business goals and objectives of the conference and we offer a wide range of support services and resort facilities to ensure every delegate obtains the maximum benefit for their personal investment in a conference at Burswood.'

Visitors to Burswood are impressed with the hotel's airy atrium lobby and its well-designed rock features, cascading waterfalls, large palm trees, lush tropical gardens, bridges, space age lifts and varied dining facilities.

The Burswood showroom theatre is located in the convention centre. Capacity ranges from 1400 for dinner shows to 2000 with theatre-style seating. The ballroom is located behind the showroom and seats approximately 800 for a banquet/formal dinner or 1000 for a cocktail reception. Three smaller meeting rooms are available and the hotel offers three boardrooms, as well as Solitudes function room for smaller seminars. Technical support facilities include an overhead projector, video conferencing, screens, whiteboards, and so on. Designed with the conference organiser in mind, the Burswood Dome is Australia's largest enclosed indoor stadium. A feature of the dome's unique design is the huge inflated teflon-coated fibreglass roof, which soars to a height of 35 metres and provides this column-free venue with unobstructed viewing from every seat in the house.

Overall, Western Australia has made significant inroads into the MICE market due to facilities such as Burswood, and achieved growth of almost 100 per cent in the number of national and international meetings hosted between 1994 and 1996. This growth was primarily in meetings of less than 100 and 100–500 in number.

Source: Convention & Incentive Marketing (April 1998)

Questions

1 What facilities at Burswood International Resort Casino have been designed to meet the needs of emerging societal trends in the external market?

2 Construct a product feature and benefit profile for Burswood International Resort Casino, targeting two separate market segments — convention clients and incentive clients.

The business of
selling and promoting conventions

LEARNING OBJECTIVES

After studying this chapter, you will be able to:

- understand the concept of destination marketing and how it relates to the Australian MICE industry

- determine how destination factor endowments can impact the service provider's marketing and sales activities

- outline the process of putting together a marketing action plan

- outline the important issues relating to direct sales

- understand the problem areas relating to contract negotiations.

INTRODUCTION

The marketing and sales action plan strategies outlined in this chapter are natural extensions of the marketing issues outlined in chapter 6. Marketing and sales are inexorably linked, but do differ in the objectives and dynamics of application.

This chapter provides a broad understanding of destination marketing as it relates to the Australian MICE industry and as a strategy on which many MICE marketing and sales activities are focused. Furthermore, the marketing action plan (a practical working strategy document) is analysed with respect to how a hypothetical primary service provider can effectively organise and focus its predetermined broad marketing and sales strategies into a month-by-month workable action plan. Many primary service provider marketers to the MICE industry do an adequate job of identifying the broad marketing issues outlined in chapter 6. However, it is in the implementation and application of resources and following through with effective marketing mix communication activities where many such marketers fail to meet the organisation's expectations, and thus its overall marketing goals. For effective marketing to occur, marketers must plan their work and then work their plan. Chapter 6 dealt with the former; this chapter outlines the latter.

Finally, related sales issues are discussed as they fit into the overall marketing action plan process. As a foundation issue, it is important to understand that there are inherent differences between marketing and sales. Being market-oriented involves having a much broader orientation than being sales-oriented (Astroff & Abbey 1995). Marketing is more strategic; its practice is one of combining, blending, integrating and organising the related factors that affect the sale of the provider's services or facilities. Sales, then, is one aspect of the marketing mix (i.e. direct sales) and fits into the overall marketing strategy as one tool to get customers to commit to buying the service or product.

DESTINATION MARKETING

Destination marketing is a strategy that is particularly utilised by service providers in the Australian MICE industry. The concept is based on the premise that tourists travel to destinations (Kotler et al. 1996). Destinations are defined as places with some form of actual or perceived boundaries — physical, political or market-created (e.g. a tour operator defining the South Pacific as including Australia). To market a recognisable 'destination' presents many marketing challenges. Destinations can be defined as entire countries — for example, the 'Australian' destination — or smaller regions — for example, the Northern Rivers region of New South Wales, which is branded as 'Tropical New South Wales'. Australia presents particular challenges with respect to destination marketing because of its physical size, system of states and territories, distance from international markets and related access problems (Richardson 1996).

The primary focus of destination marketing for all service providers is to create in the consumer or decision maker's mind a single image or brand awareness of the destination. The destination's image has a great deal of impact on the awareness and attitude of the consumer (Gartrell 1994). The more positive the perception of the destination held by the consumer, the more likely the destination will be found as a suitable convention or meeting venue or location. This positive perception can involve a variety of variables: the availability of adequate accommodation, the quality of food and beverage options and meeting space, the support/ancillary services available and the destination's 'factor endowments' (see below) that support MICE activities.

Kotler et al. (1996) have stated that a destination can identify its natural target markets in a couple of ways: first, by determining the demographics and psychographics of current visitors or customers, and second, by conducting an audit of the destination's attractions and select segments that might have an interest in them. The latter relates to the concept of factor endowments. The term has been applied primarily to describe the flow of international tourism (Vellas & Bécherel 1995); however, the theory can be applied to specific destinations within a country. When applied to destination marketing, the theory simply states that a destination might have a comparative advantage over another destination due to its superiority in certain resources — natural (historic, artistic, cultural), human (skills), and capital and infrastructure. Thus, a destination such as Port Douglas in northern Queensland has a comparative advantage because of its natural resources, such as the local indigenous culture and proximity to the Great Barrier Reef. It might also have a strong capital base in five-star accommodation, but might be somewhat weak in the human resource area due to the transient nature of the skilled population. Understanding the destination's factor endowments will better allow those service providers, primary and secondary, to more easily market the overall destination to the MICE industry.

Understanding a destination's factor endowments relates to the subject of product features and benefits, discussed in chapter 6. Such a marketing and sales focus asserts that a MICE customer does not buy the product feature (e.g. the Great Barrier Reef), but the benefits that the feature provides (e.g. relaxation, soft adventure or educational opportunities). Knowing the benefits provided by the destination's factor endowments allows the service provider to market the destination effectively, along with the service provider's individual product or service.

This knowledge of destination benefits also allows the marketer to differentiate the destination in the consumer's mind on a comparative advantage basis (i.e. no one else has a Great Barrier Reef, Uluru or Sydney Harbour.) Therefore, when designing a marketing action plan, the MICE service provider can position its product or service effectively in relation to the overall branding and differentiation basis of the destination. Thus, destination marketing is a cooperative effort between all service providers in a destination. This cooperative marketing strategy is an integral part of the marketing action plan that is discussed in the next section.

The marketing and promotion of tourism and MICE-related business for the destination of Brisbane is illustrated in the following industry insight.

Brisbane Tourism, the trading name of the Brisbane Visitors and Convention Bureau, is a membership-based non-profit organisation responsible for the marketing and promotion of tourism and conventions in the Brisbane region, both nationally and internationally. Brisbane Tourism plays a vital role in generating sustainable economic and social benefits to the region as a consequence of visitors' expenditure. These benefits result in increased investment in infrastructure, job creation and improved community services and lifestyle.

Brisbane Tourism's business plan is designed to: confirm and consolidate the organisation's priorities in respect of the goals, strategies, and performance measures for key functions of the company; emphasise the primary policies of the board of directors; and provide the main stakeholders with the strategic and business direction of the organisation. Thus, Brisbane Tourism's 'mission' is to effectively market and promote the Brisbane region as a convention and incentive destination both nationally and internationally, highlighting its unique environment, social, cultural and geographical elements, and thereby achieving sustainable economic and social benefit for the region. The organisation's priorities have therefore been designated as: leisure tourism destination marketing and promotion, emphasising Brisbane as a 'City of Sun Days'; convention and incentive marketing, promotion and sales; the strengthening of relationships with industry bodies; and membership development and servicing.

With respect to the organisation's priorities in attracting convention and incentive business, Brisbane Tourism has identified two major strategies: first, to extend the destination branding process to attract the convention and incentive segment; and, second, regarding proposals and bids, to increase emphasis on business development, identifying potential prospects and actively following them up, and evaluating bid potential, particularly in respect of the international market.

Brisbane Tourism produces a variety of collateral sales material that is used to support the above strategies. This material includes the *Brisbane International Visitors Guide*, itineraries, fact sheets, the *Brisbane Seasonal Guide*, the *Official Brisbane Visitors Guide*, the *Brisbane Leisure Guide*, an events calendar and the trade-oriented partnership advertising rate card. The *Brisbane International Visitors Guide* is a destination motivational piece that establishes Brisbane and its region in the eyes of the international market. It contains various travel tips, dining, entertainment and shopping information, and a brief overview of the region's major events. The *Official Brisbane Visitors Guide* outlines things to see and do, details the heritage of the region and provides information on dining out, nightlife, shopping and entertainment and theme parks within the region, along with a regional map. The *Brisbane Leisure Guide* highlights on a quarterly basis those events and shopping, art and craft activities occurring in the destination during a specific season. As more of a point-of-purchase sales item, it is supported by select retailers and entertainment providers in the Brisbane region.

Source: *Brisbane Tourism*

The marketing action plan is a working document. It allows the service provider to the MICE industry to put in place practical strategies in order to reach set marketing objectives. These set marketing objectives (e.g. increase incentive business to the resort through repositioning and rebranding) are arrived at on completion of the market planning process. The process involves six stages:

1. conduct situation/SWOT analysis
2. produce destination factor endowment profile/feature and benefit analysis
3. select target market and segments (level I or II decision makers)
4. conduct market research
5. produce positioning and marketing mix strategies
6. design market and sales action plan.

To illustrate this process, a hypothetical resort is used in the following marketing exercise. The facilities of the hypothetical Tropicana Beach Resort, Port Douglas, are outlined in table 7.1. As established in chapter 6, resort properties in Australia are primary service providers to the incentive and convention industry. This marketing exercise follows the six stages outlined above and indicates how a MICE service provider, the Tropicana Beach Resort, can incorporate destination and individual marketing strategies into a coherent marketing and sales action plan.

■ Table 7.1 *Facilities of the Tropicana Beach Resort, Port Douglas*

Location/grounds 100-acre five-star resort located 500 metres from beach	
Guest accommodation 100 standard rooms 100 superior ocean-facing rooms 20 deluxe self-contained rooms/bures	**Food and beverage facilities** Terrace Cafe (seats 330) Signature Restaurant (seats 80) Poolside Palm Seafood Restaurant (seats 120) Pool Bar Ninth Hole Bar
MICE facilities Pillarless conference room • seats 250 theatre-style • verandah bar/kitchen Breakout room, seats 50 • standard audiovisual equipment	**Recreational facilities** Free form 100 000 litre pool Nine-hole golf course Two tennis courts Bowling green

■ Situation: *SWOT analysis*

The resort's sales and marketing team should first establish the resort's position in the overall external marketing environment. This 'situation analysis' examines where and how the resort stands in the marketplace, its market share and its relation to its competitors (Richardson 1996). Societal, economic and political/regulatory issues, as outlined in chapter 6, should be analysed with respect to their short- and long-term impact on the operation of the resort. From an understanding of these broad areas, the service provider marketer can then produce a SWOT (strengths, weaknesses, opportunities, threats) profile of the resort. The strengths and weaknesses relate to the resort's features and benefits, whereas the opportunities and threats relate more to the resort's external environment. A SWOT analysis for the Tropicana Beach Resort is shown in figure 7.1.

STRENGTHS
- New, but established, five-star resort (only five years old)
- 100-acre land area
- Convenient access to the Great Barrier Reef
- Experienced MICE industry staff
- Strong share of inbound international holiday market to Port Douglas
- Deluxe bure accommodation
- Recreational facilities
- Group child-minding facilities

WEAKNESSES
- Small volume of MICE business
- Resort 500 metres from the beach
- Swimming limited in ocean due to jellyfish and rips
- Conventions space limited to a single large room with only one small breakout room
- Access controlled by airlines
- Low awareness of resort in domestic MICE industry
- Limited dedicated MICE food and beverage facilities

THREATS
- Declining domestic holiday tour package market
- Asian financial downturn and its effects on inbound tourism
- Increased competition, both local and domestic

OPPORTUNITIES
- Increase domestic holiday business
- Increase domestic incentive and convention business to resort

The SWOT analysis provides the marketing team with the opportunity to set the overall marketing objectives for the resort for the upcoming year. The objectives relate to the opportunities and strengths outlined in the situation analysis. An understanding of the resort's weaknesses and threats also affects how the objectives will be pursued. For example, the marketing team decides to pursue the domestic Australian incentive market (an identified opportunity) for the upcoming year in order to broaden the resort's business mix. However, such a business goal must be pursued in light of the resort's weaknesses and capacity restrictions (i.e. only 20 deluxe bures and 100 superior ocean-facing rooms, and limited F&B facilities). Therefore, it would benefit the resort to put in place a marketing and sales strategy that targets incentive groups no larger than 100–120 individuals. Such capacity problems might also be affected by a secondary service provider, such as the airline — for example, how large a group the airline can transport on any one flight.

■ Destination *factor endowment profile/product feature and benefit analysis*

In consideration of the above marketing objectives, the marketing team then compiles:

1. *Destination factor endowment profile* — MICE industry decision makers consider not only the resort/venue but also the overall destination in the choice process. Thus, it is appropriate for the resort's marketing team to investigate the destination as a whole with respect to its factor endowments and those that offer comparative benefits for MICE customers. Those that can be identified as MICE product benefits can then be incorporated within the resort's related marketing and sales action plan.

2. *Product feature and benefit analysis* — as discussed in chapter 6, a product feature and benefit analysis focuses on the specific features of the resort itself. This analysis, combined with the destination factor endowment profile, provides a list of product benefits that can be utilised in the resort's marketing and sales positioning strategies. The effective selling of incentives and other MICE events is what Hartley and Witt term a 'knowledge-based process' (1992). Resort sales and marketing individuals must understand their clients' needs and also the product benefits available to meet those needs. The example of some Australian resorts' efforts to offer comprehensive child-minding facilities and services to MICE customers is indicative of such an understanding. The child-minding facility offers MICE consumers the benefit of time to relax and enjoy the event (Varey 1998).

■ Target *market segments*

Based on an analysis of the resort's/destination's features and benefits, the Tropicana Beach Resort's broader marketing objective to target the domestic Australian incentive market next year has been determined. Now the marketing team must clarify the target segment further in order to develop a practical marketing and sales action plan.

Target markets can be segmented by geography, demographics, purpose of visit and psychographics (Richardson 1996). The marketing team chooses to segment the market geographically, targeting level II decision makers, such as PCOs and incentive houses in Sydney, Brisbane and Melbourne. This segmentation is possible because, as discussed in chapter 6, the PCOs and incentive houses are identifiable, measurable and accessible within the marketplace. Furthermore, the 'purpose of visit' criteria can be used to target mainly those PCOs and incentive houses that control substantial amounts of incentive travel business. With this segmentation process completed, the marketing team can then incorporate these objectives into a marketing mix and direct sales action plan for the year.

◼ Market *research*

Reliable market research is vital for contemporary service provider marketers in the MICE industry. Such research can be gathered in a variety of ways, including formal customer surveys, focus groups and feedback on sales calls. It can be directed to uncover customer needs or where the customer is located.

The objective of this book is not to offer a discourse on contemporary social and business research methods, suffice to say that it is, however, extremely important for the marketer to conduct some form of research in order to ascertain the needs of the targeted customers. In the case of Tropicana Beach Resort, a telephone sales survey could be conducted, focus groups could be arranged in the capital cities, or a printed survey could be administered to identified PCOs and incentive house operators.

One practical way for a resort to 'locate' its potential customers is through the use of technology, particularly the Internet. In order to access the facility and services MICE site on the Internet for the Sheraton Mirage, Port Douglas, an information menu must first be completed (see figure 7.2). This allows the PCO, incentive operator or end user access to a variety of related MICE facility and service information on the Sheraton Mirage, Port Douglas. It also allows the Sheraton to record the information into a database to be followed up at a later date by Sheraton sales staff.

◼ **Figure 7.2**
Conference organisers Web site — Sheraton Mirage, Port Douglas

NEW USER QUICK REGISTRATION

Salutation: ○ Mr. ○ Mrs. ○ Ms.
First Name:
Last Name:
Title:
Company:
Address 1:
Address 2:
City:
State: [Select... ⬍]
Zip/Postal Code:
Country:
Phone Number:
Fax Number:
Email Address:
Web Sites Address: [http://www.]
Please enter a password of your choice, twice.
You will use it to access Plan it Online on future visits.
Password:
Confirm Password:
[CONTINUE]

Another practical manner by which to identify potential MICE customers is to visit the lobby of competitor facilities. Simply reading convention notice boards will indicate who and what type of MICE business is coming to your market area.

■ Positioning *and marketing-mix strategies*

At this stage of the process the target market segments have been chosen, customer needs have been identified and appropriate product benefits have been determined. The marketing team can now position, market and sell the venue or resort accordingly through the use of a marketing action plan.

Covering a period of one year, the action plan outlines on a monthly basis designated marketing communication activities necessary to reach specific marketing objectives. These communication activities, as outlined in chapter 6, include collateral material, advertising, publicity and public relations, direct marketing, sales promotion and direct sales. Issues such as consistent product branding and product differentiation also should be considered.

In the case of the Tropicana Beach Resort, the following provides examples of related action plan communication activities that could be undertaken. All activities directly relate to the overall marketing objective of increasing the number of small- to medium-sized incentive groups to the resort. Each individual communication activity is highlighted, along with the month in which it must commence or be planned. Specific marketing actions are categorised under the relevant communication mix area (e.g. collateral material).

Collateral material

1. Produce a promotional brochure featuring the facilities, services and benefits of using the Tropicana Beach Resort as a venue for small- to medium-sized incentive groups (January).
2. Produce a variety of incentive promotional materials to aid PCOs and incentive houses in customer direct mail campaigns (February).

Advertising

1. Initiate the production of a joint CVB/Ansett Australia print advertisement, to be featured quarterly in *Convention & Incentive Marketing* (*CIM*) magazine (January).
2. Produce an individual venue print advertisement to appear quarterly in *Convention & Incentive Marketing* (February).

Public relations and publicity

1. Write consumer and trade media releases to announce new children's club facility for convention delegates (January). To be distributed in February.
2. Plan special trade media receptions/lunches in Sydney, Melbourne and Brisbane in March to promote the resort as an incentive destination venue (involve CVB and local airline representative) (January).

Direct marketing

1. Produce a database list of all possible PCOs and incentive houses in target markets (January).
2. Develop a direct mail promotional flier highlighting the new children's club facility (March).
3. Direct mail promotional flier to all identified PCOs and incentive houses (April).

Sales promotion

Develop special children's activities kit for distribution to targeted PCOs and incentive houses (tangibilising the product) (January).

Direct sales

1. Identify select PCOs and incentive house operators in capital cities to target for individual sales calls (January).
2. Conduct direct sales calls on identified PCOs and incentive houses in Brisbane (March).

These examples simply outline the types of marketing communication activities that can be planned in order to reach the service provider's marketing objectives in accessing MICE-related business. For each established marketing objective — in this case, increase incentive business and increase domestic holiday business — separate communication mix activities must be planned. These marketing communication activities are then set down in a monthly time line, as outlined in table 7.2. Communication activities are then placed in the appropriate month for action. In addition to the activity, the marketing team member responsible and the proposed budget expenditure are also indicated. Such an action plan outline will provide a focused road map for all team members for the year, in addition to allowing variations in both budget and activities to be made as deemed necessary.

■ Table 7.2
Marketing action plan: Tropicana Beach Resort's marketing communication activities for the month of January

MARKETING ACTION PLAN — JANUARY			
Communication area	**Activity**	**Action by (initials)**	**Budget ($)**
Collateral material	Produce promotional brochure	JR	8000
Advertising	Produce cooperative destination print advertisement for *CIM* magazine	MH	1700
Publicity and public relations	Write media release on new children's club for MICE customers	HD	
	Plan media receptions for March (Sydney, Melbourne, Brisbane)	HD	
Direct marketing	Develop database of PCOs and incentive houses in target markets	JR	
Sales promotion	Develop special children's activities kit for distribution to targeted PCOs and incentive houses	TR	3000
Direct sales	Identify select PCOs and incentive house operators in capital cities to target for direct sales calls	MH	

Our discussion of the marketing process is now complete. The next section of this chapter focuses on the application of the last communication mix activity, direct sales. Sales administration issues and their application to the Australian MICE industry are also discussed.

SALES

Sales is an integral part of the marketing process. An effective marketing process will result in customer awareness and a propensity to buy. To ensure the marketing process is effective, the service provider must follow through with an expedient sales action plan. Branding, advertising and promotion alone will not ensure a service provider's success in the MICE industry. The MICE industry is a people industry. The service provider is not simply a resort, CVB or venue; it is a people problem solver (Hartley & Witt 1992).

The following discussion indicates how effective sales administration can be an important part of the overall marketing process. Again, it is not the intention here to review and discuss the 'fundamentals of sales', but more to understand how specific sales issues relate to the marketing activity of a contemporary service provider to the MICE industry.

■ Sales *administration*

Primary and secondary service providers to the MICE industry must coordinate their sales activity in a careful and organised manner. This activity must be consistent with target market segments and other marketing communication objectives. Thus, sales and its administration are coordinated processes supported by the marketing action plan. For example, a service provider could conduct a direct marketing exercise to targeted PCOs in Melbourne. This could consist of sending the PCOs an elaborate information kit describing the service provider's product. Then, after the PCOs have received the direct marketing information, the service provider could follow up with a direct sales call, on the assumption that the PCOs now have some initial knowledge of the product on offer. Thus, the sales activity is linked with the select marketing action plan activities.

Sales administration involves the management of a sales force and the management of customers. Service providers historically manage and structure sales staff by activity: inside sales versus outside sales. Inside sales staff support outside sales activities and coordinate sales direction in relation to the overall marketing action plan. They also:

- provide timely follow-up on all sales leads and enquiries
- maintain customer databases
- provide quotes and contract administration
- establish an effective liaison with other departments, such as F&B, reservations, and so on, and act as a 'single' point of contact for customers
- assist in the planning of sales calls/industry promotional events
- develop collateral material

- assist in the coordination of on-site or in-house groups
- coordinate internal marketing activities
- solve problems
- conduct site inspections.

Conducting site inspections is a very important sales activity for a primary service provider to the MICE industry. Site inspections, also referred to as 'educational' or 'familiarisation' trips in Australia, form a vital part in the knowledge-base process of educating the MICE decision maker. Related research by Meeting Planners International (cited in Gartrell 1991) found that 90 per cent of the meeting planners surveyed preferred a site inspection in order to research a MICE venue. This view is supported by research by Vogt et al. (1994), who have found that prior experience is the most frequently utilised source of information when selecting a venue, and furthermore, that such MICE decision makers place a strong emphasis on this personally gained information.

Therefore, it is absolutely vital for the service provider's internal sales and marketing staff to conduct well-run, efficient and well-targeted site inspections for MICE decision makers. Well-run means clever and creative; efficient means the client's group is looked after in a capable and efficient manner; and well-targeted means understanding that all PCOs and MICE decision makers are not alike, and have different needs and different types of business, so site inspections should be designed accordingly. Designing the site inspection accordingly could also mean promoting individual stays or visits by MICE decision makers as well as group site inspections. As a sales promotion activity, the resort service provider could offer targeted MICE decision makers specially priced or FOC (free of charge) accommodation packages, to be used at their convenience to visit the service provider's venue/resort. Again, these 'individual' site inspection visits must be well-coordinated to ensure a successful visit.

Outside sales staff primarily operate in the external environment. They:
- coordinate and arrange cooperative sales and marketing activities with other destination service providers such as CVBs, airlines and entertainment venues
- obtain market feedback on sales and marketing opportunities, competitive activities and client needs
- liaise with internal sales staff in the transition from sales to the in-house operation of group movements
- support select public relations and publicity activities
- conduct direct sales calls in order to educate, develop customer 'relationships' and create sales (direct sales is discussed further in the next section).

Sales administration also involves the management of customers. This involves qualifying possible sales leads and maintaining up-to-date databases and client/customer profiles.

The following snapshot outlines the career profile of Sharlene Dadd and explores some of the activities undertaken in her role as manager, convention and incentive sales, at the SCVB.

Sharlene Dadd was appointed to the position of manager, convention and incentive sales for the SCVB (Sydney Convention & Visitors Bureau) in September 1997. For the previous seven years Sharlene was involved 'on-site' in various hotel marketing roles, including director of sales for the ITT Sheraton in Jakarta, the Regent of Sydney and the Sheraton Wentworth Hotel in Sydney. She has a Bachelor of Arts degree in language and psychology from the University of Sydney.

Sharlene is on the MIAA (Meetings Industry Association of Australia) NSW Chapter Committee, has been an active committee member of the Sydney Chamber of Commerce Sydney Policy Committee and has served on the Board of the Indonesian Chapter of PATA (the Pacific Asia Travel Association). She works with a team of seven in the SCVB conference and sales department, as well as representatives in Europe, North America and Melbourne. With annual sales targets in excess of $200 million, the SCVB sales department tracks the movement of major international events, sources opportunities to put Sydney forward as a potential host city, prepares bids and lobbying campaigns and, once successful, ensures that maximum delegate attendance is achieved.

At a time of limited resources for city convention bureaus, Sharlene feels that one of the SCVB's major sales challenges is to target its market in international congresses correctly and to improve its strike rate (with respect to win/lose) in attracting such events to Sydney. Such a market orientation coincides with the SCVB's charter. In addition, she says that cooperative sales are a big part of what her team does. Their cooperative efforts involve joint advertising and the organisation of select international trade shows. The SCVB invites members to participate in these select 'trade booths', thereby eliminating the hassle for each member in attempting to work and arrange such a sales front on its own.

Source: Sharlene Dadd

■ The sales *call*

Direct, or face-to-face, sales calls allow the service provider to:
- pursue a commitment to buy from a customer
- obtain competitive market information
- receive product/service feedback information
- develop customer relationships.

A professional sales approach in direct selling is vital. Such an approach is based on sound product, competitor and client knowledge. Effective sales of incentives and conferences is a knowledge-based process. A professional sales person has a high understanding of their product's features and benefits, and the destination's comparative advantages in factor endowments. Knowledge does not only mean credibility (Morrison 1996); it also allows the sales person to more effectively problem solve for the client. Thus, the marketing exercise of creating a feature and benefit analysis for the service provider's product links directly with direct sales activities.

The sales person also must have some authority in making on-the-spot decisions while in the presence of MICE decision makers. This gives the sales person more credibility in the eyes of the decision maker and allows them more often to 'close the sale' with the client. It is advisable for the sales person to have set boundaries in which to operate when quoting rates and committing sales support funds.

Planning is an important part of direct sales activity and involves:

- acquiring as much information as possible about the MICE decision maker prior to the actual sales call
- understanding the decision maker's particular business mix (e.g. incentive, small meeting, association)
- gaining any possible information about the decision maker from other service providers and competitors
- qualifying potential leads
- making the sales appointment — suitable and convenient times for the client should be picked when they do not feel rushed and a quiet and appropriate location should be picked to avoid distractions.

For the sales call itself the sales person must ensure they are *on time*. Remember, the sales person is their company (Morrison 1996). How the sales person presents and conducts themself will generalise to the organisation for which they work. If they are not punctual their client will think that they will handle any business in the same sloppy manner.

Good communication skills are a necessity for the professional sales person. The main communication skill utilised is to *listen*. This does not mean not taking an active part in the discussion; it simply infers that the sales person will not understand what the customer needs are and their importance if they are not an active listener. Through active listening the sales person will uncover the needs of their client, which then will allow them to satisfy such needs with one of their product benefits. Such active listening also allows the sales person to understand the level of experience the decision maker has of organising such events. Taylor (cited in Hartley & Witt 1992) stresses the importance of adapting the selling approach to the level of previous experience the organiser has in such event management.

In addition, proper body language supporting this activity will allow the sales person to close the sale effectively once a sufficient number of customer needs have been satisfied. When the sales person detects 'buying signals' from the customer, it might be time to close the sale. This is where many sales people fail in their objectives. Many do not 'ask for the business'. Selling services is an intangible activity, therefore to close the sale the sales person might receive a 'commitment' from the decision maker to use their product in the near or long term. So they should always ask for the business and never leave a sales situation by simply saying 'Call me if you need me'.

The direct sales call is also an excellent opportunity to work with other service providers in destination sales. The sales person should consider working and conducting 'joint' sales calls with the local CVB or airline/transportation provider. These service providers are not the sales person's competitors and together they can prove to be an effective and credible team. Such cooperative activities with other service providers will also allow the sales person access to potential new accounts through their databases.

Working in tandem with another service provider (e.g. a resort working with an airline) in selling to a MICE decision maker will also allow the sales person to more effectively problem solve. This problem solving ability is an important part of the sales process. Working together in the sales call may allow the service providers to overcome transportation and capacity problems. In addition, as 'cooperative' sellers, destination marketing funds in the form of tour shells, and so on, might be provided to satisfy a budgeting need for the decision maker and thus enhance the prospect of closing the sale.

After the sales call it is always important to follow up. Rarely does a sales person leave a sales call without some activity to complete or follow up for the client. When practical, the sales person should always have some reason to contact the client again. This simply might involve sending additional product information or supplying another service provider's contact details. The follow-up communication activity, if completed efficiently and in a timely manner, will further reinforce the sales person's credibility as a service provider. The follow-up process also allows the sales person to determine which MICE decision makers to develop sales and marketing 'relationships' with, and they can gain further market sales and research as the relationships develop.

■ Pricing *issues*

Various pricing-related issues can impact on the effectiveness of sales administration. Contract negotiations can be difficult for a sales person in the MICE industry. Often, sales people are eager to close the sale, but must remember who they work for. This means that selling is not merely offering the lowest price; it is getting the best possible price for the product. At times the sales person must make a decision concerning whether they can 'afford' the customer's business. As discussed in chapter 6, not all of a service provider's business is profitable.

When 'quoting' costs to the MICE decision maker, it is generally acceptable to leave some room for negotiation. MICE event organisers often work on a 'per person' cost basis, which must cover accommodation, F&B, meeting room and recreational costs. Thus, a service provider such as a resort might maintain its room rate integrity (a premium rate) by offering the meeting room space free of charge. Or, a nominal meeting room fee might be charged in order to allow the resort to maintain some rate stability in the market, with free breakfast provided daily. The challenge is how to accommodate the group within the client's budget while providing the service provider with a reasonable return for their services. The key is the problem-solving ability of the sales person.

A major concern for MICE industry service providers in Australia today is the non-standardisation of contracts, and, in particular, the absence of any universally agreed-on industry standards governing the use of cancellation fees and deposits (Abbey & Link 1994). Such a situation can place established 'relationships' with select MICE decision makers in a precarious position. There is always a desire to 'book' the business, but a grey area arises when the client must cancel or cannot offer a deposit to hold the booking.

Research conducted by Hartley and Witt (1991) has indicated the underlying reasons how and why service providers react to this situation. With respect to reasons for not operating with a standard cancellation policy, 46 per cent of hoteliers surveyed indicated cancellation charges create bad feelings and lose customers. A further 35 per cent believed that there was no reason for such a policy as cancellations were infrequent, 30 per cent were considering implementing such a policy, and 14 per cent believed that such policies were unworkable. Of those hoteliers who presently operate with a standard cancellation policy, 65 per cent indicated they did not impose the policy due to the fear of losing the customer's goodwill (particularly in the case of frequent customers). About 26 per cent of respondents indicated they would waive the cancellation fee if the customer rebooked the MICE event for a later date (an effective problem-solving approach).

Another pricing issue which emerges frequently is that often there will be more than one PCO or level II decision maker quoting for the business on behalf of the actual customer. A company such as a large car firm may tender the bidding out to one or more conference organisers who in turn liaise with competing service providers. So, it is critical for the service provider not to show any favouritism (unless intentional) in providing one PCO with a more economical price than their competing PCO. They might not get the car company's business, but they also will not alienate the PCOs involved who control a substantial amount of their future business.

And finally, a note for sales people involved in contract and related financial negotiations with MICE decision makers. Once the contract has been negotiated and the details agreed on, the sales person should begin the transition phase of handing over the operational responsibility to the internal sales and operation team. This does not mean that the sales person does not remain involved with the client, but merely allows the sales person time to chase new business and maintain a continuing positive marketing relationship with the client. This positive relationship is maintained and reinforced because the sales person then does not get involved with the specific accounting functions and transactions concerning the group movement. Sales people do not need to 'chase' deposit payments, and so on, for the accounting department. Such activity by the sales person could reflect in a negative manner and inhibit their effectiveness in the future.

SUMMARY

Destination marketing is a strategy that is particularly utilised by service providers in the MICE industry, and is based on the premise that tourists travel to destinations. To market to a recognisable destination presents many marketing challenges. By understanding a destination's factor endowments, service providers can more easily market the overall destination to the MICE industry.

Service providers' marketing objectives are implemented through select sales and communication activities. Such a marketing and sales focus is based on a sound product knowledge arrived at through an effective situation and SWOT analysis, in addition to the compilation of a product and destination feature and benefit profile. These objectives and marketing/ sales strategies are coordinated into a working document — the marketing action plan. The plan is organised on a monthly basis and is divided into select marketing communication activities: advertising, publicity and public relations, direct marketing, sales promotion, direct sales and production of relevant collateral material.

Sales is an integral part of the marketing process. To ensure the marketing process is effective, service providers must follow through with an expedient sales action plan. Direct sales activities are an important part of this process, and allow service providers to pursue commitments to buy, obtain competitive market information, receive product feedback and develop customer relationships. Contract negotiations can be difficult in the MICE industry: the key is the problem-solving ability of the sales person.

Activities

7.1 Conduct a situation and SWOT analysis for any primary service provider with which you are familiar. Develop a destination factor endowment profile for the organisation.

7.2 As a continuation of activity 7.1:
   (a) Develop a target market segment profile for the organisation. Choose market segments for the upcoming year and explain how these segment choices relate to information gained through the situation and SWOT analyses.
   (b) Develop a market research plan to identify customer needs.

7.3 From your answers to activity 7.2, design a print advertising campaign to communicate the company's MICE benefits to the target market segments. Your campaign should address, but may not be limited to, the following issues:
   - How a cooperative destination campaign would or would not be appropriate.
   - The product benefits that would be promoted.
   - The customer needs that would be satisfied by these benefits.
   - How the issue of 'branding' would impact on the effectiveness of the advertisement.
   - How the issues of product differentiation and positioning would be involved in the campaign.
   - Why the chosen media channel was selected (i.e. trade or consumer).

Discussion questions

7.1 Describe the differences between inside sales and outside sales.

7.2 What are some of the customer sales problems that can arise in the negotiation of MICE event contracts?

7.3 How is the feature and benefit analysis related to direct selling?

7.4 Explain the concept that sales is a 'knowledge-based process'.

7.5 What communication skills would enhance the effectiveness of a sales person?

7.6 Provide an example of how a sales person could be a 'MICE problem-solver' in the sales situation.

7.7 Should a sales person also act as an accountant? Discuss.

REFERENCES

Abbey, J. & Link, C. 1994, 'The Convention and Meetings Sector — Its Operation and Research Needs', in J. R. B. Ritchie & C. R. Goeldner (eds), *Travel, Tourism and Hospitality Research*, 2nd ed, John Wiley & Sons, Brisbane, pp. 273–84.

Astroff, M. & Abbey, J. 1995, *Convention Sales and Services*, 4th ed, Waterbury Press, N. J.

Gartrell, R. 1991, 'Strategic Partnerships for Convention Planning: The Role of Convention and Visitors Bureaus in Convention Management', *International Journal of Hospitality Management*, vol. 10, no. 2, pp. 157–65.

Gartrell, R. 1994, *Destination Marketing for Convention and Visitor Bureaus*, 2nd ed, Kendall Hunt, Iowa.

Hartley, J. & Witt, S. 1991, 'Conference and Function Cancellation Fees and Customer Goodwill', *International Journal of Hospitality Management*, vol. 10, no. 1, pp. 35–45.

Hartley, J. & Witt, S. 1992, 'Hotel Sales Management: Turning Conference and Function Enquiries into Sales', *Journal of Hospitality & Leisure Marketing*, vol. 1, no. 2.

Kotler, P., Bowen, J. & Makens, J. 1996, *Marketing For Hospitality and Tourism*, Prentice-Hall, Englewood Cliffs, N. J.

Morrison, A. 1996, *Hospitality and Travel Marketing*, 2nd ed, Delmar Publishers, Melbourne.

Richardson, J. 1996, *Marketing Australian Travel and Tourism: Principles and Practice*, Hospitality Press, Melbourne.

Varey, J. 1998, 'Child's Play', *The Quorum*, August, pp. 51–2.

Vellas, F. & Bécherel, L. 1995, *International Tourism*, Macmillan Press, London.

Vogt, C., Roehl, W. & Fesenmaler, D. 1994, 'Understanding Planners' Use of Meeting Facility Information', *Hospitality Research Journal*, vol. 17, no. 3, pp. 119–30.

CASE STUDY

Tourism Queensland

Tourism Queensland (formerly Queensland Tourist and Travel Corporation) was established as a statutory authority in 1979. Its primary responsibility is the marketing and development of Queensland's tourism destinations, which it achieves in association with the tourism industry. Tourism Queensland's role is to add value to the marketing efforts of the tourism industry through select cooperative and destination marketing activities. Tourism Queensland is funded by the state government to develop and market Queensland tourism destinations intrastate, interstate and internationally. Internationally, Tourism Queensland markets Queensland primarily to the travel industry through its nine overseas offices. Additionally, it works with the Australian Tourist Commission on international campaign activities through Partnership Australia to maximise Queensland's market share and create linkages for Queensland.

Tourism Queensland has a dedicated destination marketing department headed by a destination marketing manager and comprising destination marketing teams for each identified area. In addition, it operates a conventions and incentives unit with specialised staff located at the head office in Brisbane. The unit provides assistance to the Queensland MICE industry and prospective clients, with additional assistance available from the Tourism Queensland international office.

Tourism Queensland offers a wide range of cooperative marketing activities in order to promote Queensland as a destination. These activities involve:

• television advertising

• press and magazine advertising and supplements

• transit and radio advertising

• editorial coverage

• sales delegations — in conjunction with major international airlines, it can organise subsidised sales trips offering operators the opportunity to present their product directly to the travel trade in individual markets

• trade shows — for operators having some experience in the international marketplace, it will attend a wide range of trade shows throughout major international markets, providing the small service provider with an effective means of participation under the Tourism Queensland corporate banner

• direct marketing — a number of databases, developed and regularly updated by its overseas offices, are available for service providers.

Research conducted by Tourism Queensland has revealed five destinations with sufficient levels of consumer awareness and industry maturity to sustain mainstream media and brand marketing activity. They are Tropical North Queensland, the Gold Coast, the Sunshine Coast, the Whitsundays and Brisbane.

Tourism Queensland provides the industry with select 'summary' sheets that overview specific destination marketing objectives and problems that relate to the destination in question. For Brisbane this includes:

1. *The Brisbane Domestic Marketing Strategy summary sheet*
Brisbane is Australia's only subtropical capital city. A modern and diverse city, Brisbane offers visitors a stimulating city experience in a warm and friendly environment. The Brisbane Domestic Marketing Strategy identifies and addresses issues relating to the positioning of Brisbane as an attractive and desirable domestic destination. The process of implementing the strategy relies on the continued partnership between Tourism Queensland, Brisbane Tourism and the tourism industry.

2. *Market overview*
• Australia is the primary source of visitors to Brisbane.
• In the year to March 1996, Brisbane attracted 1.5 million visitors staying an average of three nights each in commercial accommodation and spending around $740 million in total. Over 50 per cent of these visitors are likely to originate from Queensland and New South Wales.

3. *Destination overview*
Tourism Queensland research has identified that Brisbane has the following image problem issues that need to be addressed:
• Brisbane has an ill-defined image and lacks a common identity.
• Knowledge as to what Brisbane has to offer to holiday makers is vague in the extreme.
• Brisbane is largely overshadowed in Queensland by nearby coastal holiday destinations of appeal.
• There appear to be many misconceptions based on a lack of information.

Source: Erszi Suranyi, Tourism Queensland

Questions

1 Formulate a positioning strategy targeted at the domestic MICE market which would overcome the select destination problems advised in the destination overview.

2 Discuss how a Brisbane hotel could work in a cooperative manner with Tourism Queensland in promoting Brisbane as a MICE destination.

Managing the
planning of conventions

LEARNING OBJECTIVES

After studying this chapter, you will be able to:

- identify and define the planning requirements of the stakeholders of a convention or meeting

- identify the stages and factors that need to be considered in the planning of a convention or meeting

- review project planning techniques and explore their application in planning, organising and scheduling a convention or meeting.

- explore the components of the convention or meeting plan

- explore the managerial and leadership skills required in the project planning of a convention or meeting.

INTRODUCTION

It takes a great deal of time, care and patience to plan, manage and organise a MICE event — even the smallest event cannot be conjured up overnight. To prepare for a convention or conference, the planning team might be in operation for over a year in some instances, but in others it might be less than six months. Major MICE events can be booked up to 10 years in advance, although the norm is three to four years. As the annual conference for one year finishes, the planning for the next year's conference begins.

So what are the ingredients for a successful convention or meeting? Obviously, they would include the identification of an appropriate venue and accommodation facilities, clarification of the catering requirements and the design and distribution of delegate invitations, along with other, smaller administrative and technical items. Such items form the component parts of the planning of a successful event. However, in order to ensure ultimate and complete customer satisfaction, the total event needs to be planned and coordinated in the most effective and efficient manner within the given time frame. The mandate is to ensure that all the activities that make up the convention or meeting are completed to the customer's satisfaction and that the needs of each group of stakeholders are met.

This chapter focuses on the planning requirements for the successful management and operation of a MICE event. It reviews the planning needs and identifies project planning techniques that are appropriate to the organisation of a convention or meeting.

THE PLANNING REQUIREMENTS OF THE STAKEHOLDERS

To ensure a successful convention or meeting a number of different stakeholders are involved: the client company, the conference organiser and the various service suppliers such as the venue and supplier of audiovisual equipment. They all require the same type of information for the planning of a MICE event, but will focus on different aspects. For example:

- The client company makes the decision to hold a convention or meeting and sets the objectives for the event with the aid of the conference organiser. It identifies the potential participants, sets the dates and establishes the budget. The client company may be open to suggestions regarding the style and location of the event and the type of event program.
- The conference organiser establishes the objectives of the event with the client company and confirms which key personnel from the client organisation will be involved in the event. They identify the site and venue, and lead and coordinate all the various facets of the event, including establishing the program and any pre- or post-conference tours. They brief and work with other suppliers such as florists, audiovisual companies and

transport companies, and identify and manage the budget for the client organisation.

- The venue liaises with the conference organiser, identifies the number of delegates and agrees the date for receipt of final numbers. It establishes the requirements for accommodation and facilities, including meeting rooms and food and beverage services and the required timing of the program for staffing the event.
- The suppliers obtain a brief of the event from the conference organiser and establish the requirements. They work with other suppliers, the venue and the conference organiser to ensure the satisfactory provision of the required goods, so that, for example, the printing is completed at the right time and specialist audiovisual equipment is available.

Planning and the use of planning techniques are essential if the conference organiser is to ensure the satisfactory coordination of all the stakeholders and suppliers and:

- identify the tasks to be undertaken
- establish the appropriate time frames
- source who is to undertake each task, by when and to what standard
- coordinate all the activities.

It is important that the people involved in actually undertaking the tasks for the potential convention or meeting are fully briefed and involved in the planning process. They are the most knowledgeable about the work and the detailed activities involved, as well as the length of time they might require. As identified in chapter 4, involving people in the decision-making process for the tasks that they will be doing for the event results in their greater commitment to the accomplishment of these tasks within the given time frame. Participation helps to build commitment.

WHAT IS PLANNING AND WHY PLAN?

Planning involves deciding what needs to be done, by whom and by when. It can be defined as 'the systematic arrangement of tasks to accomplish an objective' (Gido & Clements 1999, p. 188). A plan provides direction; it enables us to identify where we are going and how to get there — in other words, it should clarify the path that is to be taken and the outcome or end result. It also draws attention to the stages on the way (the milestones) and identifies and clarifies any sidetracks that may be necessary. A plan helps to set and establish priorities that can assist in the scheduling of activities. The plan becomes a benchmark against which the actual progress towards the final objective can be compared. As a result, corrective action can be taken against any deviations or adjustments that have occurred.

Planning assists in the setting of priorities. All managers, whatever their level of seniority or experience within a MICE organisation, need to establish priorities and identify what should happen first. A number of factors influence the setting of priorities, for example external constraints, such as the existence of imposed deadlines, the urgency of the completion of a task, activity or project and the overall amount of time required. If a task is inherently lengthy, the planning schedule must allow the necessary time for it to be completed; if a task is fairly short, then it may be possible to delay the starting date for the task. The relationship of a task to other tasks also needs to be considered — for example, the impact on other areas of the plan if the task is not completed within its specified time frame. Likewise, tasks that are dependent on the completion of other tasks need to be identified, to establish when they should be started and whether there are any consequences if the work is delayed (Quinn et al. 1996, p. 88). All of these factors assist in the prioritising and scheduling of tasks within the plan.

■ Types *of plans*

As in other business sectors, MICE organisations follow the traditional planning processes at both a strategic and an operational level.

Strategic plan

A strategic plan identifies the importance of planning and goal setting as tools for determining where a company wants to go and how it wants to get there. It is a planning process that is directed towards setting and establishing the organisation's mission and vision statement, its objectives and the process for potential achievement. A strategic plan usually is prepared for a period of three to five years and can be considered as the long-term plan for an organisation.

Operational plan

An operational plan focuses on both the planning and maintenance of the work flows that make up the operational system of a business. It verifies how the financial resources, human resources, materials, and so on, are to be monitored to ensure the most effective completion of the tasks. An operational plan is the first step in the coordination of the employees, their work and the work groups within an organisation. As a result, operational planning is very important, because it translates the future into the present and provides:

- a map of how to get there
- a mechanism for setting standards
- clarification of what is to be done and how it is to be done — that is, the standards of performance for the business and its operational areas
- identification of the work areas and the priorities of the organisation.

Operational planning is concerned mainly with scheduling and establishing timetables and milestones for the completion of tasks and activities.

Project plan

A project involves a sequence of choices or decisions that either commit or utilise resources over a period of time. To achieve success in undertaking a project, it is important to prepare a plan. The satisfactory achievement of the plan means that everything that is required is done at the right time with the efficient use of the necessary resources.

The project plan can be defined as 'an endeavour to accomplish a specific objective through a unique set of interrelated tasks and the effective utilisation of resources. It has a clearly defined objective stated in terms of scope, schedule and cost' (Gido & Clements 1999, p. 4). Many of the main activities that are undertaken by the MICE industry can be likened to the management of a project. In particular, events that are managed by conference organisers fall into the definition of a project. Many of the activities that constitute a convention or meeting can benefit from the use of project planning techniques. MICE projects range from small events, such as half-day seminars for 15 to 20 people, to major conventions, such as the World Congress of Cardiology, with over 1000 delegates. To ensure their ultimate success, such major conventions involve an extensive range of people, including PCOs, audiovisual equipment suppliers, venues, accommodation suppliers, airlines and state and national tourism offices.

■ Characteristics *of project planning*

Projects have a number of particular characteristics:
- They have a clearly defined objective.
- They have a specific time frame and a limited life. There is an identified start date and a time by which the project must be accomplished.
- They tend to be unique or one-time activities. For example, the planning of a convention or meeting is unique because of the amount of customisation that is required; no two conventions are the same.
- They comprise a series of interdependent tasks that need to be undertaken and accomplished in a certain sequence in order to achieve the objective.
- They have a certain amount of risk and uncertainty. The competing aspects of time, cost and the scope of the work need to be balanced and managed. Before a project begins, a plan is prepared to establish a set of presumptions with respect to the budgeted costs, schedule and scope of the work. Each project is unique, so the combination of estimates for these factors causes some uncertainty. Thus, for example, a conference may be provided by the required date, but the costs may be higher because of a missed printing deadline in the program production, which resulted in additional expense.
- The resources utilised are obtained from disparate sources. For example, a convention or meeting may use the services of a number of different suppliers, such as the venue, outside caterers, a transport company and a florist.
- They have a customer, that is the person or organisation that provides the funds to undertake the project. The conference organiser who manages the event and the project team who are involved in the event must accomplish the event's objectives and satisfy the customer.
- The management structures often are not hierarchical and tend to cut across established organisational structures. They also tend to be team based.

■ The project *life cycle*

Within MICE events, projects can be viewed as both separate tasks and part of the whole event. So, putting the bid together can be seen as a project in its own right, or as part of the larger project to attain, plan and organise the whole event. This is outlined in the following hypothetical example, which shows the bid as part of the convention project:

1. Putting together the bid or proposal for the convention or meeting.
2. Winning the bid.
3. Pre-event planning and organisation.
4. Managing and organising the actual convention or meeting.
5. Post-event evaluation and review planning.

Projects for events follow a life cycle that can be divided into four stages. As the projects move through the different stages of their life cycle, the roles of the different individuals and resources change. This is demonstrated in the following hypothetical example of an association event.

Stage one: *Project conception or feasibility stage — the need for a project is identified* The association wishes to increase its membership and improve the networking opportunities for its existing members. It therefore decides that it should hold an annual convention. A requirement for a PCO to organise and manage the event is identified and a convention brief is prepared and distributed to a number of PCOs.

Stage two: *Project planning or design — a possible solution is developed* In response to the brief, the PCOs prepare and submit their bid document to undertake the convention for the association. The preparation of the bid document may take several weeks or months of preparation depending on the size of the event. In their bid document, the PCOs might include their suggestions and approach to the convention, an estimate of the types of resources that would be required and an estimate of the time and budgeted cost. In determining their fee to be charged, PCOs estimate the amount of time required for the work. This includes pre-event meetings, site inspections, meetings with other suppliers, and the project team, ongoing communications and organisation of the actual event, and post-event evaluation.

Stage three: *Project implementation or execution — the project is carried out* This stage of the event is divided into two distinct phases: the pre-event planning and organisation, and the operation or execution of the event. The pre-event planning commences immediately the event has been awarded to a PCO and the letter of agreement and contract have been completed. The PCO then begins detailed planning, reviews the timelines, identifies, meets and briefs the other suppliers and undertakes activities such as site and venue selection. During this phase a variety of resources, such as individuals, materials and funds, are used at different times and at varying intensities. For example, the creative skills of an individual who specialises in themed events may be called on to design the opening ceremony for the convention, or a specialist audiovisual and telecommunication expert may be contracted to organise a satellite link for a keynote speaker. It is also important that the PCO ensures excellent communication with and coordination and integration of the various members of the event team. This includes constant updates and liaison with the association, and the frequency of these updates with all parties increases as the actual event approaches.

The actual execution of the event is the culmination of all the planning activities and the satisfactory accomplishment of the overall objective at the required quality, on time and within budget. (This is discussed in further detail in chapter 9.)

Stage four: *Project termination and evaluation* Following the completion of the event, certain 'close down' activities are undertaken. All supplier invoices are submitted and paid and the PCO prepares a final financial statement for the association. The event should be evaluated in terms of the efficiency and effectiveness of its performance and notes should be made as to how certain aspects can be improved for future events. The PCO should prepare an evaluation report on the level of participant satisfaction, to determine if the event met or exceeded expectations. Feedback and evaluations should be gathered from all members of the event team and recommendations made as to performance improvements for future events. (The evaluation phase of a MICE event is discussed in more detail in chapter 10.)

The project planning and implementation process of a MICE event therefore focuses on both the goals and objectives of the project, and the technical and managerial approach to be taken. It gathers information on the availability of the resources such as materials, finance and people. The process includes the preparation of the project schedule, considers contingency planning and identifies the standards of performance. Finally, it determines how tasks are to be tracked, reported and administered. The MICE project plan should be considered as being more complex than just scheduling all the various activities.

The management of a project can be seen to provide a well-structured method that will:

- enhance cooperation and team spirit within an organisation
- define and specify the scope and goals of the work to be undertaken and develop options to achieve these goals
- monitor and control work as it is actually done
- assist in identifying, estimating and scheduling tasks in order to carry out the project (Weeks 1996, p. 16).

PLANNING CONVENTIONS OR MEETINGS

The planning of a convention or meeting begins with the preparation of a bid submission, which is amended or updated once the bid is accepted, and continues until the final evaluation report is completed. A major part of the planning process for a MICE event is the preparation and development of the convention or meeting plan.

■ Pre-event *planning*

The preparation of the convention or meeting plan follows a number of stages. In the pre-event planning stage the tasks to be undertaken are identified, organised into a logical and understandable form and then scheduled in a systematic manner into a time line.

Task identification

The pre-event planning phase is the longest period in the preparation and execution of an event. The MICE project team needs to review whether the event design is both viable and feasible. The technique of brainstorming is extremely useful in these initial stages, as it helps to identify ideas and tasks and encourages lateral and creative thinking (Quinn et al. 1996, p. 355). In the initial proposal and bid document, the PCO will have identified the type, purpose and objectives of the event and any theme to be included, the number of days required for the event, the potential delegates and their travel requirements, and will have provided an estimation of the overall budget. However, there are a number of other issues that need to be considered in the brainstorming session, for example:

- inspection and selection of the site and venue — accommodation standard, room rates, check-in and check-out procedures, number of rooms, range and size of meeting facilities, accessibility, availability of breakout space, and so on
- food and beverage — food quality and service, menu styles, prices, and so on
- transport — venue accessibility (e.g. distance from domestic/international airport, flight frequency, road access)
- entertainment and pizzazz to support the theme (e.g. gifts, mementos, decoration)
- budgets, legal aspects, any special requirements regarding licensing, cancellation insurance, and so on
- marketing and promotion
- miscellaneous — audiovisual equipment, lighting, speakers, specialised printing, menus, and so on.

Once the brainstorming stage is completed, the ideas generated can be reviewed and organised under task areas.

In order to gain repeat business, conference organisers need to demonstrate, through their project management, that they can run a professional and smooth operation that both satisfies the client organisation and their participants and provides a healthy bottom line.

Organisation of tasks

Once the task areas and various activities have been identified, they are divided into 'work packages' so that a work breakdown structure (WBS) can be prepared. The WBS is a hierarchical tree of the tasks that need to be undertaken in the preparation of a MICE event. It identifies the organisation, supplier or individual responsible for each activity and the estimated time required to complete each activity. Table 8.1 outlines a section from a sample WBS for a convention. Figure 8.1 provides the preliminary details of the projected time line and key tasks included in the bid document for a conference for 300 delegates.

■ Table 8.1
Section from a sample WBS

ACTIVITY	ESTIMATED TIME (DAYS)	PERSON RESPONSIBLE
1. Destination and venue selection	21	J. Brown
Task	0.5	S. Smith
Contact CVB	1	S. Smith
Contact potential venues	5	S. Smith
Obtain information	0.5	S.Smith
Organise venue inspection	3	J. Brown/S. Smith
Undertake venue inspection	0.5	J. Brown
Agree venue	0.5	J. Brown
• Brief venue	1	J. Brown/K. Fields
• Organise contract		
2. Conference program	20	A. Zerrott
Task		A. Francis
Speakers		
• Select speakers		
• Notify speakers		
• Obtain A/V requirements		
Conference proceedings	10	S. Smith
• Call for papers	10	S. Smith
• Receive and process abstracts	12	S. Smith
• Receive papers	20	See list of referees
• Referee papers	4	J. Brown
• Notify authors	21	S. Smith
• Organise publishing of papers		
	7	M. Murray
Social program		
• Agree program		
• Organise welcome cocktail party		
• Organise partner program		

■ **Figure 8.1**
*Projected time
line and key
tasks for the
Australian/
American
Massage
Therapy
Exchange
Program*

OUTLINE CRITICAL PATH PLAN

February 1998
- Determine objectives of meeting
- Confirm set-up requirements at venue and number of workshops
- Select and book venue, meeting space and accommodation
- Pay deposit to venue
- Draft initial budget

March 1998
- Develop program
- Confirm and invite speakers
- Determine topics of presentations
- Brief speakers and send full agenda
- Develop exhibition floor plan
- Obtain potential sponsors and exhibitors list
- Produce and mail sponsorship and exhibition selling document
- Develop, print and mail preliminary announcement
- Develop marketing plan
- Confirm and book venues for social program
- Book tours

April 1998
- Finalise all details of sessions, speakers, social program, entertainment and registration fees
- Develop registration brochure
- Contact potential sponsors and exhibitors and confirm involvement

May 1998
- Print and mail registration brochure
- Book speakers' travel and accommodation
- Receive registrations at secretariat and develop delegate lists
- Send regular updates to client

June 1998
- Send initial accommodation lists to hotels
- Send letters to delegates confirming registration and accommodation

July 1998
- Confirm A/V requirements
- Order satchels
- Send out exhibitor manuals

August 1998
- Confirm detailed arrangements for venue, menus and timings
- Print conference program
- Purchase speakers' gifts if applicable
- Organise signage
- Obtain all insertions for satchels
- Organise pads and pens

September 1998
Week beginning 7 September 1998
- Confirm final catering numbers
- Print name badges
- Pack satchels
- Print final delegate list
- Print social tickets
- Exhibition set up and move in

Week beginning 14 September 1998
- Update delegate lists after meeting
- Develop post-meeting report
- Reconcile accounts and pay all outstanding bills
- Send thankyou letters to sponsors, exhibitors and speakers

Source: Reproduced with the permission of OCC Australia Pty Ltd

The WBS does not provide details as to the order in which the various activities should be undertaken, and does not indicate whether, for example, activity A should be completed before activity B, or whether the two can proceed at the same time (Quinn et al. 1996, p. 178). For a simple conference or meeting the interrelationships between the different tasks and activities are not difficult to establish. However, for a more complex event it is useful to portray these interrelationships graphically in the form of a network diagram, which shows the sequence of activities and any interdependencies that might influence the overall achievement of the MICE event. Popular techniques for preparing network diagrams are critical path analysis (CPA, or CPM) or programme evaluation review techniques (PERT) and Gantt charts.

CPA allows the conference organiser to see the flow of tasks required and estimate the amount of time that will be necessary to complete the overall project. It takes into consideration the interdependencies among tasks and identifies the critical points where a delay in the completion of one task could have a major effect on the overall project. In undertaking CPA it is assumed that all the tasks or activities can be identified or sequenced clearly and that the necessary time for completing each task can be estimated.

A Gantt chart is simply a bar chart that plots the time required for each task. The chart shows the expected start date and completion time for each task. There are a number of computer software packages that will calculate and produce a network diagram, such as Microsoft Project. Figure 8.2 shows a section from a sample Gantt chart for a convention.

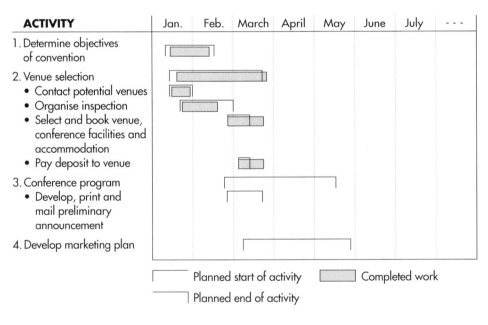

■ **Figure 8.2**
Sample section from a Gantt chart for a convention

Another task to be undertaken in the process of preparing a network diagram is to estimate the length of time taken to undertake and complete each task and the resources that will be required. In addition the cost for each task or group of tasks is then calculated. This information is prepared as one of the stages in the preparation of a Gantt chart in order to estimate whether the event can be completed in the required time, at the required cost and with the available resources. If not, then adjustments need to be made in relation to the scope of the work, the time estimated or the available resources, so that an achievable base plan is established. This 'road map' (Gido & Clements 1999, p. 11) forms the basis for the implementation of the event and its component activities. Actual progress on the various activities is monitored and measured against the plan and corrective action is taken. Corrective action is required, for example, when aspects of the event are behind schedule or over budget, such as if the design and printing of the delegate registration brochure are behind schedule or there is an overrun on the budget for the theming of the opening ceremony. If costs overrun, the original costs are reviewed and savings are made either in this area or in another area of the event.

CPA and Gantt charts are useful in the management of an event as they focus on:

- *Planning* — they pinpoint the tasks that need to be done and identify the order in which they should be done. By drawing a network diagram, the logical progression of tasks is established, and any woolly or illogical thinking is identified and thus can be dealt with.

- *Scheduling* — they calculate the total time required for the project, clearly identify the tasks to be undertaken, highlight critical jobs and indicate where there is time to spare.

- *Allocating and controlling resources* — they identify any spare time, people or funds.

- *Controlling progress and costs* — progress can be checked against the network diagram and actual costs can be recorded against planned costs. If the timetable gets delayed, the various activities affected can be pinpointed and dealt with as appropriate.

- *Communicating* — clear and concise information can be communicated to the appropriate people. Everyone knows their role and how this interacts with what others are doing.

The conference organiser can control the MICE event effectively by reviewing the Gantt or CPA chart regularly. The actual progress of the event can be measured against the planned progress, and with the assistance of the MICE team corrective action can be taken as and where necessary.

The following industry insight illustrates the value of involving local stakeholders in the planning and organisation of a national conference in a regional town. A key benefit in this instance was that, through the use and involvement of local stakeholders such as accommodation operators and an audiovisual specialist, the town was able to host a larger conference capacity than any one individual facility within the town was able to manage.

In August 1998 the National Fresh Stone Fruit Industry held its annual conference at Ballina in Northern New South Wales, a town better known for its access to surf beaches than as a mecca for the convention industry.

The venue selected to host the four-day conference, which attracted in excess of 380 delegates, was the Ballina RSL Club Ltd. The club's facilities include a main auditorium capable of seating more than 500 delegates and a range of meeting rooms, all situated on the first floor of the building and easily accessible by an escalator, lift and stairs. In addition, the RSL club provides a range of food and beverage outlets, extensive car parking facilities and an enviable location as it is situated adjacent to the river in the centre of the town. The main plenary sessions for the conference were held in the auditorium and the remaining function rooms were used for other sessions. A hockerdome was erected in an adjacent car park to house a trade show. This also provided the venue for lunch, thus enabling the delegates to view the exhibition stands on each of the four days of the conference. A number of other venues throughout the town were used to host small private sessions and dinners. A focal point of the conference was the gala dinner which was held at the RSL club and included entertainment.

The conference organising committee comprised local stone fruit growers and regional members of the industry. This committee organised the program which, in addition to formal sessions at the RSL club, provided delegates with the opportunity to visit a number of local stone fruit establishments. A 10-month planning time frame was provided, from the time that the booking was confirmed until the actual event.

The RSL club realised the importance of involving local suppliers in the event and so contact was made with, among others, the town's tourist information centre, a local audiovisual equipment supplier (for the extensive audiovisual requirements), and a Gold-Coast based exhibition company (to organise the hockerdome and supporting equipment required to house the conference trade show). The tourist information centre coordinated the accommodation operators and provided a range of accommodation both in terms of facilities and price. It established a delegate accommodation booking facility and became the focal point for delegate accommodation enquiries. In addition, it organised and coordinated a 'partner program' for the accompanying partners.

At the RSL club the manager set up an in-house conference project planning team comprising the functions supervisor, the catering and beverage managers, the marketing and advertising manager and an

(continued)

external audiovisual specialist. This group identified the tasks required and delegated areas of responsibility. The manager liaised with the audiovisual specialist and the exhibition company to determine and confirm arrangements. Approval was gained from the local council for the siting and use of the hockerdome in the car park. Regular contact was made with members of the conference organising committee to update them on progress and clarify details.

A pre-conference meeting and a post-conference evaluation were undertaken. From this event, the key points identified for effective conference management were:

- the need for extensive communication between the team, the suppliers and the organisers
- effective planning, particularly in establishing the schedule of tasks and their achievement within specific time frames
- a planning team comprising the functions supervisor, functions coordinator and the catering and beverage managers.

Source: Bill Coulter, Ballina RSL Club Ltd

■ Planning *the program*

The planning of the convention or meeting program is the next key stage in the convention or meeting plan. In forming the proposed draft program, the conference organiser needs to identify the length of both the total meeting and the individual sessions. They also need to consider and incorporate the formal conference sessions and refreshment breaks, and any social activities, free time, exhibitions and trade shows as required.

Program design

The program design should cater for the needs of the delegates while at the same time keeping in mind the overall objectives of the conference. For this reason, each session should last no longer than two hours, and preferably only one and a half hours. This is because delegates' attention spans and interest levels wane after about one and a half hours and so they need a break. Such breaks, usually for refreshments, last from 15 to 30 minutes for morning and afternoon tea, to one or two hours for lunch, dinner or a cocktail reception. The style of MICE event can influence the length of the sessions and timetabled breaks. For example, for a large convention of 300 to 400 people, a 15-minute refreshment break would be too short and would not allow delegates enough time to leave the main room, obtain their refreshments, stretch their legs or network. For a training course of 15 to 20 people, a break of 15 minutes for morning or afternoon tea may be sufficient.

In planning the program, particularly for conventions and meetings that last more than one day, time needs to be allowed for viewing the exhibits and networking, as well as for free time and entertainment. The timing of the opening session is also important. For example, an opening session that commences at 9 a.m. may be fine for a conference or meeting that is held in a central location, such as the CBD, and where the majority of delegates are based in the vicinity. However, for delegates who need to travel inter and intra state, this may mean arriving the evening before or catching a very early flight. As an alternative, the first session may be a welcome reception held the evening before the opening session. This allows those delegates who have arrived early the opportunity to mingle and network.

Pace and timing of the program

Attending a convention or meeting is an investment in time and money for the delegates. They and the organiser of the event want the meeting to be productive. In the design of the program it is important that there is sufficient time and an appropriate number of sessions to achieve the overall objectives of the event, while at the same time ensuring that the timing is not overgenerous. For example, if a program designed to cover a two-day period could have been accommodated in less than one day, delegates can leave feeling frustrated, with their feelings of accomplishment and their vision of the effectiveness and efficiency of the meeting diluted.

Other factors to be considered include the delegate profile, the need for participants to move about (particularly after sitting for a period of time), travel distance to the event and the style of event. For example, at the refreshment breaks of a corporate meeting, delegates may need to contact their office for updates. In addition, other issues such as accompanying partners, the complexity of the material being covered, the requirements for breakout sessions and costs need to be looked at. For example, some groups and companies, particularly corporate conferences and meetings or training sessions, may wish to incorporate early morning and evening sessions, increase the number of breaks and include some physical activity as a more effective use of time. Other conventions or meetings, however, such as an annual international convention or an incentive conference, may require a slower pace and more varied leisure time.

Components of the program

The components of the program tend to comprise four main areas: the formal meeting sessions; the provision of food and beverages; exhibition and trade shows; and free time and social activities.

Formal meeting sessions

For a basic meeting such as a one-day seminar, the program might comprise three to four formal meeting sessions, each of approximately one to one and a half hours in duration, morning and afternoon tea breaks and lunch. This may be a 'working lunch', where a lighter style of menu is chosen. Figure 8.3 outlines a basic program for a one-day training seminar.

8.30–9.00 a.m.	Delegate registration
9.00–10.30 a.m.	Session one
	Welcome, introduction to day
10.30–11.00 a.m.	Refreshment break
11.00–12.30 p.m.	Session two
12.30–1.45 p.m.	Lunch, e.g. light working lunch of open sandwiches, two/three salads, fruit platter, orange juice, tea/coffee
1.45–3.15 p.m.	Session three
3.15–3.45 p.m.	Refreshment break
3.45–5.15 p.m.	Session four
5.15 p.m.	Close of session
	End of day

Basic audiovisual equipment provided as part of conference delegate fee — overhead projector and screen, whiteboard, pens and lectern.
Room set up — U-shape.

Conferences or meetings normally include general or plenary sessions, which all delegates attend, and breakout sessions, where delegates break away from the main group and attend smaller group meetings. The main plenary or general sessions tend to focus on the key issues that may affect or be of interest to all participants, while the breakout sessions are more suitable for the sharing of information. Breakout sessions tend to be timetabled as round-table discussion sessions or workshops. Many programs contain general or plenary sessions for the discussion of the main topic or theme, followed by smaller breakout sessions for the discussion of a range of topics related to that theme. At some conventions, breakout sessions are repeated two or three times during the program, so that delegates can attend each session.

The opening session of a convention or conference is of utmost importance in relation to the planning of the program, for it is here that the tone, style and content of the convention or meeting is established. A welcome address is normally undertaken by someone holding a key or senior position either within or external to the organisation. In the same way, the end of a convention often signals the culmination of the event and as such there is often a gala banquet, which may be coupled with a series of presentations or awards. The conclusion of an event is just as important as the opening session because it provides the delegates' final impression of the convention or meeting.

Speakers may come from within the organisation or from outside sources, and are selected by the conference organiser to complement and achieve the overall goals and objectives of the event. At major conventions, politicians, key industry leaders and other professional speakers or personalities are often chosen to speak. For example, motivational meetings often focus their choice of speaker on a current 'motivational guru'. An ideal program offers a variety of modes of delivery and speakers in order to maintain the interest of the delegates.

The provision of food and beverages
The food and beverage components of the convention or meeting program play an important part in the overall success of an event. Many conference

organisers consider that they are critical, because the provision of quality food and beverages will be remembered and discussed long after the end of an event. Poor quality food and beverages will have a negative impact on the overall perception of the event, no matter how effective or efficient the other aspects of the conference were.

In planning the convention or meeting program, appropriate times must be scheduled for meals and refreshment breaks. These breaks provide opportunities for delegates to network and socialise, and a great deal of business is carried out informally at this time. The conference organiser also needs to consider the extent of the food and beverage requirements. For example, if a meeting is scheduled for more than two hours, a refreshment break such as morning or afternoon tea will be expected. If delegates have travelled long distances, some organisers may want to welcome them to a day meeting by organising a light refreshment such as morning tea on arrival. At a company management or training meeting, continuous tea and coffee may be required throughout the day. The form and variety of items at refreshment breaks can leave a memorable impression on delegates. Items such as freshly baked biscuits or muffins, fruit smoothies and fresh fruit platters can turn a break into an occasion. Many conference organisers use the opportunities afforded by food and beverage breaks to showcase their local, regional and national cuisine. The provision of food and beverages is discussed in more detail in chapter 9.

Exhibitions and trade shows

If the convention or meeting is to be accompanied by an exhibition or trade show, the conference organiser should schedule enough time in the program to enable delegates to view the exhibits. They should also ensure that the exhibition site is located within the convention area. In this way, delegates can freely access the exhibits.

Free time and social activities

Depending on the length of the convention or meeting, the conference organiser may wish to incorporate some social activities, free time or entertainment in the program. The style and type of activities chosen will be influenced by the nature of the event, but may include, for example, a welcome cocktail party, a gala dinner with guest speaker and/or entertainment, or a tour of the city or local area, such as a harbour cruise. In some areas, wine tasting or local winery tours are firm favourites to be included in conference programs. At incentive events, recreational or sporting activities may be incorporated, such as golf or parasailing. Many resort venues provide a number of packages that can assist conference organisers in the provision of suitable activities to complement the convention program.

■ The convention *or meeting blueprint*

During the pre-event planning stage the conference organiser and the various stakeholders involved in the convention or meeting will develop, either independently or jointly, a planning document for the actual execution of the event. This 'blueprint' (Lovelock 1992, p. 96) is a development and extension of the 'road map' mentioned earlier. Each conference organiser will have a different format for this document, but the following information generally is included:

- contents page
- information on the destination, site, venue, and so on, and the suppliers that are being used
- a detailed list of contacts at the venue, including their telephone numbers
- information on the venue such as meeting rooms, registration information and procedures, and facilities such as restaurants, amenities and sports facilities
- a delegate registration list and room allocations, together with information on their arrival and departure
- daily 'running sheets', which detail the day-to-day plan of each session and event within the conference
- closing information and check list
- evaluation information.

It is also important during this pre-planning stage that the conference organiser 'walks the course' and draws up diagrams and formats for items such as room set ups, and clarifies how the event will actually happen. This information should be included in the blueprint for the convention or meeting. Each stage of the event should be thought through carefully and any critical gaps in the logical progression or thinking should be identified and resolved. At all times, the needs of the participants should be borne in mind.

The information contained within the plan and blueprint should be developed to ensure and maintain management control of the project. The material should be written and organised so that, should it be necessary, any experienced staff member within the conference organiser's direct team could run the convention or meeting.

The snapshot on page 251 demonstrates the practical use of planning tools and indicates the skills required of a conference organiser.

■ Planning *the printed materials*

Planning the printed materials is another stage of the convention or meeting plan. Each convention or meeting incorporates a wide range of printed materials that have to be both planned and organised prior to the actual convention or meeting. This includes marketing collateral, as well as materials that are required for the actual event, such as delegate registration forms, conference brochures and programs, participant name tags, delegate lists, conference proceedings, lists and diagrams of the exhibitor stands, information on sponsors, tickets and vouchers, special invitation letters, signage, T-shirts, and so on.

Ruth McCarthy, conference manager at Axis Conference Planners, left a British university with a degree in modern languages and no idea what she wanted to do as her chosen career. A combined graduate secretarial and business studies course provided her with business skills and led her into the world of publishing, where as a personal assistant (PA) she 'learnt to work'. From publishing she moved to an advertising and promotions agency, and then, realising that she was feeling frustrated with her career as a PA, she sought career advice.

She got as far as 'conference organiser' in the alphabetical directory of career opportunities, when she realised that this was to be her future direction. One of her strengths lay in her ability to organise people and activities — a key requirement of a conference organiser. She began applying for jobs and talking to people in the conference industry and finally joined a small, London-based event management company.

This background experience in event management proved to be very useful in her search for work when she arrived in Australia. Ruth joined Tour Hosts and was contracted initially to manage the social program for a large conference. She later focused on special events and social programs and finally became responsible for the total management of conferences. The two years she spent at Tour Hosts provided a huge learning curve, both in terms of the MICE industry in Australia and the Australian culture and way of life. As a 'Brit', one of her responsibilities was to organise the 'Australiana' events for conferences! She took this seriously, researching the background to the various events and producing an on-site 'passport' and Australiana guide distributed to guests on arrival at the event.

Ruth moved from Tour Hosts to become conference manager at OCC, a medical communications company, where she organised a range of MICE activities from large conferences and educational seminars, to product launches and small events. OCC is involved in strategic marketing and publishing for a number of pharmaceutical companies. As conference organiser for the company, Ruth was involved in the organisation and management of a range of events that were included as part of the marketing package put together by OCC for its clients. Her work included, for example, organising a series of educational seminars for general practitioners and other medical specialists throughout Australia, to launch a new drug for a pharmaceutical company. However, because of the autonomous nature of the conference department within OCC, she could also bid to manage medical association conferences and events, such as the Australian Natural Therapies Association Conference. Her role at OCC was a mix of both corporate and association conference organisation.

(continued)

Reporting directly to the managing director of OCC, Ruth was responsible for the successful financial management of her department. This included monitoring the department's budget and providing a forecast of the external revenue to be generated from conferences. With a staff of one assistant conference manager, she prepared bid documents for potential association business and then, on gaining the business, organised and managed the event, including site and venue selection, pre-event planning such as appointing the venue, and the coordination of the various suppliers.

A key tool within her kitbag was the timeline and critical path for the event. These determine the critical dates for the event, such as the dates for the mailing of conference registration brochures. She sees herself as the project manager for the event, reporting to the client organisation and its conference committee with information on a regular basis. These meetings are often intense, as aspects of the conference are negotiated and information is gathered — for example, discussing details of the program or gaining approval for the brochure copy.

Ruth identifies negotiation skills as being important, as are the ability to be diplomatic and gain clients' confidence in her professional capabilities. It is also important, she realises, to remember that it is the client's conference, and the ideas generated for the conference are 'owned' by the conference committee. The conference organiser is only the facilitator and the person responsible 'for making it happen'.

Recently, Ruth has joined Axis Conference Planners where, in her role as conference manager, she focuses more specifically on the corporate market and is working as part of a larger event management team. While still responsible for some pharmaceutical events, she is expanding her experience of other industries, namely IT, and gaining valuable experience managing events off-shore in parts of Southeast Asia.

Ruth is an accredited meetings manager (AMM) as recognised by the Meetings Industry Association of Australia (MIAA) and is an active member of two MIAA committees. Ruth is currently studying for an MBA on a part-time basis at the Australian Graduate School of Management at the University of New South Wales.

So what has attracted Ruth to, and kept her interested in, her career in the MICE industry? The sense of achievement that is gained when a conference is successful and the variety in the job. Each conference is different, not only in the people she meets but also in the requirements for the event. Each conference may follow a set pattern, but they are all different.

Source: Ruth McCarthy, Axis Conference Planners

Convention and meeting collateral

The objective of the convention or meeting program, as previously discussed, is to inform and guide delegates through the event (Weissinger 1992, p. 106). The program describes the various convention or meeting sessions and gives their location and times. No matter how large or small a meeting is, it will have a program, even if it is only a single sheet listing the agenda items. In many situations, however, it will be both elaborate and varied and will include not only the itinerary but also the profiles of the speakers, an outline of the various sessions and information on sponsors and exhibitors.

At many conventions or meetings, the conference organiser arranges for the papers presented by the speakers to be collated in the form of conference proceedings, which are often printed separately or made available on CD ROM. Abstracts of conference papers also are available prior to the event, on the Internet.

The delegate registration form and brochure often are incorporated into the preliminary conference program, and the registration component usually takes the form of a tear-off slip. Many delegate registration forms are designed to be compatible with industry-specific software programs for ease of delegate data entry. This assists in the speed of data entry for the conference organisation and its secretariat. On-line registration systems, using the Internet, are in use. Potential delegates can view both the conference program and the brochure, and register for the event, via the Internet. A review of the use of technology within the operation of conventions and meetings is discussed in chapter 9.

The conference organiser and their team decide on the presentation, style and format of the convention or meeting program and associated materials. For example, an A4-folder that has been customised specifically may be used to incorporate all the documents that they wish to provide for each participant. They need to plan the design and type of name tags, special invitations, tickets and vouchers for any events outside those incorporated within the conference registration fee or for accompanying partners. Again, industry-specific software programs are available, so that, for example, name tags can be printed with both the delegates' names and the sponsoring company. Other materials that may need to be considered in the pre-event planning include place cards, specially-printed menus for the gala dinner, a daily newsletter that provides delegates with updates of activities and sessions, and promotional or specialist gifts such as commemorative T-shirts, caps, and conference satchels.

At an international convention held in Sydney, all participants were presented with the convention proceedings and program in an 'Aussie' style backpack, and were given a commemorative umbrella, toy koala and bottle of Australian wine. All items featured the logo of the sponsoring company, as well as the name and date of the convention and its location. At a MIAA National Conference held in Tasmania, the focus and theme of the conference, 'The core issues', was highlighted on all the conference materials that were distributed to delegates (see figure 8.4). To spotlight Tasmania, the logo of the conference was an apple.

■ **Figure 8.4**
*Collateral
and delegate
materials for
the MIAA
National
Conference,
Tasmania*

Source: MIAA

■ **Planning** *the registration process*

The organisation of the convention registration process is a further stage of the convention or meeting plan. This is a key area, as it is often the first time that the delegate will come into contact with the conference organiser and their team. The registration process often begins when the completed registration form and conference registration fee are received prior to the actual event. Joining instructions and individual queries are answered at this time. For a convention where the company does not predetermine delegate attendance, delegate pre-registration and payment is essential if the conference organiser is to be appraised of the potential number of participants who will be attending the event and therefore its viability. For a corporate meeting, the conference organiser may be given a list of delegates. The registration process continues when the delegates arrive to attend the event. At this time, the process is usually one of confirming their arrival and attendance details, and providing additional information and conference collateral. For a large convention, the registration process at the actual event can cause queues and potential delays.

Delegate registration systems

The management of queues for delegate registration is an important part of the planning and organisation of a convention or meeting. Queues are an integral part of service delivery and service systems, and include both physical queues and queues related to customers waiting for services, such as room service within a venue. The concept of queuing is inevitable and is seen as a problem as everyone now expects faster service. Lovelock (1992, p. 162) has noted, 'the design and management of queues can have important implications on the perceived quality and speed of the service experience and delivery'. Conference organisers need to consider not only the logistics of managing the queues but also the human issues such as how queuing delegates can pass the time quickly and pleasantly and the maximum amount of time people are prepared to wait for service.

The basic concept in queue behaviour has been identified as the fact that people do not arrive 'to enter' the service process (i.e. registration process) at a given arrival rate (Chase & Aquilano 1992). Though delegates may arrive on average every five minutes, they do not arrive at exactly the same time, that is every fifth minute. If they arrive early, they have to wait until the previous customer is processed; if they arrive late, then there is a loss in the use of the service process and a potential delay for subsequent delegates. At the same time, the process of dealing with each delegate may be longer or shorter than the stated five minutes, which causes a queue to form. To reduce the queue it is essential that the processing of delegate registrations is faster than the average arrival rate of delegates.

Conference organisers need to reflect on the processing of potential queues from the perspective of the customer, that is the delegates. Points they should consider include:
- Is it reasonable to expect delegates to wait for a particular service at that time?
- Is the period that is spent waiting reasonable and acceptable?
- Is the priority process for serving delegates fair? Should it be done on a first come, first served basis, or should another priority process be used?
- Do delegates feel in control of what is happening while they are waiting?
- Is a conducive physical environment provided in which delegates can wait?

There are a number of ways that conference organisers can structure queues to make them more efficient, particularly for delegate registrations at a large convention. Queues can be structured in the following forms at the registration desk:
1. Single channel and single stage — this is the simplest form of a queue, for example one person behind another in a single line.
2. Single channel and multiple stages — delegates go through a number of different stages to complete the service process. For example, delegates queue to register their name and collect their delegate badge and conference satchel. They then proceed to another stage to pick up additional tickets and vouchers, and to yet another stage to complete the registration process for their accommodation.
3. Multiple channels and single stage — delegates form one queue and go to the first available server as they become free. This format is very popular.
4. Parallel single channel with single or multiple stages — this format is often used for large group registrations. The group is divided alphabetically by last name and there are different queues for the different letter groups of the alphabet (e.g. A–E, F–L, and so on).

Conference organisers need to put themselves in the customers' shoes and decide on the best way to manage each queuing system. Delegates registering at large conventions can be distracted in the following ways while they wait and queue:

- They can be given something to do, such as filling in a form, or provided with some entertainment such as buskers or street theatre.
- They can be provided with comfortable waiting conditions such as suitable seating, heating, airconditioning, lighting. For example, the Hotel Nikko, Darling Harbour, has a separate group check-in area for conventions and other groups, complete with its own lounge area.
- They can be provided with refreshments.
- They can be provided with different service points for different categories of delegates. For example, airlines use separate check-in points for first, business and economy passengers as a method of queue management.

Conference organisers can also use a number of quantitative decision-making strategies, such as decision trees, forecasting methods and queuing theory from the field of operations management, for the more effective management of MICE project plans. For more details see Waller (1999) in the further reading list at the end of the chapter.

*M*ANAGING THE CONVENTION OR MEETING PROCESS

The successful management of a convention or meeting project depends on many factors, including the management process.

■ Leading *the planning team*

In chapter 4 it was identified that the employees involved are critical to the success of a MICE event. The planning tools that have been outlined are merely there to assist them to do their jobs more efficiently. It is the convention or meeting team's knowledge and skills that are key to the success of the event.

So what are the leadership qualities that are required of conference organisers in their role as project leader and coordinator of a MICE event? Their leadership style should be both participative and consultative, providing advice, guidance and coaching for the team. This relates to the roles of mentor, facilitator and coordinator outlined in chapter 4. They should provide clear direction to the team, yet not lead by directive. They need to be able to inspire the people working on the event and create for the team an overall vision of the convention or meeting. Having this vision will encourage and inspire the team to work as a group towards the successful completion of the event.

Conference organisers also need to foster involvement and empowerment and create and mould the group into a team. Team members will
want ownership and control of their own work and be able to demonstrate
that they can achieve and accomplish the goals and challenges. They should
be involved in the decision making, particularly with respect to decisions
that affect them, and be empowered and given the authority for their areas
of responsibility. The conference organiser should outline the parameters
and any guidelines on what may need to be done for the event. However, it
is the team that decides on how the tasks may be done. The extent of this
consultative and participative decision making is illustrated in figure 8.5.

■ **Figure 8.5**
*Leadership-
behaviour
continuum*

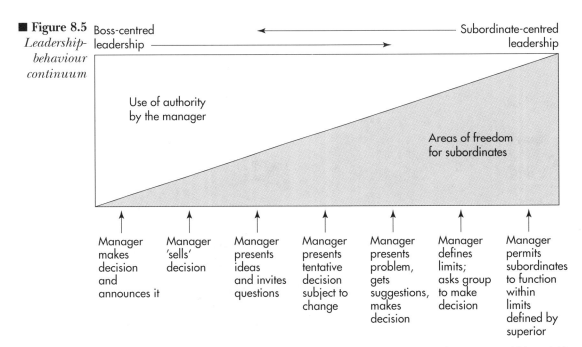

Source: Tannenbaum & Schmidt (1958, p. 164)

Conference organisers can create an environment of participation for
team members by involving them as much as possible — for example, in
presentations to the client company or by drawing on their ideas either at
individual or team meetings. In all cases, the conference organiser should
be supportive and provide mutual respect. As discussed in chapter 4,
acknowledging the contribution of both the individual and the team as a
whole can motivate the team and help team members to feel that they are
making a contribution to the success of an event. An environment of high
expectations, trust and, of course, enjoyment of the task, should be fostered. Conference organisers should set the example by following through
on commitments and living up to their word, thereby demonstrating that
following through on commitments is expected of everyone on the team.

Conference organisers must also be able to delegate, and this requires effective communication skills; these attributes and skills were discussed in chapter 4.

■ Interpersonal *skills*

Excellent interpersonal skills are very important for conference organisers, mainly because projects often lie outside a traditional business organisational structure. In the MICE industry, the project management of a convention or event can operate across areas both within an organisation and outside that organisation. Conference organisers are responsible for ensuring the satisfactory management and coordination of a group of individuals, the project team, and the successful operation of a particular event. This may involve not only team members from the conference organiser's own organisation, but also other individuals and groups from external suppliers such as the venue or audiovisual supplier (see figure 8.6).

■ **Figure 8.6**
The conference organiser and the event team

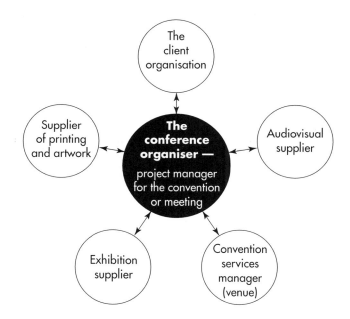

Within a venue, the convention services manager may be seen as the 'project manager', ensuring that all departments come together to provide the particular event. This can mean that the venue's project team incorporates not only the functional areas within the convention service area, but also other departments within the organisation, such as banquet operations, the kitchen, rooms division, front office and concierge.

In dealing with outside organisations, the conference organiser is seen as both the external customer and the project manager. It is their responsibility, as 'project manager', to manage and coordinate both internally within their own organisation and across other areas through the use of external suppliers. For example, a corporate conference organiser may utilise the facilities of the corporate training department and the services of the company's in-house catering department in the provision of an in-company training seminar. While this is good for creativity and innovation, it can cause some conflicts with respect to the priorities of the project team members, who may have conflicting priorities, such as other work to do, over which the project manager, the conference organiser, has no authority. In such instances, the conference organiser needs to be a good negotiator and be competent in the skills of conflict management, particularly when working with other line managers such as a convention service manager at a venue.

Interpersonal skills are required for dealings with the client organisation as well. The conference organiser has to recognise that it is the client's event and, as such, they should guide and assist to ensure that the suggestions that are made or required are successful. This can be challenging, particularly when the client organisation suggests ideas that are not viable. In such instances, the conference organiser must be able to 'turn the suggestion' around and quickly come up with an alternative that is both viable and leaves the client organisation feeling satisfied and 'owning' the suggestion. The internal and external coordination of a project is an area that often is not emphasised as much as that of the formal planning and control aspects (Quinn et al. 1996, p. 184).

While it is preferable to have well-defined outcomes for a project, this is not always possible. What is important is that there is close contact with the client organisation. There should be regular communication, either formally or informally, as to the progress of the event. It is also important to communicate regularly with the key people in the convention or meeting organisation as to the progress of the project. For example, in a venue this is achieved in many instances through the senior managers' weekly meeting, whereby the convention services manager provides an update of the status of forthcoming major conventions or events.

There are several generic project management strategies that MICE managers can use to ensure the successful management and organisation of the convention or meeting team (see Quinn et al. 1996). For example:

- In the case of a large project with well-defined outcomes but a team with little experience behind it (e.g. the annual convention of an association whose managerial advisory team has little or no experience of organising such an event) the conference organiser should depend heavily on more formal planning and control techniques.
- For a project that has a clearly-defined outcome and a high level of in-company experience (e.g. the annual sales conference of a corporate conference organiser), the conference organiser should draw heavily on the internal integration of the organisation's team.
- In the case of a large project with loosely defined outcomes and a team with little company experience behind it, the conference organiser needs to emphasise the need for external integration, formal planning and

formal control. This may well be the situation that a PCO will have to deal with in the coordination and management of a large international convention for an association. The management committee within the local association may have little or no experience and once the 'bid is won' may be given the task of ensuring its organisation and success. They may appoint a PCO who must then emphasise 'external integration' in the coordination of all the various suppliers and ensure that there is a formal planning and control system in place to monitor and coordinate the event to its ultimate success.

- In the case of a project with loosely defined outcomes but a team with much company experience behind it, the conference organiser will find their people skills at peak demand, as they will rely heavily on both internal and external integration (Quinn et al. 1996, p. 184).

In summary, conference organisers need to be highly motivated, lead by example, provide a positive, 'can do' attitude and have a desire to achieve and overcome obstacles. The MICE industry is an industry that attracts people who are confident and who thrive on challenges and getting things done. This is very evident in the role of the MICE event project managers.

𝒮UMMARY

Efficient and effective planning is extremely important for the success of a convention or meeting. In particular, it is crucial to have a structured plan. However, the management and leadership skills of the conference organiser and the ability of the stakeholders of the event to work together as a team are also integral to the success of the event.

The role of planning and, in particular, project planning, is critical in the planning, organisation and scheduling of a MICE event. There are various plans that may be prepared for the MICE organisation, each with certain characteristics and components, but key to the successful planning of an event is the preparation of a project plan that covers the various stages of the event life cycle. In addition, a number of other planning tools can assist in the successful coordination of all the activities of the event.

Conference organisers planning MICE events must remember the lead times required to undertake certain activities, be methodical, check and recheck targets, and review the plan constantly to ensure that it is on schedule. They must also prepare a contingency plan in case something goes wrong — disasters do happen.

Activity

8.1 Imagine that you have been asked to organise either:

(a) A series of evening seminars for general practitioners, to be held in the main centres of New South Wales. The client is a pharmaceutical company that wishes to promote a new range of drugs. The expected attendance at each seminar is between 200 and 250 doctors.

(b) An annual gala ball for the Australasian senior and middle managers and their partners of a blue-chip oil company. The expected number of participants is 500. The company would like the event to be held in either Melbourne or Adelaide. The event is to take place in six months time.

Identify the information and tasks that would need to be considered in the planning of one of these events. Prepare a brief work breakdown structure and a time line of the activities. Then, in groups, discuss how as project manager for the event you would organise and lead the team.

Discussion questions

8.1 Discuss the role of the MICE stakeholders in the planning and organisation of a convention or meeting.

8.2 Why is project planning an essential planning tool for a MICE event?

8.3 List and explain the main phases of the MICE event project life cycle.

8.4 Discuss the benefits of using project planning techniques in the management and planning of a MICE event.

8.5 Why should the conference organiser monitor the progress of a project event? What can be done if a convention or meeting is not proceeding according to plan?

8.6 Critically evaluate why the pre-event planning stage is paramount to the success of the convention or meeting.

8.7 Review the purpose of a MICE event 'blueprint' plan. Discuss the information that might be included in the plan.

8.8 What factors should be considered in the planning of a program for a convention or meeting?

8.9 Identify and evaluate the methods that could be used in managing the registration for 1000 delegates at a convention.

REFERENCES

Chase, R. B. & Aquilano, N. J. 1992, *Production and Operations Management,* Irwin, Homewood, Ill.

Gido J. & Clements, J. P. 1999, *Successful Project Management,* South West College Publishing, Cincinnati.

Lovelock, C. H. 1992, *Managing Services: Marketing, Operations and Human Resources,* 2nd ed, Prentice-Hall, Englewood Cliffs, N.J.

Quinn, R. E., Faerman, S. R., Thompson, M. P. & McGrath, M. R 1996, *Becoming A Master Manager: A Competency Framework,* 2nd ed, John Wiley & Sons, New York.

Tannenbaum, R. & Schmidt, W. H. 1958, 'How to Choose a Leadership Pattern', *Harvard Business Review,* March/April.

Weeks, P. 1996, *MN199 — Project Management in the Tourism Industry: Study Guide,* School of Tourism and Hospitality Management, Southern Cross University, Lismore.

Weissinger, S. S.1992, *A Guide to Successful Meeting Planning,* John Wiley & Sons, New York.

FURTHER READING

McGeoch, R. & Korporaal, G. 1994. *The Bid: How Australia Won the 2000 Games,* Heinemann, Melbourne.

Montgomery, R. J. & Strick, S. K. 1996, *Meetings, Conventions and Expositions: An Introduction to the Industry,* Van Nostrand Reinhold, New York.

Quain, W. J. & Render, B. 1990, 'A Practical Guide to Quantitative Decision Making in the Conventions Industry', in Roehl, W. S. (ed) Proceedings of the Convention/Expo Summit, 1. William J. Harrah College of Hotel Administration, University of Nevada, Las Vegas, pp. 74–83.

Waller, D. 1999, *Operations Management: A Supply Chain Approach,* International Thomson, London.

···

Australian Tourism and Hospitality Research Conference, Coffs Harbour

The Council for Australian University Tourism and Hospitality Education (CAUTHE), an organisation representing Australian universities that offer tourism or hospitality degree programs, holds an annual conference that has become the leading national forum for the exchange of information between tourism researchers and the presentation of new research results. The conference, normally held in February, is popular and well attended by university academics, researchers, postgraduate students and representatives from the tourism and hospitality industry. Held in a different destination each year, it attracts in excess of 200 delegates from Australia and overseas. Each member university has the opportunity to 'bid' to manage and organise the conference. In 1995, the responsibility for the management and organisation of the 1996 conference was given to the School of Tourism and Hospitality Management at Southern Cross University.

So, what were some of the planning processes undertaken to provide the 1996 conference?

A conference planning team was established in February 1995 (12 months before the conference) under the direction and chair of the head of the School of Tourism and Hospitality Management. A decision was taken to organise and manage the total event in-house, utilising the expertise of both the academic and administrative staff within the school. The conference planning team was divided into a number of key areas: conference organisation, conference program, conference proceedings, finance, marketing, publicity and sponsorship. The team leaders met weekly from the end of February 1995 under the guidance of the chairman.

One of the first tasks carried out by the planning team was the brainstorming of the activities to be undertaken in the preparation stage of the conference, together with the preparation of an outline time line. This provided a road map of the activities and their scheduling and was continually updated as the conference planning progressed. A section of the time line for the conference is shown in figure 8.7.

Destination and venue selection
The selection of the destination and the choice of venue were important decisions. The resort city of Coffs Harbour was selected as the conference destination. Located on the New South Wales eastern seaboard, it provided a number of venues offering conference facilities, an extensive range of

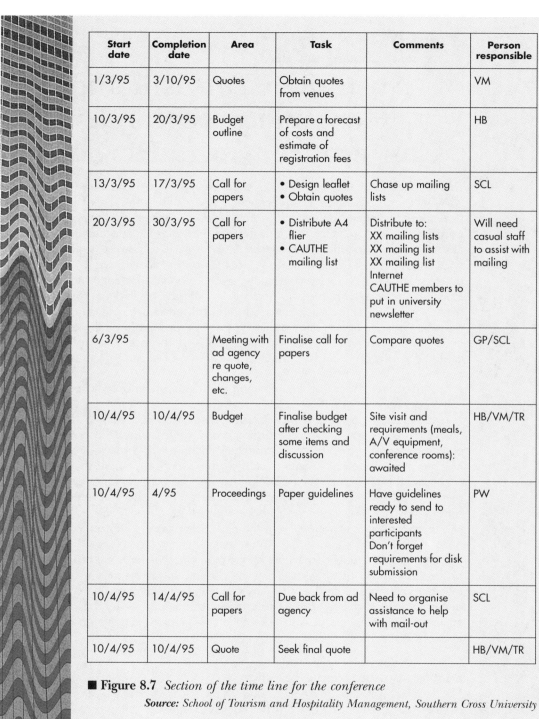

Start date	Completion date	Area	Task	Comments	Person responsible
1/3/95	3/10/95	Quotes	Obtain quotes from venues		VM
10/3/95	20/3/95	Budget outline	Prepare a forecast of costs and estimate of registration fees		HB
13/3/95	17/3/95	Call for papers	• Design leaflet • Obtain quotes	Chase up mailing lists	SCL
20/3/95	30/3/95	Call for papers	• Distribute A4 flier • CAUTHE mailing list	Distribute to: XX mailing lists XX mailing list XX mailing list Internet CAUTHE members to put in university newsletter	Will need casual staff to assist with mailing
6/3/95		Meeting with ad agency re quote, changes, etc.	Finalise call for papers	Compare quotes	GP/SCL
10/4/95	10/4/95	Budget	Finalise budget after checking some items and discussion	Site visit and requirements (meals, A/V equipment, conference rooms): awaited	HB/VM/TR
10/4/95	4/95	Proceedings	Paper guidelines	Have guidelines ready to send to interested participants Don't forget requirements for disk submission	PW
10/4/95	14/4/95	Call for papers	Due back from ad agency	Need to organise assistance to help with mail-out	SCL
10/4/95	10/4/95	Quote	Seek final quote		HB/VM/TR

■ **Figure 8.7** *Section of the time line for the conference*
        Source: *School of Tourism and Hospitality Management, Southern Cross University*

Start date	Completion date	Area	Task	Comments	Person responsible
13/4/95	ASAP		Visit potential venues	VM & TR for site inspection. Agree price with venue. Site inspection of ancillary accommodation • menus/meals • morning and afternoon teas (healthy, variety) • lunches • breakout areas • conference rooms • BBQ (calypso theme) • conference dinner Packages include: 1. Full conference Tues–Friday (cocktail party, BBQ, official dinner, morning and afternoon tea, lunch) 2. Daily rate (morning and afternoon teas & lunch) 3. Accompanying person 4. Student rate	VM, TR
15/4/95		Travel	• Need to discuss with airlines re sponsorship • DP to provide in/out Coffs flight list	Liaise with DP	SCL
15/4/95		EVENTS software	Need IBM computer specifically for running EVENTS	Prefer laptop	To go in SCL and VM's office
20/4/95		Guest speakers	• Conference dinner • Celebrity list for dinner	Who is to organise this?	GP, etc.
20/4/95		Keynote speakers	Selection of invitations	Who is to organise this?	GP, etc.
30/4/95		Meet with VCB		• Coffs brochures/ maps • Venue brochures	

accommodation at different price ranges and easy access to a domestic airport with a number of daily flights to and from Sydney.

A site inspection of a number of the venues was undertaken against predetermined criteria that included:

- a main conference room with a seating capacity of 300 people (theatre style) for plenary sessions
- a range of supporting conference and meeting rooms (minimum six) with capacity to seat 25 to 75 delegates plus breakout facilities
- exhibition space for 10 to 15 exhibitors
- the configuration of conference and meeting rooms to be in the same area to assist speed and ease of delegate access between sessions
- provision of lunch and some meals to be away from the conference area, to make the most of the resort atmosphere
- venue to be four-star standard (minimum three-and-a-half-star) and to be able to accommodate all delegates if required
- good-quality facilities and service, excellent food and beverage service.

The venue selected was not only available at the required time but was able to provide all the facilities. It offered access to all public areas, plus the use of a large foyer area overlooking the ocean for an exhibition area and breakout space for the service of refreshments. The facilities of an on-site audiovisual company were available.

Program design

The main conference held over three days was designed to include a plenary session at the beginning of each day, followed by five or six concurrent sessions examining various themes. In addition, there were a number of social activities that facilitated delegate networking opportunities and the exchange of ideas. Each session lasted no more than one-and-a-half hours and was followed by a refreshment break. The resort-style location and time of year were also taken into consideration in the design of the social activities and the provision of refreshments. For example, ice-creams and cordials were available for delegates at one of the afternoon refreshment breaks.

The social side of the program included a welcome cocktail party with a hotfork buffet, poolside barbecue, conference dinner with a celebrity speaker and a nightclub that operated on two of the three evenings. The opportunities for pre- and post-conference tours of the local area were also included, along with the facility for partner activities. It was anticipated that some partners would attend the event due to its location and the local convention and visitors bureau agreed to staff a desk at the conference so that delegates could organise additional tours.

Preparation of 'running sheets'

So that all members of the conference team were familiar with the operational aspects of the event, and to assist in communication, 'running sheets' were prepared for all conference activities and sessions. An extract from the running sheets is shown in figure 8.8. These were distributed to each member of the team plus the venue's convention services manager. In addition, a copy was included in the conference file (the conference blueprint).

Members of the conference planning team undertook the outlined tasks in the pre-planning stages. In the final few weeks prior to the event the pre-planning activities focused on cross-communication with the team and the venue and final adjustments to the program and conference operations. This included a review of all final arrangements, with some small revisions being made, and a confirmation of the final numbers.

Tuesday 6 February 1996		**Wednesday 7 February 1996**	
Conference registration		*Plenary conference session*	
Time:	10.00 a.m.–6.00 p.m.	Time:	8.30 a.m. –10.30 a.m.
Venue:	Ocean View Foyer	Venue:	Shearwater + Currawong
Set up:	Registration tables — 3 × trestles, skirted, plus chairs	No. of persons:	220
		Set up:	Stage
Signage:	'Conference registration' — yellow and blue		Theatre-style seating Top table × 4 persons.
Conference badges:	alphabetical order, plus delegate lists		Pads, pens, mints, water
Conference packs:	to be given out at registration	Audiovisual:	Slide show — sponsors plus conference logo
Need:	EVENTS software/laptop		Lapel microphone
Responsibility:	X person		Lectern plus microphone
Staffing:	X persons		Conference signage — plus banners
		Presenters:	Prof. X — opening address Prof. Y Dr. Z
		Responsibility:	X person
		Sponsor:	SCU

■ **Figure 8.8** *Extract from the running sheets for the conference as at 30 January*

Source: *School of Tourism and Hospitality Management, Southern Cross University*

Questions

1 Critically evaluate the use of the time line as a planning tool for this event. What other functions did it fulfil?

2 Discuss and explore why an effective planning system was critical in the management of this event.

9 Managing and *organising convention operations*

LEARNING OBJECTIVES

After studying this chapter, you will be able to:

- identify the factors affecting pre-conference operations

- outline a range of conference room configurations

- discuss factors affecting food and beverage services

- discuss and evaluate effective food and beverage styles

- identify and discuss the impact of computer technology on conference and meeting operations.

INTRODUCTION

As already noted in previous chapters, the organisation hosting a convention or meeting has to be confident that both the destination and its venues are able to 'orchestrate' the event successfully. Once the organisation has chosen a site or venue, and planned all the elements for the event, it is then up to the venue itself to produce what has been promised. The conference or meeting has moved from a sales imperative to an operational one. This chapter focuses on the practicalities of organising and managing operational aspects of the event, such as reserving space for the event and ensuring registration and gathering areas are adequate for the needs of the conference organiser. The chapter also examines food and beverage issues, conference room configurations and technological tools that can be incorporated into the management and operation of a successful event.

PRE-CONVENTION OPERATIONS

Long before a single delegate has arrived at the conference or meeting, the staff at the venue have begun to address the operational aspects of the event. Management at the venue has to consider the many variables that could impact on the smooth operation of the event, including:

- attendance at a similar or previous year's event
- the type of event
- the variety of styles of event (banquets, meetings, workshops, and so on)
- the timing of the various elements within the event
- the total timing of the event
- the special needs of the delegates (e.g. food items, audiovisual (A/V) equipment, and so on)
- the special needs of the organisers (e.g. themed meals)
- staffing implications
- menu types and styles
- the intricacy of room configuration
- break-down and set-up timings.

All these variables, as well as others specific to the particular venue, are taken into consideration once the venue has been selected, the several contracts exchanged and deposits received to guarantee the booking.

In addition to in-house meetings that focus on the needs of the organisation, contact with the client is a vital aspect of pre-event operations. These meetings can achieve a number of things:

- They can be an extra source of confirmation of the booking.
- They can further develop the relationship between the venue and the client.
- They can be a vehicle for the introduction of in-house personnel to the client.
- They can provide useful feedback as a post-conference evaluation.

Depending on the size, complexity and lead time involved, there could be numerous items that need further detailed discussion. These could include final room rates; food and beverage items; check-in procedures; the handling of special invited guest speakers; room configurations and their set-up and break-down times; audiovisual needs; table decorations; and, of course, any last-minute changes to the event schedule (Hoyle, Dorf & Jones, 1989, pp. 203–4).

■ Computerised *booking systems*

More and more venues, especially the larger ones such as purpose-built convention and exhibition centres and hotels with extensive conference and convention space, use current computer technology to control and manipulate many of the elements that are common to pre-event activities. While some hotel property management systems (PMS) such as Maxial and Fidelio have incorporated a simple room booking system into their overall package, programs such as EVENTS for Windows have been able to include a more complex and sophisticated booking system. In most cases, the use of computer technology has been beneficial and allowed tighter control of conference space.

The ability to trace (follow the progress of) clients from the moment they contact the venue, through the conference or meeting to its conclusion and post-event activities is one aspect of computerisation that has certainly assisted convention sales and marketing within the conference venue. With far more certainty, client account managers can provide venue management with a range of market intelligence — a critical tool in gaining repeat business and in the provision of quality client-centred service. Some of the data that can be obtained very quickly and efficiently from such systems include:

- the average number of delegates per day
- the average delegate expenditure per day
- the average delegate expenditure per period of day
- all biographical data for the organiser(s)
- full details of any previous events
- comments from both clients and venue staff
- all previous menus and room configurations.

As well as client-specific details, a computerised system also can provide management with an analysis of past, present and forecasted events. According to Shock and Stefanelli (1992, pp. 45–6) such sales and marketing information could include the following:

- total revenue
- average revenue per event
- numbers and types of events in a particular time period
- average expenditure per delegate by event type or time of year
- average number of delegates by type of event
- space utilisation percentages, overall and by room
- popularity of different types of events
- number and percentage of repeat business
- number and percentage of referral business.

■ Manual *booking system*

Computers are not used in a vast number of venues. Smaller providers such as motels, small conference centres and clubs tend to rely on a manual system for room control and client information. Many of these providers see their conference revenue as an 'extra', might only have one or two meeting/conference rooms for hire or might not consider the return on the cost for a computer system as warranting the expense. The manual system is broken down into several parts, all of which have to fit together and be very tightly controlled by management. When a client makes a tentative booking a convention enquiry sheet is completed with as much detail as possible (see figure 9.1).

The function diary (or whatever the organisation calls it) is then completed with basic details of the event, including times and room requirements (see figure 9.2). There is usually one page per day for the year and perhaps a separate diary for the following year, to accommodate forward booking. The function diary is normally considered to be 'the bible' for meeting and conference room control. When a client enquires about space, the function diary is the first point of contact for the individual charged with meeting room reservations. Once the event is confirmed, sales and marketing information is collated manually, usually in some form of filing system. Each event has its own file or folder, and all information, from original contacts, menus and room set-up to internal notes and post-conference evaluation, is contained within the event folder or file. Unfortunately, it can take a great deal of time and personnel resources to collate all the information and present management with some form of coherent and useful summary.

■ Staffing

When details of the forthcoming event are confirmed, those concerned with employee issues begin to formulate rosters and plan staffing arrangements, including not only numbers of personnel, but also various types and times when they are required. It is important to note, at this stage, that relevant industry awards and prevailing enterprise agreements must be consulted. The majority of managers are well versed in the intricacies of roster planning and control.

CONFERENCE AND EVENTS ENQUIRY FORM

Enquiry date: . . . . Taken by: . . . .
Company name: . . . .
Address: . . . . Post code: . . . .
Contact: . . . . Position/title: . . . .
Phone number: . . . . Fax number: . . . .

EVENT DETAILS

Event date and day: . . . . Proposed room: . . . . Room hire: . . . .
Type of event: . . . . Expected number of guests: . . . .
Timing: Start: . . . . Finish: . . . .

SET-UP

❏ Theatre   ❏ Classroom   ❏ Hollow square
❏ U-shape   ❏ Boardroom   ❏ Banquets
❏ Other set-up requirements: . . . .
. . . .

FOOD AND BEVERAGE

❏ Breakfast   ❏ Lunch   ❏ Dinner
❏ Cocktails   ❏ Morning tea   ❏ Afternoon tea
❏ Other information: . . . .
. . . .

AUDIOVISUAL

❏ OHP   ❏ Slide   ❏ Data projector
❏ Other requirements: . . . .

ACCOMMODATION

❏ Deluxe . . . .   ❏ Suites . . . .

PROJECTED REVENUE

Food	Beverage	Room hire	Audiovisual	Total

■ **Figure 9.1** *Sample convention enquiry sheet for the Carlton Hotel Darwin*

1999	January			February			March		
	1	2 . . .	31	1	2 . . .	28	1	2 . . .	31
Room A a.m.	///						///		///
Room A p.m.									
Room B a.m.	///								
Room B p.m.	///								
Ballroom		///			///				

■ **Figure 9.2** *Sample basic function diary*

The number of staff required for an event very much depends on the type and style of the event and the costs that are being incurred by the venue. In some cases, such as themed gala events, clients are willing to pay a premium for the venue to provide higher than average staff to guest ratios. In most cases, running an event can be a relatively cost-effective process in terms of wages and the number of employees involved.

For some events, certainly those organised predominantly through community and welfare organisations, a number of volunteers may be involved. This situation can cause friction between 'local' venue staff (paid) and the unpaid volunteers. The key here is to ensure that all meetings arranged to discuss the event, and particularly those called before the start of the event, include both staff and volunteers.

Organising any event can be made more efficient through the constant dissemination of information to all those involved. Such a policy of open communication can ensure an event that provides smooth service of the highest quality, with all staff knowing exactly what is expected of both the client and the venue.

■ Internal *marketing*

The collaborative nature of a well-organised event cannot be overestimated. From the moment that a client becomes a prospect for the venue, information about the client needs to be dispatched around the various departments likely to be involved. At the outset, those involved might be the upper echelon of the venue. In a hotel, this might include the resident manager or front office manager, the general manager, the director of sales (and/or marketing) and the financial controller. Most of these would be considered part of the executive committee that, in essence, runs a large hotel. As the event gathers pace and tentative bookings turn into confirmed space, more of the venue's staff become involved. The type and number depends on the type and size of the event and, in many cases, the importance the venue attaches to the event. However, in order of involvement, the following staff are included in the event organisation:

- convention services manager
- executive chef
- reservations supervisor (or group bookings supervisor)
- banqueting chef
- banqueting floor manager
- banqueting supervisors
- receptionists/porters (in the case of accommodation requirements)
- banqueting floor staff.

It is vital that, by the time the event begins, all staff, from management to floor personnel, are fully acquainted with the specifics of the event. As all staff are eventually privy to a cross-section of information, should there be a staffing problem (e.g. due to sickness), others can be moved from one department to another to cover the shortfall, without having to be re-appraised of all the event details.

Whether the venue uses a computerised booking system or a manual system, details of the event need to be sent around the venue to the departments and personnel involved. In the majority of cases — even within those organisations that use computerised booking and event management packages — this takes the form of a banquet event order (BEO). This handwritten or typewritten form is created in the event office and is updated as the event gets closer. A BEO is completed for every part of the event, from simple morning and afternoon tea breaks to the full gala conference dinner. About two weeks prior to the event, the BEOs are copied and sent out to the relevant departments. In most conference and meeting venues, the BEOs form the basis for all activities concerned with the event. They are used for confirmation between client and venue, for general reference, for accounting purposes, for management auditing, for post-conference evaluation and to ensure that those intimately involved with the conference carry out their duties according to the agreed program. A sample BEO is shown in figure 9.3.

CONFERENCE OPERATIONS ....

Many activities are contained in the operations of a conference or meeting, ranging from meeting and greeting the client, through to the planning stages and the post-evaluation of the event. The keys to running a quality operational department are clear and regular communication and careful planning. Having dealt with the planning function in chapter 8, this section focuses on the subsequent activities for a quality event. One of the most critical aspects of all conferences and meetings is the configuration of the meeting room.

■ Room *configurations*

In order to meet clients' requirements, it is essential that a venue has both the necessary amount of space as well as the proper type of space to service the conferences or meetings. The amount of physical space available may preclude some venues from offering certain types of event. However, even the smallest of venues has some free space that may be utilised for smaller, local community meetings. In many small motels and in some clubs, the restaurant can be utilised for such meetings outside normal trading hours.

The capacity of meeting room space is affected by a number of factors, including the physical configuration of the room itself, audiovisual equipment requirements, and other concerns such as the need for registration tables, coat racks and room set-up. The number of delegates proposed for an event will have an impact on the size and set-up of the room.

BANQUET EVENT ORDER

Date: . . . .

Account:.	Event order no.: . . . .
Contact:	Bqt coordinator: . . . .
Address:.	Telephone: . . . .
. . . .	Fax number:. . . . .

Event	Time	Attendees	Sign board
Timing	Activity	Room	Fax

Food and beverage

	Number	Price
Time: Arrival coffee ( )		$
Time: Morning tea ( )		$
Time: Lunch ( )		$
Time: Afternoon tea ( )		$

Set-up

Audiovisual

Engineering

Loading dock

Special instructions

Summary of expenses

Room hire	$
Arrival coffee	
Morning tea	
Lunch	
Afternoon tea	
Cocktails	
Dinner	
Audiovisual equipment	
Audiovisual technician	
Total	$
Less deposit	$

Total amount owing

Billing instructions: . . . .

Raul V. Hernandez
Conference and Events Manager
Carlton Hotel Darwin

Date: _____

■ **Figure 9.3** *Sample banquet event order from the Carlton Hotel Darwin*

Room layout/set-up

By way of example, figures 9.4 to 9.7 illustrate some basic seating and table layouts for conferences and meetings. The advantages and disadvantages of each are shown.

■ **Figure 9.4**
Theatre or auditorium layout

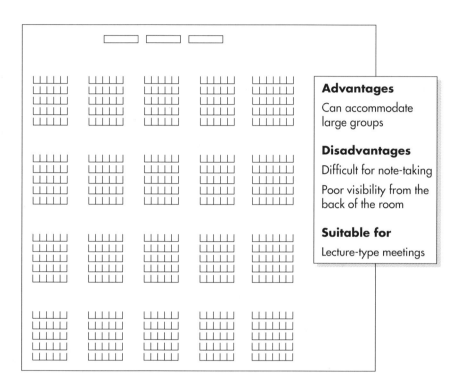

Advantages

Can accommodate large groups

Disadvantages

Difficult for note-taking

Poor visibility from the back of the room

Suitable for

Lecture-type meetings

■ **Figure 9.5**
Schoolroom or classroom layout

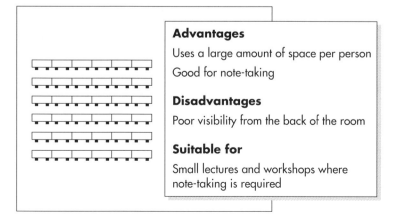

Advantages

Uses a large amount of space per person

Good for note-taking

Disadvantages

Poor visibility from the back of the room

Suitable for

Small lectures and workshops where note-taking is required

■ Figure 9.6
*Various
conference
room
configurations*

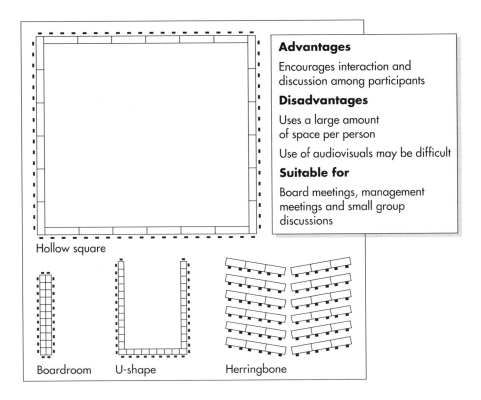

Advantages

Encourages interaction and
discussion among participants

Disadvantages

Uses a large amount
of space per person

Use of audiovisuals may be difficult

Suitable for

Board meetings, management
meetings and small group
discussions

Hollow square

Boardroom   U-shape   Herringbone

■ Figure 9.7
*Banquet or
round-table
layout*

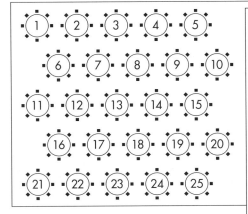

Advantages

Can be used when meetings break up into
smaller discussion groups, without
participants having to change rooms

Can accommodate food and beverage
service comfortably

Disadvantages

Uses a large amount of space per person

Use of audiovisuals may be difficult

Suitable for

Banquets, seminars and round-table
discussions

As well as ascertaining the capacity of function and meeting rooms for various types of room layouts, it is useful to develop accurately scaled drawings of each room, both for the venue's use and as a sales tool for prospective clients. As previous chapters have demonstrated, it is vital that the size and capacity of each room required for the event reflects the needs and activities of the conference. One of the recent computer innovations is software that allows conference managers to set and control room layouts on the computer screen. This is explored in more detail later in the chapter.

Set-up turnaround time

One important factor that needs to be considered when deciding on the timing and configurations for an event is the turnaround time for room set-ups. While anything is possible, given enough resources of time and staff, and some prior planning and organisation, better efficiencies for both the client and venue can be implemented. It is critical for the operational team that the venue has formulated a turnaround time schedule so that all those involved with the planning of the event know what is and is not possible. Again, the type, size and style of the conference or meeting will have a bearing on what is required.

■ Registration

When the venue has set up all the requirements for the conference or meeting, regardless of size, it then has to wait for the arrival of the delegates. Once the delegates arrive at the venue, their primary task is to register with the organisers. In some cases this may be the venue staff, but in the majority of instances staff from the client's organisation arrange registration. If there are accommodation bookings and the event is being held within a hotel or resort, there is the added complication of guest registration.

Having a large number of people check in to the venue (hotel) at the same time can cause added problems for staff requirements, with delegates and guests forced to stand around the reception desk causing snarls in the foyer. The other important factor is that of image. The venue must ensure that the delegates' first impression of the venue is one of efficiency and calm, rather than one of long queues, disgruntled guests and stressed reception and portering staff. Although conference delegates are concerned with the conference itself, positive first impressions of the venue can have a marked impact on the rest of the conference event.

One method of pre-empting such confusion and delay is to pre-register conference delegates. This is common practice within large hotels that deal extensively with large groups and tours. Rooms are allocated to guests before they arrive and their registration forms are completed from the rooming list that is supplied by the client, usually several weeks prior to the event and delegates' arrival. On check-in, delegates only need to sign their registration form and collect their room key. Another benefit can be gained from this method of registering delegates. Because the rooms are allocated ahead of arrival, the hosting organiser and the hotel/venue itself can provide relevant material in the delegates' rooms. This means delegates can be aware of any last-minute changes to conference programs and special events. The hotel also can provide sales material for the delegates, highlighting the availability of food and beverage outlets during 'free time' at the conference and providing details of other facilities that may be useful to specific conference guests.

FOOD AND BEVERAGE SERVICES ....

Food and beverage service is a significant and critical part of conference operations, and can produce a high percentage of revenue for the venue. While it can be acknowledged that this area is ostensibly part and parcel of the operational side of the conference itself, food and beverage service is important enough to warrant a more detailed discussion.

Gene Meoni, director of food and beverage at the Grand Traverse Resort Village, Michigan, has given this stark reminder of the value of food and beverage services within the convention department of a large hotel (Astroff & Abbey 1998, p. 434):

> ■ The Catering/Convention Services Department is the most profitable division of any hotel food and beverage operation provided proper planning, controls, service and creativity are utilised for an event, be it a coffee break for twenty or a five course gala dinner for a thousand.
>
> The plans, controls and teamwork involved in food and beverage service are immense. But, if effective, will lead to operational success, which I define as exceeding guest expectations, motivated employees who take pride in their accomplishments and exceeding budgeted bottom line profits. ■

Planning for efficient and effective food and beverage services for groups and functions at times can be very demanding. Some groups want very specific items, at very specific times and require special menus and out-of-hours service. However, all these demands are known to the provider well in advance of the event. In many instances, catering for such a group can be relatively painless if the venue is well organised and management has planned ahead, as discussed in chapter 8. Lead times may be fraught with stress and pressure for both staff and management at the venue, but once the group arrives, the flow of an event tends to be pre-planned and clearly structured for operational staff. Many group and function venues actively seek out more group business because groups can be serviced with minimal costs and within precise times.

In terms of increasing revenue, banquets, conferences and meetings, as well as other smaller social events, can produce additional revenue for venues. Successful events can contribute greatly to overall profitability, because the profit margin on sales can be much higher than for other, independent food outlets such as coffee shops and restaurants. In recent research, the convention services departments of several large hotels reported that revenue from their department accounted for as much as 15 per cent of total hotel revenue and up to 60 per cent of total food and beverage revenue (McCabe & Weeks 1999).

There are several reasons why the profit margin for food and beverage services for convention business might be higher than for individual customers using individual food outlets within the venue:

• In hospitality organisations that concentrate on group business, sales volume from banquets often can exceed restaurant volume by as much as two to one.

- Banquets allow greater flexibility in pricing, with the same meal often commanding higher prices than would normally be acceptable. This is because of the short time in which a large number of people need to be served and as compensation for setting up and breaking down the banquet area.
- Large volume preparation means food and kitchen labour costs are lower.
- It is unnecessary to carry the required inventory for very long, as supplies can be ordered as needed and all attendees usually receive identical meals.
- Beverage profits are high because beverage costs are controlled easily and revenues are greater due to pricing flexibility.
- Labour costs are significantly lower because employee productivity is maximised with the number of diners known in advance (Astroff & Abbey 1998, p. 433).

The types of food and beverage requirements at functions and meetings can be extremely diverse and might include some or all of the following: breakfast, lunch, dinner, dinner dances, refreshment breaks, buffets, cocktail receptions, theme parties and suppers. While most venues are willing to negotiate menu items with the client, many develop suggested menus or menu items from which the client chooses various combinations. As well as allowing the venue to pre-plan and identify appropriate items, such menus also allow the professional conference organiser or organising committee to know well ahead what is on offer at the venue and plan their meals accordingly. This means that rostering, costs and timings can be pre-set and known to management before the event takes place.

The subject of food and beverage services has been extensively covered in texts, academic journals and trade magazines. This chapter touches briefly on the main issues concerned with food and beverage service operations as they relate to convention services.

■ Food *services*

The comprehensive range of menus and menu items usually offered by a venue reflects the diversity of the function and meeting market. For example, no two functions or meetings have exactly the same objectives, type of participants, budget or expectations. By providing a range of menu options, catering facilities try to accommodate the many differing formats and durations of meetings, the number of participants, the time constraints and any group preferences. Naturally, an important consideration in menu design is the style of service that either the group prefers or the venue feels best meets the needs of the client. The type of service used also influences pricing, staffing levels and the overall atmosphere of the function.

The purpose of food events

The list of reasons for clients wanting food services is endless. It may seem a strange comment to make, but not all food services are provided just to satisfy delegates' hunger! Shock and Stefanelli (1992, p. 132) have suggested several reasons for clients wanting to include a meal function at their event:

- to create an image
- to provide an opportunity for interaction and networking
- to showcase a person, product and/or idea
- to present awards
- to honour dignitaries
- to refresh conference attendees and sharpen their attention
- to provide a receptive audience
- to keep delegates interested in other non-food activities
- to increase attendance at conferences.

Once the reason for the food service is known, planning and operational issues can be addressed so that the venue can achieve the client's objectives.

Types of meal functions

There are several types and styles of meal service available to clients. Of course, the range depends on the resources and expertise of the venue.

Breakfast

This type of meal event is becoming more popular within the corporate market. With less time available for meetings, executives and staff find that this is a useful time to hold a meeting, seminar or product launch. Breakfasts need to be well planned and timing is essential. This meal is also a useful method of getting all delegates, even those who might normally skip breakfast, in the one place at the same time (Shock & Stefanelli 1992, p. 159).

Refreshment breaks

Breaks are usually arranged to give conference attendees a respite from the scheduled conference sessions, and to provide them with an opportunity to mingle and network. Refreshment breaks are normally scheduled for mid-morning and mid-afternoon and can last from 15 to 45 minutes.

Lunch

Often light food items are used for lunches, although some organisers prefer to have at least one 'sit-down' lunch, again to get all delegates together in the one place at the one time. If costs for delegates have included lunch (which is usually the case), it is highly likely that they will attend.

Dinner

Dinners, often as the highlight of a conference, tend to be more adventurous than other meals in the choice of menu and service. The meal is often more formal than other meals served during the event and there is more time for delegates to linger. However, timing is still critical to success.

Receptions

Receptions can be held prior to the official dinner and/or at the beginning of a conference, as a welcoming, 'icebreaker' event. Most receptions include alcohol and soft drinks and some form of finger food, and are seen by delegates as an opportunity to network. For this reason, food and drink items need to be easy to carry around.

Off-premises (outside) catering

Although some organisations specialise in this activity, off-premises catering is mainly confined to events that have specifically asked for one or more activities to be held 'outside' (Shock & Stefanelli 1992, p. 169). In many cases, this is limited to the final dinner — for example, a circus themed event under the 'Big Top' — but some venues use their outside facilities for refreshment breaks and barbecue meal activities, especially lunch. Factors to be considered here include location, cost, food transportation, timing and weather.

Styles of service

After examining the different types of meal service available to clients, it is useful to look at some of the more common forms of service. Operationally, each of these carry their own specific characteristics in terms of resources, cost (to both client and venue) and image (the term 'buffet' sounds less up-market than 'silver service', although, in fact, this may not be the case). There are over a dozen differing styles of food service, for example:

- buffet-style
- family-style
- self-serve
- plated
- pre-set
- 50–50 drop
- wave.

Regardless of the style of service, there are some fundamental factors that must be taken into account when the client and venue meet to discuss operational issues. These include the venue itself, the type of client, the costs and type of meal and the number of participants. The style of service chosen should reflect the themes and objectives of the overall event and, in many cases, the wishes of the sponsoring organisation.

Menu planning

When planning event menus, management should take several factors into account: food costs; delegate requirements; the types of items required by the client; nutritional concerns; seasonality; staffing implications; and the overall impression that the meals will give to delegates. Each has a bearing on the type and content of menu that is prepared for a client. The type of meal also has an impact, as do the reasons for the meal itself. Lighter, healthy and lower fat meals have been increasing in popularity over recent years. Conference delegates tend to require smaller portions, but more meals. The impact of food styles such as 'browsing' (taking small portions from a buffet, but going up for several different servings) has moved from the traditional setting of restaurants and can now be found at conference and meeting venues. Much of the decision on food items is based on the number of delegates and the size of the venue facilities.

Truth-in-menu guidelines

The venue must not inadvertently misrepresent menu items to clients and their guests. With the incidence of legal proceedings against food service organisations increasing, it is vital that venues are careful to be truthful in describing menu items offered to convention and meeting clients. Some venues offer standard menus that can have a shelf life of more than 12 months, so ensuring that the product advertised in January is still the same when ordered at a conference in December is vital. In venue food and beverage sections, care must be taken to represent clearly to clients and delegates the quantity, quality, origin, price, brand (if necessary) and means of preparation of items within a menu.

Menu selection

The various factors that should be considered by venue management when creating menus for clients have been discussed. We now turn our attention to the client. In many cases, venues offer the client, whether a PCO or an organising committee, a selection of menus that cover the full range of food service styles and menu suggestions. Often, the client must choose the most appropriate meal styles and food items for the particular event and the specific group of delegates. For many, especially those with little or no food experience, this can be a daunting task.

Several factors can be used to guide such food choices. The type of meal will reflect the choice of dish and the number of delegates may preclude certain items not conducive to large groups. With each type of meal care must be exercised when choosing individual dishes. Colour, texture and cooking style need to be considered. Providing different types of meals may be overlooked, and delegates could be faced with the same style of cooking (e.g. fried or baked) and one-colour dishes (e.g. fish, potatoes and cauliflower) for every meal during an event.

The client must be able to provide delegates with a balance between full, heavier dishes and lighter meals. There needs to be a range of meal types (sit-down, buffet, and so on) and all dietary and personal food preferences (e.g. vegetarians, vegans) should be catered for. Our tastes in food have changed in recent years. We are more concerned with our diet and health. This should be reflected in how clients, PCOs and the like, arrange and choose meals and food items. A sample balanced lunch menu, specifically planned for 'business' delegates, is shown in figure 9.8.

Staffing considerations

Without the right staff, the service aspects of the event would be non-existent. Once the meals have been organised, it is imperative that staff are allocated to an event in advance so they can be well briefed before the event begins. Factors that might need to be considered include:
- the skill levels of staff
- the experience of floor staff
- the number of guests
- the type and style of meal service
- the timing of meal event
- the proportion of supervisory staff to floor staff.

It is imperative that convention managers ensure the continued training of their staff, be mindful of new human management techniques and implement an open system of staff relations.

MENU
BUSINESS LUNCH

Choose any two courses from the selection below

SOUPS

Curried butternut pumpkin soup with sour cream

Onion soup with cheese wheel

Smoked seafood chowder with anis

Minestrone with macaroni & pesto

Asian-style seafood soup 'Tom Yang Kung'

Chicken & mushroom broth with vegetable confetti

MAIN COURSES

Smoked pork loin in beer & mustard sauce with assorted creamed vegetables & potatoes

Panfried chicken breast with apricot & roasted almonds, madeira wine glaze, sauteed
vegetables & potatoes

Oven-baked chicken breast with a camembert & apple filling,
port wine glaze and wokfried vegetables & potatoes

Catch of the day dusted with Asian spices served with fried rice

Baked reef fish with lemon grass, coriander & vermicelli noodle salad

Roast rack of lamb provencale with chef's choice of vegetables & potatoes

Beef stroganoff with mushrooms & sour cream, tossed vegetables & pilaf rice

Creamed fettuccine with hot smoked salmon & scallions

Tuscany roasted chicken with mushroom sauce, vegetables & rosemary potatoes

Spinach & ricotta ravioli, with sauteed capsicum, zucchini & onion tossed with tomatoes

Vegetarian quiche, baked sweet potato with sour cream and chives & a side salad

Beef or lamb satays with peanut sauce & jasmine rice

DESSERTS

French crepe with raspberry filling, mango sauce & whipped cream

Rhubarb crumble with sauce anglaise

Caramel creme with a seasonal fresh fruit sauce

Profiteroles with chocolate sauce

Apple frangipan almond flan on hazelnut sauce

Mousse au chocolate served with pistachio coffee sauce

Selection of cheese & biscuits served with dried fruit (served per table)

$26.00 per person

■ **Figure 9.8** *Sample business lunch menu*

Food pricing

Most food functions are priced on a per-head basis, with the charges and menus agreed to in writing in advance. Some food functions, such as refreshment breaks, use alternative methods of pricing. Coffee or juice may be priced by the litre and pastries and hors d'oeuvres by the number of delegates or by the tray. Where function numbers are small, additional charges may be added for labour and room set-up. Some organisations charge by the menu — for example, a range of three- or four-course luncheon menus priced from 'economy' to 'expensive'. Where à la carte menus are involved (often for formal dinners) individual pricing can be attached to each menu item. In some cases, venues provide an extensive list of food items and the client can then create their own menu, priced according to each item chosen.

No matter how prices are formulated, the menu price must cover profit margins, the cost of food, payroll and other fixed and variable costs associated with the event. The final price of meal events will very much depend on venue policies regarding profit margins, the cost of food and purchasing (suppliers, quality of food, and so on). Some smaller venues will lower their prices for community-based groups in the hope of gaining further revenue at a later date, by following up delegates at the meeting to see if their company would use the venue in the future.

Confirming and guaranteeing prices for menus must be done with some caution. While many venues use a long-term guarantee for some items as a competitive tool, venues should not be too quick to promise pricing levels on items that cannot be guaranteed absolutely. Again, this tends to be part of venue policy. However, it might be circumspect for venues to include an escape clause, such as 'Management reserves the right to change prices without notice' on all written quotes.

■ Beverage *services*

The above section examined, albeit briefly, aspects of food service that often are associated with conference and meeting operations. We now turn to the beverage side of 'food and beverage services'. Again, there is not the space to detail all aspects of this facet of conference operations, but some issues do need to be raised here.

Types of beverage service

As with food events, there are several types of beverage function:

- cocktail receptions — perhaps the most common
- hospitality suites — event sponsors offering food and beverages to invited guests
- table service — part of the meal function
- special events — such as wine and cheese tastings; and wine product launches.

As with many conference operations, the final style and type of beverage function chosen is dependent on the objectives of the event, client preferences, and the number and preferences of delegates.

Beverage pricing

Beverage functions are normally priced in one of four ways:

- the open bar, where guests are free to drink the beverages and the host (the client or sponsor of the event) pays the bill at the end of the function — a 'dry till' is usually maintained to keep track of the drinks consumed
- the cash bar or no-host bar, where each guest pays for their drinks as ordered — this can cause problems, with guests spending much of their time queuing for their drinks, and special attention needs to be given to staffing and logistics of the event space
- voucher sales, where delegates purchase drink coupons from the venue or the association prior to the function and then present them to the bar staff as drinks are ordered — this eliminates the need for a cashier
- the hospitality bar, where guests serve themselves — the venue takes inventory before and after the function and the group is then billed for the amount consumed (Astroff & Abbey 1998, p. 449).

Beverage service and the prices charged for the service tend to be two of the most common causes of client dissatisfaction at functions or meetings. Thus, it is imperative that the prices to be charged and the method of doing so be put in writing and agreed on by both parties in advance. In essence, the client is entering into a contract with the supplier (in this case, the conference venue) to provide certain services and products for the group.

Beverage charges

The way in which liquor charges are set can vary quite considerably between venues and events and is different to the method of food pricing. Shock and Stefanelli (1992, pp. 177–80) have suggested several methods:

- *Charge per drink* Used in cash or open bars. Prices can be negotiated lower, depending on potential usage and total event revenues from the client.
- *Charge per bottle* A common procedure used in open bars and hospitality bars. Inventory is taken before and after the function to determine usage. All open bottles are charged to the client.
- *Charge per person* This is often used for receptions and can include the cost of food.
- *Charge per hour* Clients are charged a set price per hour of beverage function. There may be a sliding scale of prices (lower for the second and subsequent hours of the function), depending on the time allocated by the client to this type of function (see figure 9.9).
- *Flat-rate charge* The client pays a flat rate for the duration of the beverage function. The charge reflects the number of guests and the type of liquor requested by the client.

BEVERAGES
COCKTAIL PARTIES

STANDARD BAR

Draught beer (choice of two)

House white wine

House red wine

House champagne

Soft drink, orange juice and mineral water

One hour: $12 per person

Two hours: $18 per person

SUPERIOR BAR

Draught beer (choice of two)

Standard spirits

House white wine

House red wine

House champagne

Soft drink, orange juice and mineral water

One hour: $16 per person

Two hours: $26 per person

■ **Figure 9.9** *Sample cocktail party beverage menu*

Legal issues

It is important that the legal issues involved with beverage events are not ignored during operational discussions within the venue. In most countries liquor laws and related legislation have been quite severely tightened to protect both the operator and the customer. Penalties for any breaches can be quite debilitating in terms of lost revenue and, perhaps more crucially, loss of image and confidence from clients.

While laws governing sales of alcohol to minors and to intoxicated persons and other general laws have been in place for some time, increased community awareness of alcohol abuse has prompted legislation for alcohol-awareness training. Legislation regarding the responsible service of alcohol has been in the workplace for several years. The legislation covers those involved with the distribution, storage and service of liquor. Convention venues must comply with this legislation. Because of the sheer number and types of beverage and food functions that occur within conference and meeting venues, it is quite probable that at least once in a venue's lifetime, aspects of the liquor legislation will be tested, often by those who wish to bend the rules.

■ Billing *procedures*

Representatives from the venue and group (often the conference sales manager and the client or conference organiser) should meet well in advance of a function or meeting to establish the policies and procedures to be used in the billing process. It is essential at this stage to identify clearly which expenses will be met by the client organisation, which will be met by the attendees themselves and which will be covered by the venue as part of its fee. Usually, the client will be requested to send a deposit prior to the event, with other payments often made at the beginning and end of the function. After any disputes about charges have been resolved, the client is given the final invoice. Some venues may add interest charges on overdue accounts.

In order to keep track of all expenses, a master account should be established for the event, containing all the client's accrued charges. This represents an accounts receivable account. It is extremely important that the venue and the group representative establish, well in advance, exactly who is authorised to charge to the master account, what types of charges can be made and whether there is to be a maximum limit on any of these amounts.

Occasionally, some charges, particularly those to the master account, will be disputed. It is interesting to note that two of the leading causes of disputes over charges stem from poor or improper service and disagreement over the number of participants at a dinner or other function. As noted later in this chapter, it is vital that the person who has been responsible for the event goes through the total account with the client prior to the end of the conference or meeting. This is often done during the final session, on the final day. Encouraging a service orientation and establishing standardised procedures for counting attendees are essential to preventing client dissatisfaction.

TECHNOLOGY ··

While our daily lives have been inundated with technological advances for some time, the hospitality industry in general, and the convention and meeting sector in particular, have been relatively slow on the technology uptake. Many quite large organisations still refuse to use computerised systems and many of the smaller venues do not use modern technology, mainly due to cost restrictions.

However, times are changing. According to Chris Tolhurst (*Conventions & Incentives Marketing* 1999, p. 30) there are now six international-standard purpose-built convention and exhibition centres in Australia, all with built-in sophisticated technology. Many operations have continued to invest heavily in technology to meet the ever-increasing demands of clients and to protect their competitive position. The cost of computer technology is inversely proportionate to the power of the machine. In other words, as the costs have gone down, so the sheer computing power has gone up. The size of computers has been drastically reduced with the implementation of more sophisticated miniaturisation processes. The inclusion of advanced electronic communications in computers has allowed us to be in constant contact with home or office, regardless of where we happen to be in the world. Thus, sending messages and sales information from Kenya back to head office in Wellington, New Zealand, is now a simple and virtually instantaneous process.

Some caution should be added here. Although it is true that the processing and communication power of computers can be quite staggering and advantageous to many organisations, managers need to be aware of the definite possibility of drowning in a sea of information. Too much information is not necessarily a good thing. Organisations' information needs must be carefully screened and only information that is useful, timely and accurate should be used.

Before discussing the issues surrounding the implementation and use of technology within the convention sector, it is appropriate to examine a leader in this field: Trevor Gardiner. His background and views on technology are provided in the following snapshot.

SNAPSHOT
Trevor Gardiner, Amlink Technologies

Trevor Gardiner is managing director of Amlink Technologies, Australia's leading convention management software company, recently listed on the Australian Stock Exchange and exporting its product worldwide. Why is the company successful?

Following a period of computer programming, Trevor accepted the challenge to manage the computer department of Intermedia, one of Australia's largest conference management organisations. This provided an opportunity to learn two new languages — one computing and the other the language of conference management and operations. Key learning points in this process were gained from a director of Intermedia — attention to detail and quality of product — points that are integral to Trevor's whole operation and work philosophy. At Intermedia, Trevor continually gained experience in conference management and its practical operation, and at the same time developed for the company a generic conference management system called EVENTS software. This followed the company philosophy of providing a reliable product through the use of a number of checks and balances that were built into the system. The benefits of using such a system were recognised by a number of other conference organisations that purchased and adopted the EVENTS system. This provided a business dilemma for Intermedia because of the potential conflict of interest.

In 1992, Trevor bought out the EVENTS software system from Intermedia and set up Events Computing Services with a small team. They operated

(continued)

from a small inexpensive office south of Brisbane, but with a client base that was located all over Australia. The business expanded dramatically two and a half years later when the company released its Windows version of the software, which incorporated many new innovations. New markets, including the corporate sector, were opened up and the company began exporting overseas, initially to New Zealand. Trevor comments that the first time they sold their software overseas was 'daunting but exciting — going into a new market'.

Expansion overseas continued with enquiries from Southeast Asia. This again provided a number of challenges, not only in learning how to do business within the region but also in the adaptation required to the software system due to currency differences. The company has subsequently expanded and exports into North America and Europe.

In December 1998, only six years after Events Computing Services was created, the company was listed on the Australian Stock Exchange under its new name, Amlink Technologies.

So what does Trevor see as the secrets of his success?

- honesty with the company's clients, plus ensuring both the reliability of its product and customer service
- continual reinvestment of profits into ongoing developments to ensure that the company continues to be at the leading edge; clients also have confidence that they are at the forefront of technology in this area when they use the EVENTS software
- practical operational background experience in both conference organisation and operation, and computer software design
- client loyalty and support that includes many new business referrals
- involvement in the industry — the company is dedicated to education providing tertiary level scholarships for potential students of the MICE industry, sponsorship of MICE industry functions and conference presentations
- being receptive to new ideas — new ideas are embraced and clients are encouraged to suggest adaptations and innovations to the product.

Source: *Trevor Gardiner, Amlink Technologies*

■ Information *needs*

For most convention services managers, having a daily, weekly and monthly summary of events within their venue would be enough. As the needs of the various levels of management change, so too does the information taken from a computerised system. The information typically required for a convention is as shown in table 9.1.

MANAGEMENT LEVELS	INFORMATION NEEDS
Operational	• basic information about delegates/guests • events booked • times of events and other activities • creation of BEOs • number/type of meals produced by the kitchen.
Tactical	• delegate turnover levels • delegate expenditure at various events • departmental revenue • departmental costs.
Strategic	• total operational revenue • future budgets • forecasts of estimated events • economic factors that may affect budgets • future trends and analysis.

Braham (1992, p. 153) has suggested that a conference management computer system should contain the following spheres of operation, some of which are examined later in the chapter:
• trace events, clients and delegates
• enquiries, conference diary and bookings
• staff organisation and management reporting
• function list
• quotation and sales forecasting
• market research database
• marketing and mailing
• ledgers and invoicing.

■ Technology *in convention operations*

It is clear that having access to some form of computer technology can be of immense benefit to the operating functions of a convention services department, whether this is in a hotel, resort, motel or even in a purpose-built convention and exhibition centre. Now that there are several dozen useful software packages available for meeting planners, including room set-up, registration, reservations and yield management (Montgomery & Strick 1995, p. 236), all those involved in the convention and meeting sector can appreciate fully the benefits gained through the use of such technology. While there is not space here to discuss every aspect and nuance of computerisation, it is of value to summarise some of the important features, and these follow, under headings related to operational aspects of the event.

Marketing

The sales and marketing function can become a far less time-consuming activity with the use of a computerised system. All sales staff can have their own account on the system and management can gain a very accurate picture of exactly what is happening in terms of potential sales and resultant revenue. A sales and marketing package also can save account managers time, as all necessary information is constantly to hand. All package pricing, special deals and stop-sell dates (when the venue is full) can be called up with a few keystrokes. If the system used by the sales team is integrated with the PMS for the venue, sales staff can even make their own tentative, or better still, confirmed bookings into the system. This obviates the need to pass on hard copy paperwork to others to input into their own computer system.

From the PCO's point of view, having a system that will accept single-entry data input and provide a fully searchable database of delegates can be of great benefit. The EVENTS for Windows program can deliver both these key elements, as is shown in figures 9.10 and 9.11. In figure 9.10, the range of options for the organiser can be seen clearly. Input operators, managers and accounts staff can choose from data entry or custom lists through to the event notepad and budgeting and accounting. Figure 9.11 shows how the system holds a large amount of information about each delegate and how the input operator can move quite easily from demographics (delegate information) to other modules in the package such as accommodation, functions and marketing. The 'letter' section allows the PCO to create their own headed stationery and the computer merges the letters with the names on the delegate list — an enormous time-saver for PCOs.

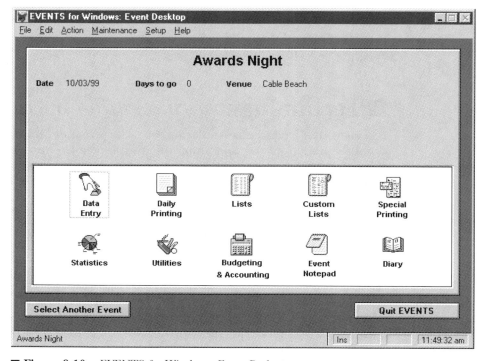

■ **Figure 9.10** *EVENTS for Windows: Event Desktop*

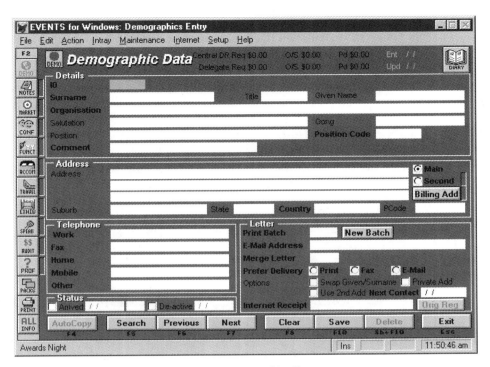

■ Figure 9.11 *EVENTS for Windows: Demographics Entry*

One further aspect of a sales and marketing package is its ability to create form letters and templates of various standard forms used by the venue. This means that the venue letterhead is always on every piece of printed material that goes to its clients. Sales staff who want to correspond with their own particular clients can create a more personalised letter (by using mail merge facilities, common to most sales and marketing packages) to include names, events, dates and times specific to a particular event or client. Such a system can also provide a list of regular clients and automatically tell the user if the client has used the venue in the past. At the end of any given time period, the system can print out reports detailing all sales figures for each individual sales manager or for the whole venue.

Reservations and registration

The impact of computer technology on these two vital areas has been touched on earlier in the chapter. Reservations can be made from any computer in the venue, as well as those taken 'on the road' by sales staff. Single entry data input reduces the possibilities of double booking — a situation feared by all venues. The ability to be able to see a variety of 'views' can maximise room usage; many programs allow the user to look at room bookings by year (the big picture) right down to an hour-by-hour view.

Registration can be speeded up using computer technology. Although there is certainly a case for good old-fashioned pen and paper systems, the use of a computerised registration system can take some of the complexities out of the process. Delegates who want to change their arrangements at the last minute, pay final amounts by differing methods or change requirements at events during the conference can all be accommodated with ease. The system, if linked to the venue system, can then inform all those involved about any probable changes to seating, meal numbers, special meals, and so on.

There are also several computer programs which allow delegates to register via the Internet. Companies having a Web presence can include an e-mail form on their Web site. EVENTS for Windows has this capability (see figure 9.12). Delegates complete the form and e-mail it to the organiser, PCO or venue. The details are then taken from the Web form and integrated into the delegate database generated for that particular conference or meeting. Again, this means less chance of incorrect input (only one source of information) and speeds up the process of booking, confirmation and revenue receipts.

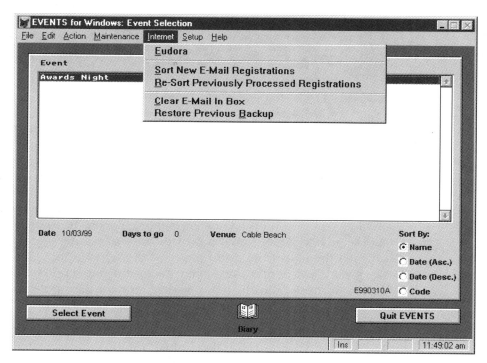

■ **Figure 9.12** *EVENTS for Windows: Event Selection, showing Internet link*

Food and beverage services

In the food and beverage area, computers are rather less visible. Much of the technology used here concerns cooking processes, and systems such as Cook Chill and microwave technologies are being used more and more in large convention venues for both local and outside catering.

However, some benefits can be gained in food and beverage operations through the use of computers. Several programs allow staff to formulate the most appropriate seating arrangements in any room, given details such as room size, table numbers, guests per table, type of food and drink service, and so on. The programs then draw a table plan utilising the available space. Figures 9.13 and 9.14 show this in more detail, using CEO software. Figure 9.13 displays a clean convention room ready to be 'set up' with tables, chairs, extra items (such as plants) and staging. This can be seen from the drop-down menu. The program allows the operator to create a room completely from scratch, and model setting based on the dimensions of the venue concerned.

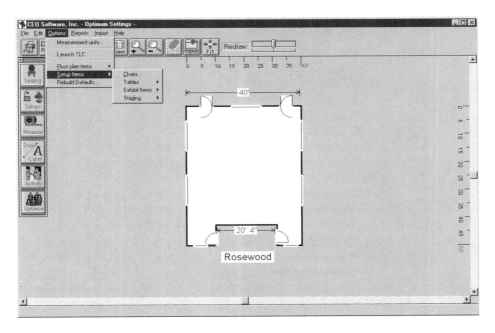

■ **Figure 9.13**   *CEO Software, Inc: clean convention room*

Figure 9.14 shows a room that has been completed. Notice that the shape of the room is not a standard 'box' and also that plants and 'stations' have been included in the diagram. Table numbers have been allocated to tables. The program will also produce and print out name tags and seating plans, matching exactly the table layout that has been created. The lower part of the screen shows a group of options that provides banqueting and several standard room layouts, similar to those identified earlier in the chapter. Being able to use such a program saves food and beverage operators time and effort and can create an image in the client's mind of an efficient and technologically-advanced organisation. The ability to create a room layout in a matter of minutes, print it out and give it to the client in a readable form must be a positive factor for convention managers.

■ **Figure 9.14**
CEO
Software, Inc:
Pre-set
dinner/dance
layout

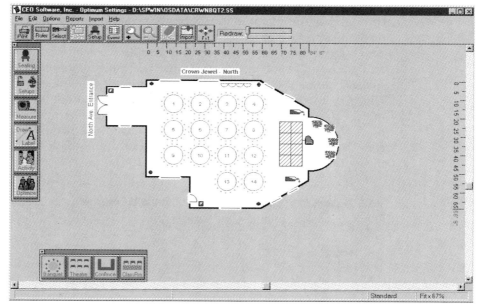

The other main use of computer technology in food and beverage operations is in inventory control and menu costing. In many large organisations, menus are costed down to the smallest teaspoon of salt (perhaps an exaggeration!). However, menu control systems have given more power to chefs to create standardised recipes together with tighter controls on costs and purchases. These controls do impact on the pricing that, in turn, is seen by the potential client.

A further use that is often forgotten by kitchen staff is the ability of most word processing packages to function as a smaller version of a full-scale printery. Using these programs, quite complex art and menus can be produced relatively cheaply. This facility also means that menus need never be set on paper for the next 12 months, as is often the case, even today. Menus can be changed as and when the chef, client, seasonal ingredients and costs dictate.

Desktop publishing

Although the use of computers to provide printed material is not common within the convention and meeting industry, it is certainly a viable alternative to third-party printers and publishers. Using the computer, venues can produce a range of printed material, from brochures and menus to name tags and other items. In many cases, the packages currently used by many venues have the power to produce such merchandise. Printing their own material allows venues to be far more flexible and client-centred than third-party printing currently allows. Menus, food items, drinks and event program notes can be tailor-printed for specific events and clients.

Management

Finally, we need to discuss briefly how the management of conference and meeting venues can best use computer technology. It is not difficult to see that having a machine that can advise what is happening in an organisation, at any time, should be a useful management tool. Systems can be set to produce summary statements each day recording event revenue, numbers and types, as well as personnel information such as staffing levels and wages. The system can also provide management with forecasted figures. Using these figures and the ability of expert systems to incorporate trends within the local community and the conference market, management can be well informed. Strategic plans can be formulated using information from the system, which may provide a competitive advantage for the venue and increase service quality.

Again, a note of caution should be made here. Not all information may be relevant for management. Managers require certain types of information and unless this is forthcoming from the computer system, managers will not be able to make policy decisions with any certainty.

In summary, an effective information system should be able to provide a range of intelligence to management. In a convention situation, software can provide production control, including scheduling, recipe costing and inventory control. The system may cover accounting processes (such as ledgers, payroll and statement generation), as well as the operational aspects of conference room control, event scheduling, cash control and productivity appraisal. Finally, management may gain information about budgets, forecasting and cash flow projection.

■ Technology *for the client*

Following on from this discussion on the use of technology within the venue for the organisation's benefit, we now focus on the types of technology that can be found in conference and meeting rooms across the country for the use of delegates and events. One of the difficulties of discussing this technology is that advances happen at such an alarming rate that it is difficult to focus on specifics. Thus, a more general discussion is provided here.

In-house purchase or outside contract?

Before discussing some of the equipment that can be found in convention and meeting venues, we should first look at whether a venue will spend the money and carry all the necessary equipment itself or whether it will use the services of an A/V specialist, who contracts equipment to clients through the venue. In some instances the latter option is made more efficient because the A/V specialist is actually located in the venue's building.

Often, hospitality venues do not carry their own equipment because:

- storage space is limited
- investment in a piece of equipment cannot be justified due to its limited use
- the cost of buying a large number of one type of A/V equipment (such as overhead projectors) is high (Astroff & Abbey 1998, p. 463).

The decision whether a venue buys in equipment or hires from a third party often depends on the predominant type of event held at the venue. For a smaller venue, for instance, with only a couple of meeting rooms and a mainly local market, purchasing an overhead projector (OHP) and a whiteboard for each room would probably be a wise investment. Astroff and Abbey (1998, p. 464) have suggested several advantages for both options, and these are shown in table 9.2.

■ Table 9.2
Advantages of using an outside A/V specialist versus buying A/V equipment

ADVANTAGES OF HIRING AN OUTSIDE A/V SPECIALIST	ADVANTAGES OF BUYING IN-HOUSE A/V EQUIPMENT
1. As A/V equipment can be extremely expensive, in the case of theft or loss, the venue would not be liable.	1. There may be a lack of suppliers in the area, or it may be difficult to rent a particular piece of A/V equipment.
2. Many A/V items are used so infrequently that the cost of maintaining inventory would be beyond many venues.	2. The venue may decide to purchase its own items that best meet its needs rather than rely on an outside contractor whose equipment may be inadequate.
3. Venues may not wish to employ specialists (who are often highly paid) to maintain and repair in-house equipment.	3. The venue has greater control over the quality of the equipment if it owns it. Rental property may have been misused and may not function properly.
4. With such swift changes in technology, some items may become obsolete and require additional expenditure by the venue.	4. The venue profits directly from hiring out its own equipment rather than directing revenue to an outside source.
	5. Hired equipment that is poor or damaged may reflect badly on the venue as a whole.

Audiovisual equipment

Having the latest A/V equipment with professional back-up support can provide a convention and meeting venue with an effective marketing tool to attract group business. Furthermore, supplying a comprehensive range of A/V equipment adds to the quality of the client's experience at the venue. Venues are increasingly investing in the latest A/V equipment for this very reason, although many smaller venues find it more cost-effective to hire equipment. It should be noted that even a basic set-up of whiteboard and overhead projector and screen might be quite sufficient for some types of meetings, especially for smaller community-based associations.

A more fundamental question that venues need to address is whether they will charge prospective clients for using A/V equipment. While many larger venues, such as hotels and conference centres, provide a basic range free of charge, the current trend is to charge group and conference organisers a fee for 'extra' equipment such as data (computer) projection, video conferencing facilities and special sound and lighting.

The difficulty for most clients, and in some cases for the venue, is to choose the very best equipment for their needs. There is now a vast array of A/V items, each tailored to a specific type of event, or part of an event. For example, just choosing a microphone for a guest speaker at an event can be quite a nightmare; the choice includes headset microphone, lapel microphone, wireless, lectern, and so on (Sheraton Pacific Corporation 1993, p. 14).

Choosing items of equipment is not a simple task. The industry insight on page 300 offers a glimpse of what one major convention venue offers in terms of equipment and labour, including sound and visual equipment, projector screens, video cameras and lighting.

As well as having all the right equipment in the right place at the right time, it is also imperative that there is a person on hand to attend to problems that delegates may experience with the technology. Re-aligning an OHP or re-setting a laptop computer with the data projector halfway through a presentation can be an embarrassing and often dreaded task for a speaker. Having a 'neutral' person who has A/V experience can defuse such a situation.

In some cases, there is an argument for venues to be quite honest with clients and contract to provide simple A/V equipment, rather than go for high-tech equipment, which they do not have the resources to back up. Although the current trend suggests an increasing use of laptop computer presentations (using programs such as PowerPoint coupled to a data projector), many of the smaller venues are just not in the market to provide clients with advanced electronic communications and global link-ups.

Video conferencing

Hotels and purpose-built convention and exhibition centres around the world have taken on the potential threat of video conferencing and turned it into a viable and productive revenue raiser. Video conferencing is basically another A/V item, or several items linked together. However, this particular A/V function is becoming more and more prevalent in the conference and meeting sector. And with the reduction of components, even small desktop computers have the capacity, given the right software, to provide video conferencing.

Video conferencing comes in two forms: receive only and interactive (Braham 1992, pp. 156–7). The former tends to be used for large international conferences where several venues around the world are 'hooked up' and a speaker using the facility in one venue, say Stockholm, can be 'broadcast' to the other venues, say Sydney and Suva. It is a one-way process, although in some cases a voice-only hook up is maintained and questions can be put to the speaker through the usual telephone system, connected to the speaker's location. The interactive system is, as it suggests, a two-way process, providing delegates with the opportunity to interact with the speaker and with each other, regardless of their location. While this technology is improving, interactive video conferencing is still somewhat stilted and movement on the screen can be quite distracting.

The interesting fact about video conferencing is that venues have cashed in, literally, on an aspect of technology that they thought would threaten their income. Venues now actively promote their ability to provide state-of-the-art video conference links to attract prestigious international conventions. Those attending in each location may still require accommodation, food and beverages and, in many cases, other events within the convention.

Stuart Haynes is the audiovisual manager at the Inter-Continental Hotel in Sydney. The reverse side of his business card reads: 'Ask us about video conferencing. Why not video tape or audio tape your next meeting? Full broadcast and ISDN facilities always available.' A timely reminder to clients that there is more to audiovisual technology than just overhead projectors, screens and whiteboards.

Stuart worked in Europe for several years before moving to Australia to take up work with local commercial television stations. He then moved to the health sector, where he was responsible for setting up studios for teaching hospitals in Sydney. After many years in the broadcasting industry, Stuart joined the Inter-Continental 11 years ago. He only intended to stay with the hotel for three months! Stuart says that coming from a broadcasting background allows him to talk the same language as many of his clients and allows him to market his product more effectively.

In 1990, the Inter-Continental was the first hotel in the world to provide analogue video conferencing. The equipment was upgraded to a digital network in 1995. The philosophy that underpins the A/V section is that this section of the conventions department is a service centre for clients and a profit centre for the hotel. Stuart feels that he is really a salesperson, required to be flexible and adapt to whatever the clients require, regardless of the short lead times. He says that A/V is really a communications tool. It allows people (delegates at conferences) to communicate not just within the four walls of a hotel meeting room, but also, in essence, with the world. The A/V department used to work with overhead and slide projectors; now it is the realm of personal computers, laptops and data projectors. The overhead is only used as a backup and the slide projector is seldom required.

When he started, the hotel had an A/V section, but only employed one person to 'look after the set-ups and someone from engineering to make sure all the equipment was working'. The situation was not satisfactory, both for the hotel and especially the client. Stuart's brief was to form a profitable and client-centred A/V department and to acquire the type of equipment that clients were requiring for their events.

The hotel owns 99.9 per cent of its A/V equipment, unlike many organisations that tend to hire in technical expertise and machines. The Inter-Continental hires out the video conferencing facility by the hour, which Stuart suggests is unusual in Sydney, where most hotels charge by the day. As he says, this can make a huge difference in terms of client costs and repeat business. The hotel has joined up with Telstra to provide guests with a 'two-way fibre optic video and audio link to full broadcast standard'. This means that the hotel can beam any television pictures directly from the hotel to a number of television stations, simultaneously and live!

As well as providing video conferencing for groups from 15 to 300, the hotel has the ability to create full multimedia production on site. They certainly have a huge amount of equipment! As well as all the 'high-tech' equipment, the hotel can supply mundane pieces such as screens, video cassette recorders, and so on. A sample list of A/V equipment and associated labour available through the hotel is shown in figure 9.15.

AUDIOVISUAL EQUIPMENT RENTAL LIST

Sound equipment
Microphone on lead
Flat table microphone (PCC 170)
Lectern and microphone
Radio microphones — hand held or lapel
Boom microphone
Speakers Pro Am 7 Bose (pair)
Equaliser
Audio broadcast splitter box
4-channel mixer/amp
8-channel Sound Craft audio desk
16-channel Sound Craft audio desk
CD player
Cassette player/recorder
Blank cassette tapes
Hybrid (microphone to telephone interphase)
Echo cancellor

Visual equipment
Kodak slide projector SAV 2050, lens to suit, carousel, lead or infrared remote, stand and tripod screen
Additional carousels
3-tier projector stand
Dissolve unit for 2 projectors
Special long or short lens

Overhead projectors
Overhead projector, Kodak 250 watt and tripod screen
Super bright overhead projector 400 watt

Video/data projectors
Ampro Espirt video/data projector
Barco super vision (video only)
Data projector DLP
Inter phase connector (connecting PC to data projector)
Switcher (data to video or data to data)

Projector screens
Tripod screen (6ft and 8ft) fast fold front or rear projected
$8'' \times 6''$ with black border
$10'' \times 72''$ with black border
Black velvet drapes includes winch ups max. 40×13 ft

Video cassette recorders
VHS PAL only, VCR
VHS PAL only plus 27" monitor on stand
VHS multi system NTSC PAL, plus 27" monitor on stand
Additional 27" monitors on stands
Video distribution amplifier (needed for 3 or more monitors)
Sony 9" preview monitor
$\frac{3}{4}$" U matic high or low band PAL only
$\frac{3}{4}$" U matic multi system
Beta cam SP PAL only player
Beta Cam SP recorder/player
(continued)

■ **Figure 9.15** *A/V equipment rental list for the Inter-Continental Hotel*

| **Vision switcher**
Sony F X E 100 broadcast
  switcher/editor with effects
Video cameras
VHS camera with tripod
Sony DXC 537 AP broadcast
  camera
Lighting
12-channel desk
Minim 23 lights
Follow spot (plus operator)
Red heads TV lights
3-channel light chaser
Table pin spotting
Sundry items
Laser pointer
Electronic whiteboard
Infrared remote mouse (for PCs)
Labour
Monday–Friday
8:00 a.m.–6:00 p.m. | Saturday–Sunday
Before 8:00 a.m. After 6:00 p.m.
Technician
Assistant Technician
Packages
Audio recording (maximum
  4 hours includes labour, desk
  and tapes — microphones
  additional)
Video recording (maximum
  4 hours, includes labour and
  VHS tapes)
ISDN lines
128 K bps connection fee
Full broadband broadcast tails
  2 way to Telstra TOC
Banner hanging
Each banner
Video conference package
(Room hire and equipment for
  max 15 people) |

When asked about his own role, as A/V manager, Stuart laughs! 'I'm really a glorified salesman', he says. He spends 30 to 50 per cent of his time each day discussing sales issues with convention sales and with hotel sales and marketing. He is responsible to the conference services manager, but does have direct lines of communication to the director of food and beverage and to the general manager.

He manages the day-to-day operation of the A/V department, with a team of five full-time and four casual staff. Most of the staff are from broadcasting backgrounds, with several currently studying audio engineering and similar courses. Stuart says that the team works well together, and he has little to do with the daily operation as his staff just 'get on with their jobs, checking the event orders every day and doing what has to be done.' He sees part of his role as trainer and mentor for those within his department. A/V staff stay with the organisation for about two to three years and he has implemented a 'buddy system' for new staff to induct them into the world of Inter-Continental A/V as quickly as possible.

Stuart feels that he has to take responsibility for clients' A/V needs and is often part of the initial contact team when clients begin the booking process for a convention or event. He does a lot of up-selling and often has to try to 'second-guess' clients' wishes, especially those who are unsure of exactly what they want. 'All they know is that they want the best event; something that stands out and is really, really memorable. And A/V can do this for them, if we do our job.' Stuart gives one example where he was asked by a client if the hotel was able to link to the BT Tower in London, download an audio and visual signal as the designated frequency and beam this into the hotel. 'And when is this happening, sir?', asked Stuart. 'Oh, shall we say in about 20 minutes?', replied the client.

In terms of issues and impacts on the A/V department, Stuart notes that many events are booked with very short lead times, making efficient operations within A/V critical. More clients are being educated through the use of A/V; they come to the hotel knowing what they want. Stuart comments that part of his role is still to anticipate what a client wants and to provide that need. He notes that the hotel expects him to produce a profit and he is happy to be able to oblige!

His contacts from previous employment have meant that much of his time is spent dealing with press personnel from a range of government offices, embassies and agencies, as well as private PR companies who bring celebrities to the hotel.

Stuart quotes from a recent survey of video conferencing in Sydney that the average weekly revenue from such events totals $90 000. With such sums being spent on this aspect alone, Stuart suggests that the A/V department is no longer just an adjunct to banqueting. The A/V department in the Inter-Continental is seen as a specialist section and is staffed and budgeted accordingly.

Source: Stuart Haynes, Inter-Continental Hotel

POST-CONVENTION OPERATIONS

In many cases, post-conference evaluation and contact between the client and the venue is a cursory discussion about the account and when the final bill might be paid. However, it is clear that evaluation and subsequent follow-up is essential for all those involved in the event: the venue, the PCO and the client organisation. Obtaining feedback from clients is a vital part of future planning. It is also a vital part of providing a quality product to the client.

Post-convention operations should include careful and critical evaluation of the food and beverage service and the response from clients regarding the technology used during the event itself. Techniques for evaluation vary from venue to venue. To ensure quality service and product, a venue could include items such as questionnaires and surveys, face-to-face meetings with clients, focus groups with delegates, and internal meetings with venue staff and supervisors assigned to the particular event. Chapter 10 discusses the evaluation process in more detail.

$\int$ UMMARY

The operational management of conventions and meetings can be a complex and intricate task. There are many variables that could impact on the smooth operation of the event. Managers must ensure clear strategies for pre-convention tasks. In addition to in-house meetings that focus on the needs of the organisation, contact with the client is a vital aspect of pre-event operations. Numerous items will need to be discussed, including final room rates, check-in procedures, and so on.

In order to meet clients' requirements, venues must have both the necessary amount and the proper type of space for meetings. There are many room configuration options, and those chosen for an event will depend on a number of factors, such as the size of the room, the number of delegates, the needs and activities of the conference and the turnaround times for set-ups.

Food and beverage service is a significant and critical part of conference operations, and can produce a high percentage of revenue for venues. No two meetings are alike, so catering facilities have to accommodate the many differing formats and functions of meetings. There are many issues to consider, from room layouts, menu styles and methods of delivery to menu planning and menu choice, staffing levels and pricing structures.

The hospitality industry in general has been relatively slow on the uptake of new technology, but times are changing. Several computer programs enable convention managers to implement ever more complex and data-rich strategies. The impact of the computer on conventions cannot be underestimated. From an increased awareness of delegates' requirements to quicker registration, the computer has changed the way events are managed.

Activities

9.1 From the sample business lunch menu in figure 9.7, choose the most appropriate items for a convention of 400 delegates. You should consider each style of food service.

9.2 Create a scenario for a one-day meeting or event, perhaps for a sporting group or a club that you know about. What types of food and beverages would you provide? Create some menus and give prices if possible.

9.3 Read the following and then complete the questions.

George is a food and beverage manager for Wiley's Motor Inn. He has been talking to Peter Richards, managing director of Jacaranda Motors, the local car dealership, regarding a one-day meeting for the dealership staff. The venue is perfect for Jacaranda Motors and Peter has been impressed with the quality of the service he has got from Wiley's Motor Inn in the past. The inn has 52 bedrooms and three function rooms — one quite large that seats 50 and two small boardrooms that are suitable for a dozen delegates. Peter wants to make the most of his booking, and has decided to have a breakfast meeting followed by three concurrent sales sessions to plan and create strategy policies for the coming year.

Jacaranda Motors has 37 staff and Peter has arranged for the dealership head office to send down two facilitators for the day. He wants to start the proceedings with breakfast at 7 a.m., for about an hour, and then go straight into the strategy meetings at 8.30 a.m., after a short break. All the rooms have been booked for the day, with the largest room booked from 7 a.m. for the breakfast.

Peter has also decided that he will put on a cocktail party for his staff and 18 of his better clients from town. The cocktail party will start at 5.30 p.m. and last for a couple of hours, and Peter wants to provide drinks and finger food.

(a) What issues are raised in this example?

(b) How might George solve these issues?

(c) Draw up several room configurations for Wiley's Motor Inn that you think would be appropriate for Jacaranda Motors' one-day meeting.

Discussion questions

9.1 A number of factors can affect pre-conference operations. Identify five such factors and their impact on operations.

9.2 Suggest solutions to the impacts you have identified in question 1.

9.3 Suggest several competitive advantages that a venue might gain by implementing a computerised conference system.

9.4 As a convention manager, how would you reflect changing trends in food and beverage consumption?

9.5 As the manager of a regional hotel with a range of convention and meeting facilities, discuss the limitations of providing a complete range of audiovisual equipment in-house.

9.6 Discuss whether video conferencing facilities reduce the need for corporate organisations to hold their meetings within venues.

REFERENCES

Astroff, M. T. & Abbey, J. R. 1998, *Convention Sales and Services*, 5th ed, Waterbury Press, N. J.

Braham, B. 1992, *Computer Systems in the Hotel and Catering Industry*, Cassell, London.

Hoyle, L. H., Dorf, D.C. & Jones, T. J. A. 1989, *Managing Conventions and Group Business*, The Educational Institute of the American Hotel and Motel Association, East Lansing, p. 169.

McCabe, V. & Weeks, P. 1999, 'Convention Services Management in Sydney Four- to Five-Star Hotels', *Journal of Convention and Exhibition Management*, vol. 1, no. 4, pp. 67–84.

Montgomery, R. & Strick, S. 1995, *Meetings, Conventions and Expositions: An Introduction to the Industry*, Van Nostrand Reinhold, New York.

Sheraton Pacific Corporation 1993, *The Sheraton Meeting and Conference Workbook*, Sheraton Pacific Corporation, Sydney.

Shock, P. & Stefanelli, J. M. 1992, *Hotel Catering: A Handbook for Sales and Operations*, John Wiley & Sons, New York.

Tolhurst, C. 1999, 'Technology Can Jazz up the Subject', *Conference & Incentive Marketing*, p. 30.

FURTHER READING

Buhalis, D. 1998, 'Strategic Use of Information Technologies in the Tourism Industry', *Tourism Management*, vol. 19, no. 5, pp. 409–21.

O'Connor, P. 1998, *Using Computers in Hospitality* 2nd ed, Cassell, London.

Peacock, M. 1995, *Information Technology in the Hospitality Industry*, Cassell, London.

Weissinger, S. S. 1992, *A Guide to Successful Meeting Planning*, J. Wiley & Sons, New York.

Wrest Point Conference Centre, Hobart

The first casino in Australia opened in 1973, when Wrest Point Hotel and Casino opened its doors to the public. The Conference Centre at Wrest Point was launched in 1984, at a time when there was only an embryonic MICE industry in Tasmania. Prior to this time, meeting facilities were provided by hotels, mainly catering for smaller conferences and meetings. From the inception of the Conference Centre at Wrest Point, Tasmania marketed itself both nationally and internationally as a convention destination. This led to the formation of the Tasmanian Convention and Visitors Bureau in the late 1980s to promote and market Tasmania as a tourist/convention destination. The industry has now grown to the stage where conference delegates inject $41 million directly into the local economy annually and is a critical economic component of the state's tourism industry.

At its opening, the conference centre was heralded as the first purpose-built conference centre in Australia. The hotel has the advantage of providing two types of guest accommodation: The Tower (197 rooms) provides five-star accommodation following a recent major upgrade of $26 million and The Motor Inn (82 rooms) gives guests a three-and-a-half-star motel-style option. The Wrest Point Hotel and Casino is owned by the Farrell family, who also own the Country Club Casino on the outskirts of Launceston.

Conference facilities at Wrest Point are located in a separate area of the complex that is linked to the main hotel/casino. The conference centre comprises 14 meeting rooms, providing flexibility to cater for groups as large as 1600, in plenary session, to smaller groups in boardrooms seating 12 people. The complex offers its delegates a casino for gaming, entertainment, restaurants, a number of bars, recreation facilities such as a swimming pool, health club, tennis courts and mini golf, and extensive gardens.

A key strength of the extensive facilities is that conference delegates can all stay on site, which enables both synergy and networking opportunities. For PCOs, this is a bonus, as there is no need for complex logistical arrangements with delegates staying in other accommodation properties. Exhibition facilities consist of a foyer plus two other large areas with a capacity for 108 exhibition booths on site. For larger conferences, trade exhibitions and catering, a hockerdome can be erected on the lawns.

Wrest Point's core business is conferences and meetings up to 600 delegates. A permanently tiered theatre can seat up to 600 delegates. MICE business is predominantly from the association market, corporate conferences and major trade exhibitions, plus multipurpose activities such as concerts and 'people mover' style events such as shows and expos, especially exhibitions aimed at the retiree market. Encouraging retiree events can provide additional benefits,

not only in accommodation sales but also additional revenue from the restaurants, casino, and so on.

Conference and exhibition organisers that use Wrest Point are mainly based in Victoria or are national associations that have representatives in Tasmania. Wrest Point has an active sales team with sales managers in Sydney and Melbourne.

The venue has a large banqueting kitchen, separate from other food production areas within the complex. The banqueting kitchen is set up in a traditional 'brigade' system, with separate sections for pastry, butchery, fish, and so on. The kitchen services the conference centre, providing dinners for up to 800 people. Another full kitchen, situated in the older part of the complex, provides catering for a further 400 delegates. To ease the flow during service times, there are a number of serveries situated throughout the conference centre.

A/V equipment and support is provided in-house by a two-person team that between them have 44 years of experience in A/V provision and production. Wrest Point holds a complete stock of A/V equipment and any items not available in-house are sourced to an external contractor. The provision of A/V support is seen as a key strength of the venue.

As with many convention providers, staffing tends to fluctuate depending on the season and the number of events being held. There are 14 permanent members of staff in the convention team, as well as several casual and part-time employees who work in the banquet services area. A team of five controls the administration of the centre and, as previously mentioned, two permanent staff manage the A/V requirements. Three other staff play important roles within the centre: one is responsible for exhibitions and trade-show coordination; one is responsible for the submission of bids and sales; and one looks after smaller, corporate meetings and social functions. There is an operations section, managed by the operations managers for conventions and exhibitions. This section is responsible for the day-to-day operations of the centre, including provision of A/V equipment and set-up and break-down of room layouts. Floor staff and crew leaders report directly to the operations manager. Management of the conference centre is through a convention centre manager, who reports directly to the general manager of the hotel casino, and an administration manager (Alfred Merse). Alfred Merse is an economics graduate from the University of Tasmania. He is the state chairman of the MIAA branch in Tasmania and is on the MIAA national council. Prior to working at Wrest Point, Alfred was with the Tasmanian Convention Bureau in destination marketing. His previous experience includes work with the Sheraton Hobart in front office, banquets and sales.

The conference centre has its own in-house exhibition booth system. As a result, it is able to offer a high standard of equipment plus a trade and exhibition coordination service. Sales and operations staff liaise with exhibitors and organise any extra facilities such as florists, display cabinets, and so on.

Initial enquiries are via sales offices in Tasmania and on the mainland (in Melbourne, for example) and through direct contact with the hotel itself. Once deposits are received, the conference is handed over to the administration

manager and a case manager is allocated to liaise with the client. Wrest Point conference staff aim to provide 'one-stop shopping' for potential organisers. PCOs, organising committees and other stakeholders deal with one person within the centre who arranges all their requirements, creating a far more effective and efficient service for clients.

Within Wrest Point there is a team approach and the family business promotes a culture of looking after employees. Many staff have been at the venue for 25 years.

The development of the hotel's water location and the inclusion of in-house exhibition services has allowed Wrest Point to enhance the range and quality of its services and it is seen as an industry leader within the convention services industry in Tasmania.

Source: Alfred Merse, Wrest Point Conference Centre

Questions

1 Discuss the strengths and weaknesses of Wrest Point Conference Centre.

2 Given the diverse range of facilities offered by Wrest Point, create a three-day program for an international convention of 420 delegates. The program should include menus, session schedules (with A/V requirements), timing and staffing requirements. Pre- and post-conference activities should be considered as well as free time for delegates.

CHAPTER 10

Managing the
quality of conventions

LEARNING OBJECTIVES

After studying this chapter, you will be able to:

■ define and identify the concepts of 'quality' and 'service'

■ evaluate current organisational practices in the provision of quality service for a convention or meeting

■ identify the stakeholders in the provision of quality customer service for a convention or meeting

■ determine the issues relating to service provision for each of the major stakeholders for a convention or meeting

■ establish methods of measuring quality service in MICE organisations.

INTRODUCTION

For the next few years, the Australian MICE industry will be under the spotlight of international scrutiny to see whether it can continue to live up to and exceed the standards of international best practice. Australia has been recognised for the quality and excellence of its venues, but some conference organisers appear concerned about shortcomings in service quality and customer service in supporting meetings (Christie 1994; Commonwealth Department of Tourism 1995). In the light of even greater competition, the opportunities provided by the Sydney 2000 Olympics and the celebrations surrounding the centenary of Federation, the MICE industry needs to ensure that it continues to deliver and exceed the current levels of excellence in the provision of quality customer service. However, to achieve this may affect not only its operational management systems but also the very way that business is conducted within this sector of the tourism industry.

This chapter reviews and discusses the concepts of quality management and the provision of service quality within conventions and meetings. The focus is on the two themes that have been implicit throughout this textbook — ensuring a consistent quality product or service and providing continuous customer service. The end result is to ensure a high level of customer satisfaction for both the client organisation and the delegates or participants who attend the event.

Achieving high levels of customer satisfaction is the ultimate goal of the conference organiser. Satisfied customers not only want to repeat the experience but also tell their friends and peers. Conventions or meetings provide the opportunity for conference organisers to satisfy the client organisation as well as the many delegates attending the event. This captive audience provides an enormous advertising potential for the conference organiser, the venue and other suppliers. The interrelationships in the provision of quality customer service between the client organisation, the conference organiser and the venue is outlined in the quality service model (see figure 10.1), together with their impacts on the ultimate customer, the conference delegate.

■ **Figure 10.1**
The quality service model

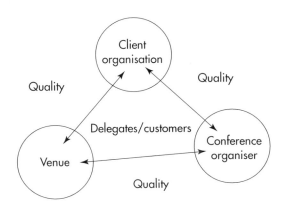

QUALITY AND CUSTOMER SERVICE IN CONVENTION MANAGEMENT

In the MICE industry today, managers are conscious of the priority for revenue generation. However, there is a trend away from mere 'money' towards a more caring attitude to the consumer. If the MICE industry in Australia is to continue to enhance its reputation for the provision of quality events, then a customer-centred philosophy to client management should continue to be adopted. Before reviewing the issues of quality and its impact on individual stakeholders, the notions of 'quality' and 'service' are outlined.

■ What *is quality?*

Quality management involves making sure that the product or service on offer is delivered at the right time and at the right place and meets the customer's requirements. It covers not only the people involved in the provision of the product or service, but also aspects such as the systems, their administration and the associated paperwork. Also tied in is the quality of the products purchased from other suppliers. This aspect is critical, because many suppliers are involved in the provision of the total service. Conference organisers therefore need to build up a network of quality providers.

Quality management and its implementation are important in today's MICE industry. Worldwide, delegate expectations are continuing to rise, and successful venues and conference organisers are addressing these rising expectations and driving them even higher. To be successful, conference organisers and venues require a positive, adaptive organisational culture that demonstrates a willingness to change. The introduction of a quality management system and a commitment to quality in the service delivery can assist in achieving these quality objectives.

There are a number of basic principles involved in the introduction of quality management within a MICE organisation (Heymann 1992):

- *Management leads the way* The CEO must communicate to the team a clear vision statement that demonstrates a commitment to quality. The establishment of a quality culture should be introduced into all areas of the organisation. All staff should be treated with respect, encouraged to contribute and recognised for their individual contribution. A team orientation should be developed in and between departments. For example, conference and banqueting sales and conference service coordination should not squabble over what can be achieved with regard to a particular service.
- *Agreement of customer requirements* Customer driven policies and procedures should be developed. Service standards need to be established for each step and each component of the service and its delivery, from the first point of contact through to the actual event and post-event evaluation. The key is to do the right things the first time.

- *Development of leadership skills*   To provide growth, continuity and stability, and avoid continual 'fire fighting', the leadership skills of managers should be developed, together with their ability to solve problems.
- *Recognition that staff are the key*   The MICE organisation should develop its human resources, from the recruitment and selection process through to training and development, performance appraisal and career development. Key staff should be empowered, and reward and recognition systems should be measured not only in dollars but also in recognition for both individuals and the team.
- *Plan for quality*   Forecast business should be planned, and the organisation should be ready to react to any changes as and when required. For example, for the registration process at a large convention, the peak check-in times should be pinpointed and plans made to ensure that enough staff are available to deal with delegates, thereby ensuring that there are no delays in the service.
- *Measure for success*   With the ultimate goal being continuous achievement, systems that measure this achievement should be built into the MICE organisation. Traditionally, the profit and loss account and delegate evaluation forms have been used. However, these are not sufficient because the organisation needs to develop and measure performance and compare actual achievement against preset standards. Feedback should be provided to the staff.

Quality management and customer service go hand in hand. 'Profitable companies learn from the people they serve and provide unparalleled quality of service and reliability' (Peters & Waterman 1982, pp. 156–7).

■ What *is service?*

Traditionally, the term 'service' has been difficult to define because of its intangibility. Lovelock and Wright (1999, p. 5) have provided two approaches that help to capture the essence of its meaning and assist in an understanding of the term:

> ■ A service is an act or performance offered by one party to another. Although the process may be tied to a physical product, the performance is essentially intangible and does not result in ownership of any of the factors of production. ■

> ■ Service is an economic activity that creates value and provides benefits for customers at specific times and places, as a result of bringing about a desired change in — or on behalf of — the recipient of the service. ■

Another approach might to be to state that service is setting standards regarding customer needs and meeting them.

Service is not just giving customers bigger and better facilities; it involves the way these facilities are given to them. Smiling, friendly faces talking about the conference and meeting facilities are far more conducive to an enjoyable hospitality experience than just a bare meeting room or venue set up for the event. As the convention and meeting industry becomes more efficient, it is important that the service factor is not forgotten or lost.

Many people take good service or adequate service for granted; yet poor service can be a powerful dissatisfier for the potential customer. For example, poor service at the conference registration desk, such as staff who are rude, lack attention, have little knowledge of what is required or appear bored or disinterested, results in customers assuming that it happens all the time.

In the MICE industry, quality management and customer service go hand in hand with service quality influencing the customers' overall attitude about the service delivery. This attitude can be formed by a number of successful or unsuccessful experiences.

Service and the provision of service within a convention or meeting consist of both tangible and intangible actions that are undertaken by people. For example, the tangible components might include the provision of a meeting or convention room with comfortable seating, adequate lighting, audiovisual equipment, morning tea, lunch and so on. Intangible actions might consist of how the service is provided and directed at the conference delegates in order to satisfy their needs, such as a welcoming smile and a cheerful good morning as the delegates arrive at the venue. The intangibility of the service provided at a convention or meeting, as elsewhere in the tourism and hospitality industry, means that it cannot be stored and sold again. If the convention room is not sold today, it cannot be sold again. In the same way, the service is not transferable. The customer (the delegate) normally comes to the convention or meeting, rather than the other way round.

Successful companies have shown that the introduction of 'customer interaction' policies, that is effective customer service and the provision of quality service, leads to improvements in the level of customer satisfaction. This in turn may result in repeat business for the company. No matter how judiciously that technology and information are used to give a competitive advantage, when a delegate walks into the foyer of the convention venue the team is required to perform up to expectations. The team has a responsibility to produce good service consistently. Good service separates the basic venues from the truly exceptional venues. In the long term, the MICE businesses that fail to adequately deliver service and quality will be severely hampered in their quest for repeat customers. The emergence of the service-centred customer has resulted in many organisations establishing improved levels of service and quality for their product or service. Their aim is to attract the more discerning customer.

Different levels of service

The style and type of convention or meeting activity can affect the level and extent of the service that is required, for example how the event is designed and customised, the extent of staff involvement and thus staff levels, the service and amount of client interaction that the conference organiser, the venue or other suppliers need to supply. Thus, the provision of a large convention for 1000 delegates within a venue could be equated to a service factory, while the design and operation of a personalised training and team-building program could be considered more as a professional service than a service factory (Lovelock 1992, p. 39). The degree of labour intensity and interaction per individual delegate in the latter case would be much higher than for the large convention, which may consist mainly of plenary sessions.

Evaluation of the service

The volatility of providing a service can cause a number of problems, for service tends to be an ephemeral commodity, which is not easily pinned down, checked or counted. Research has indicated that a customer's expectations of the quality and delivery of a service is based on a long-term evaluation of how the firm provides that service. A customer judges the quality of the service by five main factors — reliability, tangibility, responsiveness, assurance and empathy (Zeithaml, Parasuraman & Berry 1990). These factors are particularly relevant for the MICE industry because of the potential number of suppliers that are involved in the organisation of an event and the length of time over which the business for each event is conducted:

- *Reliability* Many potential conference clients are concerned about the reliability and dependability of the conference organiser in their provision of the service. The industry has low barriers to entry and a high turnover of both staff and conference organisers. Additionally, the long lead times for an event can result in many interactions between the conference organiser and the venue, or the conference organiser and the client organisation (Rutherford & Umbreit 1993). Each encounter is a potential occasion to either impress the client or cause concern. Not providing information on time and staff not knowing about the event are potential occasions for dissatisfaction. An unreliable service is no better than a poor service, despite the fact that other aspects of the total service may be satisfactory. If the provision of the core service is unreliable, then the customer may switch to another supplier. The client and delegates are both involved in the actual production of the service, that is the convention or meeting. Therefore, they experience any mistakes directly, such as the morning coffee arriving late or insufficient coffee being available for the number of delegates. Employees provide a degree of variability in the service they provide due to their different personalities, skills and attitudes. One employee can provide a radically different type of service to another, despite the provision of company manuals and training in the standards required.
- *Tangibility* This relates to the provision of the physical facilities, audio-visual equipment, and so on, within the convention or meeting product or service. As discussed previously, Australian capital cities are noted for the quality of their facilities and infrastructure, such as purpose-built convention and exhibition centres and venues, and for staff who are both competent and efficient. However, this may not be the case in some regional areas and could in fact be a weak link in the overall service provision.

- *Responsiveness* Are the conference organiser and venue staff helpful and able to provide prompt service to the client organisation or their delegates? This aspect is of particular importance currently in Australia, as many CBD venues have gained a competitive advantage by ensuring short turnaround times in their responses to conference quotations for client organisations (McCabe & Weeks 1999).
- *Assurance* Are the staff involved knowledgeable, polite, competent and trustworthy? This aspect of service provision links to a reduction in staff turnover levels, improvements in staff training and development, and effective tailored recruitment and selection policies. In a bid to highlight the 'assurance' aspects of the MICE industry, the federal government has highlighted in a number of reports the need for specifically designed training for MICE industry employees (Commonwealth Department of Tourism 1995; Office of National Tourism 1998).
- *Empathy* Does the convention organisation provide caring and personalised attention to clients and their delegates? Within the MICE industry, this has been a continuing area of development since the 1990s.

The need to strive for reliability of service is always paramount. While the other dimensions of tangibility, responsiveness, assurance and empathy provide the conference organiser or venue with the opportunity to delight customers by exceeding their expectations, if the service is not reliable, then it will overshadow all other aspects (Lovelock & Wright 1999).

Potential gaps in service quality

Certain shortfalls or 'quality gaps' can occur at various points in the performance of the service (Lovelock & Wright 1999, p. 91). These quality gaps happen when the actual quality of service falls below the level expected by the customer. Each service gap is critical in the customer's overall assessment of what is expected compared to what is actually received. For the conference organiser, the ultimate goal is to ensure that each quality gap is as narrow as possible.

Seven areas for potential gaps have been identified (Lovelock & Wright 1999, p. 93). These are outlined below.

1. *The knowledge gap* A knowledge gap can exist when there is a difference between what the conference organiser or provider of the service believes the customer expects and the customer's actual needs and expectations. For a conference organiser this is particularly relevant. Such differences can occur easily, and not only can the client organisation's requirements be different, but the expectations and requirements of the delegates can be different yet again. One method of narrowing this gap is for the conference organiser and client organisation to clearly establish and agree the aims and objectives of the event as early as possible.

2. *The standards gap* A gap in the standards can occur when there is a difference between, for example, the venue management's perception of the conference organiser's expectations and the quality standards established for the service delivery by the venue or other suppliers.

3. *The delivery gap* A gap in the delivery can occur when there is a difference between what is specified for the service standard and what is actually provided. A typical example is the 'overselling' of a banquet menu.

4. *The internal communications gap* A gap in internal communications can occur when there is a difference between what the conference organiser or a venue's advertising and sales promotion staff think are the features of the convention or meeting product, its performance and service quality levels, and what the company or venue is actually able to deliver. The convention industry, and in particular venues, suffers greatly from this gap in service quality. So, for example, convention sales staff may sell facilities and customer expectations for a conference that the convention services manager is not actually able to deliver.

5. *The perceptions gap* The perceptions gap can occur when there is a difference between what is actually delivered and what the client organisation or delegates perceive they have received.

6. *The interpretation gap* A gap in interpretation can occur when there is a difference between what the service provider's (e.g. the PCO) communication efforts actually promise and what the customer (e.g. the client organisation) thinks was provided by the communication, for example concerning the details within a contract.

7. *The service gap* The service gap can occur when there is a difference between what the customer expects to receive and their perception of the service actually delivered.

A discrepancy in any of these seven gaps can damage a relationship with a customer.

Having discussed aspects of service and customer satisfaction and the need to provide quality within the management of the MICE event, our attention now turns to specific links within the model outlined in figure 10.1. Each interactive element is explored in terms of its focus on generating quality service for the client organisation, customer or delegate.

QUALITY AND THE ROLE OF THE CLIENT ORGANISATION AND THE CONFERENCE ORGANISING COMMITTEE

The conference organising committee is often the embryo of the convention or meeting. The committee may be formed by the client organisation with a brief to investigate the possibility of holding such an event, and it will make a decision as to the viability of the event. The committee has a number of interlinkages and interactions with the other stakeholders involved in the provision of a convention or meeting, such as the PCO or conference organiser for the event (if one is appointed), the venue, other suppliers and the delegates.

The conference organising committee reports to the client organisation. The tasks that are undertaken by the committee can be quite complex, and it is essential that the group members are committed to the goals of the organisation and the proposed convention or meeting. To enhance the goal of providing a quality service and product, the committee should consider the following points when carrying out its duties:

- Members of the committee must share a common culture that is focused on quality. This belief should also be shared by the client organisation.
- As well as a commitment to a quality culture, clear and resolute leadership should be provided within the committee, as well as by the client organisation.
- Standard monitoring procedures should be put in place and conducted at various times during the planning process and actual operation of the event. The committee should agree on the monitoring procedures.
- The core service that is to be provided by the committee should be identified and delivered through leadership, monitoring and training.
- Specialist staff may need to be included within the committee. For example, some organisations employ a conference organiser as part of their workforce; alternatively, others contract the business of managing and organising the convention or meeting to a PCO.
- Training may be required for those involved within the committee, because it may be the first time that they have participated in such a specialist group activity (Williams 1998).

In order to explore the service quality issues that impact on an event and the conference organising committee, the next few sections cover the committee's interactions with the various other stakeholders.

■ The PCO

Appointing and dealing with a PCO can be quite a daunting task for many members of the conference organising committee. The PCO is seen as 'the expert', and should assist the committee in its decisions. As previously discussed, the PCO forms the 'executive arm' of the conference organising committee, but it is important that the committee identifies its requirements for the event at the outset, together with the quality of service that is required.

In many organisations, the hiring of a PCO and their expertise is seen as the most viable solution to providing a convention or meeting at the required quality, especially if there is no single employee or manager who can adequately undertake the task. The conference organising committee is responsible for ensuring that the needs and wants of both the client organisation and the delegates are met. In using the services of a PCO, the committee is delegating many of the aspects of the event to a third party. It is this third party who then briefs the suppliers and other stakeholders of the convention or meeting requirements, including the quality standards. The

PCO should therefore be monitored to ensure that quality service is being provided and the stated service requirements are being achieved.

To work cohesively with a PCO, several aspects should be taken into consideration by the committee. Initially, prior to the appointment of the PCO, the committee should contact other organisers with whom the PCO has worked to find out whether they are reliable. During the pre-event planning the committee should hold regular meetings with the PCO; these meetings should be accompanied by an agenda, and all discussions should be confirmed in writing. Members of the committee should be involved with the PCO in selecting the venue, to ensure their needs are being met.

■ The venue

Venue staff often assume that when they are about to provide convention services and facilities to a potential conference group that those people interacting with the venue have some fundamental understanding of the intricacies of venue selection, set-up and general planning of events. In some instances, particularly if there is no designated conference organiser, this is actually not the case. The delegated person, or group, from the organising committee responsible for liaising with the venue often have little or no experience and can be left rather stranded once the complexity of the planning tasks becomes apparent. In order to ensure the provision of quality customer service for the event, there thus needs to be some emphasis on training committee members in the finer points of venue selection and conference planning.

In briefing and working with the venue, the objectives of the event should be clarified, together with the general outcomes required by the client organisation and any extraordinary needs of the event participants. The conference organising committee (or the PCO) should keep detailed records of contacts with the venue and decisions about how the conference is to be organised. These should be kept in writing and filed. This system means that the PCO and other stakeholders can be quickly and reliably informed of any changes or priorities. It also provides a bank of historical information for future events.

Several practical factors should be considered by the committee when dealing with the venue and may be viewed as critical to the provision of a quality service. The committee should:
- check (and double check) the timings of each event to ensure turnover times are adequate
- test the quality of food by sampling the dishes or having a meal in the venue
- review the quality service standards set by the venue
- speak to all management staff concerned with the event
- ensure all contact is confirmed in writing
- attend a similar event and experience the venue's service.

■ The suppliers

The suppliers to the conference organising committee are a diverse group and may include transport companies, audiovisual equipment suppliers, outside catering companies and general hire companies, for items such as marquees, tents and office supplies. As they do with other stakeholders, the committee (or the PCO) should build its relationships with these suppliers and view them as a partnership. The suppliers are an essential component in the provision of a quality convention or meeting.

When dealing with such a range of businesses, it is vital that the committee confirms all dealings in writing and that only those items that will enhance the quality of the event are acquired from these suppliers. In its selection of each supplier, the committee (or the PCO) should establish the standard and performance levels required, such as quality of product, compliance with delivery schedules, reliability of contact, and so on.

Suppliers should be provided with the event requirements well ahead of the required time lines, and a contingency plan (e.g. a list of alternative suppliers) should be prepared in case of non-compliance. The specifications for the required goods and services should be quite detailed, and the suppliers should be checked to ensure that they actually can deliver the goods.

■ The delegates

Ensuring the provision of quality service and customer satisfaction for delegates is a complex process and provides a significant issue for the conference organising committee.

> ■ Important influences on the level of customers' expectations often outweigh the control of the service provider, and are noted as being the extent of personal needs, word of mouth, customers' past service experiences and finally influences of external communication (Desombre & Eccles 1998). ■

Delegates to an event may have nothing in common, apart from their reason for attending the event. Some delegates will have specific dietary needs, others will require special information, and disabled delegates may require additional services and special facilities within the venue. While the committee or PCO may not be able to adhere to every whim and request, they need to set guidelines as to what is acceptable for that specific event, in terms of requirements.

The committee or PCO must ensure prompt responses to delegate enquiries. Delegates' perceptions of the quality of service that they receive at the event are often based on the initial interaction and response to their enquiry. A pleasant telephone manner, timely written confirmation of conference reservations and smooth registration are all critical aspects seen by delegates as part of the quality of service provided by the conference organiser. In some instances, shortfalls by the venue can reflect badly on the committee, even though the lack of quality service is not its fault.

■ The client *organisation*

The key to dealing with the client organisation (i.e. the company, association or individual that has decided to hold the event) is to ensure that its requirements are seen as vital to the success of the convention or meeting. The conference organising committee or the PCO must ensure that the overall objectives of holding the event are met through the planning and organisation of the event itself.

The committee is seen as the 'person' charged with planning, organising and executing the event. In some cases there may be conflict within the management executive of the committee or the client organisation as to who should be responsible for these tasks — an internally appointed group or an external third-party organiser, such as a PCO. It is therefore important to ensure that the objectives of the client organisation are clear and that its requirements head any list of achievable goals.

The committee must ensure that the event program reflects the objectives of the conference. It must decide on a site that will allow the event to provide the best possible environment to realise the wishes of the client organisation. In some cases, members of the committee may have been taken away from their normal work duties. This may cause some conflicts between their loyalty to their normal work activities and their position on the committee.

The client organisation will have its own perceptions of the quality of service that should be provided by the conference organising committee. To meet these perceptions, the committee should take the following factors into account:

- all requirements should be in writing
- regular meetings should be held with the client organisation
- a member of the client organisation should become a member of the conference organising committee
- adequate funding for the event should be made available
- there should be commitment and leadership from the client organisation to the provision of quality service.

With such a diverse group of people attempting to organise an equally diverse group of people within an ever-changing environment, it is easy to lapse into a standardised routine. The conference organising committee must be able to adjust to its current surroundings and be as flexible as possible.

> ■ Most of us do many things, day after day, seldom questioning why. Are there better way of doing things? Has the original purpose behind certain activities long vanished? There are a number of reasons why processes become inefficient. Chief among them is the failure to continually question processes with an eye on assessing which activities add value and which do not (Marecki, Revalas & Sackler 1998). ■

The PCO has a unique role to play in the provision of quality service. They have to ensure that it is provided within their own organisation and that they provide quality customer service to both the client organisation and its delegates. They may therefore need to rethink some of their business processes so that they can provide a flexible, responsive and customer-focused workforce. In the provision of quality in event management and organisation, the PCO needs to ensure that both the venue and the suppliers selected are able to cooperate and supply the quality of service required by the client organisation. Some PCOs express the view that often the suppliers do not understand their needs or the needs of their clients. As noted earlier, creating a network of quality providers can assist in ensuring ultimate customer satisfaction and it is therefore of paramount importance. Its introduction creates an awareness and necessity to be sensitive to the pressures on the client, even if they are not related to the PCO contractually. To be successful, PCOs need to be flexible. However, how many venues and PCOs really are flexible, respond to clients' needs and work in partnership with their stakeholders? In the provision of a convention or meeting it is important to treasure every customer and let them know it.

■ Communication *skills*

Communication and cooperation are key to the planning and organisation of a successful convention. In order to achieve quality customer service, the PCO should be aware of the many elements of quality service mentioned earlier, but draw more importantly on their communication and coordination abilities.

Verbal communication skills

The PCO will need excellent verbal communication skills in their face-to-face interactions with the client, suppliers and conference organisation team. In all verbal communication, the PCO should be aware of the clarity and style of the communication, the choice of language, its appropriateness and the cultural diversity of the group. Non-verbal communication and the messages that may be displayed should also be borne in mind. In other words, the non-verbal message should complement the verbal component — for example, eye contact that is warm, positive and supportive. In telephone conversations the clarity of the message must always be paramount, as is the speed of response to the calls. For a PCO who may be dealing with a plethora of calls, the ability to respond to queries in a time efficient manner while still maintaining the level of service, empathy, and so on, is critical.

Meetings and their management are another method of communication between the PCO and the client organisation or suppliers to the event. Agendas and agreed actions should be circulated promptly to members. The PCO also should be aware of the culture of the organisation and cognisant of any hidden agendas, both of which can affect the meetings' effectiveness and outcomes.

Written communication skills

Written communication between the PCO, the client organisation and the various suppliers is extensive and comprehensive, and may be in the form of bid proposals, reports, contracts, briefs to suppliers, and so on. Fax and e-mail are now in common use. The speed of response to an enquiry that is required in today's MICE industry has implications for the PCO, particularly with respect to the choice of communication medium. For example, the use of fax and e-mail has meant that many enquiries are now dealt with virtually immediately, irrespective of the source of the enquiry. Responses can be transmitted within a matter of seconds to an organisation across the globe. However, on a more practical note, while the use of these telecommunication methods provides an added dimension to the quality of service provided, it can in some instances be detrimental. E-mails and faxes should be reviewed to ensure the same quality of presentation as in the more traditional written documentation.

■ Partnerships

The provision of a high quality of service for a convention or meeting requires that the PCO forms 'partnerships' not only with the client organisation and the conference organising committee but also with the various suppliers. All of these partnerships are important, but none more so than with the venue.

The PCO and the venue

Traditionally, many venues have followed an attitude of simply renting out space and any associated services to an organisation or PCO for a conference or meeting. They have not seen themselves in partnership with the PCO or company and thus have not focused on building relationships with their customers. However, the PCO and the selected venue need to form an informal partnership, the aim of which is to ensure the provision of an event that both meets and exceeds the expectations of the client and their delegates.

The interactions between the PCO and venue are an area of great importance in the convention and meeting industry, yet they are also one of the key areas of weakness and vulnerability. The interactions that occur with each service encounter can take place over a long period of time, in some cases up to three to five years. The total service delivery process starts with the early contract negotiation and goes right through to the post-event evaluation. The interactions involve numerous contacts with hotel or venue staff. One of the main factors that can weaken the quality of service is the level of staff turnover. Often, the PCO or members of the venue's conference team will change during the total service delivery process for the conference. This can cause difficulties in communication with the client or PCO and in the provision of the required service. A venue that has built up the confidence of the PCO can easily lose this confidence as a result of poor service, broken promises, and so on.

Rutherford (1993) has identified the major areas of interaction and the areas of the greatest difficulty between the PCO and venue staff, along with data on effective and ineffective behaviour in the provision of service quality. The key people who interact with a PCO and influence the service quality are the convention services manager, the sales manager and the catering director or manager. Examples of service problems include a number of instances where the sales manager has oversold the capabilities of the venue to the PCO or client organisation, and it has been left to the convention services manager to redeem the problem.

The PCO team

In the provision of quality service a PCO needs to focus on attention to detail, by looking at the small steps and identifying aspects that can cause dissatisfaction or inconvenience if they are not carried out well. It is the small steps that can make or break the reputation of the PCO. The PCO needs to foster a culture of quality and quality customer service within the convention team. Difficulties in using part-time staff in some areas of the organisation should be recognised. For example, in the organisation of conference registration, part-time staff need to be trained in the systems of the conference organisation so that they become familiar with the skills and the quality standards required as soon as possible. By completing such training, these staff are made aware of the commitment of the organisation to their involvement in the event. They become part of the conference team and contribute to providing a quality event. To complement quality management, best practice and benchmarking could be introduced as aids to help measure performance against the competition.

The following snapshot provides an insight into the philosophy and some of the skills required of a conference organiser who is focused on providing quality customer service.

SNAPSHOT

Peter May, Institution of Engineers, Australia

Peter May has over 30 years experience conducting meetings, conferences and trade exhibitions in Australia and overseas. Currently, he oversees the national conference operation of the Institution of Engineers, Australia, which involves working on more than 20 major events each year. He is an accredited member of the Meetings Industry Association of Australia and is a Fellow of the Australian Society of Association Executives. In 1998/99 he was awarded the 'Outstanding Operations Person', MIAA National Award for Excellence.

Peter sees himself as being professionally involved in the Australian meetings industry, initiating and managing conferences and trade exhibitions.

He is not sure why he became so involved in conferences and did not start out deliberately to make his living this way. In fact, in earlier occupations he tried to avoid becoming responsible for such activities. In spite of these efforts to choose a different direction, he often found himself on one committee or another working to achieve some collective goal by creating an 'event'. Inevitably he became 'experienced' and began to appreciate the value of what he was doing and to realise that it gave him a sense of satisfaction. He then started to learn what the meetings industry was all about.

It seems to be a basic human need to meet, to learn and exchange ideas, and to socialise. Meetings are also a recognised business activity. Large corporations meet to communicate within their boundaries. Other groups meet to project their interests beyond their 'tribal' boundaries. There are over 100 000 registered societies in Australia and many of them conduct regular conferences to achieve their objectives. Many of these organisations attract delegates from overseas and in doing so contribute to the national income. Business travellers attending conferences contribute billions of dollars to the Australian economy each year. Over the years Peter has come to appreciate the value of human interaction, the business outcomes and the economic contributions that are generated from successful events.

Peter's earlier working experience gave him a sound background in management and administration, a sensitivity to legal issues and some skill in communicating and negotiating. This background has been important, but not as important as one personal characteristic that he believes is critical for anyone who wishes to work in the meetings industry and enjoy it. That is, you must like people. Committee work can be difficult and so tolerance and team play are essential attributes for anyone who would do this for a living. Whereas knowledge, skill and talent are important, the ability to work with others, and to commit to shared goals, is the basis for respect as a professional.

He has been fortunate to work with so many skilled and talented people who have freely shared their particular knowledge and experience. Indeed, he thinks that the sharing of knowledge, skill and experience is a characteristic of the meetings industry; a rare characteristic that is seldom found in other industries. Any success that he may have achieved in creating and managing conference events reflects the talent and professionalism that has surrounded him in all his endeavours.

Peter is pleased to be part of this interesting, if sometimes challenging, industry.

Source: Peter May, Institution of Engineers, Australia

Having assessed the requirements of the PCO and conference organising committee or client organisation in providing quality service to create a positive customer service reaction, the focus now turns to the venue.

QUALITY AND THE ROLE OF THE VENUE

There are a variety of venues that are capable of holding some form of 'conference', be it a small, weekly, boardroom-style meeting for a local business or a product launch for a multinational company. The expectations and the processes for providing quality customer service for these examples are the same — that is, the customers ultimately want the best service they can obtain while the venues, with their range of facilities, are ideally placed to provide such service. From a venue's perspective, however, providing a quality product or service and providing continuous customer service may require some alternative processes and strategies from those utilised by the PCO and conference organising committee.

Venues encompass a diversity of departments. There is thus a need for venue managers to ensure high levels of internal interaction between management and staff and among staff. The incidence of customer–staff contact is extremely high and should be managed in such a way as to ensure that each point of interaction enhances rather than reduces the customer's perception of the service.

Richard Normann has borrowed the idea of 'moments of truth' from the language of bullfighting (Lovelock & Wright, 1999, p. 54). He has noted that:

> ■ [We] could say that the perceived quality is realized at the moment of truth, when the service provider and the service customer confront each other in the arena. At that moment they are very much on their own ... It is the skill, the motivation, and the tools employed by the firm's representative and the expectations and behaviour of the client which together will create the service delivery process. ■

The metaphor could be seen as rather simplistic, that is equating the final moments of a bull's life and the ultimate threat to the bullfighter's life to that of a single connection between two people. The analogy does however highlight one very simple fact — intrinsic to managing quality service is the fact that the service is only as good as the people who provide it, and providing (or losing) quality service can happen in an instant.

Ayers Rock Resort is well known as a quality successful meeting venue, and has won numerous industry awards. The following industry insight provides some background information on the effective development of the resort.

After a concerted team effort and a long lead time, Ayers Rock Resort has again won an Australian National Tourism Award for Quality and Excellence in the resort category. The resort won four categories: Tourism Marketing and Promotional Campaigns, Tourism Retailing, Meetings Industry and Tourism Restaurant. In 1998 it was awarded the Best Meeting Venue. The resort is perhaps Australia's most decorated tourism enterprise, collecting the 1994 and 1995 Australian Tourism Awards for Best Resort, plus 33 Brolga Awards (the Northern Territory Tourism Awards) and 16 other Australian tourism awards. The resort is totally committed to quality service and a quality management program is supported throughout the organisation.

The small group of motels and associated services that developed around the base of Uluru (Ayers Rock) in the 1960s soon became inappropriate for the demands of national and international visitors. As a result, in the early 1970s, the Northern Territory government resolved to develop a new resort that would be both sympathetic to the environment and able to provide an 'experience' in itself, with a range of accommodation and touring services.

Ayers Rock Resort (then Yulara Resort) was constructed in the early 1980s as a combination of tourist elements: the camping ground, the Four Seasons Hotel and the Sheraton Hotel. Initially it enjoyed a growth pattern, but in the period 1987–92 fluctuations in visitor numbers and operating losses were recorded.

In 1991, the Territory government announced a restructuring of Yulara Resort, in order to place it on a more commercial footing. The following year, a new statutory corporation, the Ayers Rock Resort Company Limited, was formed to take over as owner, manager and developer of the resort facilities. Under this new management regime, all contracts were rescinded and a complete restructuring began. A service agreement was signed with Southern Pacific Hotel Corporation to allow for specialist recruitment and to offer a career path for staff and management beyond the location of the resort. As a result, the turnaround profit was substantial.

Visiting the Red Centre offers a powerful experience — a satisfying change from the hustle and bustle, noise, pollution and population of the big cities. Uluru has unique attractions and places of historical, cultural and environmental value. The resort, which offers 640 rooms, attracts an average of 360 000 visitors a year to its range of accommodation facilities and eateries (which offer choices from superb seafood to outdoor dining). There is a retail centre and outdoor amphitheatre for meeting delegates who are looking for something a little different in their choice of conference venue. Apart from its unique location, the resort offers a state-of-the-art 'Uluru Meeting Place', custom-built to hold medium-sized conferences and special events.

(continued)

The concept of a conference to Australia's Red Centre used to conjure up images of billy tea and damper, a local entertainer and safe, if uninspiring, menus. Today, conference delegates enjoy up-to-date technology, champagne and canapés at sunset, an Aboriginal didgeridoo player performing amid the sand dunes under the stars, and menus inspired by local bush tucker and specialities such as crocodile and emu. According to national sales and marketing manager, Andrew Denman, sales in room nights generated by conferences and incentive groups grew substantially in the first half of 1999.

The renewed and continuing success of the Uluru Meeting Place and the Ayers Rock Resort has been built on a philosophy of being customer focused, through an understanding of the needs, wants, desires and expectations of the visitor. The resort is able to provide satisfaction with excellence. In 1998 Uluru Meeting Place was awarded the Best Meetings Venue at the National Australian Tourism Awards.

Source: Ayers Rock Resort

■ Differences *in service quality*

The provision of service quality may not be the same for every single delegate who comes into contact with a venue and its service. There are several elements that can impact on a venue's ability to produce continuous customer service at a quality that is acceptable to the customer. These factors can be segmented into four areas:

1. *The technical quality — what is delivered?* This includes elements such as the quality of the food that is served, the timing of the events, the image reflected by the venue's physical environment, the provision of reliable audiovisual equipment and other technology, and the provision of staff who are supportive of the needs of the customer or client organisation.

2. *The functional quality — how is it delivered?* Judging 'how' the service is delivered can be problematic and difficult. From the venue's perspective, this could include ensuring that staff are well-trained, rostered staff have the skills to deliver the exact service required for a particular client group, there is adequate staff supervision and the attitudes of the staff reflect the overall image of the venue.

3. *The process quality — judged during service* This includes all the elements that occur during the event, such as food and beverage services, the ability to ensure a seamless turn-around between the various functions of an event, and staff and management's skill in maintaining a calm and professional front-of-house appearance for clients, despite the fact that the back-of-house scene may be chaotic.

4. *The output quality — after service is performed*   Measuring the response to the service delivery is a critical aspect of MICE management. For venues it takes on an extra dimension, because of the range of services and products (from the different departments) used by event delegates. Customers often have the time after each service encounter to examine the contact in minute detail, so their post-contact perceptions can be a vital ingredient to enhancing the service provision.

■ Customer *interaction*

Customer interaction is an integral part of the core service provided by conference venues. Staff and management make contact with client organisations as well as individual delegates. The communication process for a venue's convention department can be considered as an exchange mechanism — customers and delegates express their desires, and the venue's convention department informs them of the extent to which their desires can be met (Mattsson & den Haring 1998).

Service encounters

Interactions between the service providers and their clients can occur at several levels. In the case of high-contact services, customers visit the service facility in person and are actively involved with the service provider and its personnel. In the MICE industry, and particularly in the provision of conferences within venues, high-contact service do not take place all the time. The pattern tends to be increasing contact prior to the event (the interaction between the PCO and the venue), contact is reduced during the actual conference and then there is another surge of contact at the end of the event (as venues evaluate the event with the delegates and PCO). In the case of medium-contact services, the customer is less involved with the delivery of the service — for example, the level of contact could be limited to those delegates who arrive at a venue for a short one-off meeting such as a morning seminar. There may be very little contact between the conference organiser and the client organisation and minimal interaction between the delegate and the venue. In some situations, customers want nothing to do with the service provider and prefer a low-contact service. Internet conferences and teleconferencing are two examples of a lowcontact service that are becoming more popular in our increasingly electronic world. Although only a minority of clients utilise such systems, there are opportunities for PCOs and individual organisations to arrange conferences and meetings via the Internet. It is more likely, however, that delegates would use electronic contact to make room reservations at a venue (Lovelock & Wright 1999, pp. 48–9).

Customer and server interaction

The most obvious way that delegates come into contact with the venue is through contact with the venue staff who are working for that particular event. In many cases, there is very little personal contact between the staff and the delegates. The venue is responsible for looking after two distinct 'clients' — the conference organiser (or conference organising committee) and the delegates, once the event begins. In a sense, the venue must serve two 'masters'. Unfortunately, both can have very different requirements of the venue. For example, the conference organiser might specify a particular type and choice of menu such as a traditional three-course lunch with wine, while the delegates might prefer a light, healthy working lunch and might not understand why the venue cannot satisfy their needs.

Conference organisers have to be mindful that they represent not only the client organisation but also their delegates. The client organisation has the eventual authority to approve or reject elements within the event. Delegates, however, often have no control over the event itself. They arrive at the conference, listen to the proceedings, take their meals as directed, use the venue's facilities and leave at the end of the conference. The requirements of the client organisation and the delegates can be vastly divergent. The one feature that remains similar to both is that they expect personal contact with the venue.

The service provider (server) and the customer have a relationship. This relationship is based around the amount and type of power that each possesses. (Lovelock 1992, pp. 358). Servers, for example, have the unique ability to deliver service that is highly sought after, they are customer committed and provide quality service. Servers can demand and often get rewarded for quality service and can give 'tangibles' to customers in terms of respect and care. Customers, on the one hand, authorise and pay for services received, but on the other hand can refuse to purchase and have recourse to legal action should service be patently lacking. They can demand quality and respect and can provide rewards to 'servers' in the form of appreciation.

Both servers and customers have the ability to use moral, political, social and psychological power over each other. This is illustrated in the following example (dates and names changed). The Mountain Hotel is a large five-star property on the outskirts of a popular resort region. In 1993, a top-level conference was organised through a federal government department. The number of delegates, including many senior members of political parties from around the world, meant that the hotel would have only a few rooms vacant during the weekend of the conference. For security reasons, the department decided to book out the entire hotel and its facilities, including all conference space and accommodation facilities. As far as the venue was concerned, there was no other viable alternative in the area for this type of gathering. Both the hotel and the government department were in a position of incredible power. On the one hand, the hotel could have charged the group an exorbitant rate to close down the hotel for the weekend. On the other hand, the government department indicated that there was a social and moral duty on the part of the hotel to keep prices as low as possible, due to the national significance of the event.

■ The service *delivery system*

We now turn our attention to two major components of the service delivery system: front stage and back stage (Lovelock 1992, p. 24).

Front stage

The front stage is the area most commonly associated with the provision of customer service. It includes customer–staff contact points and general contact by the customer with the organisation itself (e.g. through advertising, promotional brochures and conference kits). In the service delivery system, company statements and invoices and correspondence (mail and telephone) are all aspects of the front stage.

Customers also are part of the front stage. Customers, as delegates attending a conference, are generally thought of 'in a vacuum'. This is far from true. Delegates often discuss service issues with each other and are in contact with each other for much of the duration of an event. In addition, delegates can come into contact with other elements of the system (e.g. they may use facilities within the hotel or equipment supplied by the venue) and with other service personnel, such as housekeeping and room-service staff.

Back stage

Workers in the front line cannot deliver a quality service without top-class backup services (Clemmet 1998). The back stage is an area that delegates seldom see and have little involvement in, yet this area still impacts on the total quality service experienced by the delegates. However, it is less likely to be linked directly to them. For example, back stage elements could include the maintenance and engineering department in a hotel or the audiovisual support provided during the event. Delegates and clients generally are happy when all is well. However, should something go wrong with the equipment or other back stage elements, dissatisfaction levels can become high in a very short space of time.

■ Aspects *of quality service*

There are several aspects of the provision of service that can be managed by the venue, but that sometimes cause conflict of interest in terms of revenue generation. These aspects can be included in the design and provision of the service and in the long term can provide a greater reward for the organisation in terms of repeat business, cost control and better service provision. They are related to the concepts of capacity and productivity.

Capacity

Capacity relates to the amount of physical space that a venue has available to it and the number of staff available to service the customers. Filling a conference room to overflowing may increase revenue, but the negative response from delegates and the PCO or conference organiser undoubtedly will impact negatively on the long-term repeat business from that particular client. Similarly, a venue should not offer menus and styles of food service without a corresponding base of skilled personnel to support those services.

Venues should limit their capacity and take in only those numbers that they can comfortably serve. Venues need to be content with the long-term prospects of positive word-of-mouth advertising about the quality of the service provision rather than opting for 'quick fix' short-term revenue earners.

Tools that can assist the venue to manage capacity are yield management techniques and queuing techniques. Yield management is a useful capacity management technique for organisations that have a volatile but set capacity. With a venue it is the convention manager's task to fill the available rooms to their maximum earning capacity. This may mean not accepting a conference room booking for an event that is a low revenue earner during times of high demand. In many venues, for example, wedding receptions are not taken during weekdays, as corporate conferences can make better use of the facilities and earn more long-term revenue for the venue at this time. Yield management is discussed in more detail in chapter 11. Queuing techniques were discussed in chapter 8. By using different queuing systems to manage conference registration, for example, venues can ensure that delegates have a pleasant experience while the venues maximise their capacity efficiently and attractively.

Productivity

Productivity measurement within MICE events can be problematic. Quality service can be an ethereal concept. It follows, therefore, that measuring whether a venue is being productive while providing a service to clients can be complicated. To measure productivity adequately, a clear set of standards and guidelines must be agreed on by all those involved — for example, management, staff and, in some cases, the client. Venues are single units servicing a client base located very close by (i.e. in the actual venue), so measurement tools can be flexible and may reflect the different aspects of the delivery system.

Two other techniques that can assist venues to achieve maximum productivity are the development of a blueprint of the service process and the use of job design, which were discussed in chapters 8 and 4, respectively.

The blueprint clearly shows, on paper, the key interactions and interlinkages between the customer and the front and back stage operations, together with the support elements (such as advertising and promotional materials) and management functions. It identifies any shortcomings in the service delivery system and the levels of productivity being achieved.

The venue staff are key in the provision of quality service and customer satisfaction. Venue management should take into consideration the principles of job design and job analysis when reviewing the blueprint and productivity levels within the convention or meeting. The value and importance of job design was explored in chapter 4.

Venues have a difficult task satisfying all those involved within their operation — the staff, the client and the delegates. In order to provide quality service, a complex mix of operations, human resources, training and management must be evident. As well as dealing directly with their clients (the PCO and conference organising committee), venues must also deal with their internal stakeholders and suppliers. Venue managements' function is to mould the various stakeholders into a single, coherent and harmonious body ready to satisfy, or more importantly to excel, in providing quality customer service.

EVALUATING QUALITY CUSTOMER SERVICE

A post-convention review of the conference organiser, venue and other suppliers involved is of great importance. It provides the opportunity to review how the delegates, the conference organiser and the client organisation perceived the conference, the venue's organisation and the provision of service quality. A review of this kind can provide useful lessons and constructive suggestions on how such an event might be improved in the future. The purpose of the review is to evaluate performance prior to and during the event.

Any evaluation process should take into consideration the quality service factors of reliability, tangibility, responsiveness, empathy and assurance and the seven potential quality gaps. The evaluation process should include:

- the site and location of the event
- the venue, its facilities and food and beverage services, as well as the quality of service provided
- the convention itself, for example the program content, speakers, marketing, social activities, and so on
- the individual sessions, for example the relevance of the topics, clarity and presentation of the topics, achievement of objectives, and so on.

■ The evaluation *process*

To gain a comprehensive appraisal of the convention or meeting, it is necessary to make a '360-degree' evaluation. Such an evaluation would cover:

- the perspective of the delegates
- the perspective of the venue and other suppliers
- the perspective of the PCO
- the perspective of the client organisation.

Delegates

Feedback from delegates is sought on their perceptions of the quality of the event and the level of delegate satisfaction. This is usually gathered in the form of a questionnaire consisting of both structured and unstructured questions. The questionnaire should cover items such as accommodation, the provision of food and beverages, details of the event, its organisation and management, and the content of the convention program. These questionnaires are often distributed at the end of the event, and in some instances after each session. Figure 10.2 shows an example of a standard structured questionnaire distributed at the end of an event.

CONFERENCE EVALUATION

1. THE PROGRAM

please circle your answers   **(5 = Excellent/1 = Poor)**

Overall	5	4	3	2	1
Plenary session	5	4	3	2	1
Plenary session day 2 — MICE industry	5	4	3	2	1
Concurrent sessions	5	4	3	2	1
Conference proceedings — refereed	5	4	3	2	1
Conference proceedings — working papers	5	4	3	2	1

Comments ....
....

2. SOCIAL PROGRAM

Overall	5	4	3	2	1
Welcome cocktail party	5	4	3	2	1
Poolside barbecue	5	4	3	2	1
Conference dinner	5	4	3	2	1
Lunches	5	4	3	2	1

Comments ....
....

3. THE VENUE

Overall	5	4	3	2	1
Guest rooms	5	4	3	2	1
Hotel services	5	4	3	2	1

Comments ....
....

4. GENERAL

a. Are you employed:

    As an academic
    In industry
    In a government department
    As a student

b. Did you present a:

    Refereed paper
    Working paper
    Student paper
    Poster paper

c. How did you find out about the conference?...
....

d. On a scale of 1–5, was the conference value for money **(1 = No value/5 = Excellent)**

    1   2   3   4   5

e. Overall how would you rate the 1996 Tourism & Hospitality Research Conference?

    Excellent Good   Fair   Poor

f. What would you like to see changed for next year?...
....

g. Next year's conference is to be held in Sydney, 5–6 July 2000. Will you be attending?

    Yes   No   Maybe

Thank you for your help

■ **Figure 10.2** *Sample conference evaluation form*

Source: Southern Cross University

The venue and other suppliers

The evaluation of the venue should be undertaken 'in-house' with the key team — the convention services manager, the department heads and the sales manager. Comments from the staff should be obtained as to how the event could be improved, because their comments may provide a different perspective from those of the management. Any weak spots should be identified and suggestions should be obtained on how they might be overcome for future events. Any specific aspects that went particularly well should be highlighted.

Many venues do not undertake an in-house review unless the event is extremely large. However, the time taken is well spent, and assists in the process of continuous improvement.

The PCO and the client organisation

It is important for the PCO and the client organisation to go over events while they are fresh in everybody's mind. They should also compare what actually happened against the plan — for example, budgeted figures against actual figures, budgeted number of delegates against the actual number, check-in and check-out procedures, and so on. The strong and weak spots should be identified and a decision made as to how these should be handled in the future.

𝒮UMMARY

Quality management and the provision of service quality within MICE events are key to ensuring that high levels of customer satisfaction are achieved by both the client organisation and the delegates to an event. Obtaining high levels of customer satisfaction is a critical objective for conference organisers. Within the MICE industry, quality management and customer service go hand in hand.

In order to ensure a process of quality management for MICE events, conference organisers need to be aware of not only the management principles for introducing such a system but also the role of the stakeholders in the provision of the event. The issues relating to the service provision, and the interrelationships of the various stakeholders and how they deliver quality customer service, are critical to the success of the event.

Service, and more importantly establishing methods of measuring quality service, is a complex and intricate subject. In many instances, this aspect of the MICE event is assumed to be built into and just part of the conference package. Yet the supply of a quality service to delegates is actually a commodity that requires a great deal of planning and coordination prior to implementation. For the customer to receive a quality service, a structured and comprehensive system needs to be implemented that recognises all the facets of this process.

Activities

10.1 Undertake a quality audit of a convention or meeting facility within your region.

10.2 As a convention services manager in a venue, prepare the agenda and points for discussion for a pre-conference briefing session for key staff for a 600-delegate convention that is to be held over three days in three weeks time.

Discussion questions

10.1 Assume that you are the conference and banqueting manager of a 250-bedroom hotel with conference and banqueting facilities for 250, plus three small seminar rooms with a capacity for 25–50 delegates. The hotel is situated in a regional town. You would like to introduce a system of quality management into your area. Identify the key areas to be addressed in general, and then the key areas to be addressed with regard to customer orientation and quality standards.

10.2 Assume that you work for a firm of PCOs. You wish to put forward a proposal to introduce a quality management system into the business. Identify the key areas to be addressed in general and then in relation to supplier management and the setting of quality standards. Design a program for implementation. Identify your key areas of concern regarding the implementation of such a program.

10.3 Reliability, tangibility, responsiveness, assurance and empathy are key factors in evaluating service. Review the stages in the provision of a conference or meeting and identify the potential weaknesses in relation to these key factors.

10.4 Discuss the concept of 'quality gaps' as it relates to convention or meeting management.

10.5 Analyse the factors that you would look for as a delegate in the provision of quality customer service. In groups, discuss these factors.

10.6 Identify the communication skills required in the interactions between PCOs and conference venues.

10.7 Design a conference evaluation system for a training conference for senior managers to be held over four days in a four-star 'retreat'-style venue.

10.8 Critically discuss how you would develop the partnerships within the quality service model.

REFERENCES ....

Christie, A. 1994 'Best Practice in the Hospitality Industry', *The Quorum*, January/February.

Clemmet, A. 1998 'Dictating Customer Service', *Work Study*, vol. 47, no. 2.

Commonwealth Department of Tourism. 1995, *A National Strategy for the Meetings Incentives, Conventions and Exhibitions Industry*, AGPS, Canberra.

Desombre, T. & Eccles, G. 1998, 'Improving Service Quality in NHS Trust Hospitals: Lessons from the Hotel Sector', *International Journal of Health Care Quality Assurance*, vol. 11, no. 1.

Heymann, K. 1992, 'Quality Management — A Ten Point Model', *Cornell Hotel and Restaurant Administration Quarterly*, October, pp. 51–60.

Lovelock, C. H. 1992, *Managing Services, Marketing Operations and Human Resources*, 2nd ed, Prentice-Hall, Englewood Cliffs, N. J.

Lovelock, C. & Wright, L. 1999, *Principles of Service Marketing and Management*, Prentice-Hall, Englewood Cliffs, N. J.

Marecki, R. F., Revalas, D. A. & Sackler, W. G. 1998 'Managing Service Quality Through Process Improvement: Using Statistical Process Control Tools in a Restaurant Environment', *Praxis*, Spring/Summer.

Mattsson, J. & den Haring, M. J. 1998 'Communication Dynamics in the Service Encounter: A Linguistic Study in a Hotel Conference Department', *International Journal of Service Industry Management*, vol. 9, no. 5.

McCabe, V. S. & Weeks, P. 1999, 'Convention Services Management in Sydney Four- to Five-Star Hotels', *Journal of Convention and Exhibition Management*, vol. 1, no. 4, pp. 67–84.

Office of National Tourism. 1998, *Tourism: A Ticket to the 21st Century: National Action Plan*, Office of National Tourism, Department of Industry, Science and Tourism, Canberra.

Peters, T. & Waterman, R. 1982, *In Search of Excellence*, Harper Row, New York.

Rutherford, D. G. & Umbreit, W. T. 1993, 'Improving Interactions Between Meeting Planners and Hotel Employees', *Cornell Hotel and Restaurant Administration Quarterly*, February.

Williams, C. 1998, 'The State of Quality Management in Six Leisure Related Research Sites', *The TQM Magazine*, vol. 10, no. 2.

Zeithaml, V. A., Parasuraman, A. & Berry, L. L. 1990, *Delivering Quality Service: Balancing Customer Perceptions and Expectations*, The Free Press, New York.

FURTHER READING ....

Barsky, J. D. 1995, *World-Class Customer Satisfaction*, Irwin Professional Publishing, New York.

Bitran, G. R. & Hoech, J. 1990, 'The Humanization of Service: Respect at the Moment of Truth', in Lovelock, C. 1992, *Managing Services, Marketing Operations and Human Resources*, 2nd ed, Prentice-Hall, Englewood Cliffs, N. J.

Bowen, D. E. 1990, *Service Management Effectiveness: Balancing Strategy, Organisation and Human Resources, Operations and Marketing*, Jossey-Bass, San Francisco.

Brownell, J. 1991, 'Middle Managers Facing the Communication Challenge', *Cornell Hotel and Restaurant Administration Quarterly*, February, pp. 52–9.

Brymer, R. A. 1991, 'Employee Empowerment — A Guest Driven Leadership Strategy', *Cornell Hotel and Restaurant Administration Quarterly*, May.

Davidow, W. H. & Uttal, B. 1989, *Total Customer Service*, Harper Row, New York.

Heskett, J. I., Jones, T. O., Loveman, G.W., Sasser, W. E. & Schlesinger, L. A. 1994, 'Putting the Service Profit Chain to Work', *Harvard Business Review*, March/April.

Ingram, H., Teare, R., Scheuing, E. & Armistead, C. 1997, 'A Systems Model of Effective Teamwork', *The TQM Magazine*, vol. 9, no. 2.

James, D. 1993, *Managing for the 21st Century*, The Text Publishing Company, Melbourne.

Mill, R. C. 1986, 'Managing the Service Encounter', *Cornell Hotel and Restaurant Administration Quarterly*, February, pp. 39–46.

Riley, M. & Periogiannis, N. 1990, 'The Influence of Hotel Attributes on the Selection of a Conference Venue', *International Journal of Contemporary Hospitality Management*, vol. 2, no. 1.

CASE STUDY

Providing quality service

The Ballina Beach Resort is situated 500 metres from the ocean in the seaside town of Ballina in northern New South Wales. In the four-and-a-half-year period following acquisition, the resort's management team has developed the property into a highly successful business venture, increasing business by over 400 per cent. The resort has become identified locally as an outstanding conference, meeting and function venue, not only in terms of the facilities provided but, more importantly, for the quality of service and consistent high standard of the product provided. It has been a finalist in the meeting category of the North'wards , the local area tourism awards.

The resort's former general manager, Dale Potts, has had a lifelong involvement in the hospitality industry, from an early age in the family motel to experience gained in the hospitality service quality centres of Switzerland, Austria and Germany, learning the fine art of service.

With a recognised commitment to the provision of quality customer service, particularly in the area of conferences and meetings, how has the venue's success been achieved?

The resort's management holds a belief that quality service is going that one extra step, going out of your way to help 'above and beyond the call of duty'. This cannot be taught; it has to come naturally and be instinctive. Quality service is also seen as being able to predict what the customer wants and remember a name, their favourite room or cocktail, and so on.

Therefore, to establish quality service, the staff employed not only need to be skilled, efficient and courteous, but also should have pleasant personalities. Coupled with a pleasant personality is a good smile. You cannot teach someone to smile; it has to come naturally and spontaneously, because that member of staff is confident in what they are doing and confident in the product they are selling. The resort's management team recognises that operational skills and efficiency can be taught with good management and training, but that how a staff member walks, talks and thinks is a personal attribute. An enthusiastic, friendly approach and the right attitude are exactly what the customer wants; however, they have to come from the heart. Staff are recruited for their ability to read customers' moods and react appropriately.

Dale also believes that there is a need to lead the team in a friendly manner and to suggest rather than dictate, to maintain enthusiasm and create a good atmosphere and working environment. He recognises that most staff thrive on responsibility, which should be encouraged, and the ability to make decisions and use intuition and common sense. This will almost certainly be reflected in how staff treat their customers. As a result, staff satisfaction and levels of productivity will increase, and this will ensure ultimately that the customer gets the best service — quality service.

The resort staff follow a number of key themes with regard to the management and organisation of conferences, meetings and functions:

- *One chance* They only get one chance on the telephone to sell their facilities. The potential conference or meeting enquiry will rarely ring back a second time and ask more questions. Therefore, they need to paint the picture about the location and facilities available and be enthusiastic about the conference. Following the telephone call, they send out their marketing tool (the conference brochure, which provides a visual essay of their product), and follow up and organise a site inspection, not only to show off their facilities, but also to begin the partnership process. They also show the conference organiser their conference portfolio.

- *Only sell what you can do well* This is the first step in creating customer satisfaction. They only concentrate on conference or function business that they know they can do well. If they cannot provide what the conference organiser requires, they suggest alternatives.

- *Every item sold to the conference organiser in respect of the conference will reflect directly on the establishment* They do not drop their standards in order to make a 'cheapie type' or substitute item because of a limited budget, such as removing the homemade biscuits or muffins. Delegates will make a generalisation that all morning teas provided by the resort are of that quality. They will not be aware of the financial constraints or blame the conference organiser. In order to avoid a bad first impression by the delegates, they suggest an alternative to the conference organiser that ensures both the quality and standard of their product and yet is within the budget limitations of the conference organiser. They assist the conference organiser in identifying the needs of the delegates — for example, if delegates have driven long distances, they may be pleased to receive a cup of coffee/tea on arrival. You do not want delegates walking away saying they could not even get a cup of coffee. They may have to sell this option to the conference organiser, but the relationship is a partnership.

- *Meet and greet* On conference day, they treat the conference delegates as their VIPs — they meet and greet them, and are well presented and enthusiastic. They ensure that the front-of-house staff have great personalities, know the product and always create a positive *yes* attitude. 'No' or 'I don't know' are not in the resort's dictionary. They ensure that delegates are guided to the conference registration area, are shown the location of the welcome coffee/tea, the conference room, toilets, and so on.

- *It's all walk and talk* The first break of the conference (morning tea) provides a public relations, marketing and quality service opportunity. It is not just a cup of coffee. Many people will remember the conference by the quality of the coffee/tea break and it provides a free marketing opportunity for the resort. Staff are expected not to wait for the delegates to come to them but to anticipate their every requirement. This is recognised as an art form, which is instinctive and difficult to teach. It is all walk and talk.

- *People who attend conferences are people who organise conferences* The resort staff recognise the cost of marketing and selling the facilities to potential conference or function organisers. They also realise that proffering a platter of homemade blueberry muffins or savoury scones provides a marvellous opportunity to talk to delegates. They recognise that each delegate at the conference could wear two or three hats and that the particular service of morning tea could capture a potential conference for 50–200 delegates or a function for 150 people.
- *Planning and attention to detail* Before the conference actually starts they never take anything for granted — they check the chairs, equipment, back-up bulbs, flip-chart paper and markers (the resort and the conference presenter will look stupid if the presenter commences writing and the marker is empty). In other words, they think it is essential to check the basics. At lunchtime they service the conference room.

Three basic principles assist delegates to survive a conference and provide fatigue busters — air, light and water. The temperature in the conference room ideally should be 23°C, lighting should be effective, and chilled, filtered water should be used without ice cubes, as they cause a distraction when water is poured. Refreshment breaks should be taken outside the main conference room, and the location of the refreshment breaks should change to alleviate boredom and fatigue. The siting of the tea and coffee service stations and the flow and volume of people per service station should be considered to ensure the smooth and speedy flow of service.

Dale defines an excellent conference as a happy conference organiser who receives many compliments from delegates. He recognises that many people can run a good conference, some people can run a very good conference, but few can run an excellent conference. Delegates will judge the service and conference by whether the venue was a good or bad host, so at the end of the day, it really comes down to hospitality. Therefore, it is important to employ staff who are always hospitable, friendly and receptive and give service tirelessly.

Source: Dale Potts, Noosa Lakes Convention and Exhibition Centre (formerly Ballina Beach Resort)

Questions

1 Map the customer service system at the resort, highlighting the points of interaction that enable quality service to be provided.

2 In view of this manager's philosophy for providing quality customer service, prepare a list of attributes that would be required in the recruitment and selection of casual conference staff.

11

Managing the
financial, budgetary
and legal considerations
of conventions

LEARNING OBJECTIVES

After studying this chapter, you will be able to:

■ outline the overall financial implications of conventions and meetings to the MICE industry

■ design, produce, monitor and control a financial budget for a convention or meeting covering both expenses and potential income

■ outline the concept of yield management and explore its application to conventions and meetings

■ identify some of the legal liabilities associated with organising conventions and meetings

■ establish a system of risk management and explore its application to conventions and meetings

■ recognise the importance of ethical behaviour within the convention and meeting industry.

INTRODUCTION

The ultimate purpose of providing quality service, achieving customer satisfaction and introducing efficient and effective working practices at a convention or meeting is to make a positive financial impact on the bottom line for the client organisation, conference organiser and other suppliers. By providing MICE events, the industry and its various stakeholders are seeking to make money either directly or indirectly for the state, region, city or area, the venue, conference organiser and client organisation. Effective financial planning and control is one of the keys to the successful execution of an event and as such is an area of major importance for conference organisers. To assist in achieving this objective, financial and administrative systems, procedures and controls need to be established to identify and track costs and monitor sources of revenue. Conference organisers must be able to prepare and work to financial budgets and put into operation a system of control that ensures the financial viability of an event.

This chapter focuses on the financial and budgetary implications of providing conventions and meetings. It outlines some of the considerations in the preparation, monitoring and control of both the budget and the event in order to maximise revenue and minimise costs. These include the identification of sources of income and expenditure and the use of techniques such as yield management. It discusses the factors involved in the process of price negotiation with the various suppliers, as well as the concept of risk management and some of the legal liabilities associated with providing a convention or meeting. Finally, the chapter looks at business ethics and its relationship and importance to the MICE industry.

FINANCIAL PHILOSOPHY AND OBJECTIVES

To understand the background to the budget for a convention or meeting, it is necessary to have an idea of the financial philosophy and objectives of the client organisation, as these will impact on the structure of the budget and the style and type of event.

■ Corporate organisations

A convention or meeting organised by a corporate organisation is seen generally as a cost to the business, with the main philosophy behind the event being to review some aspect of the business such as planning, training, marketing, sales or production. As such, the costs incurred in the provision of the event are viewed as the costs of doing business. For example, a meeting might be held as an investment (e.g. a training meeting), with the overall purpose being to improve employee performance and perhaps increase their contribution to the total income of the business. At a motivational or a sales meeting the objective might be to put 'fire' into the employees to go out and conquer the world, with the overall aim being to gain more customers and increase sales. In staging an 'in-house' conference or meeting the company needs to ensure that the costs incurred do not exceed budget and that the overall implicit objectives are achieved.

The purpose of a meeting will also determine how the budget is to be spent. For example, a company might budget conservatively for a meeting for shareholders, as proof that it is spending funds wisely, while a product launch might be more lavish. What is essential, however, is that the conference organiser is aware of the client organisation's attitude to and perception of the event in respect of the quality of facilities and services required and the associated costs. The conference organiser should also be aware of the general financial situation at the company, such as a tightening of budgets.

■ Associations

Associations need to ensure that expenses incurred in the provision of a convention or meeting do not exceed the income received. An association might state that its national convention is for the purpose of continuing education and networking opportunities for its members. Yet the unstated objective might be to generate sufficient income from the event to support other member activities throughout the year. The financial goal of the event might therefore be to provide a surplus of funds that could be critical to the survival of the association. Or an association's monthly regional meeting might have as one of its objectives 'to maximise, stimulate and increase membership growth', and the financial goal in this instance might simply be to break even or even to allow a small deficit.

So, in holding a convention or meeting, an association might not make any direct monetary gain. However, the event potentially creates an environment that may assist its membership to increase their income through activities such as networking. For any convention or meeting, the business that is undertaken outside the actual meeting is often as important as that conducted within the sessions.

THE CONVENTION OR MEETING BUDGET

One of the key aspects in the financial management of a convention or meeting is the preparation of the event budget. This process involves discussions between the conference organiser and the client organisation to decide on the overall budget figure and to identify and establish potential areas of income and expenditure. There is also a need to establish an efficient and effective monitoring system to ensure that event revenue is maximised and expenditure is minimised.

■ The conference organiser *and the client organisation*

The preparation of budgets is a difficult and intricate task and often is not the favourite occupation of conference organisers. They must use their negotiation skills and interweave their knowledge of budgets and statistical information and analysis to ensure that the event meets the financial goals of not only the client organisation but also their business. Historical information from previous conferences is frequently used to provide guidelines for future events, so it is important that event record keeping is impeccable. While the client organisation's financial philosophy is important, its perceptions and expectations of the event need to be clarified. They can be completely different to the conference organiser's, and aspects such as the quality of the event will affect the required budget.

The client organisation might provide the overall budget guidelines and budget amount, or they might be estimated in conjunction with the conference organiser. Wherever possible, the conference organiser should be involved or consulted when these figures are prepared and made aware of any budgetary constraints. The conference organiser should ensure that all possible expenditure for the event is included in the budget preparation. Once the budget has been prepared and agreed on it should be monitored regularly and financial statements should be produced. Costs should be reviewed constantly and mechanisms put in place to control potential areas for cost overruns (e.g. guidelines for travel expenses). The conference organiser should be notified of and acknowledge any changes that are made during the lifetime of the convention or meeting budget. A successful convention or meeting cannot be planned and organised without the conference organiser being intimately aware of the budgetary constraints.

Once the budget has been set it may be managed on a day-to-day basis by either the client organisation or the conference organiser, or it may be managed jointly, with the conference organiser informing the client organisation of any expenditure.

■ The budget *process*

It is important that a financial framework is developed that enables all parties to identify and designate revenue and expense categories easily and establish the depth of information required.

Undertaking research
The amount of research that the conference organiser needs to undertake to compile the budget can be varied. For conventions and meetings that are

held on an annual or biannual basis, comparative data should be readily available from recent meetings that may have been similar in size, scope, and so on. For other events, such as those that are by invitation only, there may be a need to consider factors such as the location and potential dates and their impacts on attendees (e.g. the conference may be held in the holiday period or at a distant location), the program content and structure (e.g. the number of sessions and speakers) and the food and beverage and audiovisual requirements.

Compiling the budget for an in-house company event for which the number of attendees is known is relatively easy. However, in putting together the budget for an association convention, for example, the conference organiser may need to make some intelligent 'guesstimates', based on their skill and past experience, to identify the expenses and potential costs. This may include areas such as cocktail parties, welcome drinks, special events, formal dinners, audiovisual equipment hire, and so on. It is for these areas that figures from previous years or similar style events become particularly important — such as the number of delegates, payment patterns, style of accommodation preferred, general delegate expenditure patterns, number of accompanying partners, and so on. Statistics prepared by industry associations for their members can also provide assistance.

The conference organiser's experience is important in ensuring that the costs of the services provided by the venue and other suppliers are both competitive and viable. Preliminary estimates and proposals put forward by potential suppliers and venues can assist in determining the various expenditure headings of the budget and enable fairly accurate projections to be made. In addition, some contingency funds for exceptional items of expense should be incorporated into the budget.

Depth of information required

The conference organiser should implement a systematic process to establish the level and depth of information required for the planning, reporting and identification of the items of income and expenditure (Nichols 1991, p. 128). The complexity and extent of this system depends on the type of event. For example, for a small conference or meeting one overall budget may be all that is required, while for a large convention or exhibition, each component of the event may have its own separate budget within the main budget.

■ Identifying *sources of income and expenditure*

The conference organiser should determine the various areas of expenditure for any event, and, for those events that require revenue to be raised to ensure their viability, potential income sources should also be identified.

Areas of expenditure

The conference organiser should establish the potential areas of expenditure and related costs. Areas of expenditure can be separated into fixed and variable expenses. Fixed expenses are those expenses that do not alter with the number of delegates, for example advertising and promotion, hire of audiovisual equipment and speaker fees. Variable expenses fluctuate and are dependent on the number of delegates. The majority of expenses for an event fall into this category and include items such as food and beverages. Figure 11.1 outlines some areas of expenditure for a convention or meeting.

Venue
- Room hire
- Exhibition area hire
- Dinner venue hire
- Additional meeting rooms.

Printed materials
- Stationery
- Promotional material
- Media releases
- Registration forms/brochures
- Invitations/tickets
- Programs
- Name tags
- Conference proceedings.

Staging costs
- Audiovisual equipment
- PA system
- Lighting
- Operator/technical fees
- Signage
- Plants/decorations.

Speakers/entertainment
- Speaker fees
- Performer fees
- Travel costs.

Food & beverage
- Opening function
- Gala dinner
- Lunches
- Morning/afternoon teas
- Themed events.

Administration costs
- Registration staff
- Office staff
- Photocopying
- Postage
- Fax/telephone
- General stationery
- Merchandise
- Transport
- Insurance.

■ **Figure 11.1** *Areas of expenditure for a convention or meeting*

Sources of income

Once all of the expenses have been decided on and calculated, the sources of revenue to support the activities should be identified and prepared if relevant. The sources of income (revenue) for an event are as varied as the creativity of the conference organiser and/or client organisation. The basic sources include:

- delegate registration fees — this is the most constant source of revenue for any conference, and in particular for association or independent conferences
- exhibition fees — income generated from the sale of exhibition stands/ booths and space
- sponsorship — this can be in the form of dollars or 'in kind' contributions such as airfares and accommodation
- grants — from government and/or other bodies
- merchandising — money from the sale of items appertaining to the event, such as educational materials, clothing (T-shirts, hats) and cassette or video tapes
- advertising — money from the sale of advertising space, for example in the conference brochure, on clothing, and so on.

Without the various sources of funding and income it would be impossible to hold some MICE events.

Other issues

The importance of delegate attendance at conventions or meetings, particularly in the case of association or independent business conferences, is critical to both the budget and ultimate success of the event. This factor is recognised by many CVBs, and they provide delegate boosting and attendance initiatives directly linked to an event's marketing and promotion as one of their services.

For the convention or meeting that is dependent on receiving a monetary return, delegate registration fees should be maintained at a level that will not discourage participation (Nichols 1991, p. 132), yet still provide the necessary revenue to cover costs. In dealing with an overseas event or international delegates, exchange rates and currency fluctuations need to be taken into consideration. Delegate registration fees for events held within the host country should be paid in local currency.

The budget for the convention and meeting is compiled initially without the fees or salaries of the conference organiser and associated employees included. These need to be factored into the overall financial plan. The issue of the fees charged by PCOs has caused some discussion with the industry. This is examined in more detail in the industry insight on page 350. Where appropriate, the conference organiser and client organisation should consider the profit or return that is required to be generated by the event and include that amount in the budget. Figure 11.2 outlines a section of a pro-forma budget for a convention or meeting. The section illustrated focuses fairly extensively on areas of fixed costs that might be incurred. It provides an excellent 'memory jogger' of items such as the various print components of the conference (e.g. call for papers, early bird announcement and menu for the official dinner).

Fixed costs

Room hire

1. Venue	days at		
2. Opening ceremony venue		$	$
3. Executive/council meeting		$	$
4. Trade exhibit venue		$	$
5. Other room hire		$	$
	Total	$	$

Office costs

1. Rent of office space weeks at	$	$
2. Wages	$	$
– Full-time officer		
– Part-time	$	$
– Temporary staff during convention	$	$
3. Telephone Rent	$	$
Calls	$	$
4. Facsimile	$	$
5. Mailing (see printing for no.)		
– Notice of intent		
– Call for papers		
– Registration		
– Programs		
– Acknowledgement		
General office mailing	$	$
6. Photocopying	$	$
7. Travelling costs (executive)	$	$
– Airline		
– Hotel		
– Miscellaneous	$	$
8. General stationery	$	$
9. Incidentals	$	$
Total	$	$

Printing

	Quantity	Cost
1. Logo design/poster design	$	$
2. Notice of intent	$	$
3. Supplement to journal	$	$
4. Call for papers	$	$
5. Registration form	$	$
6. Registration acknowledgement	$	$
7. Program	$	$
8. Partner program	$	$
9. Mini program	$	$
10. Letterhead	$	$
11. Exhibition application	$	$
12. Envelope	$	$
13. Registration booster	$	$
14. Early bird cards	$	$
15. Posters	$	$
16. Menu for official dinner	$	$
17. Wine labels	$	$
18. Conference stickers	$	$
Total	$	$

Technical papers

1. Pre-prints pp/x copies at c per page	$	$
2. Editing charge	$	$
3. Binding and cover	$	$
4. Postage (optional)	$	$
Total	$	$

Transport

1. Daily transport from hotels to venue coaches @ $ for days	$	$
2. Transport to opening ceremony coaches @ $	$	$
3. Technical visits to days out coaches @ $	$	$
Total	$	$

Guests and speakers

1. Speakers' fees	$	$
2. Fares	$	$
3. Accommodation and meals	$	$
4. Guests at reception @ $	$	$
5. Guests at official dinner @ $	$	$
6. Printed invitations	$	$
7. Press entertainment	$	$
8. President's hospitality suite	$	$
Total	$	$

Staging

1. Hire of audiovisual equipment		
– Projectors (movie, slide, overhead)	$	$
– Screens	$	$
– Microphones	$	$
– Lecterns	$	$
– Sound recording	$	$
– Video	$	$
2. Operators' wages	$	$
3. Banners and directional signs (airport, stage, lectern registration desk)	$	$
4. Master of ceremonies	$	$
5. Ticket writing — speaker's name	$	$
6. Public relations consultant	$	$
7. Press kits and press room	$	$
8. Audiovisual presentations	$	$
Total	$	$

■ **Figure 11.2** *A section of a pro-forma budget planner for a convention or meeting*
Source: Dawsons Venue Directory

The issue of pricing and the fee structures charged by PCOs for the range of conference and exhibition services that they provide has been a cause for much discussion and debate over recent years.

The rapid rise and growth in the number of PCOs in the late 1980s and 1990s resulted in them being able to charge whatever the market allowed. Allegations were made of cost undercutting, secret commissions and a 'mark up' on everything. This led to a call for the industry to benchmark and establish a fee structure. In the wake of the recession in the mid-1990s, some PCOs in Australia heavily reduced fees in order to win business. However, as a policy there is a danger that this approach could damage the reputation and standards of the entire industry.

To provide a full conference service, a fee structure that ranges from $60 to $150 per delegate has been quoted. The full range and extent of services offered by the PCO within this fee band may vary and should be taken into consideration, as it may omit certain aspects, such as providing a delegate registration service.

Recognising that companies involved in the provision of convention and meeting services may be involved in a range of activities, the industry sees the issue of pricing as up to each individual company. Many PCO firms range in size from large operators, such as Tour Hosts or ICMS, to those that employ just a few people. Some companies deal exclusively with conference organisation; others may be involved in many activities, such as publishing, travel agency work, public relations, or may be a division or adjunct of another business. Such factors can affect their pricing structure and result in the different fee structures for their services. It is recognised that the cheapest quote does not necessarily obtain the business and that price, while important, is often not the most influential factor in a client's selection of a conference organiser. Suggestions have been made that charges should be on a per-delegate or fee-for-service basis, the format used by firms of consultants.

Source: CIM (1994, p. 5)

■ Monitoring *the budget*

The conference organiser is responsible for ensuring the viability of the budget and financial plan for a convention or meeting. In order to make sure that the final outcome is satisfactory, sound financial management practices should be undertaken, and ideally no more than one person (preferably the conference organiser) should be responsible for reviewing and approving any expenditure. Income received and expenses incurred should be monitored frequently.

The simplest way of monitoring financial transactions is to use income and expenditure statements and cash flow forecasts. The income and expenditure statement itemises and outlines the budgeted figures for each area, together with the actual figures for that item at a given time (e.g. monthly) and the accumulated figure to date (Nichols 1991, p. 134). A cash flow forecast should be prepared using a spreadsheet. It provides information on the anticipated positive and negative income and expenditure flows at any given time. Projections for the anticipated revenue streams — for example, delegate registration, sponsorship funds and exhibition stand sales — can be forecasted through the time line of the event. The payment of any expenses, such as venue deposit requirements, can then be planned.

The use of both the income and expenditure statement and the cash flow forecast will assist the conference organiser in the careful and efficient management of the financial aspects of the event. In addition, the conference organiser needs to ensure that control mechanisms are in place to highlight and assist in the identification of costs that exceed the budgeted figures established in the financial plan. The conference organiser should also be aware of and familiar with general financial and accounting procedures.

Areas for cost containment

In order to provide effective financial management for the event, the conference organiser should also be familiar with how to contain costs within the convention or meeting, such as:

- providing speakers in writing as to what audiovisual equipment is available for presentations
- reviewing the event's master account produced by the venue, including a daily check of items charged to the master account and an agreement as to the final delegate numbers for each food and beverage occasion
- checking the number of delegates attending the event and, in particular, the numbers of delegates who actually plan to attend particular activities — this may indicate a reduced number of people for some activities and result in a saving on the potential food and beverage costs for that activity
- providing guidelines on the reimbursement of travel expenses.

THE NEGOTIATION PROCESS

In any negotiation, and particularly within the MICE industry, a key point to remember is that it should be a 'win–win' situation for both parties. Negotiation is not a game where someone wins and someone loses. For it to be successful, both parties must win. The negotiators need to be aware of the points on which they will not compromise and those on which they will. The secret to success is to stand firm on the points that are important to the organisation and to concede on those that are not. The best outcome is for both parties to come out from a negotiation satisfied with their achievements, despite the fact that they may both have conceded some points.

■ The conference *organiser*

The success of a conference organiser's negotiations with a venue depends on a number of factors, including the size of the group and the potential revenue that the event will generate for the venue. A conference organiser is in a better negotiating position if the conference is for 200 delegates rather than 20 delegates — it provides greater bargaining power. A venue that is seeking business is beneficial to the conference organiser in terms of bargaining ability when negotiating convention rates. If the venue has high occupancy rates both in terms of accommodation and convention space, then it is unlikely to negotiate substantial discounts. However, new properties or properties wishing to establish themselves (in terms of market share) or who are experiencing a downturn in business are keener to negotiate.

The extent of the negotiations can vary with the area, region and venue and can be influenced by regional and seasonal factors. However, there may be room for further negotiation in the following areas:

- room rate charges for the meeting room/s — in many cases, the rates charged for the hire of the meeting rooms can be waived, mainly in the light of the income generated from accommodation, food and beverage services, and so on
- exhibition areas — the charge for the use of exhibition areas is often negotiable, particularly if a large group is involved
- parking — in venues located in inner cities or where parking costs and is at a premium, a venue often may allocate free parking for VIP guests, key organising staff and speakers
- deposits — the amount of deposit required by the venue often can be negotiated and in some instances may even be waived
- storage areas — some venues charge for storage space, and if this is the case, it may be an area for negotiation.

■ The venue

Preparation is the key factor in any successful negotiation. The convention services manager or the sales manager needs to be aware and thoroughly familiar with the venue's facilities and services and its strengths and weaknesses — for example, whether the venue is better equipped than its competitors, when the venue requires group business, and so on. They should be very familiar with the strengths and weaknesses of their competitor venues. This will assist the convention sales manager in negotiations with the conference organiser. For example, in peak business periods when demand for the venue and its services are at their highest, the highest charges can be obtained. In the low season (the 'value' season), when demand is reduced, discounted prices often attract potential conference organisers. The shoulder period between the peaks and low levels of business often links to when medium to high rates are charged and this is a time when many venues concentrate their sales and marketing efforts.

In discussion with the conference organiser, the venue staff should try to determine:

1. *The purpose of the convention or meeting* Every property has its own appeal, for example a city centre venue for a large company event and a small, secluded venue for a managing director's working party. Some venues can afford to have just one group in house at that time and this is a factor that will attract some conference organisers.
2. *Dates* When is the convention or meeting scheduled and how flexible are the dates? Are the desired dates available at the venue's competition?
3. *Capacity of the convention facilities* If the venue is the only one in the area that is large enough to accommodate the group easily, this will provide a negotiating advantage.
4. *Budget available* What is the client organisation's available budget and is price of major concern? If, for example, the client organisation has held a similar event at one of the group's other properties, then it may be pertinent to contact that venue to ascertain details of the event, spending patterns, and so on.
5. *Past problems* If the conference organiser experienced problems with another venue, such as poor food service, this may be an issue at the next event.

It is also important for the venue to try to establish the conference organiser's key concerns, for example fast check-in, special diets, natural lighting for visually-impaired delegates. Also to be considered is the 'time life value' of the account. Minor concessions offered on one occasion may result in long-term lucrative business. The successful negotiator needs to ensure that a 'win–win' situation is achieved by both parties.

■ Areas *for negotiation*

During the negotiation process, the venue and the conference organiser should be prepared to discuss the following:

- *Room rates and the number and types of rooms required* The rates should be discussed clearly for each style of room, for example premier rates for suites or rooms with ocean views and standard rates for run-of-the-house rooms. The numbers of each type of room required should be identified — for example, a total number of 100 accommodation rooms might be made up of 75 twins, 5 singles, 15 doubles and 5 suites. The release back dates of the room allocations should also be identified so that if, for example, the pre-held rooms are not taken up 21 days before the event, then the venue has the authority to release them back into general stock.

- *Complimentary and reduced rates for rooms*   It is commonplace for venues to supply a number of free or complimentary rooms. The number varies a great deal — for example, a venue may be generous if the convention is scheduled in the off-season or in the off-peak period of the week, such as one room for every 25 or 50 delegates. The number of complimentary rooms should be identified clearly in the letter of agreement or contract. The complimentary rooms or reduced rate rooms can be used by the conference organiser for speakers, and so on. However, they should not be taken for granted by the conference organiser and should be included in the negotiation process.
- *Meeting space and public space*   These areas normally attract a nominal fee or are provided at no charge. An experienced conference organiser will want to hold all public rooms until the program and resulting traffic flows have been confirmed. If the event is in the distant future, this may cause difficulties for the venue, as it may want to sell other conference space. The amount of public space to be held should therefore be negotiated. It is reasonable to hold all public rooms that might be used with the convention, but a release back date should be set by which time the conference program will have been completed and confirmed. The provision of a press room, a conference office or working space for the conference organiser also needs to be discussed and outlined in the final contract together with any associated charges.
- *Exhibition space*   The venue needs to establish whether there is to be a charge for the use of exhibition space together with the facilities that it is providing such as booths, tables, and chairs.
- *Food and beverage requirements*   The venue should outline the amount of notice it requires for final number guarantees, such as 48 or 72 hours. The menus and relevant prices should be discussed, together with the timing and content of the refreshment breaks. Liquor charges and any complimentary food and beverage items also need to be clarified.
- *Audiovisual equipment*   A list of the basic equipment that is provided by the venue should be reviewed, together with information on the range of extra facilities available and the appropriate costs. This is a key area for negotiation by the conference organiser.
- *Delegate arrival and departure patterns*   The potential for early check-ins or late departures from the venue should be discussed. This is particularly relevant for international visitors arriving for a convention. Most international flights into Sydney or Brisbane arrive early in the morning, so an early check-in at the venue is particularly welcome.
- *The availability of complimentary transport to and from the airport*   If the venue has a pick-up service for guests to and from the local airport, the form and frequency of the transport should be discussed.
- *The method of payment*   How the venue is to be paid, whether there is a deposit time schedule and the venue's terms and conditions of business should be discussed.

In order to be able to put together a quotation for the conference organiser, the convention services manager or sales manager should be familiar with the required gross profit of the venue and costs associated with labour, materials (e.g. food and beverages), and so on. They need to be aware of the break-even point and the various margins that can be reduced and the areas where costs can be contained by the venue so that the final price negotiated with the conference organiser can be competitive.

Following discussions and negotiations between the conference organiser and the venue, the details are confirmed either by means of a letter of agreement or a contract, to prevent any misunderstanding.

PRICING POLICIES

An association or other professional organisation planning a convention or meeting will need to establish the registration fee for potential participants to attend the event. This registration fee is often calculated on a full-cost recovery basis, whereby all the fixed and variable expenses for the event are determined and, where appropriate, a margin is added for the profit required. In the calculation of the fee, the revenue received from sponsorship and other sources is taken into consideration.

In addition to those factors already mentioned, the following should be considered when determining the registration fee:
* The amount that can be charged, for example considering the total budgeted expenditure; how sensitive delegates are to different prices; the prices charged by similar style events; early bird discounts for delegate bookings and payments received before a certain date; psychological pricing, such as $495.00 per delegate instead of $525.00.
* The basis of the pricing, for example what the registration fee includes (e.g. entry and attendance at convention), the length of the event (e.g. three days) and whether a single price should be charged for a bundled package attendance at the plenary and other sessions, a copy of the conference proceedings, morning tea, lunch and afternoon tea for three days, the gala dinner and welcome cocktail party).
* Identification as to whom should collect the payment, for example the conference organiser may be responsible for collecting the registration fees and an intermediary organisation, such as an airline, may be responsible for flight bookings and payment collection.
* Where and when payment should be made, for example directly to the conference organiser, with a final date set for conference registration.
* The payment method, such as credit card, cheque or international money order.
* How the price is to be communicated, for example preliminary conference announcement, conference brochure or Internet announcement (Lovelock & Wright 1999, p. 235).

Within a venue, conference facilities are often quoted on a per-delegate basis, such as day delegate rate or a 24-hour delegate rate (residential conference package). Figure 11.3 provides an example of both packages.

Day delegate rate	24-hour delegate rate (or residential conference package)
• Morning and afternoon tea • Two-course lunch/buffet • Conference room rental • Conference stationery • Basic audiovisual equipment, e.g. whiteboard or flipchart and overhead projector and screen.	• Overnight accommodation, e.g. superior city view room • Full Australian breakfast • Morning and afternoon tea • Two-course lunch/buffet • Conference room rental • Conference stationery • Basic audiovisual equipment e.g. whiteboard or flipchart and overhead projector and screen.

In Australia, some convention venues focus more on an 'à la carte package' (i.e. each item is priced separately), while in other venues or areas, perhaps where there is more competition, the focus is on the conference package, be it a day delegate rate or a 24-hour delegate rate. It all depends on the type of business. However, the conference organiser needs to be familiar with the various pricing policies.

Calculating the break-even point

Break-even analysis is a tool that assists in the setting of prices. The basic concept is that at some level of sales (revenue) there will be sufficient income to cover the expenses of the convention or meeting (Getz 1997, p. 214). In calculating the break-even point, both fixed and variable costs are taken into consideration. The variable costs are relative to the volume of conference participants. Figure 11.4 illustrates the break-even chart for an academic association conference for 250 delegates. Fixed costs include promotion and publicity, printing, brochures and satchels. Variable costs include food and beverages. The registration fee is $425.

■ **Figure 11.4**
*Break-even
chart for a
conference of
250 delegates*

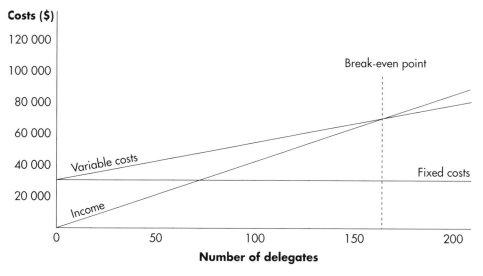

When setting the price, whether it is for the registration fee or for the prices to be charged by MICE suppliers, consideration should also be given to the various types of pricing strategies such as prestige pricing, reference pricing, price skimming, and so on (Getz 1997, p. 215).

THE BILLING PROCESS

The conference organiser needs to establish with the venue and other suppliers a process for billing for the various activities of the event. This will include setting up a master account with the venue and ensuring that all aspects of the billing procedure, including the payment schedule, are clearly identified.

The venue and the conference organiser often establish the billing requirements for an event months before the convention or meeting takes place, once the booking has been confirmed and the contract signed. Billing arrangements should not be organised after an event as errors and confusion can occur. The venue and conference organiser should discuss and agree on issues such as:

- the setting up of the master account for the event and how it is to be itemised
- the charges for the various types of rooms (accommodation rooms, meeting rooms, etc.)
- the arrangements for food and beverages and how they are to be charged
- the handling of delegate charges (the conference organiser should notify delegates about the billing arrangements in order to avoid any embarrassing problems)
- the charges for special events such as tours and transport
- the arrangements for audiovisual equipment hire and electrical and telephone charges, including whether the venue is to be billed for charges from outside companies such as florists
- any charges for security and other labour provided by the venue
- the venue's policy with regard to deposit structure
- guest credit facilities, including clarification of the accepted credit cards and policy regarding the acceptance of personal cheques, as well as who should notify the delegates on these matters
- the members of staff from the conference organisation who are authorised to sign accounts prior to and during the event.

■ Setting up *the master account*

The purpose of the venue establishing a master account for the convention or meeting is to ease the billing arrangements for the conference organiser. It is important that the conference organiser establishes with the venue and the client organisation which financial aspects of the event are to be paid through the master account and which items incurred directly by the delegates are their responsibility and should be charged to their individual accounts. For example, for some corporate events, the company will pay all delegate charges including accommodation, meals, and so on but will exclude personal items such as personal telephone calls and use of the mini bar.

All aspects of the billing process and procedures should be pre-arranged, before the event and the details laid out clearly. Within the venue, the billing arrangements for each section or activity should be outlined clearly (often through the banquet event order), so that each department, including the accounts department, is fully aware of the requirements for the event.

The conference organiser and the venue also need to establish who is to inform the delegates of the billing arrangements, particularly with respect to accommodation and ancillary items not covered by the delegate registration fee.

The main points are that the billing arrangements are outlined clearly and understood by both the conference organiser and the venue, and that clear, concise information is communicated to the delegates.

■ Payment *requirements*

The payment requirements for the master account vary a great deal, depending on the policy of the venue and the credit reputation of the conference organiser (past payment history, frequency of business, etc.). The final total dollar figure of the master account normally reflects a substantial amount of money, so to ensure effective cash flow management, the venue will want to obtain this money as quickly as possible. It is therefore common policy for venues to request a deposit or 'staged payments' during the time leading up to the event. In some instances, this can be as much as 80 per cent of the total projected bill for the food and beverage component of the event. The venue's payment requirements will be outlined in its terms and condition of business. However, the final payment of all accounts relating to the convention or meeting is usually requested at the end of the event or within a short period following the event. Increasingly, venues are charging interest on unpaid convention balances. It is common policy for a venue to undertake a credit check on the conference organiser or client organisation prior to the event.

During the convention or meeting the conference organiser should inspect the master account regularly, and particularly at the end of the event, to check the final numbers and accounts being charged. In this way they can view and agree the charges and initial their approval.

YIELD MANAGEMENT ....

Yield management is a method for managing capacity profitably (Lovelock 1992, p. 188). It can help sell the right inventory unit to the right type of customer at the right time and place. It is a very popular technique used by airlines and hotels, but is equally appropriate in convention management when the convention services manager or sales manager within a venue is managing space.

Yield has been identified as the average revenue received per unit of capacity, with the objective being to maximise the yield to improve profitability (Lovelock 1999, p. 319). Yield management and its analysis ensure that the convention services manager or sales manager recognise the opportunity cost of accepting business from one customer or market segment when another may subsequently yield a higher rate (Lovelock & Wright 1999, p. 319).

The use of yield management techniques are appropriate in the following situations:

- in businesses that operate with a relatively fixed capacity, such as hotel rooms or conference rooms
- when the demand can be segmented clearly, for example knowing which customers use the various priced services — different market strategies can then be developed and used for each segment
- when the inventory is perishable, such as accommodation and conference rooms, which if left unsold on a certain day cannot be sold again
- when the product is sold in advance, for example reserving rooms in advance when, if the venue had waited, it could have sold the rooms at a higher (or perhaps lower) price
- when demand fluctuates substantially, for example the peaks and troughs of business such as weekends and holiday periods (Lovelock 1992, p. 189).

To introduce a system of yield management within a MICE venue a clear plan should be established that is based on an analysis of past performance and current market data. This should indicate the extent of the convention or venue's accommodation capacity that can be allocated for specific dates to different types of customers at different prices. For example, the venue convention sales and accounting team may hold quarterly meetings to discuss projected sales for the following six-month period. Any gaps or peaks of business can be identified, and the convention sales team given targets to address these gaps. The trend to shorter lead times, cost competitiveness and speed of response in the booking of convention and function facilities can be used to the venue's advantage, for example by providing the opportunity for conferences to be booked two to three months or less before the event.

Some examples of yield management techniques currently used within venues that provide convention and meeting facilities include:

1. *Type and style of event* Some venues have put into place policies that restrict the type and style of event that they cater for. For example, wedding receptions are more labour intensive and therefore more costly than a conference for 300 to 400 delegates, so the venues focus on the more profitable areas.
2. *Type and length of event* Some venues discourage the booking of convention rooms for one day only, particularly during the middle of the week,

as this may limit the opportunity to sell the space to a convention that may last two to three days or more.

3. *Size of event* Convention sales staff in some venues are trained to maximise revenue from convention space bookings. For example, they may decline a potential booking one year in advance for a one-day meeting for 50 delegates if the only room available has a capacity for 200, because in the subsequent period they may be able to maximise revenue and book the room for a client requiring convention facilities for 150 people for two to three days. Some venues only accept bookings for functions, dinners or banquets three to six months before the event, in the knowledge that should space still be available three to six months out, it is unlikely to be sold for a large convention, conference or meeting.

The decision to accept or reject convention business needs to be made in the light of realistic expectations of the probability of obtaining higher rate business and the need to maintain established and desirable customer relationships (Lovelock 1999, p. 320).

LEGAL AND ETHICAL CONSIDERATIONS

A number of legal considerations can impact on MICE events and should be borne in mind by conference organisers, such as the preparation of the contract. While many are straightforward, in some situations it may be necessary to take guidance from an expert in the field, particularly where the issue or its outcome is more complex or uncertain.

■ The contract

A contract is an agreement between two or more parties that sets out their obligations and is enforceable by law. It describes the exchanges between the parties (McDonnell, Allen & O'Toole 1999, p. 190). Within the MICE industry, contracts are normally in the form of a formal letter (a letter of agreement), often used between the venue and the conference organiser and other suppliers, or a formal contract.

The conference organiser and the venue

The contract between the conference organiser and the venue is prepared once negotiations are complete. This is an area that can cause the conference organiser a great deal of concern and anguish. Before the contract can be formalised a number of details should be discussed and agreed. These are then formulated into a written proposal, sent by the venue. The written proposal is often dealt with by fax and forms the basis for future discussion. The contract is prepared by the venue, to ensure that the conference organiser does intend to honour their commitment to the venue. In many instances, only conferences and meetings with more than 10 accommodation rooms are required to sign a contract (Global Meeting Planner

1996, p. 50). For smaller meetings, often a letter of agreement accompanied by a credit card deposit is used.

The contract will include the venue's full name and address, the conference organiser's full name and address, and the start and completion dates for the convention or meeting. The exact dates of the event should be listed, together with any set-up and pull-down, start and finish times. This protects the venue against the conference or meeting tying up a room beyond the specified time or cut-off point and enables it to sell the space after that time if it should wish. A list of the services that the venue has agreed to provide, together with a breakdown of the total costs itemised per area, should also be included. The conference organiser should check the contract to ensure that the venue has included any specific discounts or agreed changes to the official charges. Any additional services that can be provided, if required, and their costs should be noted, along with whether the conference organiser is using any outside suppliers.

Details should be given of guaranteed minimum numbers for the convention or meeting. These are normally required 48 to 72 hours prior to the event, with the final charge being for the number guaranteed at that time or the final head count on the day, whichever is the highest. The contract should also include a deposit and payment schedule. The amount of the deposit required is often listed as a percentage of the total amount of the account. Some venues state that they require a deposit 'to be discussed with the group convention manager'; others state 10 per cent or a minimum of $500; and some calculate the deposit on a sliding scale of the final food and beverage figure (Hartley & Witt 1991).

A clause should be included in the contract regarding termination and cancellation of the event to cover either party if they are required to cancel the event due to circumstances beyond their control. The venue's cancellation policy should be stated clearly and concisely. It should list the penalties if cancellation does occur, together with the appropriate time frame. In many instances, the amount to be paid is determined at the time of the cancellation and appears to be negotiable, depending on factors such as the venue's relationship with the client and whether the event is to be rescheduled to a later date. Examples of cancellation fees include: for cancellation 60 days plus prior to the event — a full refund of the deposit; 30 to 60 days prior to the event — a 50 per cent refund of the deposit; less than 30 days prior — a forfeit of the deposit (Hartley & Witt 1991).

The venue's terms and condition of business should be outlined: this is normally a list of the venue's *do*s and *dont*s. It also contains details of the venue's policies regarding items such as service charges, government taxes (e.g. the Sydney CBD bed tax), staff labour surcharges, liability, security, and any other hotel regulations. Venues take no responsibility for loss or damage to equipment or merchandise left on their premises. Therefore, where appropriate, a conference organiser should take out insurance. Venues often state in their terms and conditions of business that no items should be attached, pinned or glued to wall surfaces without prior arrangement, and that event organisers are financially responsible for damage to hotel property during the function. Many venues' terms and conditions of business state that the venue's security manager will be pleased to discuss security arrangements.

If the convention is accompanied by an exhibition or a stage set-up that is to be organised by an outside contractor, then venues frequently state in the contract that this must be discussed with the hotel chief engineer. A time frame for this discussion is usually given. There may also be a clause stating that outside contractors should negotiate and liaise with key hotel staff with regard to setting up and breaking down their equipment.

The conference organiser and other suppliers

The conference organiser should outline the financial restrictions and expectations so that the other suppliers can put forward proposals that can be realistically and accurately supplied within those boundaries. The agreement between the conference organiser and these suppliers should be formalised in a legal contract, which should explain in detail the services or supplies that are being provided. The conference organiser and client organisation's financial responsibilities also need to be clarified, so that there is no room for questions. However, despite the necessity for a written contract between the conference organiser, venue and other suppliers, they should work together in partnership, dealing with each other honestly, to provide a quality product for the ultimate satisfaction of the delegates and client organisation (Weirich 1992, p. 191). Contracts are there as a safeguard, not to trick the organiser. They should always be read through thoroughly prior to being signed.

■ Risk *management*

The introduction of procedures that enable a strategy of risk management are essential to protect the conference organiser and to ensure that delegates have a safe and enjoyable experience. Conference organisers cannot function within the MICE industry without being exposed to some sort of legal liability, such as personal injury, loss of money, property damage, and so on. Conference organisers can face heavy penalties and loss of business if they do not take precautions against potential situations for legal action by dissatisfied delegates in their care. The key point is that conference organisers need to be aware of the types of liabilities that can be incurred and the action that can be taken to reduce risk. They also need to consider who will pay if something goes wrong during one of their events (*CIM* 1999, p. 3).

A risk management plan should be put in place within every conference organisation to ensure that every possible scenario is covered. Key areas of risk exposure for conference organisers might include:
- contractual liability
- injuries to customers or delegates
- dissatisfied customers or delegates
- loss of reputation, selection of suppliers, overseas operations.

For example, advertising and other promotional methods, while providing tremendous scope for creativity, can also provide a misleading or false message. Conference organisers should be aware of the laws relating to consumer protection and advertising standards and codes of practice. The information contained within the advertising material must be accurate and the illustrations, photographs and design must be realistic and appropriate. This covers issues such as the quality of the accommodation, the terms and conditions of the business, refunds, cancellation charges, the payment processes, any additional expenses that may be incurred by the delegate and booking procedures for the hotel accommodation.

All too often, conference organisers assume a limited responsibility for the delegates who attend a convention or meeting, but the extent of this responsibility is often poorly defined. This includes responsibility for their behaviour and actions that may cause damage to the property or bodily injury. Conference organisers need to define policies that deal with unacceptable behaviour and train conference organisation staff on these policies (*CIM* 1999, p. 3).

There are four basic rules to risk management:

1. *Avoid or diminish the risk*   Every situation should be evaluated for possible risks. These risks should be identified and avoided where possible. For example, hotel accommodation reservations and transport pick-ups may fall through because of a failure to make the correct booking or an inability to complete the payment procedures, perhaps due to poor financial management or general mistakes and errors. As a result, one small error could cause considerable inconvenience or aggravation and could be considered grounds for legal compensation by delegates who anticipated a trouble-free experience.

2. *Transfer the risk*   For risks that cannot be avoided and for which the conference organiser should not be held liable, the conference organiser should review and check whether they are the responsibility of someone else (e.g. a delegate slipping on a wet floor in the cloakroom). Suppliers to conventions or meetings are required to take a share in the liability for the event, but venues frequently accept no liability, and display signs to this effect in the pool area and rooms.

3. *Devise backups and alternatives*   Alternative plans should be ready to be put into place.

4. *Distribute the risk*   For example, obtaining various sources of revenue for an event, including a number of sponsors and exhibitors, can reduce the risk of shortfalls in revenue generated (Weirich 1992, p. 162; McDonnell et al. 1999, p. 201).

It is important that conference organisers anticipate the risks and consider the availability of appropriate insurance cover, for example public liability insurance, workers' compensation insurance, weather insurance and property insurance. There are many types of insurance available to cover most areas. However, the main point is to try to curtail and minimise the risks. Conference organisers should exercise reasonable care throughout the convention or meeting. Figure 11.5 shows a convention and exhibition insurance policy from AON Risk Services.

Section 1: Cancellation/abandonment

This section will protect the policy holder in the event of cancellation, abandonment, postponement, curtailment or relocation of the event due to any cause beyond their control. Perils insured include airline/transport/haulage, etc., strikes, non-appearance of guest speakers, damage to or double booking of the venue, and any other cause not excluded.

The principal policy exclusions are lack of interest, lack of financial support/financial default and claims arising from 'known developments'.

Shortfall of delegates/attendance

As well as providing protection for the total loss of an event, the policy will also automatically indemnify the policy holder in situations where there is a shortfall in the number of people attending the event due to any outside cause.

The most likely scenarios which may give rise to a claim under this extension are, in the case of conferences, airline strikes, and non-appearance of guest speakers; in the case of exhibitions, localised public transport strikes.

Weather

Cover can be provided should adverse weather conditions of any description lead directly to a financial loss in connection with the staging of an outdoor event.

Section 1 of the policy takes effect from the date that coverage is arranged (we recommend lead time of at least eight months, if practical).

Automatic extensions to the policy

Provided Section 1 is selected, the policy will provide for:

Failure to vacate — should penalty charges be imposed by the venue because of a failure to vacate the premises on time, the policy will idenmnify the policy holder up to $20 000 any one loss.

Emergency accommodation expenses — if at any time during or immediately after the event, your delegates/guests become stranded due to airline strike, engine breakdown, coach breakdown, error in departure times, etc., the policy will reimburse emergency accommodation expenses incurred up to $20 000 any one loss (net of any contribution by the airlines/coach operator, etc.).

Additional expenses: the policy will pay all reasonable additional expenses, up to the full Section 1 Sum insured selected, in order to take any action necessary to salvage the event (e.g. emergency bus/coach hire, alternative venue hire, emergency arrangements for replacement guest speakers, etc.).

Section 2: Physical loss or damage

Not many people realise that where goods are hired in order to stage an event, most often the hirer is responsible for any and all loss or damage.

This section will provide protection for such goods, or alternatively goods which are actually owned by the policy holder, not only at the venue, but also during transit to and from.

Section 3: Public and products liability

This section provides protection for the policy holder's legal liability to any member of the public (including delegates) in the event of personal injury or property damage.

The coverage provides automatic protection for:

(a) damage caused to the venue

(b) damage or injury incurred by third parties caused as a result of goods sold or supplied by the policy holder during the event

(c) third party goods within your legal control (e.g. exhibitors' goods), where loss or damage arises out of the policy holder's negligence up to $200 000 any one loss

(d) Cruise vessel liability up to $1 000 000 any one loss.

Important note: The fact that the venue may have its own liability protection has no bearing on the need for the organiser to effect this coverage.

Section 4: Money

This section will provide for protection in respect of loss of gate takings, petty cash, registration monies, etc., at the event, but not while left unattended unless contained within a cash register or securely locked away.

Section 5: Personal accident

This section will provide protection for death or serious injury incurred by organisers and their staff, voluntary workers and committee members while engaged in the organisation or conduct of the event.

■ **Figure 11.5** *AON conference/exhibition insurance scheme*

Source: AON Risk Services Australia Ltd

■ Business *ethics*

Within all sectors of the business environment, moral standards and business ethics have become increasingly important and an integral part of everyday business operations. The MICE sector, as other areas of the tourism and hospitality industry, can be prone to unethical behaviour, with the pressure to achieve a healthy financial bottom line often overtaking a company's code of ethics. The commitment to ensure ethical behaviour within an organisation begins with the CEO. If the CEO does not believe or display ethical behaviour, then it is hard for the team to exhibit and implement ethical behaviour. In this situation, individual employees tend to fall back on their own framework and personal code of ethics. In the same way, if employees believe that they are not being treated fairly and that the company is more concerned about the 'bottom line' than about their customers and employees, then they will be less likely to be concerned about their ethical behaviour (Montgomery & Strick 1994, p. 213).

The very nature of the MICE industry produces many situations that can be prone to unethical behaviour. This can cause concern for both the conference organiser and the industry stakeholders who may find it difficult to agree or disagree as to what constitutes ethical behaviour. Yet delegates to a convention or meeting have a right to expect fair and equitable treatment from the conference organiser, the venue and other suppliers; to expect the truth from items stated (e.g. on a menu or in a conference or venue brochure), and to expect good service. Therefore, organisations should introduce a code of ethics that reflects their own goals and objectives, and this should be communicated to all of the team.

So, what are some of the ethical situations that face conference organisers in the management and organisation of conventions or meetings?

Famil tours

When CVBs or venues invite prospective conference organisers or client organisations to visit a location or venue for free, they hope to influence them and demonstrate the capabilities of the location and its facilities, so that they will hold a convention or meeting there in the future. For conference organisers or client organisations potentially seeking to book a convention or meeting in the area, it is perfectly legitimate to accept the visit. A question of business ethics is raised, however, for those organisers that may accept the famil tour but have no clear intention of holding an event at that destination in the near future. They see the visit as a free weekend.

Overbooking

An ethical dilemma that frequently occurs within a venue is the practice of overbooking the guestrooms. In reality, a guest is not guaranteed a room despite having made a reservation. Failure by a venue not to overbook may result in a loss of profit when a number of rooms 'no show'. More recently, the practice of overbooking has expanded to convention and meeting rooms.

Commissions

The practice of taking commission on services 'sold on' by conference organisers has become accepted practice within the industry. However, ethically and legally it is important that conference organisers and others who act as 'agents' do not accept hidden commissions on any goods or services and their supply, such as hotel accommodation, conference satchels, delegate name badges and audiovisual equipment (*Secret Commissions Act 1905*). Clients should be made aware of the commission and reference should be made to it in documentation such as invoices and contracts.

Gift giving

Gifts within the industry are commonplace, from a simple basket of fruit or a bottle of champagne to a room upgrade or an elaborate and expensive piece of jewellery. While it might be appropriate to accept the basket of fruit or bottle of champagne, when does a gift become a bribe? Receiving expensive jewellery is definitely not acceptable (Weirich 1992, p. 192). Many companies and organisations have established rules that staff who are in a position to make purchase decisions or are in a position to influence outcomes should not accept gifts. This is a useful guideline for MICE organisations.

Employment, rates of pay and working conditions

The MICE industry employs a large number of part-time and casual employees. Ethically and legally, it is important to ensure that working conditions and enterprise agreements establishing standard wages are adhered to and that these employees are not taken advantage of. As stated earlier, people are a key resource to ensure quality of service and customer satisfaction with the convention or meeting.

Ethics is a way of life, and depends on honesty, integrity and common courtesy. Individuals should develop their own code of ethics, while MICE organisations need to develop and maintain both good business and ethical practices. The code of ethics developed by the MIAA is outlined in the following snapshot.

SNAPSHOT
A code of ethics for conference organisers

In order to encourage a high standard of ethical behaviour within the convention and meetings industry in Australia, in 1996 MIAA introduced a code of ethics for the Association. Association members accept the responsibility to follow this code as part of their membership of MIAA.

The MIAA Code of Ethics

Each member of the Association shall conduct their business with integrity and in an ethical manner to earn and maintain the confidence of clients, colleagues, employers, employees and the public.

Article 1

Members shall pursue and maintain high standards of personal and professional conduct, and:

a) Comply with the laws of Australia or of the country in which work is being performed and operate within the spirit of those laws.

b) Ensure that all contracts and/or terms of business are clear, concise and are honoured in full unless terminated or modified by mutual agreement.

c) Maintain professional skills by continued personal development and education and encourage colleagues to do the same.

d) Uphold at all times the standing of the Association and its Code of Ethics and actively encourage colleagues to do the same.

Article 2

In their relation with clients or employees, members shall:

a) Act as faithful agents in both professional and business matters.

b) Advise them of any conflict of interest situation as it may occur or as it is perceived.

c) Give professional opinion as objectively as possible when asked to do so and accept responsibility for advice given, actions taken and omissions.

Article 3

In contact with others, members shall:

a) Protect the safety, health and welfare of employees and the public.

b) Respect the confidentiality of information which comes to them in the course of their duties.

c) Not harm or attempt to harm, maliciously or recklessly, directly or indirectly, the professional reputation of others.

Breach of ethics

The National Council of MIAA acts as a Disciplinary Tribunal to deal with any breach of ethics cases. Members against whom complaints are filed are given the opportunity to put their case. Complaints must be in writing and must be able to be substantiated. Ethical matters are dealt with in confidence by the National Council. Breaches may result in a warning to a member that any further transgression from the spirit of the Code will likely cause cancellation of membership and removal of any rights and privileges to which he or she may hitherto have been entitled by virtue of membership. Serious breaches can result in immediate expulsion of a member.

Source: MIAA (1999)

$\mathcal{S}$UMMARY

The value and importance of effective and efficient financial and budgetary procedures cannot be underestimated in the overall success of the convention or meeting. Conference organisers within MICE organisations need to be familiar with budgets and conversant in developing and managing budgets for MICE events. This includes gathering background research data to prepare the budget, identifying sources of income and areas of expenditure, and monitoring not only the budget but also the actual expenditure for the event. In addition, they should be able to use their negotiating skills and be able to interweave their knowledge of statistics, budgets and accounting to ensure that the financial goals of the event are achieved. Yield management techniques are important for venues, as they enable them to maximise their revenue.

The legal aspects involved in the management and organisation of an event should be given full consideration. All too often, conference organisers do not realise the potential extent of their liability. A basic awareness of the risks and liabilities is of considerable value. However, in some situations the advice of a legal specialist may be beneficial. Conference organisers should prepare and implement a risk management plan within their operation and take out the necessary insurance as appropriate.

The MICE industry faces a number of ethical dilemmas in its business practices. As the industry enters the new millennium, it is essential that it embraces the concepts of business ethics and develops and implements an appropriate code of conduct.

Activities

11.1 As a conference organiser, design a system for monitoring the budget for a three-day convention and exhibition. Discuss the key areas to be monitored.

11.2 Design a code of ethics for a small firm of PCOs.

Discussion questions

11.1 Discuss the value and importance of undertaking research in the preparation of a budget for a MICE event. Identify the sources of information that may be used.

11.2 In the negotiation stage of a convention, how can the participants ensure a 'win–win' situation?

11.3 Critically discuss why a letter of agreement or contract is necessary between a conference organiser and a venue.

11.4 Discuss the concept of business ethics within the MICE industry.

11.5 As a conference organiser within a small organisation that specialises in the corporate training market, identify the key areas that should be evaluated in the preparation of a risk management plan for the business.

11.6 Outline the budget expenditure headings that may be incurred in a two-day corporate sales conference.

11.7 As a conference organiser within an association, what factors should be considered when setting the delegate registration fee for the association's annual conference?

11.8 As a convention services manager in a resort-style convention venue, discuss the potential advantages of utilising yield management techniques to increase revenue.

REFERENCES

Convention and Incentive Marketing. 1999, 'Operators Could Face Heavy Penalties', vol. 25, no. 1, January.

Getz, D. 1997, *Event Management and Event Tourism*, Cognizant Communication Corporation, New York.

Global Meeting Planner. 1996, 'Negotiating Rates and Contracts', June.

Hartley, J. S. & Witt, S. F. 1991, 'Conference and Function Cancellation Fees & Customer Goodwill', *Journal of International Hospitality Management*, vol. 10, no. 1, pp. 35–45.

Lovelock, C. H. 1992, *Managing Services; Marketing Operations and Human Resources*, 2nd ed, Prentice-Hall, Englewood Cliffs, N. J.

Lovelock, C. & Wright, L. 1999, *Principles of Service Marketing and Management*, Prentice-Hall, Englewood Cliffs, N. J.

McDonnell, I., Allen, J., & O'Toole, W. 1999, *Festival and Special Event Management*, John Wiley & Sons, Brisbane.

MIAA. 1999. *Who's Who in the Meetings Industry*, MIAA, Sydney.

Montgomery, R. J., & Strick, S. 1995, *Meetings, Conventions and Expositions: An Introduction to the Industry*, Van Nostrand Reinhold, New York.

Mooney, J. 1994. 'Something's Rotten in the Politics of Pricing', *Convention and Incentive Marketing*, vol. 20, no. 10, October.

Nichols, B. 1991, 'Sound Financial Management for Successful Meetings', *Journal of International Hospitality Management*, vol. 10, no. 2, pp. 127–36.

Weirich, M. L. 1992, *Meetings and Convention Management*, Delmar Publishers, New York.

FURTHER READING

Leiberman, J. H. 1993, 'Debunking the Myths of Yield Management', *Cornell Hotel and Restaurant Administration Quarterly*, February, pp. 34–41.

Weissinger, S. S. 1992, *A Guide to Successful Meeting Planning*, John Wiley & Sons, New York.

CASE STUDY

Conference and exhibition insurance: AON Risk Services

Philip Sunshine has been in the insurance business for many years. After six years working as an underwriter in London, Philip moved to AON Risk Services in 1986. AON is the largest insurance broker in Australia with over 40 branches nationwide. AON is the only insurance company endorsed by the main bodies of both the meetings industry and the events and exhibitions industry. Philip has been involved in risk services relating to the convention and meeting sector since joining AON. He has a wealth of experience and can readily suggest elements of any event, conference or meeting that may go wrong at any given time.

The policies that have been generated to cover conference and meeting activities are very detailed and include a range of elements that can cause litigation, frustration and loss of business image for any PCO, conference organising committee and venue. The factors that can go wrong for conference organisers are not limited only to cancellation or abandonment of the event itself. Philip suggests that organisers and venues need to be covered for elements such as a shortfall of delegates and physical loss or damage. The weather can play havoc with outdoor events, even if they are small components within a larger conference; adverse weather can lead to loss of revenue.

Other elements may include personal accident, loss or theft of money, public and product liability, failure to vacate and emergency accommodation expenses. There are times when serious injury or even death is incurred by organisers, staff, volunteers or committee members while working at a conference event. Loss of monies collected by conference organisers can be averted through risk management procedures, but theft often happens. Public liability usually is mandatory, but product liability, when damage or injury incurred through third-party goods (such as exhibitor's goods or convention items), is often overlooked by organisers. Failure to vacate and emergency expenses are two items that all conference organisers hope will never happen to them. If a conference or meeting runs over time and there is an added cost associated with this, or if delegates are forced to extend their accommodation through no fault of their own (such as an airline strike) then there is insurance to cover these possibilities.

There are several common questions that conference organisers and venues ask of Philip in relation to insurance coverage and liability. These include:

- Will a venue's liability policy protect me?
- Are off-site events covered?
- If I hire equipment, who is responsible if it is lost or damaged?
- If I provide a creche, am I covered?

The use of hockerdomes raises interesting questions of liability and responsibility for damage caused by and to the structure. In most cases, the hirer is liable, even if the hockerdome or marquee is not correctly erected. By using a reputable insurance company, the conference organiser or venue is able to find solutions to these questions and may be able to insure against incidents that can occur.

Over the years, Philip has been involved with over a million dollars worth of claims, for events such as illness of the promoter, non-appearance of the guest speaker, equipment stranded by strike and damage caused by weather. Some conferences have had to be completely relocated, and as a result of the pilot's strike of 1989, there were many claims lodged for delegate shortfall. As a guide for conference committees, PCOs and conference venues, Philip and AON provide a checklist, so that nothing is left to chance. This is shown in figure 11.6.

Most conferences and exhibitions happily proceed without incident — *some do not*. In our long experience in the conference/exhibition insurance field, we have dealt with payments in the thousands of dollars to policy holders who responsibly chose not to adopt the 'it's not going to happen to me' approach.

Some examples of potential problems include:
1. *Airline strikes* — involving not only pilots, but air traffic controllers, ground staff, baggage handlers, cabin crews, etc.
2. *Fire damage to venue or conference room*
3. *Train or bus strike*
4. *Industrial action* — by venue staff or essential support staff such as removal contractors.
5. *Venue unready* — obviously affecting new venues, but more often established venues undergoing renovations.
6. *Illness or whim of guest speaker*
7. *Adverse weather conditions* — affecting functions in marquees, for example.
8. *Loss of profits* — more often applicable to an exhibition than a conference.
9. *Double booking by venue* — highly unusual but not impossible.
10. *Bomb hoax or threat*
11. *Legionnaire's disease* — this will cause isolation of the venue.
12. *Food poisoning by caterers* — involving the calling off of the event and possible allegations from delegates.
13. *Interruption of power supply* — e.g. remember Auckland?
14. *Additional expenses* — e.g. alternative venue hire, emergency bus/coach hire, alternative guest speakers, etc. incurred to salvage the event.
15. *Failure to vacate* — should you fail to vacate the venue by the designated hour, it is standard practice for the venue operators to impose a penalty fee (this can be significant should a separate event be planned immediately after your own).
16. *Emergency accommodation expenses* — what happens in a situation where the bus or aircraft breaks down or you have simply mistimed the return of delegates to the airport, etc? (continued)

■ **Figure 11.6** *Checklist of essential insurance: what can go wrong?*

17. *Theft of equipment from event* — by the public, delegates or venue staff — even if it is not your equipment, the exhibitors or the hire company may hold you responsible.
18. *Loss of goods in transit* — to and from the event.
19. *Accidental damage to equipment* — e.g. misuse of a projector.
20. *Robbery/loss of money* — gate takings, petty cash, etc.

THIRD PARTY (LIABILITY) CLAIMS

i.e. claims brought by third parties (litigation trends show that even if the organiser of an event is visibly innocent of any wrongdoing, they may still be 'brought into an action').

21. *Slip and fall* — people often fall over (particularly at conference dinners, etc.)
22. *Damage to the venue*
23. *Theft of exhibitors' displays* — a claim would be instituted by a disgruntled exhibitor alleging 'lack of reasonable care' (e.g. inadequate security arrangements).
24. *Display injures delegate or member of the public* — particularly 'dynamic' displays.
25. *Overhead sign falls*
26. *Marquee collapses*
27. *Libel and slander by guest speaker* — you never know exactly what they might say!

Source: AON Risk Services Australia Ltd

Philip's final word on insurance is that insurance premiums are never wasted. 'If you are lucky and nothing goes wrong, they have bought you peace of mind. If you are unlucky, the insurance premium is probably the best money you ever spent.'

Source: Philip Sunshine, AON Risk Services Australia Ltd

Questions

1 Discuss the types of risks that may be incurred in organising and managing a three-day corporate convention for 200 delegates to be held at a resort island venue in the Whitsunday's.

2 Identify the particular risks for which it would be beneficial to obtain insurance.

12 Strategic
management of
conventions

LEARNING OBJECTIVES

After studying this chapter, you will be able to:

- define strategy in relation to convention management and related businesses; recognise emergent, deliberate, managed and unmanaged strategies; and list the various forms that strategies can take

- describe ways that strategies can be created, showing awareness of competitive strategies and cooperative strategies and noting how both are used in the MICE industry

- present a three-dimensional analysis of conference products, and show its strategic relevance

- show how business organisations in a multisector convention industry can be classified by type and how this can guide management

- discuss the pros and cons of teamwork and individual work in strategic management

- discuss strategies for managing work-related stress among employees in the MICE industry.

INTRODUCTION

People with career aspirations in virtually all fields of business, and certainly in the MICE industry, are giving increasing attention to the practicalities and theories of strategies. Researchers interested in business and management have also become more interested in the subject. This chapter draws on recent developments and discusses a number of topics relating to the strategic management of conventions and similar kinds of meetings.

Illustrative examples are taken from the MICE industry as well as other types of industries such as retailing. To study a topic such as strategy by focusing on one industry would be unproductive. Practising strategists learn by observing all sorts of industries and various types of human activity, such as sport and war, in order to borrow and adapt ideas for strategies to use in their own domain.

To simplify the presentation, the term 'organisation' is used as it occurs in writings on management to represent all kinds of collectives such as business firms, partnerships, companies and public sector agencies. Likewise, 'conference' is used as a generalisation, embracing conferences, conventions, congresses, forums, symposiums, seminars, exhibitions, and other kinds of meetings. Subtle variations between these different meetings can be found in the glossary and are outlined by Astroff and Abbey (1995, pp. 8–12).

This chapter does not discuss incentive travel. This is because it is a specialised business, with rather different activities and strategies in traveller-generating regions compared to those in destination regions, where visitors on incentive programs might be serviced by conference organisers in conference venues in a similar manner to conference delegates.

FUNDAMENTAL ASPECTS OF STRATEGIES

Why is strategy important to many business managers? What do strategies achieve? What are strategies? Are all strategies managed, and if so, how? Who is involved? Is it only company directors and top managers, or are employees at all levels actively involved in strategy making and implementation?

Such questions can be thought of as pointers to primary issues for understanding the subject. If asked to say what strategies are, many people might be vague or unsure. The following definition should not be regarded as 'the' definition, since other useful examples can be found. However, this one has been widely quoted since it first appeared.

> ■ A *strategy* is the pattern or plan that integrates an organisation's major goals, policies and action sequences into a cohesive whole. A well-formulated strategy [contributes to] marshal and allocate an organisation's resources (Quinn 1991, p. 5). ■

The following alternative definition is slightly different in two ways: it regards strategies as conscious behaviour and it links them to resource use, seeking some kind of objective. 'Integrates' and 'coordinates' are essentially similar key concepts in both definitions.

> ■ A *strategy* is a conscious act that coordinates resources to help achieve objectives which seem important for improved performance, defence, or some other purpose (Leiper 1998, p. 35). ■

These two definitions should be helpful in a number of ways. A complex word or phrase that is central to a subject being studied or discussed can be defined in order to make it clear what it means and what it refers to, with some degree of precision. The twin definitions are fairly precise, and they specify the component parts or processes, the main functions and relationships in a strategy. Furthermore, a clear definition helps to focus thinking and develop a fuller understanding. A definition can also help communication among people with a common interest in a subject, if everyone in the group is aware of the same definition.

This does not require everyone to agree absolutely. For example, the standard definition of 'tourist' that is followed by many tourism institutions can be regarded as too broad, and also biased against the public interest (Leiper 1995, pp. 7–14) but that opinion can be put aside while using the institutional model for the purpose of a discussion or research.

The twin definitions can be applied when thinking analytically about strategies for conferences. Illustrations of this are set out below, after consideration of Mintzberg's article 'Five Ps for Strategy' (1991a), which shows how strategies can occur in five different forms or manifestations: plans, ploys, patterns, positions and perspectives. These five are 'definitions', according to their author. However, they lack the precision of the two definitions given above and could be more accurately termed descriptions of five forms that strategies can assume.

■ Strategies *as five Ps*

Often, a strategy is expressed as a plan. A plan is a process setting out steps, which are shaped by rational and analytical thinking, for guiding future actions. Tossing a coin to decide what to do next is one way of deciding actions, but it is not a plan because it does not involve rational thinking. Forming a vision for a business venture is another way, but it too can be achieved without a plan. Copying successful methods is another way of guiding future actions, but it is not planning either; it is merely imitative behaviour.

While many people initially are inclined to think of a strategy as a type of plan, when asked if they would conclude that an organisation without a plan had no strategy, they often respond in the negative, and are then induced to revise their first idea that all strategies are plans. In practice, strategies often exist without planning.

A ploy or stratagem is a variety of plan, designed to trick an opponent or competitor. They can be effective, but the wrong sort can be risky and can rebound on the perpetrator.

Strategies in the form of patterns are common in the MICE industry. Conference organisers tend to follow consistent methods in the way they go about seeking new business and, having secured a contract, in the way they conduct conferences. Such patterns are repeated because, apparently, past experiences have been successful. The nature of these strategic patterns is not described here in detail, but some aspects are discussed in the section on products of conferences.

There are many possible positioning strategies. Some convention venues in large cities seek a position at the top of the market by offering top quality facilities in a stylish location, promoting an image of exclusiveness and by setting prices high in comparison to other convention venues in the same city. In Sydney, this sort of positioning strategy can be seen in a handful of five-star hotels with well-developed convention venues, including the Inter-Continental and the Sheraton on the Park.

Not all successful positioning strategies require up-market aspirations. Consider successful retailers such as Target, Best & Less and Kmart, which are successfully positioned around the cheaper end of the retail market. Conference venues following a similar positioning strategy include universities, which offer on-campus accommodation to conference organisers during the vacations, when most students are absent. These are sometimes used for association meetings, but seldom in the corporate meeting market.

'Position' can relate to other things besides position in a market hierarchy. Some conference organisers specialise in particular kinds of meetings and in that sense are using a positioning strategy. For example, OCC (see chapter 8) is a professional conference organiser specialising in the medical industry. The OCC example represents a niche strategy, which is a form of positioning. Niche strategies often are described as effective competitive strategies for small-scale businesses. In fact, this is a misleading description. A genuine niche strategy is not normally a competitive strategy; rather, it is a strategy for avoiding competition from larger or stronger potential opponents, by positioning an organisation where those potential opponents do not go.

Another way that strategies can take the form of positioning is when an organisation positions its operations in a particular location. This could be linked with the niche principle. Consider a conference venue offering a full range of conference facilities located in a city or town where there are no other conference venues of that kind. The Ballina Beach Resort is a case in point (see chapter 10). Several of the 30 motels situated in or close to Ballina have conference facilities, but only the Ballina Beach Resort has a full range. To some extent it has a niche strategy. When dealing with customers who want an event in Ballina supported by full facilities, Ballina Beach Resort does not have to compete with other conference venues. In this strategic position, it can enjoy the benefits of a quasi monopoly. The condition exists because other investors in full-facility conference venues have either ignored Ballina or decided that the city's potential as a location does not justify the risks of investment.

Strategies in the form of perspectives occur when an organisation forms a particular way of looking at the world and its business relationships. An interesting case is the professional conference organisation, World Research Group. The organisation is described in its own Web site (*http://www.worldresearchgroup.com*) and also, for those who prefer an objective view, in an article by journalist Barbara Ehrenreich (1997). World Research Group's perspectives on society include a view favouring the ideology of privatisation. This is a belief that governments should abandon public utility programs so that private sector interests can make a profit from them — for example, by taking over prisons, airports, motorways, hospitals, educational institutions and welfare programs. (The large profits enjoyed by corporations active in privatised industries come from ongoing government subsidies, as well as the monopolistic advantages that can be exploited by the owner of an airport, hospital or similar facility.) One segment of the conference market that World Research Group targets is business conferences for investors seeking information about opportunities from privatisation schemes.

Listing five Ps should not be inferred as a recommendation for managers to select and focus on just one. Rather, good strategic management requires thinking about all five, recognising that effective strategies can have several Ps in a mix.

■ **Emergent** *strategies and deliberate strategies*

Strategies can stem from deliberate acts and non-deliberate acts. The latter are termed emergent strategies and come about, not from a plan or other conscious behaviour, but as patterns or positions that an organisation might have drifted towards. Writers on the subject do not claim that deliberate strategies are superior to emergent strategies, nor do they say that relying on emergent strategies is always problematical.

Indeed, successful strategies can emerge in strange ways. An example is the Amex credit card, a strategic initiative launched in 1958. For years, American Express' top managers had rejected suggestions that they should enter the credit card industry. They saw the business of American Express as traveller's cheques and they regarded credit cards, then dominated by Diners Club, as something American Express would be wise to avoid for it could lose money and a new credit card might induce people to forgo traveller's cheques. The strategic decision to launch the Amex card was, in a real sense, imposed on American Express (Grossman 1987). Despite an illegitimate origin, the Amex credit card was soon highly profitable in its own right and also led to greater success for American Express traveller's cheques.

In other words, a strategy can stem from what happens to an organisation, irrespective of its managers' plans and deliberations. Besides the Amex card, many similar cases can be found. Consider Ugly Duckling Car

Rentals. Fucini and Fucini (1987) have described how the founder established a small-scale enterprise with its major resources comprising six used cars. Without a plan or other deliberate activity by Tom Duck, this small venture began developing into a giant, multi-outlet chain. The business environment virtually imposed a growth strategy when investors copied Tom's initiative and offered payments for the right to use the brand name.

■ Managed *and unmanaged strategies*

A weakness in some writings on strategy, including the important articles by Mintzberg and Quinn noted above, is that in remarking that strategies are deliberate or emergent, writers fail to distinguish clearly between managed strategies and unmanaged strategies. An emergent strategy can be an unmanaged strategy while it is emerging. What this suggests is that managers should continually look out for emergent strategies affecting their organisation, and attempt to decide objectively whether such strategies should be fostered or resisted. Once a decision is considered, a conscious and potentially managed strategy, a deliberate strategy, comes into existence. This is what happened at Ugly Duckling and American Express. Based on this issue, here is a definition of managed strategy:

> A managed strategy comprises the conscious activities of coordinating and otherwise managing the application of resources to help achieve objectives that seem important for success or survival.

Strategic management or hard work?

Managed strategies are important because, without them, an organisation is likely to have to depend on luck or hard work by employees. In practice, hard work has never been a path to success for human civilisations; to imagine that this is so is 'a doubtful argument which relies heavily on comparing humans to insects, such as ants' (Saul 1995, p. 157). Managed strategies add a conscious, intellectual, thinking component to human organisations, a factor that can raise productivity while reducing reliance on hard work. The motto 'Work smarter, not harder' captures this principle and is demonstrated in the industry insight on page 379.

■ Objectives *and resources in strategic management*

Strategies are related to major goals, often termed objectives. They should be expressed with a degree of precision, concerning what and when they are to be attained. To have as an objective to be 'highly profitable' is too vague. On the other hand, an objective to earn a profit of $300 000 after tax in the year 2001 is meaningful. A conference organiser might express a strategic objective as receiving a 98 per cent favourable response rate from delegates surveyed for opinions about the year's conferences.

Amlink Technologies, a Brisbane-based company specialising in conference management computer software (see figure 12.1 and chapter 9) shows how conference organisers can apply the 'work smarter' motto. The services it offers conference organisers include technologies that can handle on-line processing of delegate registrations, obtain credit card validations automatically for registrations indicating that form of payment, and process the papers written by conference speakers. All these technological innovations not only save time, but also provide faster service to delegates. Importantly, in addition they save a lot of money that would otherwise be spent on processing these items manually.

■ **Figure 12.1** *Amlink Technologies Web site*

Resources are a key concept in definitions of strategy. An organisation's resources are all the things that its staff can use and manage to help achieve its objectives. For example, at the Black Stump Convention Centre, the management team has divided its resources into several categories:

- *physical resources*, including its function rooms, public areas, equipment such as audiovisual appliances, seating, catering, airconditioning and recreational facilities

- *financial resources*, including money in the bank and credit available
- *human resources*, comprising the employed personnel and directors, as well as regular part-time contractors who are engaged during busy times
- *supplier resources*, comprising the companies that routinely supply the centre with goods or services (such as audiovisual and exhibition equipment), and with whom ongoing relationships have been established
- *marketing resources*, including any established relationships with clients and marketing intermediaries.

Each of these domains can have its own strategies. For example, to survive and thrive a business needs strategies for human resource management. These concern issues such as staff recruitment, selection and development, fair treatment, and appropriate pay and working conditions (see chapter 4). As another example, conference organisers need carefully designed financial strategies, because of the irregular inflows and outflows of cash that normally occur. The overarching concept of a managed business strategy is that it combines all the domains, integrating them into a reasonably cohesive whole.

■ **Why** *are strategies important?*

Strategies are important because of what they can contribute to an organisation. They give direction, leadership and ideas. This applies to all kinds of strategies, managed and unmanaged. In effect, American Express was led into the credit card industry not by its official leaders — its top managers — but by an emergent strategy. Without an effective strategy of some kind, an organisation's resources would not be used in a cohesive way; rather, they would be used haphazardly and, possibly, quite inefficiently. Without an effective strategy, an organisation is unlikely to achieve its objectives, because it will lack direction. A common example of a strategy aiming for efficiency is the custom of hotels and resorts entering the convention and meeting market seasonally, at off-peak times, when, without conventions and meetings, their occupancy rates would be at unprofitably low levels.

While much discussion revolves around business growth, in practice this is only one direction. Some organisations do not seek growth but stability and survival. Not every professional conference organisation can grow into a large business with the capacity to arrange several events simultaneously, and a strategy that overstretches resources in chasing unrealistic goals carries a high risk of failure.

Effective strategies also are important because they help organisations to fit into their environments. Some people view business environments as a mix of potentially threatening conditions that can only be faced by unrelenting competitive strategies. In practice and in theory, this can be a myopic and unworldly view, for no functioning industry can survive unless its component business units cooperate in appropriate ways, besides competing where appropriate (Burton 1990; Leiper 1995, pp. 121–34; Brandenburger & Nalebuff 1996).

■ Competitive *and cooperative strategies*

Competitive strategies are discussed in countless books on strategic management and the generic strategies described there are broadly useful in any kind of industry. There are a number of well-established generic competitive strategies. For example:

- *market penetration strategies* attempt to take market from competitors, using a range of techniques in a marketing mix
- *product development strategies* attempt to improve products so that consumers' preferences for the improved products give the innovator a competitive advantage
- *market development strategies* include attempts to expand a market, usually via informative and persuasive promotions — these strategies have considerable potential in the convention and meeting industry: the idea is to induce more associations and corporations to stage conferences of various sorts
- *diversification strategies* occur when an organisation attempts to broaden its range of products — there may be considerable scope for this strategy within the MICE industry, for example World Research Group (see above) is a professional conference organisation following this strategy
- *cost leadership strategies* involve moving prices (up or down) ahead of competitors in order to take some advantage
- *differentiation strategies* require making changes to products and/or promotional messages in ways that create a competitive image
- *focus strategies* involve specialisation in a particular line of products or markets — they are closely aligned to niche strategies, discussed above.

Cooperative strategies are not so widely discussed, but their fundamental importance should be recognised: well-managed businesses normally require a blend of competitive and cooperative strategies. Contrary to first impressions, they are not mutually exclusive and can be followed simultaneously. In business, as in sporting contests, competition occurs within the bounds of cooperation. In a football or tennis match, being competitive does not mean breaking the conventions and rules of the game; recognising those conventions and rules amounts to tacit cooperation by the players. Of course, the fact that players are now commonly termed 'competitors' tends to disguise this reality. In most industries, many kinds of cooperative strategies can usually be identified. Sixteen examples have been identified as being common in tourism industries (Leiper 1995, pp. 125–34). In a well-developed convention and meeting industry, there are a number of cooperative strategies. For example:

- items in formal and augmented products can be packaged into a single conference product offered at a single price
- standardised products exist when various conference venues provide broadly similar facilities and when various conference organisers are able to stage broadly similar events — the practices might contradict competitive principles, but they have advantages for all parties, including delegates

- intra-industry networks are common because most employees of conference venues and conference organisers in a city get to know one another and meet to share information of various sorts
- groups such as MIAA have several functions, all pertinent to the cooperative theme found in working industries: information on matters of common concern can be shared and representations can be made to governments and allied industries — liaison between the AACB, the MIAA and the ATC exemplifies this function (see chapter 2)
- intra-industry careers are common, and staff employed by conference organisers and venues tend to change employment by taking up new jobs within the industry, rather than moving out to work in other industries — intra-industry careers lead to knowledge and skills being spread across the industry, a process which has attributes of cooperation as an emergent strategy.

This list is not comprehensive. One way that the MICE industry will develop is by innovative people devising new and better ways for industrial cooperation. These need not restrict competition, any more than new rules introduced to improve tennis are likely to reduce competition between players.

■ Who *creates and makes strategies?*

Company directors and top managers are the principal creators of strategies in some organisations, especially among small-scale businesses. In conference industries this is quite common. However, the image of strategy as the exclusive concern of the people at the top is misleading, for in most businesses employees at all levels are involved in the creation of strategies as well as their implementation. There are several explanations for this, including emergent strategy, the trend to empowerment, and the increasing reliance on teamwork, which is discussed in more depth later in the chapter. The following snapshot looks at a successful firm based in Adelaide, and indicates how its foundation strategies came from Ann Ewer's experience and ideas.

SNAPSHOT
Ann Ewer, Staffords Conference Management

Ann Ewer established one of South Australia's leading conference management businesses, Staffords Conference Management, in 1989. Before then, Ann was employed in an executive secretarial position and was asked, in 1978, to provide secretarial assistance (effectively act as conference manager, but that term did not exist then) for a legal convention of some 875 delegates and 550 accompanying partners. This was in the days of typewriters (no computers), with no large convention and exhibition centres and only one major hotel in the city of Adelaide. Having retired to the country after that event, which was the most successful legal convention ever held at the time, Ann realised that she loved the work and decided to establish her own business when she returned to the city in 1989. Soon Staffords was established and enjoying an excellent reputation. Staffords employs five staff, though the number fluctuates depending on workflows, and has managed a variety of conferences for a wide range of industries, including garden nurseries, urban development, scientific research and insurance, taxation and legal companies.

Ann believes the keys to Staffords' success include:

- being thorough — working from a detailed planning schedule prepared as soon as they are awarded a conference
- detailed and accurate budget preparation with tight control of additional expenditure and constant knowledge of the precise situation at any given time
- excellent follow-up systems to ensure nothing is overlooked
- good procedural systems in the event of staff changes
- looking after staff so they have few staff changes — there is nothing worse than a client having to deal with two or three different conference managers during the planning process
- absolute honesty with the client — if they make a mistake or haven't done something, they admit it
- nothing is too much trouble — they do whatever their clients need and do not complain even if they feel or know the task is a waste of time.

She believes a conference can be considered a success when three groups form certain opinions:

- organising committees deem a conference successful if registrations exceed expectations, there is a healthy profit and they feel that they contributed to the conference but did not have any hassles/worries leading up to the event; it all seemed to take care of itself
- delegates deem a conference successful if the hotel they booked (via the conference manager) had a room for them and check-in was effortless; they heard some good speakers and learnt something; the social functions were fun, providing ample opportunity to network; and the food was of a good standard
- a conference manager knows it is a success when the sponsors and speakers say 'Thanks. You did a great job', and when all the above are achieved!

Source: Ann Ewer, Staffords Conference Management

While the notion that strategies are intrinsically linked to plans has spread in the past 30 years, plans are often unnecessary and can cause problems when applied in this way. Planning can have a useful role in strategic management, however. The key is recognising where and when plans are useful.

■ A widespread *illusion and its fallacies*

Imagine the answers that would be obtained were a large sample of people employed across a range of industries asked to supply the missing word(s) in this sentence: 'All businesses should have strategic …' Quite likely, many would add the word 'plans'. Better answers would be 'management' or 'thinkers and leaders'. The fact that many people carry misleading illusions like the one that links plans with strategy creation exemplifies the fact that what can appear to be common sense is not always reliable. This condition is widespread in the present age, a time when misleading myths and illusions are proliferating (Shermer 1997).

The theory that business strategies should be created by planners and based in plans was, for a while, a fashionable idea in the business world. In the 1980s, the trend faltered as companies found that the idea was not always practical. The trend went into reverse when companies began eliminating their strategic planning departments. Researchers investigated the problems with planning, and Mintzberg's book, *The Rise and Fall of Strategic Planning* (1994), contains the most thorough project. He found that attempts to plan strategy often fail because of interrelated factors, which he summarised into four fallacies:

- The fallacy of predetermination is the misleading assumption that the future can be predicted with sufficient accuracy to serve as a foundation for strategic plans. It can, but only if stable conditions prevail, as was the case with the global economy in the 1960s. However, the global economy has been in turbulence since 1974. Few predicted the Asian economic downturn that began to emerge in mid-1998, but it has had drastic impacts on tourism (Leiper & Hing 1998). Any strategic plan based on predictions of continued economic growth across Asia has lost its utility.
- The fallacy of detachment is the false assumption that planners can somehow detach their thinking from day-to-day business issues and produce a plan that will inform business about key decisions in some future period.
- The fallacy of formalisation is the naive assumption that once a plan has been formed, it represents something realistic and reliable as an indication for future actions. Routine committee meetings often proceed under the same fallacy; some people view them as being productive work merely because of two facts: they are official assemblies of apparently busy people and they are structured around an agenda.
- The grand fallacy is the combination of the other three, and it amounts to unreasonable and unfounded faith in planning as a process for

strategy formation. The work of creating strategy is like all creative behaviour: it cannot flourish if subjected to programming and tight management, which is what planning tends to do.

Strategies and flexibility

A common confusion about strategic planning is allied to the first and third fallacies. There is a general agreement in business that strategies should be flexible, a principle carrying more importance now, in uncertain times, than it did 30 years ago. Some people react to the principle by seeking security in a strategic plan, without realising that the more a business is subjected to planning, the more it loses its flexibility. A hidden cost of a strategic plan is some degree of inflexibility.

■ How *strategies are created*

As described above, strategies emerge frequently without any plan or other deliberate source. Managers should be watching for these occurrences so that they can make an appropriate response. This is not an adequate theory: sitting around waiting for strategies to emerge is not the ideal way to run a business. And if formal planning has been found to be a less than ideal way to devise strategy, what remains? Close observation of successful business indicates that strategy often is devised by persistent thinking about strategic issues. Anything that encourages creative thinking in an organisation might help to produce good strategy. Teamwork, using various techniques to stimulate and focus thinking, can be useful, although it has limitations (discussed later).

Retreats as a source of strategy

Many organisations take teams away for a 'retreat' to think about strategies. While retreats can be effective, there is a possibility that proper holidays lead to more productive thinking on strategic issues. This has not been thoroughly researched, so far as is known, but preliminary investigations might be indicative (Leiper 1995, pp. 65–7). A proper holiday in this sense requires at least two weeks away from the routines of work and home life, and gives time for rest and relaxation. Proper holidays have two advantages over executive retreats as a medium for fostering creative thinking. First, they are longer, allowing time for rest and relaxation, which are normal priorities before individuals are ready for creative thinking. Second, they take individuals away from work colleagues, who tend to be reminders of routines. Creativity requires the breaking of routine.

■ What *to think about while devising strategies*

Strategy is often devised by persistent thinking about strategic issues. But thinking about what specifically? Broadly, several themes can be recommended. Porter (1980) and Voyer (1995) are among the theorists who have provided useful models for thinking about the contexts of business strategy. Voyer's approach, which incorporates Porter's model for analysing an industry's environments, is summarised in figure 12.2.

■ Figure 12.2
An outline of the steps for devising a strategy

1. Specify a mission statement
   - a precise definition of the business
   - the long-term objectives
2. Scan the external environments
   - the industry's environments (use Porter's model)
   - the macroeconomic environment (social, economic, and so on)
   - assess opportunities and threats to the business
3. Scan the internal environment
   - value chain analysis
   - financial analysis
   - assess the strengths and weaknesses of the business
4. Statement of business strategy
5. Integrated programs for strategy implementation

Source: *Adapted from Voyer (1995)*

This is not a planning approach. Plans and planners only play a role towards the end, in step 5, when integrated programs refer to the scheduled combinations of various resources. Earlier in this chapter, resources were described in reference to conference industries.

Ways of thinking about competitive possibilities, and about cooperative possibilities, are outlined later in this chapter. Competition and cooperation are not mutually exclusive; instead, both conditions normally exist together. Healthy competition occurs within the bounds of a cooperative framework; it does not compete with it.

A problem with this model is that it is prone to lead into the fallacy of detachment. To combat this, two more ways of thinking can be recommended. First, effective strategists spend time thinking about things that have no obvious link to business or strategy. This helps bring about detachment. To stimulate such thoughts, they read novels and newspapers, watch movies, and converse with colleagues over lunch about anything interesting. Useful ideas about business can arise during these intervals, from sources that have no obvious link to business issues. Second, and most importantly, effective strategists stop thinking periodically, and do so regularly. This can be very difficult for busy people, who tend to be preoccupied with issues, and are always thinking, preoccupied by busyness. Mental rest (not thinking) can be as useful for regenerating productive thinking as physical rest (no movement) is for regenerating physical energy. The history of creative discoveries has countless cases of people whose creative ideas came to them while idly contemplating natural phenomena.

The roles *of planning in strategic management*

Merely because planning might not be the best way to create strategy does not mean that planning should not be used for other functions within the scope of managing a business. In the MICE industry, planning is important for implementing strategies. Principally, this is because the major activity involves projects with unusual attributes. Conferences can be viewed as a series of projects, rather than a flowing process. Thus, theories of project management are more applicable than theories of process management. While many conferences share characteristics, every conference is a one-off event; it requires managing as a project (see chapter 8).

Project-based activities (such as conferences, building construction or routine medical surgery) use planning to help the effective and efficient implementation of strategies. For successful completion, each project requires a complicated mix of resources to be assembled, and then combined in an appropriate manner. The more complicated the project, the more complex the mix and the more useful a plan for managing the project.

Earlier, a list was provided showing the resources used at one convention centre. A conference plan would itemise a more comprehensive list of resources, with details for each as to the quantities and standard required, the sources of supply, the time required and the person responsible for the acquisition. As the project begins, the planning document becomes a monitoring and control document, allowing each item to be checked off. The sequence of directing (strategy creation), followed by planning, monitoring and controlling, can be regarded as steps in a management system for each conference.

An unusual attribute of the MICE industry is that projects cannot be delayed easily. In this regard, conferences are unlike other projects such as building construction. If a conference is scheduled and advertised to commence on 1 February, and problems with resources arise during January, the event cannot be postponed and re-scheduled to commence a week later, on 8 February. In most instances, many delegates would cancel if that were to occur. In conference management, everything must be ready on the scheduled date. This characteristic places extra value on careful planning.

Action *planning and critical path planning*

Plans used in business organisations are more effective if they have the qualities of an action plan. Action plans:
- specify the person (or, less effectively, people) who bear responsibility for each item in the plan — this identifies who can be held to account if things go wrong, and praised when things go well

- state precisely when each step is to be started and when it is to be completed — this allows the schedule (the sequence of steps) to be managed (a good technique for this is critical path planning: see chapter 8)
- state unambiguously how each step is linked to one or more other steps — this allows problems to be traced to their causes if things go wrong (again, critical path planning is useful).

Many so-called 'strategic plans' prepared in the 1990s for governmental agencies in Australia lacked these vital attributes. Examples can be found among the 'strategic plans' published by the Office of National Tourism. This deficiency might reduce the effectiveness of these plans.

For complicated projects, a more intricate form of planning is required. The most useful technique in such cases might be the critical path method (CPM, or CPA) (see chapter 8). This technique uses network analysis and is quickly learnt (Vitalis, Monin & Holland 1988).

■ Planning *for VIPs at conferences*

The presence of VIPs (very important persons) at conferences can pose tricky issues for conference organisers, specifically how they should be addressed and introduced, and how they should be ranked for seating arrangements, and so on. To plan for such matters, all major conference venues in Australia have on hand Joel's book, *Australian Protocol and Procedures* (1988). VIPs include heads of state, government ministers, government ambassadors, highly prominent religious leaders, and so on. The term does not apply to individuals who are looked on as token VIPs within their own circle, but who are in fact merely prominent members of some profession, trade, association or industry.

CONFERENCE PRODUCTS

In any business, a central factor in strategic management is having a good understanding of the products. The following discussion explains how this can be done and why it is helpful in relation to strategies for conferences.

■ Three *dimensions of conference products*

Authorities on business such as Kotler (1972; 1989) emphasise that products can be perceived by marketers and managers in a multidimensional way and that this is useful for strategic management. Conference products can be broken down to reveal three dimensions: formal products (the most obvious); augmented products (which some writers have called extended products); and core products.

Formal products were termed 'tangible products' in early writings (Kotler 1972) and have long been known as 'product features' by advertisers and sales personnel. To replace 'tangible' this dimension was later re-named 'formal', to include products based around intangible services. A custom of dividing outputs into products and services misses this point. The conference industry is a services industry and the key issue is to think of what is produced by the servicing.

■ Formal *products*

A formal product is one dimension or facet of a bundle of goods and/or services. The formal products of a conference comprise the essential events of the meeting, along with those major aspects of its physical setting that can be managed. A meeting might have several formal attributes, including:

- an explicit theme and purpose
- a physical setting, specifically the building(s) and room(s) where the event is staged
- a duration, usually expressed as so many days
- a schedule, such as the times given for plenary sessions, breakout sessions, coffee intervals, lunches and dinners, and entertainment
- one or more keynote speakers and other speakers.

To illustrate theme and purpose, consider, for example, the 1999 CAUTHE (Council for Australian University Tourism and Hospitality Education) conference, staged that year in Adelaide. Each annual conference has around 300 delegates representing a dozen countries. The main purpose is to provide an opportunity for people interested in research and education on tourism and hospitality to meet for informal discussions and to listen to research reports. The theme of the Adelaide conference was 'Delighting the Senses', and food and wine were featured in the promotional messages.

■ Augmented *products*

An augmented product comprises a formal product plus a cluster of services and goods that might accompany it. Some of the augmentations might be optional extras, while others are provided regardless of consumers' wants. Augmentations are not essential, but might be helpful. A conference's augmentations can include:

- packaging transport to the venue, accommodation and rights to attend the conference as a single booking and billing facility
- hospitality at airports and other transport terminals
- hospitality at the main venue
- information and local transport provided specifically for delegates
- entertainment included as part of the event
- lunches, dinners and in-between snacks included as part of the event
- sightseeing tours or other tourist, recreational or cultural activities offered as optional add-ons
- name badges
- souvenirs provided at no direct cost or sold at the venue, such as a T-shirt displaying the conference title

- a printed program of the scheduled events and, in many cases, a published version of the principal talks presented
- a list of delegates' names and addresses
- a satchel or bag displaying the conference title, used to contain the program and other documents
- jugs of iced water and mints on tables during sessions.

There might be a temptation to regard features of the city, town or region where a conference is staged as part of the conference's formal or augmented product. While these features certainly can be important for the popularity of conferences (Sydney or Auckland as a venue might attract more delegates than, say, Lismore or Eketahuna) it is not strictly speaking part of the product. Location is related to another facet of a strategic marketing mix; location can be an important feature of a conference's promotion.

■ Core *products*

The core products of any business are the psychological impacts of the formal and augmented products on the consumers. If these impacts are positive, in the sense that consumers are satisfied to some degree, the core product can be described as a product benefit.

The president of Revlon Cosmetics pinpointed the nature of core products when describing the different dimensions of his company's products: 'In the factory we make cosmetics; in the drugstores we sell hope' (cited by Kotler 1972, p. 423). Consumers buying lipstick or other cosmetics are not, in a psychological or behavioural sense, buying a tangible set of chemicals. Instead, they are buying the hope or expectation of feeling more beautiful or presentable when wearing the product.

Two terms often used to distinguish between a product's formal and core dimensions are 'features' and 'benefits'. Features are the things most easily recognised. Several items in the above examples of formal and augmented products could be described as a conference's product features. A conference's core products or product benefits are not so easily recognised. They exist in consumers' minds, but are most important in business strategy, more so than formal and augmented products. This is because, unless a product goes at least part way to satisfying consumers' needs, giving a psychological sense of benefit, delegates will feel that a conference has not been worthwhile.

So what are the core products of conferences? Earlier, chapter 5 identified a number of purposes behind conferences, drawing on research by Montgomery and Strick (1995). Those purposes give insights into the core products. Thus, the core products of a conference include, in part, the successful attainment of its purpose(s), which might include providing a medium for creating changes in the attitudes, skills and knowledge of the delegates. Montgomery and Strick have indicated several ways that a conference can do this, including generating new ideas, disseminating facts and ideas from a pool of knowledge, and generating a spirit of cooperation among delegates who are, in most cases, people with some shared interest, and members of some sort of community.

A conference essentially is a set of shared experiences, typically supported to some extent by services and, as with any experience or service industry focused on people, the core products are changed people. The core products of a conference are represented by changes in the delegates.

Montgomery and Strick's list of purposes gives insights into parts of the core products of a conference. But other parts are often more important strategically. To identify these parts, and to gain a more comprehensive and deeper understanding of core products, we can think (and possibly research into) how delegates might be changed as a consequence of participating in a conference. This deeper line of analysis can be pursued by asking: Why do so many people like going to conferences? Why has conference-going become a popular custom? Why do employers pay for employees to attend conferences? The answer is not merely because large numbers of people want or need to gain new ideas, and want to access a pool of knowledge. If this were so, public libraries would be selling tickets for standing room in the non-fiction shelves.

When core products are described as 'benefits' derived by consumers, the descriptive word should not be inferred in any moralistic manner, which would limit core products to things that everybody might publicly endorse as being respectably proper. A deeper reason why conference-going has become a popular custom is that many people enjoy themselves by going on trips to conferences and this has little or nothing to do with gaining new ideas, communicating in a pool of knowledge or entering a spirit of cooperation. Certainly those factors are paramount for some delegates, but for most delegates at many conferences they are only excuses for attending.

So, what is special about conferences that gives many delegates a sense of recreational leisure? This vital part of the core product flows from a combination of three factors. First, some conferences offer opportunities for leisure, away from home life and normal work routines. Leisure is more than free time; it involves some mix of recreational and creative experiences — the mix depends on the individual's preferences and the opportunities at hand. Second, delegates at a corporate conference normally do not pay for the major conference expenses since these are met by their employer. Any recreation that comes at no personal cost tends to be quite enjoyable.

Third, because many conferences are work-related, the recreational benefits they provide are given a legitimate cover. Fun at a conference is authorised fun, but it must be given a cloak of respectability; it must not be given too much prominence. Thus, in many conferences, there is ambivalence in both the strategic design of the event and its promotion. Sometimes, the recreational theme is given more than a hint in promotions — one leading American cruise line targets conference organisers using advertisements featuring photographs of a cruise ship and the statement, 'The hardest part is remembering you're here on business'. More on this subject can be found in a collection of short stories by Moorehouse (1978) or an article on Las Vegas by Bing (1995). Of course, not all conferences are the same. At some, there is virtually no leisure for delegates; at the other extreme, there might be nothing but rest, relaxation and entertainment.

■ A multidimensional *view of products in business strategies*

Conference managers and their employees should try to develop a multi-dimensional view of their products. A conference is more likely to succeed and a conference-related business is more likely to prosper if there is an appropriate mix of formal and augmented products. This is how positive core products are generated. To achieve this requires careful attention from conference planners, managers and support staff. Employees can be trained to recognise the three dimensions and how each affects the ability of the business to satisfy the needs of consumers.

In addition to the fact that each dimension has relevance, there is a strategic possibility that one dimension can make up for deficiencies in another. For instance, augmented products can be used to disguise shortcomings in formal products. And since augmented products are often cheaper and easier to devise than formal products, this can have twin advantages — marketing and economic — for a business. This is illustrated in many ways within the MICE industry.

ORGANISATIONAL TYPES

Just as business organisations in general can be classified into types, so can the MICE industry, particularly MICE businesses in large cities operating on a national or international scale with large numbers of organisational units specialising in various functions, such as conference organisers or convention venues.

■ Classifying *conference organisations into types*

Analysing an industry's organisations into types has practical relevance, because each type is best managed in a particular way. Awareness of this allows managers to avoid the deficiencies of using the wrong approach, if they erroneously assume that certain ideas about management are relevant to all types of business organisations. Introductory textbooks on business tend to ignore this issue. Instead, they present an approach to classification based on legal forms such as sole traders, partnerships, companies, and so on. Such categorisation has little significance for managerial issues. Another approach has more significance. Devised by Mintzberg (1979; 1991c, 1991d, 1991e), this arranges organisations into seven sets that its author calls 'configurations' but which can be more simply described as types: entrepreneurial, bureaucratic, professional, ad-hoc, diversified, missionary and political.

If managers recognise the type they are trying to manage, their efforts can be more effective and more efficient. So, which types are found in conference industries? Which are most appropriate for these industries? Real organisations are unlikely to match one of the seven theoretical types precisely; instead, a real organisation will exemplify one type in particular but have traces of others.

A preliminary step is to identify the various forms of organisations in conference industries. For the purpose of this discussion, three forms are noted. Across Australia and New Zealand, many examples of each can be observed. This list is not comprehensive, since conference industries include other forms, such as hotel conference departments. The three forms are:

- purpose-built convention and exhibition centres
- professional conference organisers (PCOs)
- amateur organisers of conferences (AOCs).

These three forms can potentially be classified within Mintzberg's scheme of seven organisational types; but this requires avoiding the stereotypical images of 'professional', 'bureaucratic', and so on, as the terms are used in everyday language. In Mintzberg's scheme the expressions have specialised meanings. So, while there might be a natural inclination to say that PCOs are examples of the 'professional' type of organisation, in Mintzberg's scheme for understanding strategy, in fact they are not, as explained below.

Purpose-built convention and exhibition centres

Purpose-built convention and exhibition centres tend to match the bureaucratic type of organisation and overall, seem more like this type than others. This does not mean that these centres typically display the negative characteristics associated with the term 'bureaucrat' in popular imagery (slow in response and overly burdened with regulations). It means instead that they tend to be organisations working to routines, with a sizable capital investment — two characteristics that shape the way they are normally managed. Other examples of bureaucratic organisations can be seen in airlines, large-scale hotels, the national post office, prisons, large-scale chains of restaurants and public service departments.

The business of purpose-built convention and exhibition centres is fairly routine. They provide space and facilities for conferences and exhibitions and, from the perspective of centre management, each conference or exhibition follows a fairly similar routine, including common steps such as: promoting the centre as a venue; contracting for an event; assembling facilities in some quantity and the standard required for each event; overseeing the arrival of delegates; hosting the delegates; attending to changes in requirements and to problems; cleaning up afterwards; preparing accounts for payment; and following up with clients to seek feedback on the centre's performance. Certainly there are variations, but a routine exists, repeated for successive conferences. Another term for the bureaucratic type is the machine organisation, a label that connotes routine, reiterated operations.

The centres are relatively capital-intensive organisations (in contrast, for example, with PCOs, which are labour intensive). A centre's main capital is in its building and associated facilities, an investment that can amount to millions of dollars or, if it is not owned, to substantial leasing costs. Capital intensity requires a management style emphasising tight control; if a centre were to be grossly underutilised, large sums would be lost in idle capital and fixed expenses.

Awareness of these characteristics is only the start of understanding what purpose-built convention and exhibition centres as a bureaucratic type might mean in terms of a managerial approach. Implications flow from the match; they can be inferred by aligning Mintzberg's (1991c) theories about this type with knowledge about the centres. One implication is that managing these centres involves heavy emphasis on the control functions of management. The purpose is to make the routines run smoothly. Another implication is a heavy reliance on personnel assigned to support roles of various sorts that have the same purpose. Employee initiative is not a major factor in the success of a bureaucracy. More important is employees' reliability. This factor should shape strategies for staff recruitment and training.

Professional conference organisers

To an outsider, PCOs might seem similar to purpose-built convention and exhibition centres in terms of the model of seven types of organisations, since both work on conferences, a field characterised as routine work. There is a subtle difference, however (see below). PCOs cleverly use the term 'professional' to create an image of competence and service. While this term is quite useful for marketing the business, for managing PCOs there is more to be gained by thinking of another type of organisation, the ad hoc (or innovative) type (Mintzberg 1991d). This type has many characteristics of the entrepreneurial type, but differs in certain respects.

PCOs as organisations typically have a structure that can be described as highly organic. They are flexible, and so should be able to avoid the trappings of bureaucracy. In smaller organisations particularly, there is usually no sharp division of employees into fixed specialised jobs, even though some employees need a high level of expertise in particular aspects of conference organisation. Instead, the employees should be flexible and innovative, ready and capable of doing one or more specialised jobs when needed and being deployed into project teams and task forces when required.

Well-trained personnel are needed in effective PCOs, and they must be individuals with fluid attitudes, capable of working alone but also adept at fitting quickly into cohesive teams. Because a PCO might work on conferences of vastly different sizes, and simultaneously on multiple conferences in different purpose-built convention and exhibition centres, the teams for PCO operations are truly ad hoc, in that a new team might be assembled every few days for each new conference. Part-time and casual employees are vitally important in these circumstances. Like part-timers and casuals in some other hospitality industries (except for recruits on work experience), these individuals are not hired merely as helping hands, but because they have skilled competencies for a particular field of PCO work.

While there is superficial routine in the work of PCOs, their success depends on their skills in responding well to the opportunities, needs and problems of each conference, and this crucial factor dominates the underlying routine of the work. That is one reason why PCOs are best viewed as an ad hoc or innovative type.

Amateur organisers of conferences

AOC seems an apt term for this discussion, referring to the temporary committees established within a group that wants to run a conference. In practice, AOCs are often called conference organising committees. AOCs are amateur in several senses: the people forming them are not full-time conference organisers earning an income for that work, and normally are involved as volunteers with an enthusiastic desire to help the conference to successfully achieve its designated purpose.

As organisations, AOCs have traces of several types — entrepreneurial, ad hoc and bureaucratic — but the type they most closely resemble is the missionary type. A pure missionary organisation forms when its members come together because they share a common ideology. They coalesce because all have a strongly felt common set of values.

Missionary organisations tend to be newly formed. They seldom last long as that type. Each AOC does not have to survive beyond the time required to design and stage the conference. They tend to be small and, unconstrained by tradition, they can be innovative to some degree. They tend to be led by charismatic individuals. Individuals' roles in missionary organisations are often supplementary to their routine roles: it is often a part-time role, for a short interval. The classic form of missionary organisation is the Israeli kibbutz and perhaps AOCs can learn from this example. An analysis of the kibbutz in terms of organisational theory might be useful in that endeavour (Mintzberg 1991e).

Cohesion or conflict?

Successful conferences require, among other things, contributions from purpose-built convention and exhibition centres, PCOs and AOCs. Because these are different types of organisation, there is potential for misunderstanding and conflict. Awareness of this issue is the responsibility, first and foremost, of the people with professional experience in conference strategies and operations — those in the PCOs and purpose-built convention and exhibition centres. They have to lead the AOCs in this respect — a role that might require tact and diplomacy. The ultimate goal is a successful conference.

*T*EAMS OR LONE RANGERS?

Should the MICE industry assign responsibility for strategy to individuals or teams? And if teams are best, what size is optimal? Is the best strategy achieved by small, exclusive teams of top managers, or by larger teams taking in virtually all employees?

Until recent years, there was widespread belief that strategy was and should be the exclusive preserve of a few people at the top. The word 'strategy' stems from the ancient Greek expression for an army general: *strategos*. From that origin, and from its long association with military matters, three ideas gathered wide belief: first, that strategy was bound up with leadership; second, that leadership was the exclusive preserve of a few people at the top; and third, that only unusual individuals had the ability to lead in a strategic sense. Ability in this respect was widely seen as a talent — something possessed by a fortunate few, not something that the majority could acquire.

One of the first to show that these ideas were misleading was Leo Tolstoy in his great novel, *War and Peace*. A brief interlude from the story of the 1811–12 war between France and Russia discusses strategic issues. One hundred years after *War and Peace* was published in 1869, the same perceptions about strategy began permeating the minds of people interested in business management. Some of them have gone further; Tolstoy did not identify teams as a source of strategy.

■ Advocates *for teams*

The theory of teamwork being a medium for strategic management spread greatly in the 1980s. In recent years countless articles and books have promoted the idea, such as Wall and Wall (1995). The Walls have rejected the idea that strategy is or should be the sole responsibility of CEOs (chief executive officers) or their associated top managers. Certainly, CEOs and their assistants often have a great influence on strategies (sometimes too much), but in increasing numbers of organisations, almost all employees have inputs into strategies. Like many other recent writers on the topic, the Walls have extended that point to dismiss the idea that strategies are best derived by people on their own ('in the shower') and instead, have pushed the benefits of teams as the ideal seedbed for germinating good strategies.

Teams have three apparent advantages. First, they allow everyone to contribute, recognising that each individual potentially has worthwhile ideas. Second, by getting everyone involved in strategy, they can understand why and how the strategy is supposed to work. Third, as a result, everyone will feel committed to making the strategy effective. All three advantages make sense.

■ Problems *with teams*

Despite its good sense, the line of thinking that promotes teams as the best medium for strategy creation is problematical. Teams are useful in many ways, but what the Walls have described enthusiastically as 'a headlong rush towards team-based organisations ... in the 1980s and 1990s' (1995, p. 17) is a depressing and misleading picture. Putting individuals into teams tends to suppress individuals' creativity, which is needed to devise innovative strategies. Creativity is more likely to flourish when an individual is given space and time alone for a while, away from any team or other kind of organisation.

This assertion can be demonstrated by careful observations inside sporting teams, political parties, work teams and social clubs, where creativity tends to arise not while members are present in a team ensemble, but when individual members have thinking time away from the team. Creativity is individualistic. Is it possible to name one passable play or novel written by a committee? Major scientific discoveries, in the main, also have been advanced by individuals (Koestler 1959, 1970; Medawar 1969), as have been most creations in broader fields (France 1996). The fact that teams in laboratories normally are involved in developing scientific breakthroughs should not be confused with the fact that the creative work often stems from one or two individuals.

This is an age when most people seem to enjoy watching team sports, so perhaps the theory that teams are the best model for structuring work organisations has a foundation in sporting myth. The fact that teams are advocated by many organisational theorists might be based not so much in a belief that teams foster creativity, but in a desire to foster harmony and compliance among workers — conditions that normally help managers, but that do not necessarily help organisational performance. Moreover, many so-called 'teams' in the business world are not true teams; they are just groups or collectives given the label of 'team'. The label gives organisations a democratic gloss and a sporty image, which possibly deceives some workers into imagining that they are part of a true team, so making them more compliant and submissive.

The great psychologist Sigmund Freud, who discovered the fact that much human behaviour is shaped by unconscious events, described groups as 'impulsive, changeable and irritable', where people often become 'slaves to emotion ... led almost exclusively by the unconscious' (Freud 1965, pp. 13–16).

◼ A place *for individuals and a place for teams?*

How can the contradictions be resolved? Are teams or individuals the optimum approach? The answer depends on precisely what aspect of strategic management is being considered. For creating or formulating ideas about strategy, often the best source is individuals, given time and space away from fellow workers and organised structures. For assessing and reviewing strategic formulations or visions, after an individual has devised and introduced them, teams are certainly useful. And very often teams are essential for implementing strategies, especially in organisations where a complex set of resources needs to be assembled and coordinated.

◼ Implications *for conference managers*

There is a distinction between two phases of strategic management: formulation and implementation. Teams are less useful in the formulation stage, but have great utility after formulation, before decisions and during implementation. Ad hoc or innovative types of organisations are important in conference industries. Every conference is a new and distinct event, and a new (or re-formed) organisation must be assembled to manage it.

Moreover, in terms of what can be managed, a conference can be viewed as a set of formal and augmented products. Thus, before a conference, a series of teams can be established, each one responsible for managing specified items in the mix of formal and augmented products. There is also a need for a general management function, overseeing the conference as a whole. Frequently, there are three groups involved in this role. One represents the venue or conference centre; another represents the client, association or company whose members are coming to the conference; and the third is the conference organiser.

STRATEGIES FOR MANAGING WORK-RELATED STRESS

Basic to the management of anything is knowing what can and cannot be managed. The resources of an organisation (or an individual) are those things or factors that can be managed by that organisation (or individual). Environments cannot be managed. Principles flowing from this distinction, between resources and environments, are as relevant for business managers as they are for individuals managing their personal lives and personal work. This was expressed 2000 years ago by a Stoic philosopher: 'It is only after you have learned to distinguish between what you can and cannot control that inner tranquillity and outer effectiveness become possible' (Epictetus trans. 1995, p. 3). Schumacher's classic book (1974) contains a useful analysis of what can and cannot be managed, in its discussion about future acts and events.

Stress management is a problem that is growing in importance, in all industries. As with other industries, there are some employees within the MICE industry who find work stressful. Some degree of stress is not problematical and can actually stimulate people to feel good and work better. But too much stress can be very problematical, both for the individuals who suffer personally and for their employer organisations who bear the costs when work deteriorates or when employees go on sick leave or resign because of too much stress.

So far as is known, no research studies have compared the MICE industry with other industries to measure incidences of work-related stress. Quite possibly, incidences are relatively high in the MICE industry. Time constraints and expectations of high quality service are crucial factors but these are not causes of stress. Certainly, the fact that conferences cannot be postponed and that most employees try to provide high standards of service are part of the conditions that can give rise to unhealthy levels of personal stress, but they are not the cause. Work-related stress is manageable, and accordingly, stress management should form part of a conference organisers' strategic management.

Drawing on scientific research projects conducted by laboratory scientists in the United States into the causes of stress, Leiper and McTavish (1998) have suggested several strategies for reducing work stress, including:

- Empowering employees can reduce stress. Empowerment is discussed extensively in the management literature and is already being practised widely in conference industries (but probably not because it can reduce stress).
- More importantly, managers can reduce stress by creating conditions that allow their subordinates (lower level managers and other employees) to avoid having to make excessive numbers of important decisions. Stress is caused by having to make too many important decisions over a short period of time and by not getting appropriate feedback for those decisions. (This explains why relaxation is a short-term remedy for stress: it is a state when people are not making important decisions.)
- Appropriate feedback for stress reduction has two necessary qualities. First, it should occur soon after a decision is made. Second, it should not come from a source of stress; appropriate feedback must come from an external origin, not the stressor(s).

■ Applications *in conference management*

Strategic application of these principles by managers in the MICE industry is a complex art, but it is widely applied by managers who use good common sense, even if they are not fully aware of the underlying science.

A clearly expressed and detailed operations plan (an action plan) for a conference can reduce the number of on-the-spot decisions that employees need to make during an event. Appropriate feedback for decisions is a subtle issue. At conferences, opportunities for stress-reducing feedback for employees working for the conference organiser and venue can come from various sources. These can be summarised into several categories: the workers, the employees of the conference organiser and venue; the delegates; the client organisation; and managers of the conference organisation and venue.

Teams of employees working at a conference can be coached by managers to encourage all members to give immediate support to fellow members during stressful conditions. We all see this principle in action when we watch team sports. In speeches of welcome by the client organisation and in announcements of 'housekeeping' matters, delegates can be encouraged to thank the conference workers 'who are doing a great job under stressful conditions'. Courteous delegates do this anyway, without encouragement. Superficially, delegates might seem an inappropriate source of stress-reducing feedback because delegates are stressors. In fact, individual delegates are not causes of stress for conference workers, so when one personally remarks to the workers that they 'are doing a great job', the remark can serve as a stress barrier.

Managers of professional conference organisations or venues should be careful when and how they give feedback to conference workers if the aim is to reduce levels of stress. If managers are themselves active as part of a busy team of workers, they can, like the captains of sporting teams, give effective feedback during the action. If, on the other hand, they are acting in a supervisory role, any remarks they make might merely serve to remind workers that they are being watched and under pressure. Thus, attempts to relieve stress might, instead, add to stressful conditions. Appropriate feedback must come from a source that is not perceived by workers as a source of stress. A manager who is directly sharing in the work is not a source of stress. A manager who is merely present and observing is probably a source of stress.

After a conference has ended, most employees appreciate expressions of thanks from delegates, sponsors and managers, but after the event might be too late to have any impact on stress reduction.

SUMMARY

A strategy can be defined as a conscious act that coordinates resources to help to achieve objectives that seem important for improved performance, defence or some other purpose. Occasionally, a strategy is expressed as a plan, but not all effective strategies require plans. Strategies in the MICE industry also come in the form of patterns, positions and/or perspectives. Strategies can be managed or unmanaged. The former are important because, without them, an organisation will probably have to depend on luck or hard work by employees. Resources are a key concept in strategic management. An organisation's resources are all the things that its staff can use and manage to help it to achieve its objectives. Strategies are important because of what they can contribute to an organisation. They give direction, leadership and ideas.

Effective managers recognise competitive strategies and cooperative strategies. Both varieties normally exist in conference industries, each contributing particular values to a business and the industries in which it participates. Strategic management is helped by a good understanding of products. Conference products can be broken down to reveal three dimensions: formal products, augmented products and core products. Analysing an industry's organisations into types also has practical relevance because each type is best managed in a particular way. Awareness of this helps managers to avoid the deficiencies of using a wrong approach, if they erroneously assume that certain ideas about management are relevant to all types of business organisations.

The problem of work-related stress is growing. While some level of stress is beneficial to people within the convention and meeting industry, too much stress can result in a deterioration in work and potential labour turnover. Managers in the MICE industry should therefore be aware of and utilise strategies to reduce levels of stress.

Activity

12.1 Review a number of conference organisations in your area (e.g. venues, PCOs or other suppliers) and compare the competitive and cooperative strategies that they use within their business.

Discussion questions

12.1 What is a strategy? Describe five forms a business strategy might take for a conference organiser or convention centre.

12.2 Describe ways in which analysing a conference's products can help the managers of conferences.

12.3 What are some of the problems that can arise when a company tries to plan its strategies?

12.4 What is the difference between an emergent strategy and a deliberate strategy? Is one or the other always better? Illustrate your answer with reference to conferences and conventions.

12.5 Describe the three main features of an action plan, with examples from conferences.

12.6 Discuss at least two strategies that conference managers can use to reduce the impacts of stress on their employees.

12.7 Describe at least five generic competitive strategies and suggest how each could be applied in conference management.

12.8 Describe at least four cooperative strategies that might be found in conference industries.

12.9 Review the advantages and disadvantages of teamwork in the strategic management of the conference organisation. Identify and discuss the potential situations when individual work may be more appropriate in the strategic management of the conference organisation.

REFERENCES ··

Astroff, M. T. & Abbey, J. R. 1995, *Convention Sales and Service*, 4th ed, Waterbury Press, Cranbury, N. J.

Bing, S. 1995, 'Scenes from a Mall', *Esquire*, vol. 123, no. 5, pp. 56 & 61.

Brandenburger, A. M. & Nalebuff, B. J. 1997, *Co-opetition*, Doubleday, New York.

Burton, J. 1990, 'Composite Strategy: The Combination of Collaboration and Competition', *Journal of General Management*, vol. 21, pp. 1–23.

Ehrenreich, B. 1997 'Spinning The Poor Into Gold: How Corporations Seek to Profit from Welfare Reform', *Harper's Magazine*, August, pp. 44–52.

Epictetus trans. 1995, *The Art of Living*, Harper, San Francisco.

France, P. 1996, *The Insights of Solitude*, Pimlico, London.

Freud, S. 1965, *Group Psychology and the Analysis of Ego*, Benton, New York.

Fucini, J. & Fucini, S. 1987, 'Tom Duck: Ugly Duckling Car Rentals', in *Experience Inc.: Men and Women Who Founded Famous Companies After the Age of 40*, The Free Press, New York, pp. 185–91.

Grossman, P. Z. 1987, *American Express: The Unofficial History of the People Who Built the Great Financial Empire*, Crown, New York.

Joel, A. 1988, *Australian Procedures and Protocol*, 2nd ed, Angus Robertson, Sydney.

Koestler, A. 1959, *The Sleepwalkers: A History of Man's Changing Vision of the Universe*, Grosset and Dunlap, New York.

Koestler, A. 1970, *The Act of Creation*, Pan, London.

Kotler, P. 1972, *Marketing Management: Analysis, Planning and Control*, 2nd ed, Prentice-Hall, Englewood Cliffs, N. J.

Kotler, P. 1989, *Marketing in Australia*, Prentice-Hall, Sydney.

Leiper, N. 1995, *Tourism Management*, RMIT Publishing, Melbourne.

Leiper, N. 1998, *MN417 Strategic Management for Tourism and Hospitality Enterprises: Study Guide*, Southern Cross University, Lismore.

Leiper, N. & Hing, N. 1998, 'Trends in Asia Pacific Tourism; From Optimism to Uncertainty', *International Journal of Contemporary Hospitality Management*, vol. 10, pp. 245–51.

Leiper, N. & McTavish, M. 1998, 'Stress at Work: A Method for Dealing with Problematical Stress, Not in the HRM Literature But Useful in Many Industries Including Hospitality', unpublished paper, Southern Cross University, Lismore.

Medawar, P. 1969, *The Art of the Soluble*, Penguin, London.

Micklewait, J. & Wooldridge, A. 1996, *The Witch Doctors: What Management Gurus Are Saying, Why It Matters And How To Make Sense of It*, Heinemann, Oxford.

Mintzberg, H. 1979, *The Structures of Organizations*, Prentice-Hall, Englewood Cliffs, N. J.

Mintzberg, H. 1991a, 'Five Ps for Strategy', in Mintzberg, H. & Quinn, B. J. (eds), *The Strategy Process: Concepts, Contexts, Cases*, 2nd ed, Prentice-Hall, Englewood Cliffs, N. J., pp. 12–19.

Mintzberg, H. 1991b, 'Generic Strategies', in Mintzberg, H. & Quinn, B. J. (eds), *The Strategy Process: Concepts, Contexts, Cases*, 2nd ed, Prentice-Hall, Englewood Cliffs, N. J., pp. 70–81.

Mintzberg, H. 1991c, 'The Machine Organization', Mintzberg, H. & Quinn, B. J. (eds), *The Strategy Process: Concepts, Contexts, Cases*, 2nd ed, Prentice-Hall, Englewood Cliffs, N. J., pp 630–45.

Mintzberg, H. 1991d, 'The Innovative Organization', Mintzberg, H. & Quinn, B. J. (eds), *The Strategy Process: Concepts, Contexts, Cases*, 2nd ed, Prentice-Hall, Englewood Cliffs, N. J., pp. 731–45.

Mintzberg, H. 1991e, 'The Missionary Organization', Mintzberg, H. & Quinn, B. J. (eds), *The Strategy Process: Concepts, Contexts, Cases*, 2nd ed, Prentice-Hall, Englewood Cliffs, N. J., pp. 352–57.

Mintzberg, H. 1994, *The Rise and Fall of Strategic Planning*, Prentice-Hall, Hemel Hempstead.

Montgomery, R. J. & Strick, S. K. 1995, *Meetings, Conventions and Expositions: An Introduction to the Industry*, Van Nostrand Reinhold, New York.

Moorehouse, F. 1978, *Conferenceville*, Penguin, Melbourne.

Porter, M. 1980, *Competitive Strategy: Techniques for Analysing Industries and Competitors*, The Free Press, New York.

Quinn, J. B. 1991 'Strategies for Change', Mintzberg, H. & Quinn, B. J. (eds), in *The Strategy Process: Concepts, Contexts, Cases*, 2nd ed, Prentice-Hall, Englewood Cliffs, N. J., pp. 4–12.

Saul, J. R. 1995, *The Doubter's Companion: A Dictionary of Aggressive Common Sense*, Penguin, Toronto.

Schumacher, F. E. 1974, *Small is Beautiful: A Study of Economics As If People Mattered*, Sphere, London.

Shermer, M. 1997, *Why People Believe Weird Things; Pseudoscience, Superstition and Other Confusions of Our Time*, W. H. Freeman, New York.

Vitalis, A., Monin, J. & Holland, P. 1988, *Network Analysis*, Dunmore Press, Palmerston North.

Voyer, J. 1995, 'Strategy Design and Planning', in Mintzberg, H., Quinn, B. J. & Voyer, J. (eds), *The Strategy Process, Collegiate Edition*, Prentice-Hall, Englewood Cliffs, N. J., pp. 49–65.

Wall, S. J. & Wall, S. R. 1995, *The New Strategists: Creating Leaders at All Levels*, The Free Press, New York.

Wilson, P. 1997, *Calm at Work*, Penguin, Melbourne.

FURTHER READING

Argyris, C. 1977 'Double Loop Learning in Organizations', *Harvard Business Review*, September/October, pp. 115–25.

Holsigner, R., Jordan, C. & Levenson, L. (eds). 1971, *The Creative Encounter*, Scott, Foresman & Co, Glenview.

Morgan, G. 1986, *Images in Organizations*, Sage Publications, Los Angeles.

Santayana, G. 1906, *Life of Reason* (various publishers).

CASE STUDY

The 19th Annual Conference

This case study is based on a conference staged by a hypothetical trade association. Although it is hypothetical, this conference is probably not all that different from some actual events. The purpose is to highlight analytical issues relevant to strategies for conference management.

The 19th annual conference was staged last year in a hotel in a provincial town of New South Wales. Because the association is relatively impecunious, it does not use a professional conference organiser but leaves all the arrangements to a subcommittee of the association's members. The hotel was (and still is) lucky to be hanging on to its official two-star rating. Architecturally stylish, it has decayed in recent years. Its rooms are shabby and overdue for refurbishment. The audiovisual equipment in the conference room (which doubles as an extension of the dining room) is prone to break down. The airconditioner rattles in its old age, struggling against the heat and muggy humidity that is typical of the climate. The conference schedule had to be rearranged every day because several speakers failed to show. In summary, in certain respects this conference was a failure.

However, from the point of view of most of the delegates, the hospitality seemed wonderful, in all respects. The employed staff representing the conference organiser and host hotel did a great job to make the delegates feel welcome. So did the team of volunteer hosts, comprising a committee from the sponsoring association. The food was good, the bar and disco remained open and crowded with delegates and partners until 2 a.m., and the sightseeing tour on the free afternoon was hugely enjoyed by all. The partners' program pleased everyone. Consequently, almost all the delegates and partners felt, during and after the event, that yes, there were a few problems, but so what? The conference was deemed enjoyable and a success.

Questions

1 How can theories about products be used to analyse what was effective and what was problematical at this conference?

2 In terms of theories about the multidimensional nature of products, why on balance did the delegates regard the conference as a success?

3 Discuss the types of conferences or meetings that might have felt different about the outcome if their annual event had been staged in the hotel described in this case.

4 Imagine that you are employed as a professional conference organiser and are asked by this association to arrange its 20th annual conference. You are told that a minority of influential members were dismayed with certain aspects of the 19th conference. How would you begin the task?

À la carte menu: A menu that allows customers to choose from a range of food items.

Account managers: Staff within the sales team and/or convention sales team who are responsible for specific clients. Clients may include individuals and/or industry types such as medical, government and corporate.

Action plan: A type of plan that is designed in such a way as to help its effective and efficient implementation. It specifies the person(s) who will bear responsibility for each item, when each step is to be started and completed, and how each step is linked to other steps.

AOC (amateur organiser of conferences): A person or committee responsible for planning and managing a conference, because they have been asked to do it on top of their routine work duties, or because of altruistic motives.

Beverage: Any drink taken by conference delegates, including both alcoholic and non-alcoholic drinks.

Break-even analysis: A financial calculation to estimate the level of income required to cover the fixed and variable expenses.

Bureaucratic: A type of organisation, common in business and the public sector, characterised by several features, particularly routine work processes.

Buying centre: A group of people (or an individual) who decide on the destination or venue for a convention or meeting.

Cash flow forecast: An analysis of the projected positive and negative income flows at any given time.

Clinic: A small group meeting where the participants focus on analysing and solving problems or acquiring specific skills or knowledge.

Collateral material: Any printed promotional, sales or marketing material, such as product brochures, fliers, newsletters, and so on.

Competitive strategy: A strategy that gives an advantage, making the business more efficient in some way. There are several generic competitive strategies, used across many industries.

Conclave: A totally private and secret meeting.

Conference: A forum for participation, consultation and discussion of matters of common concern and the interchange of ideas. Attendance may be large or small.

Conference organising committee: A group formed by the client organisation with a brief to organise a MICE event.

Conference resort: A resort or accommodation facility whose purpose is to cater exclusively for small- to medium-sized MICE events.

Congress: A term often used in Europe to denote a meeting of national and particularly international participation. A formal meeting for discussion and speeches. It can have political implications, but can be held by any group of people on any subject.

Convention: A gathering, often international, of people to meet and discuss. It covers not only the business for which the meeting was called, but also social activities and interchanges among attendees.

Convention services manager: Responsible within a hotel or venue for the coordination of the servicing of a convention or meeting.

Cooperative strategy: A strategy that enables or encourages a business to work in tandem with others to make them all more effective in various ways. Normally, cooperative strategies transform individual businesses into a functioning industry. Cooperative strategies allow for some degree of competition among the businesses.

Core product: According to marketing theory, core products are the most important way for managers to think of products. In a service-based industry, the core product is the change(s) brought about in the person or thing being serviced. Thus, the core products of conferences are the delegates who have been changed in some way(s) as a consequence of their experiences.

CPA (or CPM): A technique that results in the production of a network diagram. It assists in the identification of the various activities of a project and the relationships and interdependencies among those activities.

Delegates: Participants in a MICE event.

Deliberate strategy: A strategy that has been activated in a conscious and purposeful manner, occurring as a consequence of systemic behaviour.

Desktop publishing: Due to the increased ease of use, capacity and complexity of computer programs, smaller computers are now able to carry out publishing tasks once seen as the domain of printers and large publishing companies.

Destinations: Places with some sort of actual or perceived boundary — physical, political or market created.

Direct marketing: A form of marketing where services or products are marketed from the producer to consumers without an intermediate channel of distribution.

Emergent strategy: A strategy that has not been activated in a conscious and purposeful manner, and occurs not from systemic behaviour but as a consequence of environmental influences.

Enterprise agreements: Terms and conditions of employment agreed to by an organisation (management) and staff as a whole, or individually.

EVENTS for Windows: A proprietary brand, computerised event management system for large and small convention organisations. Mainly used by conference organisers, rather than venues.

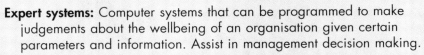

Expert systems: Computer systems that can be programmed to make judgements about the wellbeing of an organisation given certain parameters and information. Assist in management decision making.

Facilities guides: Dossiers produced by convention and visitors bureaus and distributed to potential conference organisers. They cover the full range of MICE facilities available within an area that are provided by members of the bureau.

Factor endowments: A destination may have a comparative advantage over another destination due to its advantage in certain resources — natural (historical, artistic, cultural), human (skills), and capital and infrastructure.

Famil tour: A number of executives from differing organisations are brought to a city or area and shown an overview of the destination, its facilities and capabilities.

Fixed expenses: Those expenses that do not vary with the number of delegates attending the event.

Food service: Meals taken during a conference, usually breakfast, lunch and dinner.

Forum: A public program of panel discussion and audience participation with all sides of a question discussed by both the panellists and the audience.

Gantt chart: A bar chart that combines the two functions of planning and scheduling.

Human resource planning: The process by which an organisation ensures that it has the required quantity and quality of employees available when and where necessary.

Incentive house: An incentive company whose business objective is to increase productivity from its clients' employees through a variety of motivational and other reward measures.

Industry awards: Terms and conditions of employment agreed to by the relevant union body, industry association and government.

Job analysis: A process of obtaining information to determine the essential duties, tasks and responsibilities of a job.

Job description: Outlines the purpose of a job, the major duties and activities that it involves and the conditions under which the job is performed.

Job or person specification: Provides information on the skills, experience, personal qualities and competencies required to undertake a particular job.

Labour demand forecast: An estimation of the number and type of employees required by an organisation.

Labour supply analysis: An audit of the internal supply and availability of staff in the external environment.

Labour turnover/staff turnover: The process where employees leave an organisation and are replaced.

Managed strategy: A deliberate strategy that is managed to some extent, which means that resources are being used in a coordinated way with a strategy in mind; the coordination might involve a mix of innovating, directing, facilitating, planning, monitoring, controlling, and so on.

Market segmentation: The grouping of potential customers within a market in such a way that their responses to marketing initiatives will be about the same.

Master account: The main account for an event, set up by the venue for the conference organiser. All key chargeable items incurred in the provision of the event are posted to this account.

Niche strategy: A strategy that avoids competition from more powerful adversaries. If all businesses followed niche strategies, no industry would develop.

Operational plan: A plan that focuses on planning and scheduling the workflows of the business. It establishes the activities to be undertaken and how they should be performed.

Plan: A process setting out steps, shaped by rational and analytical thinking, for guiding future actions.

Positioning: The development of an appropriate marketing orientation, service or marketing mix to occupy a specific place in the minds of the customers within the market segments targeted. Involves communicating product or service benefits that meet the needs of the particular segment targeted.

Press conference: Specialist gathering to which members of the media are invited, to hear information on some new event or development. A government press conference may provide information of national or international importance.

Product differentiation: A marketing strategy where one company attempts to position a product or service in a manner in which it appears different and distinct from that of a competitor.

Product feature/benefit profile: A list of product features (i.e. facilities and services) that relate to specific benefits that satisfy the needs of a particular customer segment.

Professional conference organiser (PCO): An intermediary who acts on behalf of a company or association in the organisation of a convention or meeting. Their main business is to organise conferences.

Project plan: A plan to achieve a specific task of a limited duration that comprises a number of interrelated activities through efficient and effective use of resources.

Property management system (PMS): A fully integrated computerised system that manages various tasks and functions within an organisation such as a hotel.

Purpose-built convention and exhibition centre: Sometimes referred to as a dedicated convention centre (or DCC). A purpose-built, stand-alone facility used principally for meetings, conventions, trade shows and exhibitions. It will normally have catering facilities but need not include accommodation.

Quality gap: A shortfall that occurs when the actual quality falls below the service level expected by the customer. There are seven potential quality gaps (the knowledge gap, the standards gap, the delivery gap, the internal communications gap, the perceptions gap, the interpretation gap and the service gap).

Quality management: Making sure that the product or service is right all the time and meets the customers' requirements.

Resident manager: Management position, usually in large hotels, often equivalent to assistant general manager. This position is usually responsible for room division (front office, housekeeping, etc.) and the general day-to-day operation of the property.

Resources: An organisation's resources are all the things that its staff can use and manage to help achieve objectives. Can be divided into human, financial, technical and other categories.

Responsible service of alcohol: A government-lead initiative that mandates training for all personnel involved in the purchase, sales and service of alcoholic beverages.

Retreat: Often held for intense problem solving, introspection and study. The term is often used for religious retreats, but it is becoming more popular in the business world. Customarily, only a few people attend retreats, which are a mixture of business and relaxation, without the normal business interruptions.

Sales promotion: A marketing mix strategy where customers are given a short-term inducement to make more of an immediate purchase.

Satellite service kitchen: Forward kitchen located near convention or function facilities but away from the main kitchen. Used for the finishing and distribution of food.

Seminar: A meeting that promotes an exchange of ideas or disseminates information, usually on a specific subject/s. Usually a smaller type of meeting. It may be open to the public whereby the people attending may have nothing in common except the common interest of the seminar.

Service: Setting standards regarding customers' needs and meeting them.

Set menu: A menu for conference delegates that does not allow for any choice. The food items are decided by the conference organiser and the venue convention services staff.

Site inspection: A visit by an individual or individuals from an organisation to view a venue and its facilities.

Situation analysis: Examines where and how the product stands in the market place, its market share and its relation to its competitors.

Strategic plan: The long-term plan for an organisation.

Strategy: The pattern or plan that integrates an organisation's major goals, policies and action sequences into a cohesive whole.

Stress: Excessive work-related stress is a pathological condition caused by having to make too many important decisions over a short space of time without getting appropriate feedback for those decisions.

Symposium: A meeting where a particular topic is discussed by several specialists in the form of presentations. Rather formal in conduct. Some audience participation, though much less than a forum.

Tour operators: Organisations that package other people's products. They operate as an intermediary between the principals of the industry (i.e. hotels, airlines) and the retail travel agency network.

Transition point: The point at which the client organisation or conference organiser is introduced and transferred from convention sales to convention services or banquet operations.

Travel agency: An intermediary organisation that links travel principals (i.e. service providers) and consumers through the provision of a range of services associated with the sale of travel products.

Turnaround time: The time it takes banquet floor staff to break down a room, and lay out and reset the room for the next event.

Variable expenses: Expenses that fluctuate, dependent on the number of people attending the event.

Work breakdown structure (WBS): A hierarchical tree of the tasks or areas required to be undertaken in the preparation of a MICE event.

Workshop: A brief session involving a small group of people from a particular field. The emphasis is on participation in problem solving.

Yield management: A capacity control mechanism that effectively manages revenue and inventory by pricing differences on the elasticity of demand.

APPENDIX

Key findings of the ICCA 2000

■ **Table A.1** *The top 20 international association meeting countries, 1996–2000*

	NUMBER OF MEETINGS PER COUNTRY				
COUNTRY	1996	1997	1998	1999	2000°
1 United States	230	200	192	148	100
2 United Kingdom	181	170	161	125	112
3 Spain	129	138	160	95	48
4 France	148	123	132	85	59
5 Germany	139	139	131	114	53
6 Italy	126	114	114	72	56
7 Australia	117	125	109	91	118
8 Netherlands	130	121	104	77	53
9 Japan	122	87	104	73	41
10 Austria	91	66	91	42	25
11 Finland	85	74	83	83	43
12 Sweden	75	70	83	65	36
13 Denmark	102	61	79	56	31
14 Canada	73	76	69	62	43
15 Portugal	41	40	62	28	16
16 Belgium	70	66	59	38	17
17 Israel	71	38	53	37	20
18 Switzerland	68	56	52	41	16
19 Korea (Republic)	36	40	46	44	16
20 Brazil	27	42	46	49	35

Source: ICCA (2000)

■ **Table A.2** *The world's top 20 convention cities, by number of meetings per city, 1996–2000*

CITY	NUMBER OF MEETINGS PER CITY				
	1996	**1997**	**1998**	**1999**	**200**
1 Madrid	33	46	76	15	10
2 Vienna	60	44	75	29	12
3 Copenhagen	76	41	65	49	24
4 Paris	50	47	46	23	26
5 Amsterdam	50	47	46	31	15
6 Stockholm	45	36	42	36	26
7 Singapore	27	21	42	13	11
8 Lisbon	25	23	40	17	8
9 Jerusalem	46	22	39	23	12
10 Barcelona	51	52	38	34	22
11 Helsinki	39	36	35	32	20
12 Seoul	29	29	34	38	13
13 Budapest	60	29	33	43	15
14 Edinburgh	31	34	33	28	22
15 Sydney	35	46	30	38	43
16 London	36	50	29	30	26
17 Melbourne	29	25	27	22	31
18 Berlin	26	20	26	26	14
19 Taipei	16	23	26	15	11
20 Brussels	27	31	25	19	10

Source: ICCA (2000)

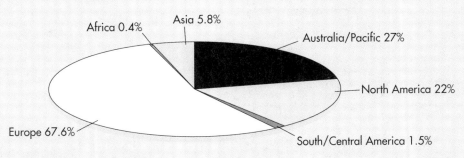

■ Figure A.1 *Headquarters of international organisations (associations with meetings post–1998)*

Source: ICCA (2000)

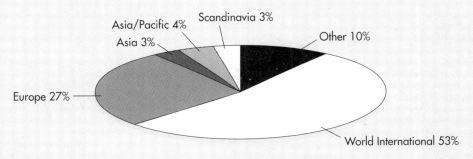

■ Figure A.2 *Rotation area of international meetings, 1998*

Source: ICCA (2000)

Source of appendix data: ICCA 2000, *The International Meetings Market, 1991–2000*, ICCA, The Netherlands. Information from this report can also be found at *www.icca.nl.*